Ruling by Other Means

What do states gain by sending citizens into the streets? *Ruling by Other Means* investigates this question through the lens of state-mobilized movements (SMMs), an umbrella concept that includes a range of (often covertly organized) collective actions intended to promote state interests. The SMMs research agenda departs significantly from that of classic social movement and contentious politics theory, focused on threats to the state from seemingly autonomous societal actors. Existing theories assume that the goal of popular protest is to voice societal grievances, represent oppressed groups, and challenge state authorities and other powerholders. The chapters in this volume show, however, that states themselves organize citizens (sometimes surreptitiously and even transnationally) to act collectively to advance state goals. Drawn from different historical periods and diverse geographical regions, these case studies expand and improve our understanding of social movements, civil society, and state-society relations under authoritarian regimes.

Grzegorz Ekiert is Laurence A. Tisch Professor of Government at Harvard University.

Elizabeth J. Perry is Henry Rosovsky Professor of Government at Harvard University.

Yan Xiaojun is Associate Professor of Politics and Public Administration at the University of Hong Kong.

Cambridge Studies in Contentious Politics

General Editor

Doug McAdam *Stanford University and Center for Advanced Study in the Behavioral Sciences*

Editors

Mark Beissinger *Princeton University*
Donatella della Porta *Scuola Normale Superiore*
Jack A. Goldstone *George Mason University*
Michael Hanagan *Vassar College*
Holly J. McCammon *Vanderbilt University*
David S. Meyer *University of California, Irvine*
Sarah Soule *Stanford University*
Suzanne Staggenborg *University of Pittsburgh*
Sidney Tarrow *Cornell University*
Charles Tilly (d. 2008) *Columbia University*
Elisabeth J. Wood *Yale University*
Deborah Yashar *Princeton University*

Rina Agarwala, *Informal Labor, Formal Politics, and Dignified Discontent in India*
Ronald Aminzade, *Race, Nation, and Citizenship in Post-Colonial Africa: The Case of Tanzania*
Ronald Aminzade et al., *Silence and Voice in the Study of Contentious Politics*
Javier Auyero, *Routine Politics and Violence in Argentina: The Gray Zone of State Power*
Phillip M. Ayoub, *When States Come Out: Europe's Sexual Minorities and the Politics of Visibility*
Amrita Basu, *Violent Conjunctures in Democratic India*
W. Lance Bennett and Alexandra Segerberg, *The Logic of Connective Action: Digital Media and the Personalization of Contentious Politics*
Nancy Bermeo and Deborah J. Yashar, editors, *Parties, Movements, and Democracy in the Developing World*
Clifford Bob, *The Global Right Wing and the Clash of World Politics*
Clifford Bob, *The Marketing of Rebellion: Insurgents, Media, and International Activism*
Robert Braun, *Protectors of Pluralism: Religious Minorities and the Rescue of Jews in the Low Countries during the Holocaust*
Charles Brockett, *Political Movements and Violence in Central America*
Marisa von Bülow, *Building Transnational Networks: Civil Society and the Politics of Trade in the Americas*
Valerie Bunce and Sharon Wolchik, *Defeating Authoritarian Leaders in Postcommunist Countries*
Teri L. Caraway and Michele Ford, *Labor and Politics in Indonesia*

(continued after index)

Ruling by Other Means

State-Mobilized Movements

Edited by

GRZEGORZ EKIERT
Harvard University

ELIZABETH J. PERRY
Harvard University

YAN XIAOJUN
University of Hong Kong

CAMBRIDGE
UNIVERSITY PRESS

University Printing House, Cambridge CB2 8BS, United Kingdom

One Liberty Plaza, 20th Floor, New York, NY 10006, USA

477 Williamstown Road, Port Melbourne, VIC 3207, Australia

314–321, 3rd Floor, Plot 3, Splendor Forum, Jasola District Centre,
New Delhi – 110025, India

79 Anson Road, #06-04/06, Singapore 079906

Cambridge University Press is part of the University of Cambridge.

It furthers the University's mission by disseminating knowledge in the pursuit of education, learning, and research at the highest international levels of excellence.

www.cambridge.org
Information on this title: www.cambridge.org/9781108478069
DOI: 10.1017/9781108784146

© Cambridge University Press 2020

This publication is in copyright. Subject to statutory exception and to the provisions of relevant collective licensing agreements, no reproduction of any part may take place without the written permission of Cambridge University Press.

First published 2020

A catalogue record for this publication is available from the British Library.

ISBN 978-1-108-47806-9 Hardback
ISBN 978-1-108-74561-1 Paperback

Cambridge University Press has no responsibility for the persistence or accuracy of URLs for external or third-party internet websites referred to in this publication and does not guarantee that any content on such websites is, or will remain, accurate or appropriate.

Contents

List of Figures		page vii
List of Tables		ix
List of Contributors		x
Acknowledgments		xii
1	State-Mobilized Movements: A Research Agenda *Grzegorz Ekiert and Elizabeth J. Perry*	1
2	Manufactured Ambiguity: Party-State Mobilization Strategy in the March 1968 Crisis in Poland *Dominika Kruszewska and Grzegorz Ekiert*	24
3	Suppressing Students in the People's Republic of China: Proletarian State-Mobilized Movements in 1968 and 1989 *Elizabeth J. Perry and Yan Xiaojun*	57
4	State-Mobilized Community Development: The Case of Rural Taiwan *Kristen E. Looney*	86
5	Enforcement Networks and Racial Contention in Civil Rights–Era Mississippi *David Cunningham and Peter B. Owens*	110
6	Social Sources of Counterrevolution: State-Sponsored Contention during Revolutionary Episodes *Mark R. Beissinger*	140
7	Occupy Youth! State-Mobilized Movements in the Putin Era (or, What Was Nashi and What Comes Next?) *Julie Hemment*	166
8	State-Mobilized Movements after Annexation of Crimea: The Construction of Novorossiya *Samuel A. Greene and Graeme B. Robertson*	193

9 Mirroring Opposition Threats: The Logic of State
   Mobilization in Bolivarian Venezuela   217
   Sam Handlin

10 Mobilizing against Change: Veteran Organizations as a
   Pivotal Political Actor   239
   Danijela Dolenec and Daniela Širinić

11 The Dynamics of State-Mobilized Movements: Insights
   from Egypt   261
   Ashley Anderson and Melani Cammett

12 State-Mobilized Campaign and the Prodemocracy Movement
   in Hong Kong, 2013–2015   291
   Eliza W. Y. Lee

13 The Resurrection of Lei Feng: Rebuilding the Chinese
   Party-State's Infrastructure of Volunteer Mobilization   314
   David A. Palmer and Rundong Ning

Index   345

Figures

2.1	State-mobilized movement: March 8 to June 24, 1968	*page* 30
2.2	State-mobilized movement by repertoire: March 12 to June 24, 1968	32
2.3	State-mobilized movement across the country: Number of reported rallies and demonstrations	33
3.1	Workers of the Xinhua Printing House and Xinhua Bookstore deliver printing materials with Chairman Mao's latest instructions to the Workers' Propaganda Team setting out to Tsinghua University campus	61
3.2	Workers at Beijing Knitting Mill admire mangoes from Mao Zedong	64
6.1	Political groupings in the Orange Revolution (KIIS survey)	150
6.2	Political groupings in the Orange Revolution (Monitoring survey)	152
6.3	Attitudinal profile plot for three clusters of counterrevolutionaries in the Orange Revolution	161
8.1	Donbas–Russian Spring network activity, 2011–2016	204
8.2	Topics over time	206
8.3	This country can't be beaten!	209
8.4	Republic of Novorossia, June 2014	209
8.5	News front	210
9.1	Arenas of operation and dominant types of mobilization	223
10.1	Share of MP questions on veteran-related issues from 2000 to 2015. Source: Croatian Policy Agendas Dataset (Širinić et al., 2016)	248
10.2	Density of veteran NGOs and HDZ vote share in 2013 local election	250
10.3	Veteran protests between 2000 and 2017. Source: Dolenec et al. (2019)	253

11.1	State-sponsored and contentious mobilization in Egypt, 2011–2013	276
11.2	Kaplan-Meier survival estimates for SMMs by organizational presence	283
11.3	Kaplan-Meier survival estimates for SMM by regime identity	284
13.1	The iconic image of Lei Feng	321
13.2	Propaganda poster for sent-down youth in the Cultural Revolution	335
13.3	Banner for the Go West Programme's website	335

Tables

4.1	Community development policies in Taiwan, 1955–1981	page 95
4.2	Results of the Community Development Campaign in Taiwan, 1969–1981	100
6.1	The demography of counterrevolution in Ukraine, 2004	155
8.1	Authorities at peak periods of activity	208
8.2	Top ten media – Russian Spring movement	211
9.1	Major elections and referenda during the Fifth Republic, 1999–2017	220
9.2	Opposition threats and state mobilization responses across four phases	224
11.1	Cox proportional hazards model for SMMs, 2011–2013	281
12.1	Public support of the Occupy Movement	306
12.2	Survey on whether the Occupy Movement should continue or stop	306
13.1	Frequency of key terms in the *People's Daily*	337

Contributors

Ashley Anderson is Assistant Professor of Political Science at the University of North Carolina, Chapel Hill.

Mark R. Beissinger is Henry W. Putnam Professor in the Department of Politics at Princeton University.

Melani Cammett is Clarence Dillon Professor of International Affairs in the Department of Government at Harvard University and Chair of the Harvard Academy of International and Area Studies.

David Cunningham is Professor and Chair of Sociology at Washington University in St. Louis.

Danijela Dolenec is an Associate Professor in the Faculty of Political Science, University of Zagreb.

Grzegorz Ekiert is Laurence A. Tisch Professor of Government and Director of the Minda de Gunzburg Center for European Studies at Harvard University.

Samuel A. Greene is Director of the Russia Institute at King's College London and a Reader in Russian politics.

Sam Handlin is Assistant Professor of Political Science at Swarthmore College.

Julie Hemment is Professor of Anthropology at the University of Massachusetts Amherst.

Dominika Kruszewska is a Postdoctoral Fellow with the Weatherhead Center for International Affairs at Harvard University.

Eliza W.Y. Lee is Professor of Politics and Public Administration at the University of Hong Kong.

Kristen E. Looney is Assistant Professor of Asian Studies and Government at Georgetown University.

List of Contributors

Peter B. Owens is a Research Technician in the Office of Institutional Research at California State University, Chico.

David A. Palmer is a Professor jointly appointed by the Hong Kong Institute for the Humanities and Social Sciences and the Department of Sociology at the University of Hong Kong.

Elizabeth J. Perry is Henry Rosovsky Professor of Government at Harvard University and Director of the Harvard-Yenching Institute.

Graeme B. Robertson is Professor of Political Science at the University of North Carolina at Chapel Hill.

Rundong Ning is a Ph.D. Candidate in the Department of Anthropology of Yale University.

Daniela Širinić is an Assistant Professor in the Faculty of Political Science, University of Zagreb.

Yan Xiaojun is Associate Professor of Politics and Public Administration at the University of Hong Kong and Director of the Research Hub on Institutions of China, HKU.

Acknowledgments

This was a complex research project, and we could not possibly have completed it without generous support from multiple research institutions at Harvard and the University of Hong Kong (HKU). We are grateful to the Harvard Asia Center, the Harvard-Yenching Institute, the Minda de Gunzburg Center for European Studies, the Radcliffe Institute for Advanced Studies, the Weatherhead Center for International Affairs, and HKU's Faculty of Social Sciences and Research Hub on Institutions of China for their support. Three conferences that were a core part of the project required major organizational efforts. We would like to thank in particular Sarah Banse, Laura Falloon, Tommy Fan, Darren Fung, Elaine Setser, Lindsay Strogatz, and Rebecca Wassarman for their expert assistance in making these events successful.

At our initial conference where the basic ideas for this book emerged, we benefited greatly from the help of an extraordinary group of graduate research assistants. We are grateful to Jared Abbott, Chris Carothers, Jingkai He, Li La, Matt Reichert, Grains Gu, and Zhu Zichen. Throughout the project we were assisted by the input and advice of many colleagues. Our special thanks go to: John P. Burns, Cheris Chan, Jan Kubik, Richard W. X. Hu, William Hurst, Zhan Jinghong, Gary King, Steve Levitsky, Wolfgang Merkel, Joel Migdal, Kacie Miura, Jennifer Pan, Scott Radnitz, Zhao Suisheng, and David Zweig. We are also grateful to the editor and staff of Cambridge University Press for their work on this book.

1

State-Mobilized Movements: A Research Agenda

Grzegorz Ekiert and Elizabeth J. Perry

1.1 INTRODUCTION

On April 10, 2016, an agitated crowd gathered in the center of Warsaw. The demonstration, dubbed the "million people march," followed the customary Polish protest repertoire. The usual sea of Polish national flags and emblems of the Solidarity movement were on display. The march began with a mass in the Warsaw Cathedral before the crowd moved across the old town to the Presidential Palace. Heavily equipped police secured the perimeter of the demonstration, and small groups of counterprotesters were separated from the main gathering. Yet, there was something odd about this "protest" event. The angry demonstrators did not make any claims against the government in power. There were no specific demands or claims against the ruling party. Moreover, the main organizer of the demonstration – the Law and Justice party – was in power in Poland. The PiS enjoyed a majority in parliament and exercised full control of the government. The Polish president was also a PiS member. The public television and other media were in ruling party hands, and the powerful Polish Catholic Church hierarchy supported its policies. The protesters did not deliver fiery speeches against the government. Instead, they listened to fiery speeches by the president, the head of the ruling party, and other top government officials condemning the previous government and those who supported it as traitors and enemies of Poland.

The demonstration was organized to mark the sixth anniversary of the plane crash in Smolensk that had killed Poland's president and scores of top officials of the government, parliament, and armed forces on their way to participate in an event commemorating the slaughter of thousands of Polish prisoners of war by the Soviet regime in 1940. The marchers in Warsaw carried placards stating "We remember Katyn and Smolensk" and images of the deceased president and his wife. But this was not simply a commemorative event. It was also a contentious gathering that formed part of a cycle of protests organized by

1

the current Polish ruling party on a monthly basis since the plane crash. The unrest was fueled by a conspiracy theory alleging that the former government, in collusion with the Russians, had assassinated the president. Participants in the current round of protests were not only fully supported by the government, the ruling party, and various organizations allied with it: they were also actively mobilized and funded by the party. The Polish parliament even changed the law on public gatherings in order to privilege demonstrations organized by supporters of the government and to prevent counterdemonstrations by groups allied with the political opposition. In short, the entire institutional machinery of the Polish state was arrayed behind these protest events.

This case takes us to the heart of questions to be explored in this volume. Why had the crowd gathered in Warsaw? What were the people protesting? Who were the protest participants and what had motivated them to join the protest? How were they organized and mobilized? What were their grievances and demands? Who were their adversaries? And, most critically, why were organs of the state acting as facilitators rather than as targets or repressors of a protest movement?

For almost two decades, the field of social movements and contentious politics has been in "a post-paradigm phase" (Goodwin and Jasper, 2004). Most of the recent debates have focused on the relative utility of various theoretical perspectives, pitting advocates of structural approaches against adherents of cultural interpretations, constructivism, and psychological explanations of collective action. As illuminating as these theoretical debates have been, the present volume proposes a different approach. Following a pioneering effort of Aminzade et al. (2001), we seek to chart an understudied empirical domain of social movements: the state's active role in mobilizing social actors and in shaping contentious politics.

The chapters to follow examine a wide range of such state-mobilized movements (SMMs), asking what states seek to achieve by sending citizens into the streets and how successful these efforts are. Does the state's deployment of existing or newly invented organizations and movements stimulate public support and contribute to everyday governance? What kinds of meanings, identities, and social cleavages are strengthened or constructed in the course of SMMs? Who joins SMMs, and what motivates these participants? What types of states in what situations are likely to use such mobilization technologies? And what are the short- and long-term consequences of inciting popular protests for purposes of regime legitimacy and stability?

The research agenda suggested by these questions departs significantly from that of classic social movement and contentious politics theories, which focus on the threat of challenges from seemingly autonomous societal actors against those in power. A stereotypic scene in the literature on contentious politics pictures a herd of angry protesters marching against a surprised yet much stronger ruling elite and the state apparatus under its control. Contentious politics, we are told, is by nature a claims-making process in which societal challengers deploy various "weapons of the weak" to press demands upon the mighty state – a modern institutional machine equipped with advanced surveillance technology, coercive forces complete with armored trucks and state-of-the-art anti-riot gear, and a penal system poised to punish any transgression of state regulations and public order. States, governments, ruling parties, and political leaders are conventionally conceptualized as the principal targets of protest actions. The authorities, in turn, accept, ignore or reject protesters' demands, responding with a range of accommodative or repressive tactics.

But this expected scenario is clearly not applicable to the 2016 Warsaw demonstration, which was organized by the ruling elites themselves and supported by the Polish state to advance a specific political agenda of those in power. Crowds on the streets were mobilized from above to present the appearance of popular spontaneity and enthusiasm and to intimidate the opposition. In the Warsaw protest, contention was not a desperate weapon of the weak but a carefully selected and scripted tactic of the state to exercise power and promote its own objectives. Rather than posing an unexpected and unwelcome challenge to state rule, the "million people march" was a case of the state *ruling by other means*.

The Polish event was not an unusual exception in the wider universe of social movements and protest events. Major demonstrations and sustained movement activities around the world are frequently state-initiated, state-sponsored, and state-subsidized. Government involvement in sparking and sustaining social movements is sometimes open and obvious; yet, more often, it is covert and circuitous. Movements and civil society organizations may appear as the genuine expression of autonomous social interests, grievances, and emotions, when in fact they are largely constructed and manipulated by state agents. This was the case with consequential historical events such as the pogrom of the Kristallnacht in Germany in 1938 and the Rwandan Genocide of 1994, as well as more recent protests directed against opposition or foreign organizations and powers in China, Russia, Turkey, Venezuela, and Poland (not to mention their forerunners under communist and other authoritarian regimes). Similar phenomena can be found in many other countries and under a wide range of political regimes, including even well-established democracies. The roots of both domestic and transnational social activism – mediated by ostensibly "autonomous" NGOs and other civic associations – are often traceable to state agents.[1] Russian interference in the 2016 US presidential election, which included setting up movement organizations, opening fake websites, and organizing both rallies and counter-rallies, provides a poignant contemporary example of clandestine transnational involvement by a foreign state in the social movement domain. As Moises Naim (2009, p. 96) notes, this is "an important

---

[1] See, for example, Vojtiskova et al. (2016).

and growing global trend that deserves more scrutiny: Governments are funding and controlling nongovernmental organizations (NGOs), often stealthily."

Existing theories of social movements generally assume that protest is the expression of grievances, interests, and identities embedded in society at large and that popular protests arise to articulate such grievances, to represent disadvantaged and oppressed groups, and to confront and contest the state and power holders. Charles Tilly's (1978) influential conceptualization of movements as claims-making outsiders challenging members of the polity has constituted the foundation for theory and research on protest movements for the past four decades.[2] Similarly, research and theorizing on civil society assumes that civil society organizations are basically separate and autonomous from the state, able to counterbalance state power, make demands on the state, and hold government officials accountable.[3] In short, from the perspective of the dominant literature on contention the state is fundamentally passive or reactive, rather than proactive. As the most prominent scholars in the field put it, "*Contentious* politics ... is episodic rather than continuous, occurs in public, involves interaction between makers of claims and others, is recognized by those others as bearing on their interests, and bringing in *government as mediator, target or claimant.*"[4]

The classic social movement agenda (and the study of contentious politics in general) has focused on the societal side of the state–society equation, operating under three basic assumptions: a confrontational dichotomy between state and society; a reactive state that is the principal protest target; and social actors whose agency is circumscribed yet autonomous in their campaign against state power. Moreover, the state has often been conceptualized "as a unitary actor – a 'structure' – rather than as a complex web of agencies and authorities, thoroughly saturated with culture, emotions and strategic interactions."[5] Such theories, while recognizing that the state may be "brought in" to the protest arena, do not usually emphasize the premeditated and proactive agency of the state in deciding the agenda and forms of movement politics. Historical and contemporary evidence shows, however, that not only do social movements emerge to challenge other movements (in a movement–counter movement dynamic) but modern states themselves organize citizens to act collectively in order to promote specific state goals and interests.

Students of civil society are well aware of the GONGOs (government-organized non-governmental organizations) and their role in shaping the organizational landscape of civil society and advancing state interests. The

---

[2] According to Tilly (1984, p. 306), "A social movement is a sustained series of interactions between powerholders and persons successfully claiming to speak on behalf of a constituency lacking formal representation, in the course of which these persons make publicly visible demands for changes in the distribution or exercise of power, and back these demands with public demonstrations of support."
[3] See Keane (1988); Diamond (1999). [4] McAdam, Tarrow, and Tilly, 2001, p. 5; italics added.
[5] Goodwin and Jasper, 2004, p. viii.

existence of such organizations is not confined to authoritarian regimes; GONGOs are common in democracies as well.[6] Moreover, as the recent civil war in Ukraine graphically illustrates, states may establish and sponsor movement-like organizations beyond their own national borders. Walerij Gierasimow, Russia's top military official, noted in 2013 that "widespread disinformation combined with the potential to mobilize people for protests is the key weapon of the twenty-first century."[7] Such a strategy was employed in Russian military intervention in Ukraine in 2014. Three years later, Russian interference in the US election, which included not only the spread of "fake news" via social media but also the surreptitious mobilization of protests and counterprotests in American cities, offered ample evidence of the power of transnational SMMs. Although there is growing awareness in the social movement literature that the boundaries between institutionalized and non-institutionalized politics are "fuzzy and permeable,"[8] the dynamic and determinative role of the state in movement politics – both domestically and cross-nationally – has not been fully appreciated, investigated, or analyzed.

In short, in contentious politics the causal arrow goes from the state to the social movement domain (and back) as often as the other way around. We find moreover that movement politics consists not only of two arenas (institutionalized and non-institutionalized) but of multiple overlapping arenas positioned along a continuum in terms of the degree of institutionalization: infrapolitics (forms of everyday resistance),[9] grassroots politics (weakly institutionalized domain of social movements), civil society politics and transnational activism, and the formal political domain of parties, elections, and parliamentary politics. Accordingly, we must investigate not one but many boundaries, all of which are fuzzy and permeable. Once we acknowledge that agency resides in both state and society with their multiple actors and overlapping political domains, the picture becomes richer and more realistic. This volume is an initial effort to encourage just such a research agenda.

The subject of the volume is what we refer to as *state-mobilized movements* (SMMs), an umbrella concept that encompasses an array of collective social and political actions instigated or encouraged by state agents for the purpose of advancing state interests. Such actions may be conducted via peaceful marches as well as rowdy rallies and undertaken by idealistic young volunteers as well as hardened thugs and vigilantes. Although SMMs can be observed (in different forms and with differing degrees of frequency) under a variety of political regimes throughout recorded history, they have assumed particular political importance in the contemporary era due to the modern state's reliance upon citizen support to legitimize its claim to a right to rule. We may think of the full set of SMMs as reflecting a broad spectrum of state–society relations; in some

---

[6] See Naim (2009), p. 95.   [7] Quoted in Kokot (2017).   [8] Goldstone (2003), p. 2.
[9] See Scott (1985); (1990).

cases, these movements are essentially top-down and evident creations of state actors, whereas in other instances they reflect considerable social agency and ingenuity and are only gently prodded by state agents. Not included within this definition, however, are the extremes on either end of the state mobilization–social movement spectrum: state-conscripted warfare or coerced expressions of loyalty, on the one hand, and spontaneous social protests and demonstrations in support of state policies or leaders on the other. Yet in this latter case, as Anderson and Cammett argue in Chapter 11 of this volume, it is often difficult to distinguish between SMMs and autonomous displays of popular support for the state. Our main interest lies in phenomena that are located in between these two poles and for that reason demand serious attention to both the societal and state sides of the relationship. Although SMMs may occur under all types of regimes, they are especially common in authoritarian and semi-authoritarian contexts. Whereas democratic regimes derive legitimacy from free and fair elections and a universal franchise, nondemocratic regimes typically stake their claim to legitimacy by manipulating elections and demonstrating popular support in other ways. Exploring this phenomenon, empirically and theoretically, promises not only to expand our analysis of social movements but also to enlarge our understanding of the social bases of authoritarian rule, past and present.

We are not the first to notice that SMMs point to a significant blind spot in the contemporary social movement literature. Throughout modern history, social movements and mass contentious gatherings have been instruments of state governance as much as means of articulating societal grievances. In a seminal work, Eric Hobsbawm (1959) identified a specific form of resistance in peasant society that he termed "social banditry." While Hobsbawm viewed social banditry as a cry for social justice by the weak and oppressed, his critics[10] pointed to the frequent use of bandits by state authorities to protect and expand their power. More recently, other scholars have noted the role of the state and powerful elites in generating protest movements. According to Radnitz (2010, pp. 15–16), for example, "protest is not a tool of the weak alone ... Historically, governments used their vast means to coerce and cajole people to participate in mass collective endeavors, where protest serves a counterintuitive purpose – to display (purported) popular support for the regime." Similarly, Jackie Smith (2004, p. 315) notes, "There is a tendency within social movement research to conceptualize movement actors as opponents of the state. But a comparative and global perspective demands that we abandon this a priori assumption and conceptualize the state as one of several actors within a field, and there are times when the state (or elements thereof) will be allies of social movements in their struggles against other actors in the broader political field." As Jack Goldstone (2015, p. 227) observes, "there are no clear lines separating the roles of challenger (protestors or social movement activists), incumbents

---

[10] See, for example, Blok (1972); O'Malley (1979).

(those engaged in routine acceptance and membership of the polity defined by a policy field), and governance units (agents or institutions of the state)." Our task involves illuminating and explicating these state–society interconnections.

Modern states depend upon supportive, and often orchestrated, displays of citizen activism for both propagandistic and pragmatic purposes. Indeed, in many countries the domain of civil society itself has become a major arena of state–society cooperation and contestation. Just as "primitive rebels" were often tools of state power, so sophisticated "modern rebels" may enjoy cozier relations with states than is sometimes assumed. Savvy authoritarian regimes encourage and incorporate social movements as a key instrument of rule with considerable symbolic and political benefits. An argument along these lines has been put forward for the case of China.[11] As far as we are aware, however, this volume is the first effort to explore these relationships both cross-nationally and historically. We are under no illusion that this collection will provide the last word on this complex and opaque issue. The cases discussed in the chapters to follow by no means exhaust the full range of SMMs. They are meant to be illustrative rather than comprehensive. Our aim is not to present a parsimonious theory but rather to indicate the rich lode of research possibilities to be found within this relatively unexplored yet highly consequential terrain. We believe that the exercise holds considerable promise for enlarging the empirical foundations and the analytical horizons of social movement and civil society research, as well as expanding our understanding of the bases of authoritarian rule, by encouraging debate and stimulating new research on this critical domain of state–society relations. The case studies which follow, drawn from very different historical periods and regional contexts, focus on four general questions: Why and when do states seek to mobilize social movements? What are the technologies of state mobilization (symbolic, materialistic, and coercive), and how do they evolve over time? What are the dynamics of state–society interaction to be found in these movements? And, finally, what are the consequences – for state and society alike – of relying on SMMs as a mechanism of governance?

1.2 WHY AND WHEN STATES SEEK TO ACTIVATE SOCIAL MOVEMENTS

In observing that all modern states actively seek to mobilize non-state collective actors in order to promote specific goals and secure vital state interests, we certainly do not mean that states are unitary actors. The state is a complex entity shaped by its historical development, regime type, specific institutional design, governing capacity, and leadership. In order to understand its active role in the domain of social movements and civil society organizations, a careful

---

[11] See Perry (2002).

distinction among differently situated state agents is crucial. Not only do different state actors often facilitate different types of mobilizing efforts and support different societal forces; social mobilization may be a dimension of intra-state conflict as well. The capacity to mobilize various publics can be a signal of strength among contenders for power within the state (see Kruszewska and Ekiert's Chapter 2 in this volume). Hegemonic or ruling parties may assume the role of mobilizing agency, or, alternatively, we may see a complex matrix of conflict and competition across the state–society divide.

The extent of state intrusion into the social domain has traditionally been linked to regime type, with mass mobilization techniques seen as a hallmark of fascist and communist regimes[12] as well as certain populist authoritarian regimes.[13] In democratic regimes, mobilization is usually depicted as the domain of political parties and civil society organizations, especially in times of elections.[14] History suggests that nondemocratic states have indeed been more frequent and skillful mobilizers of social movements than democratic states. In general, this has been understood as an effort to compensate for the deficit of infrastructural power that despotic states often face.[15] But, as our case studies illuminate, other motivations – from shoring up legitimacy to implementing policy priorities – may also prompt the deployment of SMMs by authoritarian and democratic regimes alike.

As recent Hindu nationalist demonstrations in India make clear, democracies are not immune to SMMs. Yet the different roles played by courts, legislatures, parties, and police under democratic and autocratic regimes generate differences in the protest arena as well.[16] Historically we find SMMs to be more common in authoritarian contexts. In this volume we focus on a range of authoritarian and semi-authoritarian examples. Our cases include classic communist regimes (1968 Poland and the People's Republic of China), classic authoritarian regimes (Taiwan in the 1950s–1970s), contemporary post-communist regimes (Russia, Ukraine, and Croatia), and an assortment of hard-to-categorize quasi-democratic regimes (the American South under Jim Crow, Bolivarian Venezuela, Mubarak's Egypt, and the Special Administrative Region of Hong Kong). We discover, however, that neither the motives nor the modes of SMMs are easily explained by regime type. All sorts of regimes (as Mark Beissinger's Chapter 6 points out, going at least as far back as the English, American, and French Revolutions of the seventeenth and eighteenth centuries) have sought to forestall revolutionary challenges by sponsoring counterrevolutionary contention.

A simple typology of state motivations covers the various cases examined in this volume. The first type is a *defensive or reactive mobilization* which occurs

---

[12] See Linz and Stepan (1996). [13] See, for example, Brennan (1998); Finchelstein (2017).
[14] See Rosenstone and Hansen (1995).
[15] For the distinction between infrastructural and despotic power, see Mann (1984).
[16] See Goldstone (2015).

when the state responds to a threat posed by genuine protest movements and opposition forces. Many of our cases, from the party-state response to student protests in 1968 Poland studied by Kruszewska and Ekiert in Chapter 2 to the recent Occupy Central movement in Hong Kong described by Lee in Chapter 12 and pro-state mobilizations in Egypt analyzed by Anderson and Cammett in Chapter 11, are of this sort. In these instances, SMMs are intended to combat challengers and slow down or stop the threatening mobilization process. Mobilizing counter-movements is a strategy to maintain the appearance of popular legitimacy and social support. Enlisting societal actors in defense of the state carries more symbolic and ideological weight than simply deploying the state's coercive resources. In Perry and Yan's discussion in Chapter 3 of Cultural Revolution China, we see the importance of both charismatic authority (with Mao Zedong's personal intervention) and ideological authority (with the deployment of the "politically correct" proletariat to defuse student unrest). The second type is a *spoiler or proactive mobilization* in which the state mobilizes societal actors to intimidate opposition forces and to preempt potential challenges by opposition movements. It is often used to undermine the diffusion of contention across national borders, as was the case with the Russian state's response to the Orange Revolution in Ukraine. Hemment's analysis of the Nashi youth movement illustrates this pattern. The third type is one in which states mobilize societal actors to enhance control over local or regional authorities or as a tool of factional *intra-state conflict* and struggle. In Handlin's case of Bolivarian Venezuela in Chapter 9 and Dolenec and Širinić's example of Croatian veterans' organizations in Chapter 10 we observe party-led mobilization for both electoral and interest group ends. The fourth type uses mobilization and contention as a *signaling device* to show displeasure at actions originating from other countries or taking place beyond the borders of the (local or national) state. In federalist or decentralized political systems, local governments may engage in this type of activity to indicate their opposition to political developments occurring elsewhere in the country. The case of Civil Rights–era Mississippi, analyzed by Cunningham and Owens in Chapter 5, signaled the intention of local authorities to resist the Civil Rights reforms being promoted in other parts of the United States. The fifth type is the use of mobilization techniques for *infrastructural development* to accomplish tasks that are not easy to carry out by routine bureaucratic policy implementation strategies. Looney's discussion in Chapter 4 of rural development programs in authoritarian-era Taiwan illustrates the value of campaign methods in effecting faced-paced change. In the case of contemporary China, Palmer and Ning in Chapter 13 show how state-sponsored volunteerism delivers social services while at the same time depoliticizing the younger generation. Finally, states may seek to mobilize collective actors *across national borders* in order to support territorial claims, destabilize international adversaries, or otherwise advance geostrategic interests. We can find this in Greene and Robertson's discussion in Chapter 8 of the Novorossiya movement, in which large numbers of sympathizers supported Russian military action in Ukraine.

Although regime type per se does not predict the precise modes of mobilization adopted by various states, our cases do suggest that some states use particular mobilization technologies more often and to greater effect than others. What accounts for variation in the routinization of certain mobilization techniques over time? Should we seek the reasons in a historical legacy of state-building through ideological diffusion and revolutionary mass mobilization, or should we investigate instead the institutional configuration of the state itself, regardless of its origins? Are weak or strong states more prone to the use of mobilization techniques? Are communist or populist authoritarian regimes especially likely to rely on mobilization as a method of governing? Is regime type a factor in explaining the success of state-led mobilization, with certain kinds of authoritarian states better able to reach their objectives through mobilization technologies than others?

Alternatively, to what extent are the frequency and effectiveness of state mobilization dependent upon the characteristics of society rather than of the state itself? Do dense civil society networks and robust movement sectors limit the state's capacity to penetrate and organize society for its own ends? Do these connections enable social actors to thwart or redirect state mobilization efforts for purposes quite different from those intended by state officials? Or, conversely, does a high degree of societal connectivity actually ease states' ability to channel social activism in directions favorable to their own designs?

In illustrating the broad contours of SMMs through a range of assorted twentieth- and twenty-first-century examples, drawn from a variety of regions and regime types, we do not mean to suggest that all our cases are best understood as fundamentally the same. Rather, our goal is to understand distinctions reflecting different political, cultural, and temporal circumstances. As has been frequently noted, the third wave of democratization gave birth to new forms of authoritarianism. These "hybrid" or "competitive authoritarian" regimes are distinct from classic communist and authoritarian-bureaucratic regimes and personalistic dictatorships.[17] The end of the Cold War also altered the ways in which surviving authoritarian regimes function. Some authoritarian regimes have incorporated the entire universe of representative institutions and relatively autonomous political space, including multiparty elections, legal political opposition, independent civil society organizations with transnational ties, and some independent media. Many have also embraced open borders and free trade and accepted international investment, travel, and information flows. A number have abandoned hard coercion in favor of more "friendly" or "vegetarian" forms of repression.[18] Some have

---

[17] See Schedler (2002); Schedler (2010); Carothers (2002); Levitsky and Way (2010); Brownlee (2007); and Krastev (2011).

[18] See Krastev (2011).

shifted from centralized, bureaucratic instruments of control and coordination to flexible strategies based on networks of social organizations linked in a variety of (often opaque) ways to the state apparatus. Centralized state propaganda and censorship have largely been superseded by public relations strategies, electronic surveillance, and "astroturfing." Schedler (2002, p. 59) notes that "these regimes represent the last line of authoritarian defense in a long history of struggle that has been unfolding since the invention of modern representative institutions. Rather than suppressing representative institutions altogether, or accepting only some of them, the new electoral authoritarian regimes of the post–Cold War era have embraced them all." Increasingly, however, it seems that these phenomena are not simply the last stand of a soon-to-be-extinct regime type. The resilience of Chinese authoritarianism, the consolidation of authoritarian rule in Russia, and the return of authoritarian politics to newly democratized Hungary and Poland call such a conclusion into question. Moreover, democratic regimes are also eagerly adopting and adapting elements of the authoritarian mobilization tool kit for purposes as diverse as combatting terrorism and capturing elections. Democracies with relatively recent authoritarian pasts are perhaps the most adept at societal mobilization,[19] but the practice is not limited to them. While this volume focuses on SMMs in authoritarian and semi-authoritarian contexts, we hope that other scholars will be inspired to extend the investigation to a range of democratic regimes.

The analytical move we endorse, from treating the state as a target of protest and social mobilization to seeing it as a proactive agent in the domain of social movements and civil society, raises a number of important questions about state motivations and mobilization technologies. States are skillful and resourceful mobilizers because – as political analysts from Hobbes to Huntington have observed – the state's most basic raison d'être resides in its capacity to ensure social order. As Migdal (1988, p. 21) pointed out, the state enjoys a "fantastic advantage over other political entities in mobilizing and organizing resources for war, as well as for other purposes." Social movements and civil society organizations (from nationalist groups in Russia and India to the Tea Party Movement in the United States) constitute attractive resources for the state – or more often for various factions within the state – as they combat one another and defend against competitors and challengers from both outside and inside the state.

This intrusion into the social realm is in part the result of a modern enlargement of the domain of the nation-state together with a reframing of political culture that accepts movements and protests as a legitimate way of expressing interests, passions, and identities. Although in the case of China we may trace the origins of this "modern" view all the way back to the ancient Confucian idea of the Mandate of Heaven, the concept underwent significant

---

[19] Garon (1997) traces continuities in "moral suasion" campaigns from wartime to postwar Japan.

transformation in the course of China's twentieth-century revolutions. Moreover, across the globe we see an increase in state intrusion as a result of new technologies of surveillance and mobilization. Our comparative investigation asks whether such mobilization strategies follow an indigenous historical tradition or are instead standardized and diffused transnationally. Are the precipitants, participants, and purposes of state-mobilized social movements best analyzed in terms of national, regional, or regime specific patterns, or are they better understood as global phenomena?

1.3 MOBILIZATION TECHNOLOGIES – FROM ORGANIZATIONAL WEAPONS TO SUBSIDIZED PUBLICS

Philip Selznick (1960) highlighted mobilization technologies of communist parties in which labor unions and other social associations and institutions were organizational targets for communist penetration and control to accomplish a range of political and economic goals. According to Selznick, the communist parties' strategy was first to infiltrate nonpolitical organizations and then to manipulate their activities for partisan advantage. During the takeover phase the capture of organizations was stealthy, but, following the consolidation of communist power, these previously autonomous organizations were used for state-led and state-sanctioned mobilization campaigns. In the process, the invisible hand of the communist party became a visible and sinister hand of the authoritarian state.

Over time, as states have matured in experience and sophistication, the mobilization technologies of governance and organizational infrastructure of state-led mobilization have graduated from bureaucratic enforcement and patronage networks to diffused techniques based on new communication technologies and decentralized networks of organizations. The results can be seen, for example, in the creative use of oppositional street tactics and corporate-world techniques. Hemment's description in Chapter 7 of the Nashi movement, with its use of both mass rallies and project design opportunities, illustrates this powerful admixture of mobilization technologies. The mature state, thanks to highly developed security sectors, is able to dispense with dependence on traditional bureaucratic organizations such as hegemonic parties or trade unions and other mass associations in favor of direct social mobilization. But it does not always choose to do so. As Palmer and Ning show in Chapter 13, in the case of contemporary China the use of semi-official "mass associations" (such as the Communist Youth League) continues to be a reliable means of mobilization for state ends. Often these state-promoted movements and purportedly "civil society" organizations use thuggish methods to intimidate and deter grassroots opposition – a phenomenon seen in the Jim Crow American South (Cunningham and Owens, Chapter 5) and contemporary Hong Kong (Lee, Chapter 12) alike. In several of the chapters to follow, off-duty police officers play a critical part in organizing SMMs, further muddying the distinction between state and societal actors.

Accordingly, state mobilization strategies are frequently less than transparent. Post-communist regimes may revert to a tactic of manufactured ambiguity, with regimes actively hiding the agency of the state in a manner reminiscent of their communist predecessors (see Kruszewska and Ekiert's Chapter 2 on 1968 events in Poland) and further blurring the boundary between state and non-state sectors. Moreover, state mobilization strategies mimic the form and style of independent movements and organizations, with mutual borrowing of tactics and technologies between pro- and anti-state actors (as shown in Chapter 7 by Hemment). In contemporary mobilization technologies, cultural and symbolic resources are critical, as was true in earlier eras as well (see Perry and Yan's Chapter 3 on the Cultural Revolution in China) and are often highly contested. State-sponsored organizations may hijack oppositional symbols and discourse to stir up historical memories and mobilize ethnic and religious prejudices. We find this in the nostalgia for Eurasianism promoted by the Russian state in calling for the "return" of Crimea (discussed by Greene and Robertson in Chapter 8).

A critical question concerns the recruitment strategies and target groups selected by mobilizing state agents. The state creates avenues for actors with preformed sentiments and grievances to express them against targets selected by the state. While the classic communist playbook was focused on the mobilization of concentrated social forces (industrial or agricultural workers, students, public sector employees, etc.), today's technologies are more likely to encompass diffused social elements. In this process, once powerful but now disadvantaged populations, such as laid-off workers in de-industrialized regions, are often among the key targets of recruitment. The patron–client relationship between veteran groups and the right-wing party HDZ, which as Dolenec and Širinić explain in Chapter 10 has dominated Croatian politics since that country's independence, is of this sort. Traditionally marginalized populations, whether for reasons of poverty or ethnicity, may also be targeted to cooperate with the state, as is the case, for example, in Bolivarian Venezuela (see Handlin's Chapter 9).

In short, contemporary state-mobilized social movements are frequently opaque in terms of both motives and methods. New social media, sophisticated surveillance techniques, and decentralized GONGOs often play a critical role. In many regimes, there has been a notable move from bureaucratic to market strategies, with the adoption of slick Madison Avenue–style appeals to disparate social elements, the offer of lucrative competitive financing to participating groups, and the encouragement of bottom-up movement entrepreneurship in place of top-down management. We can detect the use of these mixed techniques by democratic as well as authoritarian and semi-authoritarian regimes. In the United States, for example, President Trump (with the help of Fox News as well as his own

Twitter account) returns repeatedly to rowdy "campaign rallies" to promote his agenda, while in India Prime Minister Modi looks for ideological validation from right-wing Hindu nationalist groups such as the RSS (whose demonstrations are also fueled by social platforms and media feeds).

These disturbing examples are illustrative of a much broader tendency for contemporary states, authoritarian and democratic alike, to mobilize social movements as a form of "rule by other means." What are the sources of this evolution and convergence in mobilization technologies? Does it reflect the general transformation of modern states, regardless of regime type, in response to new, interconnected global challenges? Current debates in the United Kingdom and other democracies over increasing state control of the Internet to counter the threat of terrorism is perhaps one indication of such a development. The use of new social media to stimulate protest from Seoul to Shanghai suggests the growing political influence of cellular and wireless technology. Is the revolution in communication and information simultaneously expanding both state and societal capacity in ways that radically redraw long-standing boundaries between state and society? Or are we witnessing instead simply an elaboration and intensification of a familiar pattern of state-mobilization of social movements that (as Beissinger's Chapter 6 explains) emerged alongside the revolutionary advent of the modern nation-state more than two centuries ago?

New social media, once hailed by many as a weapon for civil society to forge powerful national and transnational networks of activism and thereby hasten a seemingly inevitable global march toward democratic governance, have of late largely lost their erstwhile glow. Initial reports of the Arab Spring had credited social media with a catalytic role in triggering the anti-authoritarian uprisings across the Middle East; subsequent analyses suggested a more complicated scenario, with considerable unevenness among countries. Rather than provide an open platform for a more inclusive public sphere, social media often accentuate and exacerbate existing political divisions, favoring tribalism over tolerance. Government authorities, like social activists, have recognized the utility of social media for targeting subgroups of the population with narrowly framed resonant messaging. President Trump's daily tweets, tossing out "red meat" to his Republican base, are a case in point. China and Russia are perhaps the most seasoned and sophisticated state sponsors of digital propaganda, with blogging factories that design and produce multiple lines of messaging, tailor-made for different audiences. If new social media once promised to empower autonomous civil society vis-à-vis the state, the balance now appears to have shifted decisively in favor of the latter. The overwhelming advantage that states (and a few large companies) enjoy in terms of financial and technological resources permits them to dominate the digital domain. Increasingly, states exercise this dominance through covert Internet and cellular governance techniques conducive to SMMs.

1.4 THE DYNAMIC OF STATE–MOVEMENT INTERACTION

The cases presented in this volume suggest that classic ideas about the incidence, importance, and nature of state-led mobilization may need to be reconsidered. The link between state-led mobilization and regime type is not as clear-cut as once assumed. In the literature on totalitarianism, high mobilization capacity was considered to be a defining characteristic of communist totalitarian regimes.[20] In addition, communist mobilization strategies were usually conceived as highly centralized, top-down, and bureaucratically managed campaigns coordinated either by the communist party or by state-run mass organizations, such as trade unions or youth organizations.[21] The involvement of party-state agents was transparent, and their strategies highly scripted. Participation in such campaigns was seen as coerced and ritualistic, and their ideological framing as non-resonant. Scott described this condition as the maintenance of a "public transcript" in which subordinate classes were forced to participate in the ritual of power legitimization.[22] According to Linz, in contrast to totalitarianism, authoritarian regimes in general sought to demobilize citizens and limit their political participation. Subsequent literature on authoritarian rule suggested, however, that SMMs are a staple of the governance tool kit, especially in populist and highly institutionalized authoritarian regimes (see, for example, Lisa Wedeen's study of Syria, *Ambiguities of Domination*).[23] Contemporary authoritarian and hybrid regimes seem more willing to make use of SMMs, thanks in part to the ready availability of new communication technologies.

A one-dimensional view of totalitarian state mobilization was challenged in later studies which showed that, far from being a straightforward top-down strategy, state-led mobilization efforts may dovetail with popular challenges from below and reflect multifaceted and often contradictory goals of state agents. Analyzing strategies of the Hungarian party-state, Hankiss (1989) describes the dynamic interaction among four processes inherent in any SMM: mobilization, demobilization, self-mobilization, and quasi-mobilization. Simultaneously, fostering mobilization of state-sponsored collective actors and pursuing demobilization of movements that rise to challenge the state is a balancing act with multiple unintended consequences. Thus, what were once considered to be straightforward cases of state-led mobilization under totalitarian regimes (such as the workers mobilized in Communist Poland and China and described in Chapters 2 and 3 of this volume) become more complex and nuanced phenomena under closer examination.

In short, SMMs under all regime types need to be understood as operating in a dynamic and interactive field with boundaries that extend beyond standard state–society channels and include outside actors as well. Such movements are

---

[20] See Linz (2000). [21] See Selznick (1960). [22] See Scott (1990). [23] See Wedeen (1999).

often decentralized, prone to diffusion, and weakly coordinated, as they originate not only from the top echelons of the state but also from competition among bureaucratic agents operating in multiple structural and spatial locations. Furthermore, both the mobilization technologies and the symbolic framing of SMMs are not automatically inherited as traditional "repertoires" of contention but involve considerable innovation, imitation, and adaptation on the part of state and society alike. In order to be successful, they must contain elements of authenticity and resonate with actual normative orientations and preferences of targeted audiences. From the charismatic aura of Chairman Mao in Cultural Revolution China to the anti-Semitism of protesters in Communist Poland to the nationalism of contemporary Russia, we see the convergence of state messaging with prevailing popular dispositions. Yet popular sentiments are themselves protean; during China's Tiananmen Uprising, which occurred after two decades of market reform, authorities mobilized public counterprotests on the basis of materialistic, rather than charismatic, appeals (see Perry and Yan's Chapter 3).

States need not always undertake direct mobilization in order to achieve their goals. Often the state (or elements of the state) can simply open sufficient political space to permit societal actors to engage in contestation that serves state interests. We may think of this process as creating a conducive "political opportunity structure" (to borrow the language of classic social movement theory), but in this case the opening reflects a conscious technology of rule rather than an unanticipated and unwelcome byproduct of elite division or state weakness. Under these circumstances, states may facilitate the emergence of new movements as well as co-opt and empower existing societal organizations. The result is a highly dynamic field of state–society interaction.

Chapters 6 and 7, by Beissinger and Hemment, draw attention to an issue that was largely overlooked by the classic approaches – individual motivation to participate in state-led mobilizations. The assumption that such participation must be either coerced or based on structural locations of individuals or on self-serving calculations and attractive selective incentives cannot be sustained. We cannot assume that bottom-up movements are inevitably authentic[24] whereas top-down movements are not. Participation in SMMs is seldom entirely forced or fabricated; these movements can also reflect genuine sentiments, identities, and interests on the part of significant segments of the populace. Successful state-led mobilization requires identity-formation processes that cannot take place without some degree of complicity and concurrence. As with any social movement, the framing of SMMs must echo elements of extant normative preferences (whether long-standing or recent in origin) in order to be persuasive (as Chapters 7 by Hemment and 8 by Greene and Robertson on Nashi and Novorossiya clearly show).

[24] See Goodwin and Jasper (2009).

State-Mobilized Movements: A Research Agenda

Our cases indicate that individual motives for participation vary significantly. People may feel pressured to participate by peer groups or patronage networks (as we find in examples from Croatia to Venezuela). They may be motivated by material concerns and selective incentives (as was the case to some extent in 1989 China), but equally they may respond to symbols, values, or partisan preferences or personal commitments to individual leaders (as was true in Cultural Revolution China or in Mubarak's Egypt). Our case studies point to the need for state-mobilizing agents to carefully consider preexisting preferences and normative orientations among targeted groups and craft appropriate technologies of mobilization in response. The mobilization process is a dynamic and often transformative experience in which initial identities, preferences, and normative orientations can be significantly reconfigured – sometimes along lines that contradict the initial goals of state agents (see Hemment's analysis of Nashi).

This mobilization can moreover take on disparate forms in different regions even within the same country. Local governments, it turns out, may react quite differently to common challenges. In China, Perry and Yan (Chapter 3) find that the cities of Beijing and Shanghai launched distinctive SMMs in response both to Red Guard unrest during the Cultural Revolution and to student protesters during the Tiananmen Uprising two decades later. In the American South, Cunningham and Owens in Chapter 5 observe varied reactions among local Mississippi communities to the Civil Rights Movement of the 1960s. Such subnational variation reflects dissimilarities in the underlying political economies, political cultures, and "enforcement networks" that characterize different places within the same national political system. This points to a rich potential for further exploration into the political geography of SMMs.

While we are primarily concerned here with SMMs directly created and coordinated by (various levels of) the state, a number of other possibilities exist. First, there are *accidental travelers*: movements that for the most part propel themselves and pursue their own agendas and goals without much reliance on state resources. When they do interact with the state, they do so in largely unplanned ways. From time to time they discover common goals and causes with the state and therefore mobilize on its behalf but in a largely autonomous way. Second, there are *fellow travelers*: groups and movements that are ideologically sympathetic to the state's goals and projects and share a similar agenda. They consciously cooperate with the state to advance the state's goals and help realize its projects. Such cooperation can be open and public but may also be less transparent. Yet these movements are not built by the state, nor are they financed or directed by the state. Finally, there are *delegated travelers*: groups constructed, financed, and directed by the state. These may be ersatz movements or what Jan Gross has described as "spoiler civil society."[25] Even they, however, have a tendency to stray from the official itinerary determined by the state.

In sum, our cases make clear the need to focus on agency on both sides of the state–society relationship, unfolding in complex interactive fields with profound uncertainties, internal contradictions, and unintended outcomes on the individual/participant level as well as on the organization/collective level. Our research must take into account the fuzziness and permeability of state–society boundaries, the complexity of modern states, and the multiplicity of mobilizing agents that often include actors from outside the state apparatus or even from beyond the national territory (see Dolenec and Širinić's Chapter 10 and Greene and Robertson's Chapter 8 in this volume). SMMs are often improvised and based on ad hoc innovations that go beyond the boundaries of previous strategies while at the same time being attuned to contextual factors and familiar legacies. A research agenda designed to take these concerns into account goes against the structural bias that has dominated classic theories of social movements and well as the simple coercion–concession dichotomy that has formed the basis of most theories of authoritarian resilience.

Implicit coercion and explicit inducements are not entirely absent from the realm of SMMs. Fear of losing one's pension or one's job at a state-owned enterprise or worry over future difficulties in procuring various government services for oneself or one's family may work to persuade otherwise indifferent citizens of the wisdom of participation. Similarly, the allure of an immediate handout or the promise of a promotion or improved access to state-supplied benefits may serve as a powerful positive incentive for participation. But SMMs depart from our stereotypic image of "totalitarian mobilization" in that these sorts of sticks and carrots are applied subtly, sparingly, and often surreptitiously.

Overt repression of civil society of course also remains an option for authoritarian regimes that deploy SMMs. Indeed, as the examples of China in 1968 and again in 1989 graphically demonstrate, military suppression may proceed hand in hand with SMMs. Regimes vary in the degree and circumstances under which they regard SMMs and coercive repression as complementary or contradictory strategies for restoring political order in moments of crisis. In some instances the two approaches are deployed simultaneously and are clearly intended to reinforce each other; in other cases they are seen as tradeoffs, while in yet other situations (when different elements of the state work at cross purposes) they may actually undermine one another. Here, too, is an area ripe for further empirical and theoretical exploration.

---

[25] See Gross (1989).

1.5 OUTCOMES AND CONSEQUENCES OF STATE-MOBILIZED MOVEMENTS

SMMs are a powerful weapon in the arsenal of the modern nation-state, but they can also backfire. State encouragement of societal engagement can give voice to previously unspoken disaffection. A public which grows accustomed to street demonstrations is not easily demobilized and may in time redirect its populist activism against the powers-that-be. The possibility of defection is real, as illustrated in the famous episode at the beginning of the Romanian Revolution in 1989 when the crowd, which had been mobilized to support Ceausescu, turned against the dictator. For this reason, nationalist protests – even when undertaken with clear state support – are usually regarded with a certain degree of ambivalence and anxiety by the sponsoring state itself. As the history of the Chinese Revolution illustrates, a public display of patriotism can escalate into a call for a change of political leadership or political system in the event that the state is perceived as unresponsive to popular demands for a decisive show of resolve. The Chinese Communist Party was itself a product of such a development when the nationalism of the May Fourth Movement of 1919 intensified into demands for revolution. Under such circumstances, state agents – succumbing to the temptations of fraternization with dissidents – may themselves defect, thereby converting a movement intended to augment state strength into its opposite. Contemporary Chinese regimes – even as they stimulate nationalistic protests for purposes of foreign policy signaling and regime legitimation – remain aware of their own history and quick to pull the plug on patriotic demonstrations that threaten to get out of hand.[26]

Many, though by no means all, of the SMMs presented in this volume rely upon appeals to nationalism as an organizing principle. In multiethnic societies, however, nationalism is an inherently ambiguous frame that can easily estrange some segments of society. This is especially true of ethnonationalist movements whose core cultural symbols resonate strongly with the sentiments of a particular subset of the populace. The effect of state sponsorship may be to alienate other social groups whose participation is required to fashion the sort of composite coalition that Beissinger (Chapter 6) sees as necessary for a successful counterrevolutionary offensive. Secession or revolution may be the unintended consequence of a nationalist movement that serves to splinter rather than to solidify the citizenry.

Less dramatically, state-sponsored social movements may simply fall short of desired objectives. Defensive/reactive mobilization may fail to weaken existing opposition forces or may even strengthen support for the opposition. Spoiler/proactive mobilization may not manage to prevent potential challengers from arising. Factional conflict on the part of both state and society may intensify rather than abate, producing entrenched polarization. The political cleavage in

---

[26] See Weiss (2014); Reilly (2012).

Hong Kong between "yellow" and "blue" sympathizers as a result of the anti-Occupy Central Movement, described by Lee, appears to be of this sort. And extra-bureaucratic campaigns do not guarantee sound and sustained infrastructure development (as Looney in Chapter 4 suggests was the case with rural development campaigns in South Korea and the PRC, in contrast to Taiwan).

The efficacy of technologies of mobilization is one variable in the likelihood of a movement's success or failure, but it is by no means the only one. Contextual factors, including the extent to which state and societal goals are closely aligned and mutually reinforcing, are also key considerations.[27] Although new digital technologies enable the state to mobilize a wider and more diffuse social constituency, the resulting cultural and ideological diversity can easily undermine the coherence and commitment of a movement.[28] The case of Nashi, discussed by Hemment (Chapter 7), illustrates the rise of individualized agency. Often, moreover, the outcome lies beyond the control of either state or society; as in Greene and Robertson's discussion (Chapter 8) of Novorossiya, larger international forces may work alternatively to further or to frustrate the objectives of SMMs.

"Ruling by other means" exhibits both the advantages and the disadvantages of circumventing the regular bureaucratic machinery of state in favor of a less routinized and institutionalized mode of governance. Under some conditions, such as 1989 China, SMMs may help to prolong a regime's lifespan by demobilizing a threatening opposition and demonstrating popular support for state resolve. Given the right circumstances, they may succeed in harnessing mass enthusiasm and energy toward important political or developmental objectives shared by state and society alike (see Looney's discussion of Taiwan in Chapter 4). Under less auspicious conditions, however, state-mobilized social movements may prove ultimately ineffective and may presage the decay or destruction of the sponsoring political system itself – as was the case with Communist Poland or, for that matter, the Jim Crow American South.

Whether SMMs represent the last gasps of doomed political and economic systems or the dynamic expression of powerful developmental states, they are a crucially important arena of state–society interaction. Not only do they challenge prevailing theories of social movements and state–society relations; they can have momentous – if sometimes monstrous – consequences. The Kristallnacht (or "Night of Broken Glass") in 1938 Germany, when Nazi leaders acting under the guise of a spontaneous demonstration incited a series of devastating pogroms against the Jewish population, was one

---

[27] In the case of Japan, Garon (1997) argues for a pervasive mobilizing spirit that unites state and society in pursuit of shared policy objectives.
[28] See Bennett and Segerberg (2012).

such instance. The Rwandan Genocide of 1994, spearheaded by Hutu members of the presidential guard and militia and directed against the minority Tutsis, was another. In both of these cases, high-level government officials helped to mobilize civilian supporters for protests that set off a spiral of violence with far-reaching results. Like cases analyzed in this volume, the incidents in Nazi Germany and Rwanda reflected authorities' desire to preempt opposition and build support for their own policies while at the same time leveraging issues and emotions replete with popular appeal. It is the (often unhappy) confluence of state–society concerns that imbues SMMs with such power. For better or worse, SMMs have been and will surely continue to be of world-changing significance. For that reason, we believe they should also constitute a vibrant research agenda for social scientists.

REFERENCES

Aminzade, Ronald, Jack Goldstone, Doug McAdam, Elizabeth J. Perry, William Sewell, Sidney Tarrow, and Charles Tilly. 2001. *Silence and Voice in the Study of Contentious Politics*. New York: Cambridge University Press.

Bennett, Lance, and Alexandra Segerberg. 2012. The logic of connective action: Digital media and the personalization of contentious politics. *Information, Communication and Society* 15 (5): 739–768.

Blok, Anton. 1972. The peasant and the brigand: Social banditry reconsidered. *Comparative Studies in Society and History* 14 (4): 494–503.

Brennan, James P. 1998. *Peronism and Argentina*. Wilmington, DE: SR Books.

Brownlee, Jason. 2007. *Authoritarianism in an Age of Democratization*. Cambridge: Cambridge University Press.

Carothers, Thomas. 2002. The end of the transition paradigm. *Journal of Democracy* 13 (1): 5–21.

Diamond, Larry Jay. 1999. *Developing Democracy: Toward Consolidation*. Baltimore, MD: Johns Hopkins University Press.

Finchelstein, Federico. 2017. *From Fascism to Populism in History*. Oakland: University of California Press.

Garon, Sheldon. 1997. *Molding Japanese Minds: The State in Everyday Life*. Princeton, NJ: Princeton University Press.

Goldstone, Jack A. 2003. *States, Parties, and Social Movements*. Cambridge Studies in Contentious Politics. New York: Cambridge University Press.

Goldstone, Jack A. 2015. Conclusion: Simplicity vs. complexity in the analysis of social movements. In Jan Willem Duyvendak and James M. Jasper (eds.), *Breaking Down the State: Protestors Engaged with Authorities*. Amsterdam: Amsterdam University Press, pp. 225–238.

Goodwin, Jeff, and James M. Jasper. 2004. *Rethinking Social Movements: Structure, Meaning, and Emotion (People, Passions, and Power)*. Lanham, MD: Rowman & Littlefield.

Goodwin, Jeff, and James M. Jasper. 2009. *Social Movements Reader: Cases and Concepts*. New York: John Wiley & Sons.

Gross, Jan T. 1989. Social consequences of war: Preliminaries to the study of imposition of communist regimes in East Central Europe. *East European Politics & Societies* 3 (2): 198–214.

Hankiss, Elmer. 1989. Demobilization, self-mobilization and quasi-mobilization in Hungary, 1948–1987. *East European Politics and Societies* 3 (1): 105–151.

Hobsbawm, Eric. 1959. *Primitive Rebels: Studies in Archaic Forms of Social Movements in the 19th and 20th Centuries*. Manchester: Manchester University Press.

Keane, John (ed.). 1988. *Civil Society and the State: New European Perspectives*. London: Verso.

Kokot, Michal. 2017 (January 13). Jak Kreml na nowo podbija Europe metodami KGB. *Gazeta Wyborcza*, www.gazetawy borcza.pl, accessed November 20, 2018.

Krastev, Ivan. 2011. Paradoxes of the new authoritarianism. *Journal of Democracy* 22 (2): 5–16.

Levitsky, Steven, and Lucan A. Way. 2010. *Competitive Authoritarianism: Hybrid Regimes after the Cold War*. Cambridge: Cambridge University Press.

Linz, Juan J. 2000. *Totalitarian and Authoritarian Regimes*. Boulder, CO: Lynne Rienner Publishers.

Linz, Juan J., and Alfred C. Stepan. 1996. *Problems of Democratic Transition and Consolidation: Southern Europe, South America, and Post-communist Europe*. Baltimore, MD: Johns Hopkins University Press.

Mann, Michael. 1984. *The Sources of State Power*. Vol. 1. Cambridge: Cambridge University Press.

Mcadam, Doug, Sidney Tarrow, and Charles Tilly. 2001. *Dynamics of Contention*. Cambridge: Cambridge University Press.

Migdal, Joel S. 1988. *Strong Societies and Weak States: State–Society Relations and State Capabilities in the Third World*. Princeton, NJ: Princeton University Press.

Naim, Moises. 2009 (October 13). What is a GONGO? *Foreign Policy*, https://foreignpolicy.com/2009/10/13/what-is-a-gongo/, accessed November 5, 2018.

Perry, Elizabeth J. 2002. *Challenging the Mandate of Heaven: Social Protest and State Power in China*. Armonk, NY: M. E. Sharpe.

O'Malley, Pat. 1979. Social bandits, modern capitalism and the traditional peasantry: A critique of Hobsbawm. *Journal of Peasant Studies* vi: 489–501.

Radnitz, Scott. 2010. *Weapons of the Wealthy: Predatory Regimes and Elite-Led Protests in Central Asia*. Ithaca, NY: Cornell University Press.

Reilly, James. 2012. *Strong Society, Smart State: The Rise of Public Opinion in China's Japan Policy*. Contemporary Asia in the World. New York: Columbia University Press.

Rosenstone, Steven J., and John Mark Hansen. 1995. *Mobilization, Participation and Democracy in America*. New York: Macmillan.

Schedler, Andreas. 2002. The menu of manipulation. *Journal of Democracy* 13 (2): 36–50.

Schedler, Andreas. 2010. Authoritarianism's last line of defense. *Journal of Democracy* 21 (1): 69–80.

Scott, James C. 1985. *Weapons of the Weak*. New Haven, CT: Yale University Press.

Scott, James C. 1990. *Domination and the Arts of Resistance: Hidden Transcripts*. New Haven, CT: Yale University Press.

Selznick, Philip. 1960. *The Organizational Weapon*. Glencoe, IL: The Free Press.

Smith, Jackie. 2004. The World Social Forum and the challenges of global democracy. *Global Networks* 4 (4): 413–421.

Tilly, Charles. 1978. *From Mobilization to Revolution*. Reading, MA: Addison-Wesley Pub.

Tilly, Charles. 1984. Social movements and national politics. In Charles Bright and Susan Friend Harding (eds.), *Statemaking and Social Movements: Essays in History and Theory*. Ann Arbor: University of Michigan Press, pp. 297–317.

Vojtiskova, Vladislava, Vit Novotny, Hubertus Schmid-Schmidsfelden, and Kristina Potapova. 2016. *The Bear in Sheep's Clothing. Russia's Government-Funded Organizations in the EU*. Brussels: Wilfried Martens Centre for European Studies.

Wedeen, Lisa. 1999. *Ambiguities of Domination: Politics, Rhetoric, and Symbols in Contemporary Syria*. Chicago, IL: University of Chicago Press.

Weiss, Jessica Chen. 2014. *Powerful Patriots: Nationalist Protest in China's Foreign Relations*. New York: Oxford University Press.

2

Manufactured Ambiguity*
Party-State Mobilization Strategy in the March 1968 Crisis in Poland

Dominika Kruszewska and Grzegorz Ekiert

2.1 INTRODUCTION

In January 1968, Poland's communist government banned *Dziady*, a Romantic play by Adam Mickiewicz, Poland's national poet, from the stage of the Warsaw National Theater due to its alleged anti-Russian and anti-Soviet undertones. After its last showing on January 30, a couple of hundred students gathered to protest the government's decision, ending with a demonstration in front of the poet's monument. The police responded with force, beating the protesters and arresting thirty-five participants. Two students, Adam Michnik and Henryk Szlajfer, were expelled from the University of Warsaw. On March 8, students from UW organized a rally at the university in their defense, expressing their solidarity and condemning the government's cultural policies. This protest also ended violently – the People's Militia (Milicja Obywatelska, MO) and plainclothes Voluntary Reserves of People's Militia (ORMO) dispersed the demonstration and brutally beat up participating students and bystanders.

This repressive action triggered a protest wave that swept through the country. In the following few weeks, university students and high school students came out in solidarity with Warsaw students in cities all over Poland (Eisler, 2008). Students won the support of part of the country's academic and intellectual elite, the Polish Church, and members of the Catholic caucus in the Polish parliament. Yet, facing state's strong-minded repressive actions, protests gradually died out with the last student rally staged at the University of Warsaw on March 28.

The communist state responded to protests with coercion and repressions. Student gatherings everywhere were brutally dispersed by uniformed and

---

* All translations are authors' own. We thank participants of the Mobilized Contention Workshops at Harvard University and Hong Kong University, Piotr Osęka, Liz Perry, and Dariusz Stola for helpful comments and conversations throughout the development of the project.

plainclothes security forces and party activists. In the process, hundreds were arrested and thousands expelled from universities. Those supporting the students were purged or ostracized. The party authorities threatened to close down universities, and, in fact, the faculties of Economics, Philosophy, and Sociology at Warsaw University were disbanded, while professors who supported student protests lost their positions. The state relied not only on repressive police actions against students, intellectuals, and members of the country's elite; it also launched the biggest wave of mobilization against its real and imagined enemies with hundreds of thousands of participants. These state-mobilized events ranged from street demonstrations and rallies in factories and public institutions to petitions and letters in support of the country's leadership. While the state and party involvement in organizing these mass events is apparent, the participation of the masses was not entirely coerced and staged. The Polish party-state employed a complex framing strategy to legitimate repressive actions, settle conflicts within the top communist elite, and secure a modicum of genuine popular support.

Was the state-mobilized movement (SMM) in response to student protests in 1968 a case of a classic communist campaign that is centralized, scripted, and based on communist-controlled mass organizations? How was it organized and coordinated by the communist party? Who participated in counterprotests? Was participation voluntary or coerced? What was the framing strategy employed by the Polish party-state? How resonant was that framing strategy? In this chapter, we will show that the actions of Polish authorities were strategic, nuanced, and designed to activate genuine political preferences and identities that persisted in Polish society. However, we will also show that, unlike in earlier communist campaigns, actors behind the mobilization were not just following central directives. The campaign relied to a large degree on diffusion and imitation. Initiatives taken by lower-rank officials and horizontal communication within party structures were common, taking a form that some party leaders in the Central Committee found worryingly extreme.

2.2 LITERATURE AND THEORY

The crisis in March 1968 in Poland is a case of *defensive countermobilization* by the authoritarian (communist) state challenged by mass protests in a situation of deepening intra-elite conflicts and divisions. The state-mobilized contention was very swift, took a number of specific forms, and was structured by a hybrid political frame combining a traditional nationalist discourse with elements derived from the communist ideology and classic populist rhetoric. While state-led mobilization was coordinated through bureaucratic channels and enforcement networks[1] of the party-state, there was room for local

---

[1] For more discussion of the role of enforcement networks in state-mobilized movement, see Chapter 5 in this volume.

experimentation and bottom-up initiatives. Contentious events were also not evenly distributed across the country, indicating the significant role of local agency. Moreover, the specific mobilization agents and the nature of participation in these events were not fully transparent, reflecting the state strategy we describe as *manufactured ambiguity*. This specific nature of state-led mobilization in Poland does not fit well the classic image of a mobilizing communist totalitarian state.

In the classic literature on totalitarianism, high mobilization capacity is considered to be a defining characteristic of communist totalitarian regimes (Linz, 2000). Communist mobilization strategies are usually conceived as highly centralized, top-down, and bureaucratically managed campaigns coordinated either by the communist party or by state-run mass organizations, such as trade unions or youth organizations (Selznick, 2014 (1952)). They are transparent and scripted. Participation in such campaigns is seen as coerced and ritualistic and the ideological framing as non-resonant. Scott (1990) described this as maintenance of the "public transcript," in which subordinate classes are forced to participate in the ritual of power legitimization.

This simplistic view of state-led mobilization was challenged in the subsequent literature on state socialism. Far from being a straightforward top-down strategy, state-led mobilization efforts not only interact with popular challenges from below but also reflect different and often contradictory goals of the mobilization agents. Analyzing strategies of the Hungarian party-state, Hankiss (1988) describes the dynamic interaction among four processes – mobilization, demobilization, self-mobilization, and quasi-mobilization – that are inherent in any state-led mobilization efforts. Simultaneously fostering mobilization of state-sponsored collective actors and pursuing demobilization of collective actors who challenge the state is a balancing act with multiple unintended consequences. In short, state-led mobilization strategies need to be considered as taking place in the interactive field with boundaries that often go beyond state–society relations and include outside actors as well. Moreover, such mobilization efforts are often decentralized and weakly coordinated as they originate not necessarily from the top of the party-state hierarchies but from competition among bureaucratic agents from multiple structural locations. Finally, both technologies and framing of mobilization involve innovations, crafting, and diffusion. In order to be successful, they also need to contain elements of authenticity and resonate with actual preferences of targeted audiences.

The 1968 campaign in Poland represents well the strategic dilemmas of SMMs. It shows dispersed crafting by mobilizing agents and horizontal diffusion. These agents used innovative framing departing from classic communist themes and mostly supplied by state-controlled media. It also involved multiple mobilizing actors with often-contradictory goals reflecting conflicts and divisions within Polish communist elites. Although the agency was clearly embedded in the party-state mobilization and enforcement networks, including hierarchies of the communist party, mass organizations and media, the campaign was not a strictly top-down process. It was decentralized, with many local initiatives, featuring diffusion of strategies across different locations, as well as experimentation by local party and mass organizations agents. It also involved sophisticated use of various framing strategies that borrowed not only from the communist arsenal of ideas and symbols but also from resurrected and reformulated historical and national discursive elements and populist idioms in order to appeal to various groups in Polish society. In fact, it was based on genuinely resonant cultural frames and activated identities that have been shared among the Polish population. Mass participation in contentious events was not fully coerced but had a significant element of volunteerism based on interests for some and identities for others. In short, mobilized contention not only was designed strategically, involved a complex framing strategy, and was implemented with a high degree of precision to make an impression of spontaneous and wide support for the communist party; it was also, to a large degree, spontaneous, voluntary, decentralized, and diffused across the country.

While the SMM in 1968 is not a simple case of a top-down strategy, it nevertheless shares affinity with mobilization campaigns in bureaucratic and highly repressive communist one-party states. Although the process of mobilization was not strictly top-down or centralized, existing bureaucratic and organizational mobilization and enforcement networks were used, following a familiar pattern. This created the conditions for almost instant mobilization and demobilization of state-mobilized actors when the state goals were accomplished. In short, classic state-led mobilization was episodic – crowds were rallied and disbanded in an instant. Our event analysis shows this dimension of state-led contention very well. Moreover, the role of media and framing strategies, involving resurrection of collective memories, resentments, and hybridization, were at the heart of mobilization efforts.

In the following sections, we place March 1968 in the larger context of SMMs in communist Poland, a comparison that highlights the unique features of this case. Then, we analyze this state-led mobilization strategy by discussing the unfolding of the campaign over time, its organizational patterns, technologies of mobilization, and the framing strategy.

2.3 CONTEXT

March 1968 was one in a series of crises of the communist regime in Poland. Waves of protest challenging the state organized by different social groups swept through the country in 1956, 1968, 1970, and 1976 (Ekiert, 1997). Occasionally, the party also engaged in mobilization campaigns against real or perceived international and domestic enemies, such as the 1965 campaign against American imperialism in Vietnam or the 1966 campaign against the

Roman Catholic Episcopate. Among these campaigns, party-state response to student protests in 1968 stands out as unique on a few dimensions: the scale of propaganda and mobilization, its relatively decentralized character, the channeling of popular discontent to scapegoat political enemies, expand party support, and make sweeping personnel changes, as well as an innovative and resonant framing strategy based on "historical work" activating genuine cultural preferences and preexisting resentments, in particular nationalism and anti-Semitism.

Unlike other campaigns, such as for example, the campaign in support of the North Vietnamese communist regime, which could be characterized as "merely state-driven, controlled" mobilization, "routinized and emptied of meaningful political content" (Mark et al., 2015, p. 440), the March 1968 campaign was innovative in discourse, repertoire, and organization. "The regular top-down procedure of preparing and launching campaigns was altered" with a much more bottom-up, horizontal organizational style, in which the "initiators employed other channels of communication with lower-level echelons" (Stola, 2005, p. 289). In fact, at the beginning there was no central directive: "there apparently were no specific instructions from the party's Central Committee departments as to who in particular was to be targeted and what the exact content of the slogans should be." Instead, "the mass media in particular provided models of behavior to be adopted" by publicizing descriptions of early rallies, which were then imitated throughout the country (Stola, 2005, p. 289). This decentralized organizational pattern, which activated horizontal structures in the party and in which spontaneous diffusion and imitation played a more important role than instructions from the top, differentiates the March campaign from previous and subsequent SMMs in Poland.

Another unique feature of the March 1968 campaign is the defensive character of the mobilization in reaction to a threat posed by protesting students who were the first generation born and raised in communist Poland. It is important to note, however, that at that point in time the party, though threatened, was still acting from a position of dominance. Party mobilizing agents did not fear that the mobilization they facilitated and encouraged might spiral out of control and turn against them.[2] After 1980, when the party authorities realized that the mobilizational capacity of the opposition exceeded their own, such campaigns were no longer undertaken. The March 1968 campaign is also the last mass campaign, which might be characterized as a deliberate hate campaign. Subsequent campaigns took a more positive tone and did not create a powerful image of an enemy, perhaps because campaigns fueled by anger, frustration, and prejudice are

---

[2] Although notes from the meeting of the Political Bureau do reveal concerns among top leadership that the rhetoric used against the students might also place the party in a negative light (Garlicki, 1993).

more difficult to control than routine calls for support or increases in production and can only be managed by a party with a firm grip on power.

The student rebellion in March 1968 unfolded against the background of a deeper political crisis within the Polish communist elites. During the previous ten years, concessions offered to various groups in Polish society as a result of the de-Stalinization crisis of 1956 were gradually withdrawn. The leadership of Władysław Gomułka, First Secretary of the Polish Workers' Party, reversed liberalizing trends, and the "small stabilization" program brought economic and political stagnation. Thus, the revisionist forces within the party, emboldened by the reform movement in neighboring Czechoslovakia, hoped for policy changes and return to October 1956 promises of liberalization and reforms. At the same time, a nationalist and conservative faction within the party led by Mieczysław Moczar (so-called Partisans, since they were members of the communist underground during the war) sensed the opportunity to strengthen and consolidate their power within the party leadership and oust Gomułka and his allies. Therefore, the 1968 crisis comprised of two rebellions: first, by a generation of disaffected university students supported by a part of the intellectual and academic elite demanding cultural and political liberalization; and second, by the generation of party activists in their forties representing various political options, whose upward mobility was blocked by the stagnant political and economic system (Interview with J. Eisler, 2013).

2.4 STATE-MOBILIZED MOVEMENT – EVENT ANALYSIS

The state-mobilized response to events at the University of Warsaw on March 8 and 9 began with mass rallies and resolutions on March 11. On the same day, the first article with the party's interpretation of events appeared in *Trybuna Ludu*, the regime's official daily, and on March 12 the newspaper began reporting on countermobilization events. From mid-March to mid-April the country was engulfed by a wave of official rallies, manifesting support for the party and calling for punishment of the protesters. Relying on an enormous party apparatus and organizations infiltrating all aspects of life, the party went on an offensive, not only countering (or rather denouncing) criticisms issued by the protesting students and intelligentsia but also mobilizing society against the challengers and in support of the party. Figure 2.1 plots the number of counterprotest events between March 8 and June 24 – the duration of the campaign – across the country as reported by Trybuna Ludu (with dates signifying date reported).

According to the classified report of the PZPR Central Committee,[3] the countermobilization was massive – as of March 26, local party organizations (POP) organized over 1,900 meetings and close to 400 rallies and adopted about 1,150 resolutions to condemn the organizers of the student protests and express

---

[3] Information nr 64/A/4402 from March 28, 1968, Warsaw.

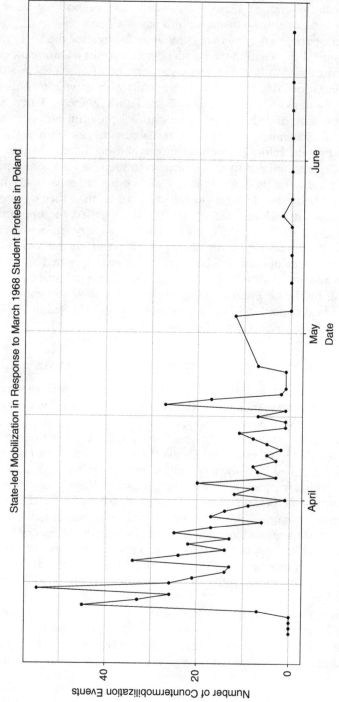

FIGURE 2.1 State-mobilized movement: March 8 to June 24, 1968

support for the party (Kula et al., 1998, p. 242). The report of the Gdańsk Voivodeship Party Committee from March 14[4] states: "in workplaces, party organizations are still organizing party meetings and mass rallies. Since yesterday organization of meetings in groups and – on a large scale – individual agitation began. Party members are getting more and more engaged and taking on more combative and offensive stances" (Kula et al., 1998, p. 101).

Figure 2.2 plots the counterprotest events by type of event starting on the date of the first report of a countermobilization rally – March 12.

One of the main forms of countermobilization to student protests was a mass rally, usually organized in factories and workplaces. Most rallies culminated in an adoption of a resolution condemning the protesters and expressing support for the party line. This is why, in Figure 2.2, incidences of rallies and resolutions trend together with differences likely stemming from reporting: resolutions were not always mentioned in reports about rallies and vice versa. However, party organizations in workplaces across the country continued issuing resolutions even after rallies had died down following about a week of fervent activity. The rallies began with the meeting of Warsaw party activists on March 11, which gathered about 6,000 people coming straight from work. The protests diffused quickly: within a week, hundreds of lower-level party organizations and all voivodeship secretaries organized rallies resembling the Warsaw event. Remarkably, the initial similarities between the rallies "most likely did not stem from centrally given directions, but from mimicry and information exchange among different party committees" (Stola, 2000, p. 108). This involved an activation of horizontal structures in the party, particularly given "a kind of political vacuum caused by the silence of the leadership" (Stola, 2000, p. 108). Diffusion happened without instructions from the party's Central Committee, mostly through officials at the lower levels of the party, who – familiar with prior campaigns – could almost mechanically recreate previous patterns of behavior: "there were also telephone calls to trustworthy comrades in provincial committees and a good deal of imitation and 'horizontal' consultation between midlevel apparatchiks on what to do" (Stola, 2005, p. 289). The speeches and slogans at local meetings throughout the country mostly mirrored the press propaganda and the initial Warsaw meeting (Stola, 2000).

For example in Katowice, the capital of Upper Silesia, Poland's industrial southwestern region, "since March 12 – from the inspiration of Voivodeship Committee of the Polish Workers' Party – an action condemning student protests in Warsaw began. Neither in the press nor during organized mass rallies and meetings – what is very characteristic – was there a mention of demonstrations and gatherings of students that were taking place in the Katowice voivodeship" (Miroszewski, 2009, pp. 83–84). Only the state-led

---

[4] Information nr 34/A/4371.

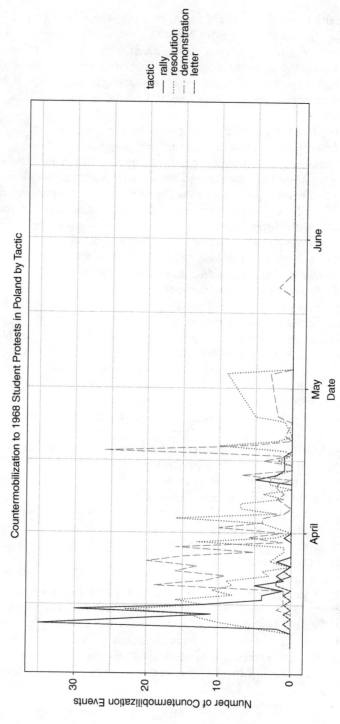

FIGURE 2.2 State-mobilized movement by repertoire: March 12 to June 24, 1968

Manufactured Ambiguity: March 1968 in Poland

response was being covered. Mass rallies of workers in major steelworks, coal mines, and factories were organized in solidarity with Warsaw workers, condemning "the culprits of irresponsible disturbances" and demanding "restoration of calm and order in Warsaw and consequences for the instigators." Workers would yell "Work! Calm! Work! Calm!" and express support for the party (*Trybuna Robotnicza*, nr 62–63, 1968).

The mass rallies, which took place on March 14 in a range of cities in the Upper Silesia region, were similar to each other in organization and slogans. At the end, participants were bused to Katowice, where about 100,000 people gathered in and around a square in the city center to hear a speech by Edward Gierek, who was a party leader in the province at the time. Gierek's words made their way into the resolution read by one of the miners and adopted during the manifestation (Miroszewski, 2009).

Geographically, as Figure 2.3 shows, distribution of state-led rallies and demonstrations suggests that countermobilization was not a simple reaction to student protests. Some of the sites with multiple rallies – such as Łódź or Szczecin – are cities that did not experience substantial student protests. Rather than in places with high student mobilization, counterprotests seem to have taken place in the largest, industrial cities, where coal mines and factories were located. It is possible that in many cities, for instance of the Upper Silesia region

FIGURE 2.3 State-mobilized movement across the country: Number of reported rallies and demonstrations

(Katowice and neighboring cities), organizing rallies and demonstrations was a signaling game in which potential contenders for power showed their ability to mobilize support. Thus, SMMs can be a powerful factor in intra-elite conflicts.

On March 19, Gomułka gave a speech to the party activists in Warsaw. This is a point where – as Figure 2.2 shows (with a reporting lag), an increase in letters as a tactic began. Gomułka's address, according to the official propaganda, triggered an outpouring of support: party activists everywhere – in factories, mines, schools, villages – sent letters to the party leadership and Gomułka personally, expressing their support for the party line. *Trybuna Ludu* eagerly reported on those letters, some of them sent directly to their offices, coming from all corners of Poland, citing passages from them and highlighting their overwhelming number.[5] Headlines like "For Poland and Socialism – against the instigators" dominated the paper for weeks.[6]

By early April, the countermobilization began to decline. Letters of support and, to a lesser degree, resolutions – as reported by *Trybuna Ludu* – spiked briefly in mid-April in response to a controversy over the behavior of Znak, the Catholic Caucus of nominally independent deputies in the Polish parliament. On April 11, Znak used a parliamentary question to oppose the brutal use of force against the students. The party's propaganda machine responded by reporting on renewed outpour of support for the party's stance and letters and resolutions disagreeing with the position of the Catholic Caucus. But by the beginning of May, the press had moved on to Labor Day parades, commemoration of victory over fascism, and production targets, striking a much more positive tone. Throughout May, articles about anti-Polish activities and Zionist propaganda in the West would appear periodically, peppered with testimonies of Poles who aided Jews during World War II[7] and political speeches that drew on themes related to March events.[8] The countermobilization to March events did not fully end until June 24, when Gomułka made a speech in which he officially condemned the anti-Zionist campaign, bringing it to a stop.

---

[5] In interpreting Figure 2.2, it is important to note that letters were likely reported in "bursts": even if they continuously trickled in over a number of days, the newspaper would report many of them in one article, demonstrating overwhelming support.

[6] See, for example, *Trybuna Ludu* (March 19, 1968).

[7] See, for example, a call from the Polish diaspora in Canada, "Piętnujemy akcje szkodzące Polsce" [We are condemning the actions hurting Poland], *Trybuna Ludu* (May 22, 1969), for an article about anti-Polish campaign of the Western Zionist organizations. See, for example, "Świadectwo prawdy" [Testimony to the truth], *Trybuna Ludu* (May 22, 1968), for discussion of Poles helping Jews during the war intended to highlight the supposedly ungrateful and anti-Polish behavior of Jews involved in the events of 1968.

[8] See, for example, a speech by Marian Spychalski, leader of the Front of National Unity, on June 8. "Rozwój Polski Socjalistycznej celem wszystkich patriotycznych sił Frontu Jedności Narodu" [The development of Socialist Poland the aim of all patriotic forces of the Front of National Unity], *Trybuna Ludu* (June 8, 1968).

2.5 STATE-MOBILIZED MOVEMENT – TECHNOLOGIES OF MOBILIZATION

The Polish party-state's response to student protests was a case of reactive or defensive mobilization. To launch it, mobilization agents relied on legacies of previous campaigns combined with innovations, among which the most important was the shift to nationalism as a framing strategy. "From the communist repertoire of previous purges and hate campaigns" from the 1950s, the March 1968 campaign took "in addition to some slogans and stereotypes of the enemy, also ready-made schemes for behavior of units and institutions, organizations practiced in their realization and the typical Orwellian newspeak" (Stola, 2004, p. 66). As in the case of previous campaigns, classic mobilization and enforcement networks were used to stage rallies and demonstrations across the country. Thus, with the party-state as the primary organizer, the campaign started quickly and developed efficiently with a consistent and coherent message. As Figures 2.1 and 2.3 show, within a span of a month hundreds of events were organized across the entire country. Party activists, experienced in mobilization campaigns, relying on preexisting scripts and behavioral patterns (typical of communist regimes), combined with innovation and emulation (more typical of social movements), could be mobilized and demobilized rapidly. Unlike in the case of all but the most massive social movements, when the state, or even some elements of the state, throws its weight behind the mobilization, the access to resources is unparalleled. Before the end of March 26, over 1,900 meetings of local party organizations (Podstawowa Organizacja Partyjna, POP) and their subdivisions (Oddziałowe Organizacje Partyjne, OOP) dedicated to the March events took place throughout Poland (Kula et al., 1998, p. 242). From state- and party-controlled organizations present in schools and workplaces, through thousands of committed and/or motivated party officials and activists with bureaucratic resources, to a massive propaganda apparatus, the range of resources at the state's disposal put classical concepts such as resource mobilization into a new light.

2.5.1 Mobilizing Networks: Party Structures, Trade Unions, and Mass Organizations

The party relied on unions and party activists in factories to organize mass rallies (so-called *masówki*), which were "carefully planned and staged by regional PZPR committees, closely cooperating with party organizations and the management of factories" (Eisler, 2008, p. 117). Together, they ensured high attendance and strategic distribution of party activists in the room, provided banners, slogans, and text for the speeches, and created appearances of enthusiasm and engagement for the sake of televised reports. The practice of organizing the rallies at the workplace, often during work hours, presumably under threat of job loss and even transporting the demonstrators to the event is reminiscent of some the tactics still used in hybrid regimes where autocrats induce employers to mobilize their employees to vote for the regime's party (Frye et al., 2014).

The resolutions adopted by workers were often "presented for approval," and factory managers would "receive" them prior to the meeting or rally, presumably from regional party officials. Documents from the Ministry of Interior reveal that, in some cases, informers reported that resolutions enjoyed very little support, and there were voices in the crowd "undermining the critical text of the resolution draft." Names of those who criticized the resolution or party politics were carefully noted. An opposing vote on a resolution condemning student protests could cost a worker his or her job, as could expressions of support for Israel or a claim made "during the mobilization of party activists in case student riots needed to be put down" that one "will not follow party orders and go beat the students up"[9] (Dąbrowski et al., 2008, pp. 531–532). Both carrots and sticks were used to encourage workers' actions against students. At one point, Lech Wałęsa remarked bitterly that "a bonus for the willingness to beat up students at the time was two thousand per person," not a small amount considering that for many workers this was their entire monthly salary (Eisler, 2008, pp. 117–118).

The party also took measures to control the content of speeches made during the rallies. Interviews conducted twenty years later by Marek Zieleniewski (a journalist from a weekly "Wprost") with two workers who spoke or read resolutions during March rallies and whose names made it into the newspapers reveal that the party ordered and staged at least some of the performances at mass rallies, even if the sentiment was indeed shared by a subset of workers. Jerzy Niedziałkowski, who worked as a locksmith at the time, recounted that "a secretary of the party organization (POP) approached me and said I had to make a speech. 'I don't have to but I can' – I responded. I did not use the paper that was slipped to me but in a few of my own words I expressed what I thought [...] then I spoke with a clear conscience. I heard that the youth was listening to provocateurs and destroying the common good. The press wrote a lot about it" (Eisler, 1991, p. 349).

The party apparatus also ensured that a sufficient amount of cheering and applause took place during the rallies. For instance, Hillebrandt (1986) notes that, during Gomułka's speech in Warsaw's Congress Hall, cheers in support of Gierek were coming from groups strategically distributed among delegates of workers from Wola, a district of Warsaw. Hillebrandt (1986) also suggests that the subsequent career of the First Party Secretary in that neighborhood could be

---

[9] The case of Helena Rey from CHZ "Minex" provides an example of the former, and of Stanislaw Malejonek from CHZ "Motoimport" of the latter. Steps were also taken to exclude Malejonek from the party. See document number 402 with notes from informants in the IPN collection. Source AIPN, 0236/160, k. 188–192, mps.

an indication of the source of the first pro-Gierek demonstration. First Secretaries of the Voivodeship Committees would also often appear at mass rallies in factories and shipyards. "The tone was almost identical" across rallies all over Poland: "an attack on intellectuals" in which "a constant set of names" appeared and the "demand to cleanse the apparatus of Zionists" were recurring themes (Eisler, 1991, p. 358).

In some cases, speakers were drawn from different socioeconomic groups to represent the breadth of support – e.g. at a rally in the Gdańsk shipyard on March 16, speeches were made first by the First Secretary of the Warsaw Committee, then by a worker, an engineer, and a vice-rector of a university (Kula et al., 1998, p. 129). Wałęsa's description of another rally as carefully planned with seating charts, including special forces, party secretaries, workers and directors, provides another clue for how scripted the countermobilization to civil unrest at universities was (Eisler, 1991, p. 349).

Even if the workers agreed with the party's spin on March events – uninformed about the events, unaware of student postulates, influenced by the propaganda in the press or because it expressed some of their grievances – the party attempted to control the organization and the course of rallies. Moreover, as Osęka (1999) points out: "[R]egardless of whether the gathered worker activists expressed their genuine feelings or whether they were forced to act out a spectacle, organizing a manifestation of loyalty on such a broad scale serves as a testimony to a considerable efficiency of the party apparatus" (p. 7).

2.5.2 The Role of State Media

As much as hierarchical mobilization and enforcement networks were instrumental in mobilization strategy, state media provided the language and framing for mobilization. The mass rallies were accompanied by an intense propaganda campaign in the press: reporting on the demonstrations; printing speeches, resolutions, and letters sent to the party executives, citing declaration of support; exposing the backgrounds and connections of organizers of student protests; and commenting on the events. Although evidence of party directives sent to the press is missing, there are many indications that the narrative was shaped, if not directly dictated, by the party's relevant committees and propaganda units.

First, the language of press articles and printed rally speeches was almost identical to that of internal party documents – be it reports from the Ministry of Interior or propaganda bulletins. "The materials used by March publicists," writes Osęka (2010), "in particular about the private lives of 'Zionists' and their family connections ... did not come from investigative journalism. Today we know that some threads, and even entire fragments of March articles were word for word taken from reports and operational materials of SB," Poland's security service. It is evident that journalists copied them verbatim because "even syntax and grammatical errors were copied" (p. 153). Furthermore, the "compact and uniform image of the enemy, which emerges out of the propaganda discourse" makes it "hard to suppose that journalists out of their own initiative conducted such a large-scale campaign." This seems to be a case especially given the consistency and coherence of themes: "in different texts appear not only the same incarnations of the enemy or similar patterns of accusations, but even identical phrases, and even entire paragraphs" (Osęka, 1999, p. 89).

Historian Dariusz Stola also makes a claim about language similarity as an indication of the origin of the documents – the comparison of anti-Zionist leaflets and newspaper articles with the "Internal Bulletin" of the Ministry of Interior makes it clear that the Ministry was the source of propaganda. The blueprint for accusations, information about involved students and their families, and again common mistakes – such as including names of people who could not have been present or the same misspellings of names (Stola, 2000) – can be traced back to Security Service (SB) and Ministry of Interior (MSW). Though internal propaganda bulletins of PZPR were not intended for wider circulation, they "were undoubtedly read by many journalists and lower-level party functionaries, and the concepts included in them were mimicked in rally speeches and hundreds of high-circulation articles" (Osęka, 1999, p. 13). However, "we do not know how confidential documents were passed to the journalists and to what degree their contacts with security service were formalized" (Osęka, 2010, p. 153).

Second, even if there is no evidence of party orders directing the press to conjure a particular image of the enemy, there is evidence of pressure put on editors reluctant to join the hate campaign. For instance, Stanisław Brodzki, assistant editor-in-chief of weekly *Świat*, which was not publishing anti-Zionist articles, was called in to the Press Bureau and instructed to participate because "the Fatherland calls" (Eisler, 1991, p. 368). The Ministry of Interior created a special team to evaluate the positions of journalists, expressed not just publicly but even privately, on the Six-Day War, resulting in dismissal of most of the journalists under investigation (Stola, 2000).

Also the anti-student sentiment was strongly shaped by the press propaganda. In the articles of the state's newspaper, *Trybuna Ludu*, students were always portrayed as not only not united with the workers but also hostile to them.[10] Moreover, likely in an attempt to discredit the demonstrators, student protests were described as organized by "small but very rowdy groups" and their "anti-people and anti-nation" character was stressed, implying that it is "the party and national obligation to counteract it."[11] The allegedly small number of protesting students was contrasted with numerous declarations of support for the party, also from academic circles, and

---

[10] "Wokół zajść na Uniwersytecie Warszawskim" [Around the events at Warsaw University], *Trybuna Ludu* (March 11, 1968).

[11] "Co się kryje za ulicznymi awanturami?" [What is behind the street fights?], *Trybuna Ludu* (March 12, 1968).

overwhelming turnout at rallies. The propaganda also juxtaposed descriptions of limos belonging to the protesting students' parents with workers' sweat; complaints of spoiled children with sacrifices made daily in factories; distant intellectuals with their gaze toward the West with patriotic workers and farmers toiling for a better future of the People's Republic. Students' militant and disruptive behavior was contrasted with restraint and calm of the workers, limited and mostly misguided support for the student demonstrators with unquestioning and broad support for the party.

The propaganda also focused on the theme of laborers working so that the country can provide universal education for the ungrateful students, brainwashed by Western media and pampered by learning conditions created by the People's Republic, engaging in anti-state activity. For example, *Trybuna Ludu* reprinted a speech made by Edward Sanecki at the Warsaw Committee meeting in which he stressed that "we will make effort to ensure that those who study for our money do not have the opportunity to conduct hostile activities."[12] Press articles about scholarships received by university students, outlining the percentage of students on stipends, the amount of money dedicated to student support, and scholarships granted by factories, reinforced this discourse.[13]

In addition to articles describing the party's narrative of events, "exposing provocateurs," printing workers' resolutions and speeches by party officials, the press also published letters or fragments of letters of support, sent in large numbers to Gomułka and the Central Committee of the party, which resembled the resolutions in form and content – expression of solidarity with the party and disapproval of students' actions, often ending with a pledge to increase production above targets.[14]

2.6 STATE-MOBILIZED MOVEMENT – FRAMING

The propaganda offensive launched in response to student rebellion was innovative by the standards of communist Poland. It was founded on three interlocking political idioms: xenophobic nationalism directed against the West and in particular against Germany; anti-Semitism; and anti-elite and anti-intellectual Marxist populism. Nationalism and anti-Semitism were resurrected strands deeply embedded in Poland's pre–World War II experience. The populist idiom was based on the glorification of productive

---

[12] "Głos aktywu partyjnego Stolicy" [The voice of the party aktiv in the capital], *Trybuna Ludu* (March 13, 1968).
[13] With headlines like "Over 190 thousand students receive scholarships" (p. 4) and "Milliard PLN for the student care" (p. 9) on March 16 and 17 respectively. See also Gomułka's speech on March 20: "Stanowisko partii – zgodne z wolą narodu" [The stance of the party – in line with the will of the nation], *Trybuna Ludu* (March 20, 1968).
[14] See for example "Całkowite poparcie dla stanowiska partii" [Full support for the party stance], *Trybuna Ludu* (March 23, 1968).

versus unproductive labor as well as the juxtaposition between the working class making sacrifices for the state and the idle intellectual elites supported by it. Like in a few other cases analyzed in this volume (see Chapters 3 and 13), the state relied on genuinely resonant frames to organize countermobilization, creatively playing to both interests and historically embedded identities (see Chapter 6) of groups targeted for mobilization.

2.6.1 Anti-Semitic/Anti-Zionist Frame

While anti-Semitism became a powerful tool in SMMs, the anti-Semitic campaign preceded March 1968 protests. First Secretary of the Polish Communist Party Władysław Gomułka used the Six-Day War (5–10 June 1967), in which Israel defeated Egypt, Syria and Jordan, and Soviet bloc countries' condemnation of Israel as a pretext to attack his real and potential competitors for power. On June 19, 1967, Gomułka gave a speech at the VI Congress of Trade Unions in which he condemned Zionism as a part of international imperialism and famously stated: "[E]ach and every citizen of Poland should have only one homeland – Polish People's Republic."

Gomułka's speech empowered nationalists within the Polish ruling elite and commenced a wave of meetings and rallies condemning Zionists and cosmopolitans. Purges directed against the Polish citizens of Jewish origin in the party-state apparatus, the army and security police, and media and cultural institutions followed. As a result, some 20,000 people were forced to emigrate from Poland.

With the backdrop of the Arab–Israeli War and the USSR's support of Palestine in the conflict, Jews in Poland were portrayed as agents of Israel, disloyal to their Polish fatherland and ungrateful for the sacrifices Poles made for Jews persecuted during the war. Some of the most popular slogans at the time included "out with Zionism – agency of imperialism"; "we will rip off the head of the anti-Polish hydra"; "everyone has only one Fatherland"; "purge the party of Zionists" (Stola, 2000, pp. 112, 115); and "remove Zionists from posts" (Kula et al., 1998, p. 91).

Banners with slogans such as "Zionists represent Israel, not the Polish people" carried at rallies in Warsaw or statements by workers reported in propaganda newspapers such as "If someone cares more about the interests of Israel and West Germany than the interests of the People's Poland, then they should not usurp the right to speak on behalf of the Polish nation"[15] reveal that one of the main accusations was the lack of loyalty to Poland and suspicions that Polish Jews do not act in the best interest of the

---

[15] "Ludzie pracy Warszawy i całego kraju potępiają inspiratorów i prowodyrów ekscesów" [The working people of Warsaw and all the country condemn the instigators and leaders of the excesses], *Trybuna Ludu* (March 14, 1968).

country. The allegation of serving foreign powers also provided an excuse for removing Jews from positions of power within the party.

The targeting of the Jewish population was a new and distinctive feature for a communist campaign in postwar Poland, where anti-Semitism was typically combined with anti-communism. The anti-Semitic campaign of March 1968 innovatively brought together symbols and slogans borrowed both from the Polish prewar radical right and from the arsenal of early communist purges and hate campaigns (Stola, 2005). These historical elements activated preexisting prejudice to create a new and resonant mobilizing frame.

As in the counterrevolutionary cases analyzed by Beissinger in Chapter 6 of this volume, in March 1968 in Poland deep social divisions provided fuel for state countermobilization. However, in contrast to those instances of mobilization, threatened minorities, instead of serving as potential recruits for counterrevolution, became the target of state-sponsored attacks. Instead of playing into the fears of insecure minorities to mobilize them in its support, the state leveraged preexisting *anti*-minority prejudices among the populace at large. This difference likely stems from distinct conditions and status of the minority group in 1968 Poland and 2004 Ukraine. As Beissinger notes, in Ukraine the Russian minority feared the potential consequences that revolutionary change could have for their position in society, making them an attractive base of support for counterrevolutionary efforts. In Poland, on the other hand, the Jewish minority was represented both in the ranks of the communist party and among the opposition and had no reason to believe any potential reforms would be to its disadvantage. Moreover, the existence of long-standing prejudice and resonance of anti-Semitic rhetoric made it an attractive tool for the communist regime, particularly that, unlike in the Russian case, if channeled toward targeted enemies, it was unlikely to provoke a backlash against the state itself.

2.6.2 Patriotism/Nationalism Frame

The patriotic frame comprised of three themes, which overlapped with both the anti-Semitic and the populist frames: the question of loyalty to the Polish nation; references to the destruction of Poland by Germany during World War II and Polish heroism; and everyday patriotism of hard work for the betterment of the nation. Within this framework, student protests were characterized as, first, initiated and manipulated by foreign and hostile powers; second, undermining and unappreciative of efforts to rebuild Poland; and third, indulgent, ungrateful, and dismissive of hard, physical work. Thus, the protests and their organizers were condemned as "eagerly fulfilling orders from Tel Aviv," as anti-Polish and steered by foreign influences, taking advantage of the Polish solidarity with the Jews during common suffering of

Nazi occupation.[16] Students were frequently portrayed as naive and susceptible to influence and manipulation by external forces using them to advance their own agenda.[17]

To play into feelings of national pride, the propaganda also often used heroic images from Polish past such as resistance against Nazism or postwar rebuilding of Warsaw, which had been leveled to the ground during wartime, to discredit "the instigators," "vandals," and "hooligans" who were destroying these achievements and disrespecting sacrifices made by the Polish nation.[18] For instance, First Secretary of PZPR Central Committee Kazimierz Łoś, in a speech at a rally in an ironwork in Warsaw, said: "We, the residents of Warsaw, who with our own hands raised it from ruins and brought it to its current state, cannot look away indifferently from these acts of self-indulgence and vandalism."[19]

Moreover, the protesters were portrayed as "the enemies of People's Poland." For example, a resolution issued by a coal mine in Katowice, ratified by 100,000 workers, proclaimed: "We are determined to cut off any hand raised against our beloved Homeland and trying to strike against the fruits of our labor. The enemy of People's Poland, the enemy of socialism, whether under the patronage of imperialism, revisionism, or international Zionism, or anyone else, cannot count on tolerance in our country."[20]

In the socialist discourse, patriotism was often equated with hard work. To be a good citizen meant to be a productive member of society. To disturb work and order, to disrupt production, was to engage in anti-state activities, to stand in the way of the progress of the Polish nation. This rhetoric permeates for instance Gierek's speech in Katowice: "[T]he concept of work has been tied into one unbreakable whole with the concept of patriotism, the love of the fatherland."[21] These ideals could be used to turn the toiling working class – the backbone of the socialist society and its pride – against the intellectuals. They were additionally reinforced by extensive press coverage of industrial promises to increase production as a manifestation of solidarity with the party.[22]

---

[16] "Potępienie inspiratorów i sprawców zajść" [The condemnation of instigators and leaders of the events], *Trybuna Ludu* (March 14, 1968).

[17] See, for example, "Ludzie pracy Warszawy i całego kraju potępiają inspiratorów i prowodyrów ekscesów" [The working people of Warsaw and all the country condemn the instigators and leaders of the excesses], *Trybuna Ludu* (March 14, 1968).

[18] See, for example, *Trybuna Ludu* (March 13, 14, 15, 1968).

[19] "Potępienie inspiratorów i sprawców zajść" [The condemnation of instigators and leaders of the events], *Trybuna Ludu* (March 14, 1968).

[20] "Komuniści Górnego Śląska i Czerwonego Zagłębia manifestują poparcie dla polityki partii" [The communists from Upper Silesia and the Red Basin demonstrate their support for the politics of the party], *Trybuna Ludu* (March 15, 1968).

[21] "Jesteśmy niezachwianie z narodem, za partią i jej kierownictwem!" [We stand unwavering with the nation, the party, and its leadership!], *Trybuna Ludu* (March 15, 1968).

[22] See, for example, "Cały kraj w pełni popiera stanowisko partii wyrażone w przemówieniu towarzysza Wiesława" [The whole nation fully supports the party position expressed in Comrade Wieslaw's speech], *Trybuna Ludu* (March 21, 1968).

2.6.3 Populism/Anti-intelligentsia and Anti-elite Frame

Much of the outrage directed against the students and intellectuals who supported them had populist roots in the perceptions of their privileged position and their access to university education and Western goods and travels (often through their parents' high posts in the regime). The language and symbols present in rallies and resolutions centered on the resentment against the elites. Students were described as ungrateful and unpatriotic, despite their privileges and opportunities, particularly given the small portion of students of working-class and farming backgrounds at universities. In the official party narrative and in the slogans of workers, students were continuously portrayed as idle, spoiled children of well-positioned parents who do not appreciate the toil of the working class and capriciously disturb public order (Kula et al., 1998, p. 95).

Professors were described as remote from society, "living in the high intellectual Alps." The word "elite" was "used by the March propaganda as an insult," and intellectuals were called "mafia" and a "clique" to emphasize their distance from physical workers (Osęka, 2010, p. 151). Banners carried by workers during rallies bore slogans such as "Writers to Their Pens, Students to Their Studies" and "More workers' and farmers' children to the universities."[23] This sentiment was also expressed in resolutions issued by workers. For example, in a car factory in Warsaw (FSO), the resolution explicitly states: "With the efforts of the entire nation, with the efforts of our working hands – a universal education system was built in the People's Homeland [...] We stress simultaneously that among the main organizers of the provocative rallies and demonstrations there are no working-class children, who know the best how much worker's sweat and effort it takes to cover the costs of education of each student." In the article in *Trybuna Ludu*, which describes the FSO rally (6,000 participants) and resolution, the workers are portrayed as "knowing the best the value of human labor" and as individuals who can "best evaluate the destructive activity of the sowers of unrest."[24]

The Organization Bureau of the Central Committee,[25] when reporting on the situation in Katowice and other Upper Silesian cities, condemned students for disturbing public order and expressed a conviction that their actions were organized by external enemies, inspired by Zionists and "political bankrupts." In line with the rhetoric in the official press, it contained information that well-off students, spoiled by excellent learning conditions, stood behind the civil unrest and that students with worker and farmer backgrounds were not involved, concluding that increasing their percentage at

---

[23] See, for example, "Warszawskie załogi domagają się przywrócenia spokoju w Stolicy" [Warsaw crews demand restoring peace in the Capital], *Trybuna Ludu* (March 12, 1968).

[24] "Warszawskie załogi domagają się przywrócenia spokoju w Stolicy" [Warsaw crews demand restoring peace in the Capital], *Trybuna Ludu* (March 12, 1968).

[25] Information nr 28/A/4365 from March 14, 1968, Warsaw.

universities would improve student attitudes in general. Approval for firing the parents of protesting students employed in high official posts was combined with the stance that the government had so far been too tolerant of the "excesses" of students (Kula et al., 1998).

A similar stance was reflected in rallies and resolutions, in which full support for the party and the Political Bureau and their actions was expressed. Calls for punishment of "instigators" and their parents and for "purifying" the party and the party apparatus of Zionists and hostile elements were common. For instance, on March 13, mass rallies took place in a number of ironworks, coal mines, etc., with 800 to 3,000 participants each; "during each rally a few workers would speak, with the majority of physical workers" (Kula et al., 1998, p. 85). In a speech printed in *Trybuna Ludu*,[26] Józef Kępa, the First Party Secretary in Warsaw (KW PZPR), describes an encounter of students with the workers, in which reminding students that their demonstrations are being watched by workers who toil for their comfortable lives was met with laughter and ridicule. The students also purportedly threw coins at the workers "like charity" and acted provocatively toward worker activists, who showed restraint and "avoided physical clashes." Students' claims about students hurt or in one case killed by the police forces are discredited in the speech as lies, and instead the wounds of workers and their sacrifice are highlighted. They are praised for keeping their calm "despite insults and physical attacks" with pieces of pavement, stones, and chairs (p. 4).

This anti-intellectual current can be understood as "clothing 'anti-Zionism' in an egalitarian costume" (Stola, 2006, p. 192) to appeal to many ordinary people who were not particularly swayed by anti-Semitic and anti-Israel rhetoric but with whom anti-elitist messages found more resonance. But, even though the high proportion of Jewish professors and students was definitely emphasized, glorification of productive versus unproductive labor also served another important purpose – preventing civil unrest from spreading to different groups of society (Stola, 2006). By presenting "degenerate intellectuals" as "traveling around the world, spread out in their daddies' limos, wearing the most expensive foreign clothes, full of distance and contempt for the hard labor of the workers" and putting them in stark contrast with the "people's patriotism" (Osęka, 2010, p. 151), the newspapers were driving a wedge between the intelligentsia and the working class, making a coalition between the two impossible.

Protesting students at the time recognized the state's propaganda efforts to turn the workers against them by portraying them as advancing anti-Polish interests. This recognition found reflection in students' response and attempts to convince the workers that they were in fact on the same side. These efforts can be gleamed from postulates and student materials confiscated by the Security

---

[26] "Co się kryje za ulicznymi awanturami?" [What is behind the street fights?], *Trybuna Ludu* (March 12, 1968).

Service (SB). Students' slogans included calls such as "Workers! Do not let them provoke you against us" in Gdańsk and leaflets distributed in Kraków stating "Workers! Do not give in to the government's hostile propaganda." The students would protest against a "fabrication of nonexistent contradictions between the working class and students," assuring the workers that "it is not true that our activity has an anti-state character." In Gliwice, on March 14, students at the Silesian Polytechnic Institute issued a call to the president and the senate of the University: "We ask to appeal to the relevant government organs not to drive a wedge between the workers and students by organizing rallies where the general student body is represented as opponents of the people's government and the Polish nation" (Instytut Pamięci Narodowej, n.d.).

In the official discourse, any attempts by the state to turn workers against students were denied. "It would have been preposterous nonsense for someone to claim that our party attempts to, or has intentions to pit workers against students or students against workers," said Gomułka in his speech on March 19. He insisted that resolutions proclaimed by workers are "not against students but against reactionary instigators," as the overwhelming majority of students undoubtedly support socialism.[27] The Ministry of Interior and the People's Militia (Milicja Obywatelska, MO) were carefully monitoring any attempts by students to contact the workers, be it through personal conversation or leaflets intended to convince them to join them in protest. When such information was obtained, as for instance in the case of a radio plant in Warsaw, "the administrative-party units of the plant were informed and took adequate safety precautions"[28] to prevent contact (Dąbrowski et al., 2008, pp. 404–405).

2.6.4 Frame Makers: Party Elites and Lower-Ranking Apparatus

A power struggle within the party was at least in part responsible for the escalation of the anti-Zionist campaign. Mieczysław Moczar, a Minister of Internal Security at the time, used the regime's campaign against student protests to consolidate his power within the party and strengthen the "Partisan" faction. Anti-Semitic attacks in combination with denouncement of political tactics during Stalinism allowed Moczar to get rid of many political opponents (Kurlansky, 2005). According to Eisler (1991): "Moczar and his supporters then did not miss any opportunity to get rid of their opponents. Where obvious evidence was missing, they did not shy away from activity of provocative character, eagerly using deletions and fabricated evidence" (p. 130).

---

[27] "Stanowisko partii – zgodne z wolą narodu" [The stance of the party – in line with the will of the nation], *Trybuna Ludu* (March 20, 1968).
[28] Document number 397 in the IPN edited collection. Source number AIPN, 0746/6, cz. I, k. 100–103, mps.

Even though he might have used it to his benefit, there is no historical evidence that Moczar staged the anti-Semitic campaign or that he did so as a result of a power struggle with Gomułka. Dahlmann (2012) points to the fact that in June 1967 anti-Zionism was not an important theme for the Moczar-led Ministry of Interior. In his interpretation, it seems more likely that the campaign originated with lower- and mid-level bureaucrats. Voivodeship secretaries organized the mass rallies, and officials from party organizations in enterprises provoked the expulsion of party members with Jewish origins (p. 203). Yet, the question remains to what extent splits and conflicts within elites created incentives for SMMs. Our analysis of the geographic distribution of events suggests that they were more common in powerful regions led by leaders who were contenders for top positions in the party apparatus.

As Osęka (1999) notes, the March campaign is still "a mysterious event" because "we do not know who started the witch-hunt and how its course was being steered." Moreover, "party guidelines written in documents from the time are surprisingly laconic and appear to restrain rather than incite the 'anti-Zionist' fury" (p. 149). In fact, the anti-Semitic or anti-Zionist theme of the March propaganda was initiated in an atypical manner, with an anonymous article, which appeared in *Słowo Powszechne*, a second-rate newspaper, and portrayed events at Warsaw University in a language that soon dominated the party interpretation of the protests: as foreign-inspired, led by Jewish students, with Zionist and anti-Polish motivations. Until this date, the author of the article is unknown (Stola, 2009). This contradicts a simplistic view of top-down mobilization.

Minutes from a meeting of the Party's Political Bureau on April 8, 1968, indicate that the leadership also did not know the origins of the article. In the meeting, Artur Starewicz, Party Secretary responsible for the press, discussed his role in dictating an article for the official party mouthpiece, *Trybuna Ludu*, which provided the same list of names of protest organizers as *Słowo Powszechne* but without the anti-Semitic tones. However, he expressed complete lack of knowledge and disapproval of the article in *Słowo Powszechne*, saying that, while it went through the Press Bureau, he personally did not see it and calling it "a one-sided article; it outdid the party press."[29]

The article spread like wildfire: "It was reproduced in many voivodships, even in the form of a poster in Kielce. Some polemical articles went through my hands, but many articles did not," said Starewicz. Notably, as stated by another member of the Bureau, Stefan Jędrychowski, "in the first period, our propaganda trailed behind *Słowo Powszechne*," indicating not only that the campaign originated at the lower levels of party organization – without the

---

[29] Of course, as multiple members of the Political Bureau noted, the article must have been approved by some party officials to go through censorship and appear in the press. See discussion during the meeting; minutes printed in Garlicki (1993).

Manufactured Ambiguity: March 1968 in Poland

directive or even knowledge of the top leadership – and spread in a horizontal manner but that the party was late in stepping in to control the message. Jędrychowski saw this as a concerning phenomenon: "I think these are centrifugal tendencies, which are not helping us consolidate the party, and might negatively affect the life of the party, the attitude of members, also in the future" (see meeting minutes published in Garlicki (1993), pp. 342–343).

Without doubt, the communist party was at the time facing an impeded bureaucracy problem. The regime forged a new middle class by promoting loyal supporters of the regime, but over time these bureaucrats began to lack opportunities for advancement. Faced with too many employees, in order to create open positions, the regime would typically either expand bureaucracy or use purges. In 1968, neither had been done in the previous twelve years, leaving the party with a number of ambitious, frustrated bureaucrats, many of whom became an important force in Moczar's Partisan faction (Eisler, 1991, p. 140). Thus, one of the motivations behind stoking the flames of anti-Semitic protest was turnover in the cadres, with young apparatchiks standing to benefit the most from these personnel changes.

As Stola (2004) puts it, in March 1968, party members were suddenly "allowed to loudly express their discontent and call for changes, under the condition that those expressions of dissatisfaction and demands fitted the permissible forms" – one of the discursive frames described in Sections 2.6.1–2.6.3. The accusations against the apparatus of power – of "alienation, use of unjustified privileges, arrogance etc." – were "in fact accusations against the establishment of Polish People's Republic (PRL)" but formulated in a language sanctioned by the party (p. 68).

The "old guard" eventually rejected the campaign, and in June 1968 Gomułka ordered the censorship office to ban the Zionist theme from the media because "the propaganda started having a negative influence on party activists and society" (Osęka, 1999, p. 11). Minutes from the meeting of the Party's Political Bureau indicate that the party leadership was divided on the use of the anti-Zionist language,[30] but that it was this frame that allowed the party to generate an unprecedented response from party members. As Loga-Sowiński, one of the Political Bureau members, put it, if the party had taken a more moderate or nuanced stance on the anti-Zionist elements of the campaign as some members of the Bureau advocated, "we would have alienated the worker aktiv and would not have the current results [...] [S]ome might be annoyed by the word Zionism, but it played a large role" (Garlicki 1993, p. 344).

In the end, Gomułka's team, despite some reservations, did let the campaign run wild for over three months, even though, as another member of the Political Bureau expressed in the April 8 meeting, "in practice, the actions of the party

---

[30] Especially Edward Ochab expressed concerns about the anti-Semitic propaganda, asking, "Do we not have a possibility to defend Jewish comrades from wrongful insinuations on TV, in the press etc.?" (Garlicki, 1993, p. 341).

organizations in TV and press went beyond the reasonable limits and proposals presented in Comrade Gomułka's speech" (Garlicki, 1993, p. 341). Not until June 24 were instructions issued banning the "exposure and accumulation of publications about Zionism" (Paczkowski, 1995, p. 370). For the time from March to June, "Zionists, revisionists, and incorrigible 'reactionists', mixed in together became a classic 'scape goat,' blamed for the existing – and evoking popular discontent – state of affairs" (Paczkowski, 1995, p. 370).

The immediate implementation of instructions from June 24 indicates that, with the ability to call off the campaign – at least in the press – at any time, Gomułka and surrounding officials chose to let the propaganda continue. At the same time, the fact that the Political Bureau considered the hysterical atmosphere of March to be detrimental to the party and that, following the conference speech, the tone of the propaganda calmed down and mass firing of employees accused of Zionism ceased (Osęka, 1999, p. 11) could indicate that the unrest was fermented by lower-level party apparatus whose careers benefited from personnel purges but who could be reigned in by direct orders from the top.

2.7 MANUFACTURED AMBIGUITY

We argue that the actions of the Polish party-state in March 1968 may be characterized as *manufactured ambiguity* – that is, the intentional creation of a significant level of confusion about authenticity of the countermobilization strategy and the extent of genuine support received for it from various social and professional groups. To this day, historical accounts cannot confidently assess how much of the support for the party was manufactured, whether participation in demonstrations and rallies was voluntary, and whether expressed anti-Semitic and nationalistic views were pushed from the top or were coming from local organizations and how they resonated with the views and believes of ordinary participants.

For example, despite the official narrative, which placed the students (the protesters) in opposition to the workers (the counterprotesters), many workers joined the students, as arrest records from the time reveal. In fact, according to documents from the Ministry of Interior, at the height of protest mobilization, workers were the largest social group arrested during the demonstrations, more sizable than the students themselves. As Eisler suggests, in some ways the March mobilization could be characterized less as a student/intellectual mobilization, in which labor did not participate, than as a generational rebellion of the young – students and workers alike – against the party-state (Eisler, 2008). This is not the picture, however, that emerges out of the official documents, neither published nor internal, in which not even students of the working class background, not to mention workers, support the protesting students.

The official narrative also contradicts accounts provided by some of the participants. For instance, worker aktiv was involved in dispersing student

Manufactured Ambiguity: March 1968 in Poland

demonstrations, most famously during the March 8 rally at the University of Warsaw, where workers clashed with students. However, what percentage of them was actually comprised of workers is a contentious issue in the historiography of March events, and it seems that workers who belonged to the militia (ORMO) faced social disapproval in their workplaces because of their involvement. According to one witness to the March 8 protests, workers who didn't belong to the militia asked professors to hide on campus for the time of the rally because they did not want to confront the students (Eisler, 2008).

As Beissinger notes in Chapter 6 of this volume, a strategy of "masking responsibility for repression by using civilians to repress revolutionary threats rather than the military or police" can make it harder for the public to attribute blame for the violence and lower the likelihood of backlash. Thus, generating ambiguity around the identity and motivations of actors mobilized to suppress protests can be a useful tactic for the regime to prevent an upsurge in opposition. Any resulting violence might then also be used to discredit the protesters as disruptive and aggressive, as shown in Section 2.6.3 of this chapter, and justify the regime's punishment of the dissidents.

In the case of March 1968 in Poland, not only the participation of different social groups but also the voluntary nature of that involvement may be disputed. Even though "in the reports to the PZPR's Central Committee, the spontaneity of those events was described" (Miroszewski, 2009, p. 84), some reports of the Secret Service reveal comments that seem to deny it. For example, one report documents a comment made by a worker bused to a demonstration in the main square in Katowice: "They transport us like sheep because their jobs are uncertain and they want to clench to power through forced solidarity" (Miroszewski, 2009, p. 85). Eisler (2008) cites Zbigniew Bujak, a foreman at Ursus factory at the time, later involved in Solidarity:

It was the hardest for them to find people willing to carry banners and slogans. They only managed to force them into the hands of party aktiv and youth aktiv. But even they, as soon as they reached the destination, tried to put all the slogans against the wall; the banners would later be overturned and trampled by others. Part of the aktiv would be gathered around the stage: those were the ones being filmed and only they applauded. Others, especially young people, running around on tin roofs and stairs (the rally took place in an old foundry), tried to drown out some of the speeches with noise. The rest standing around the stage would take in all what was said in deaf silence. (Eisler, 2008, p. 117)

Many of the protesting students, the targets of the state offensive, saw the rallies as staged. Correspondence intercepted by the People's Militia (Milicja Obywatelska, MO) reveals this perception. A memo from MO's division in Warsaw dated March 14 cites excerpts from the documents: "Warsaw is indeed with us, despite anti-student agitation and attempts to drive a rift between us and the workers" and "It's boiling also in the workplaces. All those resolutions adopted by the workplaces are products of agitation by the party. They want to pit the students and the workers against each other"[31] (Dąbrowski et al., 2008, pp. 404–405).

A different memo[32] relates that an informant heard a lawyer working in the headquarters (CHZ) of Polimex, a construction company, "condemn generally the government's strategy and the organization of so-called herded[33] rallies with uniformly pre-determined resolutions" (Dąbrowski et al., 2008, p. 628). Another intercepted document by an unknown author[34] from March 21 is even more telling:

> What the workers are saying, what the newspapers are talking about, the workers aktiv at the rallies, it is just a big farce. They gather at the rallies grudgingly, get painted slogans and stand with expressionless faces, yet one can tell that it's not their opinion. I watched a few film reports from the rallies shown on TV. In an institute, where over 3,000 people work, an enormous rally takes place, at which about 300 people gathered, where is everyone else and what are the men in fur hats intermingled in the crowd doing – are they also workers? One can hear loud applause, but cannot see any clapping hands – yes, there is applause, but from an opening night at the Grand Theater. (Dąbrowski et al., 2008, p. 622)

Although Eisler (2008) notes that attendance was not an issue because rallies were organized during work hours[35] and allowed a respite from labor, the workers in televised rallies often seemed sad and tired of endless speeches from party activists. He also claims, in line with the memo recorded by SB already cited, that "TV crews filming the rallies had trouble with recording sound because there was not enough applause" (p. 117).

At the same time, many reports from the Ministry of Interior discuss anti-Semitic and anti-Zionist declarations and moods among the workers and statements of support for the party. Like with other sources from a non-democratic government, it is difficult to assess the veracity of these reports due to lack of, for example, credible public opinion polls. While many of those documents were internal or classified, clearly not intended for propaganda purposes and hence perhaps more trustworthy, one should not forget incentives for members of the socialist bureaucracy to report favorable information to their superiors regardless of whether verified or not. Tendency to rely on rumors and widespread preference falsification among the population

---

[31] Document number 368 in the IPN edited collection. Source number AIPN, 0746/7M K. 37–42, mps.

[32] Document number 434 in the IPN edited collection. Source number AIPN, 0236/160, k. 232–234, mps.

[33] The Polish word is "napędzać," which could also be translated as "to goad."

[34] Document number 431 in the IPN edited collection. Source number AIPN, 0746/7, k. 55–58, mps.

[35] Similarly, Paczkowski (1995) claims that the success of March propaganda "indicating the culprits for poor state of the economy and everyday troubles, condemning those 'living in luxury' at the expense of a hard-working nation" ensured high turnout at rallies in factories, but "just in case they were organized during work hours" (p. 370).

(Kuran, 1987) further put into question the reliability of this information. It is thus very hard to determine the extent to which these sentiments were actually prevalent among the population.

Particularly in the case of the anti-Zionist campaign, the degree to which it was orchestrated as opposed to being driven by prejudicial sentiments among the population is debated both by scholars and émigrés who left Poland following the repressive campaign (Stola, 2004). According to one survey (Chylińska, 1970) conducted among émigrés, opinions were split between those who believed it to have been a top-down campaign and those who thought it was a bottom-up mobilization.

It seems that the party did try to channel the current of discontent against external enemies allegedly involved in diversionist actions in Poland. By finding scapegoats for the numerous economic and political problems, by providing outlets to express anger, by reshaping the students' narrative, and by staging large-scale demonstrations of support, the party attempted to achieve a number of goals: harnessing anger and prejudice to discredit and eliminate opponents; intimidating and deterring current and potential challengers through ostentatious shows of overwhelming support for the regime; mobilizing party members; and reclaiming legitimacy on the basis of socialist ideals and feelings of nationalist pride.

2.8 LONG-TERM CONSEQUENCES OF THE MARCH 1968 CAMPAIGN

At the same time, as Ekiert and Perry note in the Introduction to the volume, "ruling by other means" often has long-term consequences that work against the goals of mobilizing agents. The campaign we analyzed revealed multiple divisions and conflicts within the Polish party-state: between generations, among various ideological factions, and between central and local authorities. It also signaled potential for alliances among disgruntled students, intellectuals, the Catholic Church hierarchy, workers, and reformers within the Polish communist party. In fact, the opposition to the communist regime, which eventually contributed to its downfall in 1989, had its origins in the 1968 student protest. Although the disillusionment with the possibility of liberalizing reforms of communist regimes was mostly related to repression employed by the state – a conventional state response – the full-force mobilization and propaganda campaign against the intelligentsia left a mark on the emerging opposition movements and organizations.

On the side of the party-state, the perception of the anti-Semitic campaign spinning out of the party's control was a considerable concern. This may explain why hate campaigns were never employed again as a response to subsequent societal challenges to the regime in the 1970s and 1980s. At the same time, the strategy of pitting the workers against the students had enduring weakening effects on the resistance – not until 1980s did the two social groups bridge their divides to unite against the communist regime. For the party, the internal turnover of cadres brought new people to the positions of power, but the firing and exile of citizens of Jewish descent meant a significant drain of human capital both for the party apparatus and for the country.

2.9 CONCLUSIONS

The reaction of the communist party in Poland to a challenge from student protesters in March 1968 follows patterns discernible in both reactive and proactive responses of nondemocratic regimes to current and potential challenges from self-mobilized social actors. A few of the comparative themes which can be identified in our case study and analyzed in a larger cross-national and cross-temporal perspective are: 1) the state employed framing strategy relying on political idioms and resentments that resonate in specific historical and cultural conditions – in 1968, this took a form of reinvented nationalist mobilization against external enemies and their domestic collaborators as a means of strengthening the eroded ideological legitimacy of the regime and was combined with a populist, anti-elite theme reflecting the communist ideological underpinnings of the regime; 2) using a vast arsenal of resources available to the state and existing enforcement networks – in the Polish case, the mobilization strategy relied on a vast communist party infrastructure in workplaces across the industries, social services and administration; and 3) using state directed mobilization not only as a tool against political opposition from below but also as an instrument to settle conflicts within the ruling elite and eliminate internal challengers to top position in party and state institutions.

First, though one of the supposed goals of the campaign was to unload social tensions which arose due to difficult economic conditions and assign blame, "another plausible goal was strengthening the much weakened legitimacy of the regime ... [I]n the 1960s, there was a visible tendency to replace eroded utopian-communist legitimacy by the nationalist one" (Stola, 2000, p. 142). This is not an uncommon problem for nondemocratic, often revolutionary, regimes built on ideology. As the revolutionary or ideological legitimacy fades and everyday politics begins, they often need to replace it by either performance legitimacy or nationalist legitimacy. Given the poor state of the Polish economy in 1960s, the attempts to tap into nationalist feelings by striking exclusionist and prejudicial tones and even drawing on interwar right-wing, nationalist-ethnic themes could be seen as efforts by the party – despite communism's foreign imposition on Poland – to tie patriotism with support for the party and hard work for the progress of the People's Republic.

Second, in 1968 the technologies of mobilization still resemble tactics often used by the dual party-state throughout nearly fifty years of communist rule in the region but also show a shift to a different set of strategies. Mobilization of society with multiple campaigns, forcing various professional groups to pledge to increase production targets was frequently used during the Stalinist period (Hankiss, 1988), as were hate campaigns against internal and external enemies that resulted in purges and show trials during that period. Yet, the Polish case of the 1968 countermobilization shows the moment of transition from a visible hand of the communist state using its bureaucratic enforcement networks in fully visible and blatant way to mobilization, in which that state tries to make its involvement less transparent and ambiguous, to present pro-state gatherings as widespread, genuine, and spontaneous. We call this strategy manufactured ambiguity.

Third, state-led contentious mobilization against political opposition is also used for reforming and purifying the party and settling intra-elite conflicts. In the Polish case, March 1968 was an important moment when the process of generational turnover within the communist party begun. It culminated two years later with the ousting of the first secretary of the party (Gomułka) and many of his close allies, alongside a significant shift in communist economic and social policies. It opened bureaucratic bottlenecks within the party and state administration, allowing hundreds of younger communist functionaries to move upward. The implicit possibility of mass personnel changes played a role in both the escalation of the anti-Semitic propaganda and intra-party criticism of communist bureaucracy for lack of efficiency and accountability. Both provided incentives for lower-level party members to use it for their own personal goals. In fact, as a result of 1968 some 8,000 people were expelled from the party, including 80 high level functionaries and 14 current or former government ministers. The purges moved down the entire party-state structures, media, and the higher education system.

March events were not only associated with mass firings and personnel changes but also with mass new entry into the communist party of people sensing the opportunities to advance their careers. According to the Central Committee of PZPR's internal documents,[36] over 600 people declared their desire to join the party in the two weeks of highest protest activity, between March 8 and March 25, 40 percent of whom were workers (Kula et al., 1998, p. 242). The inflow of new party members was eagerly reported in the press as an expression of support for the party and condemnation of protests in even higher numbers at the end of the month and in the following months.[37] On April 21, 1968, the regime's

---

[36] Information nr 64/A/4402 from March 28, 1968, Warsaw.
[37] See, for example, the following articles in *Trybuna Ludu*: "Czują sie potrzebni partii" [They feel needed by the party] (March 20, 1968); "Zwiększony napływ kandydatów do partii" [Increased inflow of candidates to the party] (March 30, 1968); and "Rosną szeregi PZPR" [The ranks of PZPR are growing] (March 31, 1968).

mouthpiece, *Trybuna Ludu*, reported that, in the first quarter of 1968, party organizations in all of Poland admitted over 2,300 more candidates than in the same time period the previous year, with 44 percent of them admitted in March.[38] This rush to join the party can be understood as a rush to newly vacated state positions (instrumental) or belief that, now that the party has been purged of all influences, it will genuinely represent the working classes (ideological) (Osęka, 1999, p. 88).

The case study of the communist state's response to 1968 student protests in Poland provides insights into some of the complex ways in which nondemocratic regimes react to challenges to their power. The availability of many internal party and secret service documents, as well as press sources and witness accounts, provides rich material from which to examine tactics that are likely often used in other contexts, where such information might not (yet) be readily available. Yet even in this case, nearly fifty years after the events, there is much ambiguity around the mobilization of society by the party apparatus – indirectly through propaganda and directly through demonstrations staged using a mixture of persuasion, coercion, and rewards.

However, the examination of materials from the time indicates that the wave of countermobilization to unrest at universities was hardly as spontaneous and sincere as portrayed in the official propaganda and that the party strategically used its resources and infrastructure to launch an offensive campaign in reaction to the challenge posed by student protests. Patterns of regime behavior in crisis, which can be discerned in this case study, open up fruitful avenues for future comparative research on forms of SMMs.

REFERENCES

Chylińska, Kamila. 1970. Emigracja polska po 1967 r. *Kultura* 11: 17–55.
Dąbrowski, Franciszek, Piotr Gontarczyk, Paweł Tomasik, and Mirosław Biełaszko. 2008. *Marzec 1968 w dokumentach MSW*. Vol. 2. Warsaw: Inst. Pamięci Narodowej.
Dahlmann, Hans-Christian. 2012. *Antisemitismus in Polen 1968: Interaktionen zwischen Partei und Gesellschaft*. Osnabrück: Fibre Verl.
Eisler, Jerzy. 1991. *Marzec 1968: geneza, przebieg, konsekwencje*. Warsaw: Państwowe Wydawnictwo Naukowe.
Eisler, Jerzy. 2008. *"Polskie miesiące" czyli kryzys (y) w PRL*. 47. Warsaw: Instytut Pamięci Narodowej.
Ekiert, Grzegorz. 1997. Rebellious Poles: Political Crises and Popular Protest under State Socialism, 1945–1989. *East European Politics and Societies* 11 (2): 299–338.
Frye, Timothy, Ora John Reuter, and David Szakonyi. 2014. Political machines at work voter mobilization and electoral subversion in the workplace. *World Politics* 66 (02): 195–228.

---

[38] "Wyraz aktywnego poparcia dla polityki partii: Tysiące nowych kandydatów wstępuje do PZPR" [The expression of active support for the politics of the party: Thousands of new candidates join PZPR], *Trybuna Ludu* (April 21, 1968).

Garlicki, Andrzej. 1993. *Z tajnych archiwów*. Warsaw: Polska Oficyna Wydawnicza "BGW".
Hankiss, Elemer. 1988. Demobilization, self-mobilization and quasi-mobilization in Hungary, 1948–1987. *East European Politics & Societies* 3 (1): 105–151.
Hillebrandt, Bogdan. 1986. *Marzec 1968 (Fakty, Relacje, Pamiętniki)*. Warsaw: Wydawn. Spółdzielcze.
Instytut Pamięci Narodowej. N.d. http://marzec1968.pl/m68/. Accessed May 27, 2015.
Interview with J. Eisler. 2013. *Gazeta Wyborcza*.
Kula, Marcin, Piotr Osęka, and Marcin Zaremba. 1998. *Marzec 1968: Trzydzieści lat później*. Vol. 2. Warsaw: Państwowe Wydawnictwo Naukowe PWN.
Kuran, Timo. 1987. Preference falsification, policy continuity and collective conservatism. *The Economic Journal* 97 (387): 642–665.
Kurlansky, Mark. (2005). *1968: The Year that Rocked the World*. New York: Random House Trade Paperbacks.
Linz, Juan. 2000. *Totalitarian and Authoritarian Regimes*. New York: Lynne Rienner Publishers.
Mark, James, Peter Apor, Radina Vucetic, and Piotr Osęka. 2015. "We are with you, Vietnam": Transnational solidarities in socialist Hungary, Poland and Yugoslavia. *Journal of Contemporary History* 50 (3): 439–464.
Miroszewski, Kazimierz. 2009. Stosunek władz województwa katowickiego do wydarzeń marcowych. In S. Feracz & K. Miroszewski (eds.), *Marzec 1968 roku w województwie katowickim*. Katowice: Wydawnictwo Uniwersytetu Śląskiego, pp. 71–92.
Osęka, Piotr. 1999. *Syjoniści, inspiratorzy, wichrzyciele. obraz wroga w propagandzie marca 1968*. Warsaw: Żydowski Instytut Historyczny.
Osęka, Piotr. 2010. *Mydlenie oczu: przypadki propagandy w Polsce*. Kraków: Znak.
Paczkowski, Andrzej. 1995. *Pół wieku dziejów polski 1939–1989*. Warsaw: Wydawn. Naukowe PWN.
Roszkowski, Wojciech. 2003. *Najnowsza historia polski*. Vol. 2: 1945–1980. Warsaw: Świat Książki.
Scott, James. 1990. *Domination and the Arts of Resistance: Hidden Transcripts*. New Haven, CT: Yale University Press.
Selznick, Philip. 2014 [1952]. *The Organizational Weapon: A Study of Bolshevik Strategy and Tactics*. Vol. 18. New Orleans, LA: Quid Pro Books.
Stola, Dariusz. 2000. *Kampania antysyjonistyczna w Polsce 1967–1968*. Warsaw: Inst. Studiów Politycznych PAN.
Stola, Dariusz. 2004. Antyżydowski nurt marca 1968. In K. Rokicki & S. Stepień (eds.), *Oblicza marca 1968*. Warsaw: Instytut Pamięci Narodowej, Komisja Ścigania Zbrodni przeciwko Narodowi Polskiemu, pp. 65–72.
Stola, Dariusz. 2005. Fighting against the shadows: the anti-Zionist campaign of 1968. In R. Blobaum (ed.), *Anti-Semitism and Its Opponents in Modern Poland*. Ithaca, NY: Cornell University Press, 284–300.
Stola, Dariusz. 2006. Anti-Zionism as a multipurpose policy instrument: The anti-Zionist campaign in Poland, 1967–1968. *The Journal of Israeli History* 25 (1): 175–201.

Stola, Dariusz. 2009. Jak i dlaczego kampania marcowa stała się antyżydowska? In G. Berendt (ed.), *Społeczność żydowska w PRL przed kampanią antysemicką lat 1967–1968 i po niej*. Warsaw: Instytut Pamięci Narodowej, 107–118.

Trybuna Robotnicza, nr 62–63 [czasopismo]. (1968, March 13–14). Silesian Digital Library. Śląskie Wydawnictwo Prasowe RSW "Prasa". Accessed June 7, 2015.

3

Suppressing Students in the People's Republic of China
Proletarian State-Mobilized Movements in 1968 and 1989

Elizabeth J. Perry and Yan Xiaojun

3.1 INTRODUCTION

State-mobilized movements (SMMs) can be found among all regime types, democratic and nondemocratic alike. But certain types of regimes are more likely to generate certain types of SMMs. Communist regimes are partial to proletarian SMMs, calling on the moral authority of the "vanguard revolutionary class" to defuse challenges from other social elements at moments of internal crisis. In light of the signal importance of the proletariat in Marxist-Leninist ideology, it is not surprising that regimes controlled by communist parties should elect to enlist the participation of loyal workers in countermovements intended to delegitimize and demobilize threatening opposition. Unlike repression by the police or military, proletarian action has the advantage of political correctness. Relying on squadrons of workers to neutralize other social forces also promises more pragmatic advantages, especially when the social movement in question is composed largely of students. In responding to contention on the part of idealistic students, whose movements typically generate widespread sympathy among urban residents, intervention by unarmed workers is less apt to alienate the populace than naked military suppression.

This is not to say that workers in communist countries are mere pawns in the hands of Machiavellian party leaders, amenable to being deployed at will. Nor is the working class unconditionally trustworthy and reliable in the eyes of communist leaders; workers naturally have their own concerns that authorities must consider when deciding whether or not to enlist the proletariat as an ally. Even if the state chooses to elicit working-class collaboration, mobilizing the proletariat remains a challenge. Official trade unions are a useful but limited vehicle for recruiting worker support, since their reach generally does not extend much beyond the workplace itself. At times, *charismatic mobilization*, or "the ability of a leader to mobilize people without the benefits or constraints of formal organization" (Andreas, 2007 p. 437), can play a critical role in this process. Effective use of resonant symbolic resources to create a strong emotional bond to the supreme leader may move the proletariat to rally as a counterweight to other social groups in support of the regime. At yet other times, however, communist leaders may resort to the more prosaic discourse of material interests, communicated through regular bureaucratic channels, to persuade workers to join countermovements against regime opponents.

Appeals and technologies of SMMs vary significantly across time and space, even within a communist country as tightly controlled and politically centralized as the People's Republic of China (PRC). The contrasting experiences and positions of workers in different places, along with the distinctive cultures and calculations of various subnational governments, mean that the methods of proletarian countermobilization diverge systematically from one locale to another and from one critical juncture to the next. This chapter explores regional and temporal variation in suppressing the two most politically consequential cases of popular contention in the history of the PRC: the Cultural Revolution Red Guards of 1968 and the Tiananmen Democracy Movement of 1989. Conventional accounts of these suppression efforts stress the pivotal role of the armed forces in restoring order to a country teetering on the brink of civil war. These accounts are not incorrect, but they are incomplete. In both instances proletarian SMMs were also a major part of the story.

From its earliest days to the present, the Chinese Communist Party (CCP) has regarded proletarian mobilization as essential for attaining and retaining political power. Although industrial workers comprised only a small portion of the Chinese labor force at the outset of the revolution, they were an important focus of mobilization. This was particularly true in the birthplace of the CCP, the city of Shanghai, where factory workers were active throughout the revolutionary years (Perry, 1993). Conveniently, moreover, the Chinese term for "proletariat" (*wuchan jieji*, 无产阶级), which literally means a class lacking in property, can also refer to landless peasants and agricultural laborers. Thanks to this conceptual capaciousness, the CCP could claim that its rural revolution, while based predominantly on poor peasants, was nonetheless a "proletarian revolution." After the establishment of the PRC in 1949, the role of the proletariat – industrial and agrarian alike – was transformed from that of revolutionaries into guardians of the communist state (Perry, 2006).

The PRC has tapped the proletariat for crucial support at several critical junctures in its tumultuous history. Demobilizing student Red Guards during the Cultural Revolution and demobilizing student democracy activists in the Tiananmen Uprising both involved state sponsorship of large-scale proletarian countermovements. Although previous scholarship on these suppression efforts has focused on the Chinese state's bold deployment of the People's Liberation Army, in both cases proletarian SMMs played a key role in the battle to win over public opinion. These movements varied greatly over time and from one city to another – most notably between the political capital of Beijing and the industrial capital of Shanghai. Examining such critical junctures as they played out on the ground at different moments in different places reveals significant sources of variability and fluidity in SMMs even under a unitary communist regime. In other words, subnational diversity with important political consequences can be found not only in federal democracies (see Chapter 5 by Cunningham and Owens on Civil Rights–era Mississippi) but also in unitary dictatorships. The ingenuity and flexibility that the PRC has demonstrated in organizing proletarian SMMs, we suggest, has contributed to its impressive ability to emerge intact from episodes of chaotic contention that would surely have sounded the death knell for less dexterous regimes.

3.2 WORKERS' PROPAGANDA TEAMS IN THE CULTURAL REVOLUTION

The PRC is not alone among communist party-states in using proletarian counterprotests to subdue dangerous student movements. In the preceding chapter, Ekiert and Kruszewska show how workers in Poland were mobilized by the state in the spring of 1968 to repress student protests at the University of Warsaw. Throughout its history, the PRC has been a keen observer of events elsewhere in the communist world. Although it is uncertain whether the CCP consciously borrowed Polish techniques of counterprotest, the suppression of unruly Red Guards in China by state-organized "Workers' Mao Zedong Thought Propaganda Teams" bore an uncanny resemblance to the scenario that had unfolded in Warsaw just a few months before.

The Chinese case occurred two years into the "Great Proletarian Cultural Revolution," Mao Zedong's ultimate effort to save his revolution from slipping into Soviet-style routinization by cultivating committed "revolutionary successors" among the youth of China (MacFarquhar and Schoenhals, 2006). Initially Mao pinned high hopes on idealistic students as the best guarantee that his own revolution would not follow the "revisionist" path of the Soviet Union, but by the summer of 1968 antagonism among competing Red Guard units – all claiming to represent Chairman Mao's true revolutionary line – had escalated into violent struggles at schools and universities around the country (Walder, 2012). At Peking University, armed conflict using handmade spears, iron bars, and giant slingshots fashioned from bicycle tires had claimed the lives of several students. At neighboring Tsinghua University, home of the country's premier engineering school, the weapons manufactured by rival student factions were more sophisticated – and even more deadly. Guns, grenades, and tanks had caused 18 fatalities and 1100 injuries (Li, 2011, p. 33). With even Mao having grown tired of the Red Guards' fratricidal battles, the stage was set for a presumably less fractious force – the proletariat – to quell the campus unrest and attempt to put Chairman Mao's revolutionary crusade back on track.

When the first contingent of workers' propaganda teams entered Tsinghua University, the reaction from contentious students in Beijing was no less hostile than that experienced by Polish workers at the hands of student protesters at the University of Warsaw a few months earlier. Tsinghua had just endured more than three months of violent conflict between warring Red Guard factions in which a radical contingent known as "the Regiment" had gained the upper hand. The dramatic confrontation between students and workers was recounted by William Hinton, an American leftist who received a detailed briefing on the incident during a visit to Tsinghua:

Suddenly at 10 a.m. on the morning of July 27, 1968, huge crowds of workers ... appeared before the campus gates. Each carried a little red book of Chairman Mao's quotations ...

The workers, many of them clad in T-shirts and shorts, just as they had come off the night shift, surged forward. They took up positions around selected campus buildings, especially those that were important to the respective factions. With shirts clinging to perspiring backs and sweat dripping on the open pages of their red books, they began to read aloud and punctuate their reading with slogans shouted in unison. "Use reason, not violence. Turn in your weapons. Form a big alliance!" ...

At three o'clock, a signal shot unleashed a hail of rocks, bolts, nuts, and bottles of black ink from all the strongholds of the Regiment. Before the workers could even assess the injuries on numerous stunned and wounded comrades, detachments of spearmen charged their ranks. In the ensuing melee, the center of which shifted with lightning speed and chaotic illogic from one section of the campus to another, spears found their mark, hand grenades exploded, pistol and rifle shots rang out, and workers' blood began to flow. "Black above and red below" was the way veterans of the incident described their appearance in the eerie hours that followed – black from the ink bottles that broke on their heads and red from the blood that flowed from their wounds ...

When peace finally returned to Tsinghua in the early morning hours of July 28, five workers lay dead, 731 nursed serious wounds, 143 had been taken prisoner, and many of the prisoners had been beaten. Yet no group of workers had counterattacked, no students had been harmed. (Hinton, 1972, pp. 185–187; see also Tang, 2003, pp. 1–14)

Hinton's account, faithful to the political orthodoxy of the day, may well have exaggerated the degree of restraint exhibited by the workers' propaganda teams. Even so, it reflects the state's presentation of the working class as the righteous antidote to student protest run amok.

The workers' propaganda teams that showed up unexpectedly at the gates of Tsinghua University (see Figure 3.1) were far from a spontaneous development. Composed of employees from more than sixty factories in the Beijing area, they were led by soldiers from the 8341 Army, the central security regiment that answered directly to Mao Zedong.

The propaganda teams, it soon became clear, operated not only with the assistance of the military but with the approval of Mao himself. While state leaders had probably initially hoped to present the propaganda teams as a bottom-up proletarian upsurge – similar to the "manufactured ambiguity" described by Ekiert and Kruszewska in the Polish case – the unfriendly reception that the workers encountered at Tsinghua triggered a more transparent

Suppressing Students in China: 1968 and 1989

FIGURE 3.1 Workers of the Xinhua Printing House and Xinhua Bookstore deliver printing materials with Chairman Mao's latest instructions to the Workers' Propaganda Teams setting out to Tsinghua University campus

approach. In the early hours of July 29, Mao summoned five of Beijing's most influential radical student leaders to a face-to-face meeting to reveal his own role in the counterprotest. In response to the charge by Tsinghua's Regiment leader that the workers' propaganda team was being manipulated by a sinister hand, Mao famously replied, "If you are looking for a sinister hand, I am that sinister hand. I sent the team. You will have to blame me" (Hinton, 1972, p. 213). In this moment of extraordinary uncertainty and turmoil, Mao elected to dispense with deception in favor of direction.

Reflecting this top-level sponsorship, workers' propaganda teams were well organized from the start. The day before the teams marched on Tsinghua, Mao had convened a meeting at his residence of members of his personal armed guard. Pointing to a map of the Tsinghua campus spread out on the carpet, Mao issued instructions on how to advance on the university (Tang, 2015). That evening, delegates from dozens of local factories were called to a strategy meeting at the Xinhua Printing Plant, chaired by members of the 8341 Army and the Beijing Garrison Command. The printing plant was selected as the staging ground for the operation because it had recently overcome severe factional strife with the aid of soldiers from the 8341 Army. The sixty-two factories that agreed to participate in the Tsinghua takeover were asked to provide transportation for their own workers; in cases where factories lacked the necessary vehicles, however, the Beijing Municipal Revolutionary Committee offered to supply them. In this way more than 30,000 workers – separated according to industrial sector into seven "columns" plus one "regiment" under the direct command of the 8341 Army – were rapidly assembled. Despite, or rather precisely *because* of, this high level of central organization, this SMM was not without an element of spontaneity. In addition to the officially organized workers, thousands of other workers in the Beijing area streamed to the university gates on their own once they learned of the centrally approved plan to pacify the conflict-ridden campus and put an end to Tsinghua's "Hundred Day War" (Hinton, 1972, pp. 189–190).

News that the workers' propaganda teams were operating with the blessing of Chairman Mao greatly bolstered their authority. A former deputy party secretary at Tsinghua recalled, "I thought, the propaganda teams were sent by Chairman Mao, the 8341 Army is Chairman Mao's personal guard, I ought to trust them" (Liu, 2010, p. 126). Thanks to such sentiments, the teams succeeded in quelling the violence at Tsinghua within less than twenty-four hours. However, it would take another full year of intensive political work before the workers' propaganda teams declared victory in subduing the deep-seated factional hostilities that had riddled the university community since the heyday of the Red Guard movement (Hinton, 1972, p. 215). Even after their proclaimed victory, the teams – charged with conducting a thoroughgoing "education revolution" that would inoculate Chinese intellectuals from "bourgeois" tendencies – exercised control over the university until the death of Mao and arrest of the "Gang of Four" (comprised of Mao's widow, Jiang Qing, and three fellow radicals from Shanghai) in the fall of 1976 (Tang, 2015).

Despite their novel mission, the Tsinghua teams employed familiar propaganda techniques, relying on loudspeaker broadcasts, big-character posters, mass forums, and smaller meetings to disseminate Chairman Mao's latest instructions. Soon after their arrival, they divided into approximately 100 smaller units to fan out across campus to publicize their undertaking (Peking Review, 1968, pp. 13–16). Students, faculty, and staff were assigned to political study groups in their respective departments, each of which reported to a column of the Workers' Propaganda Team. Column Three, the largest, comprised of machinists, assumed responsibility for mechanical engineering – the premier academic department at the university. Column Five, made up of construction workers, supervised civil and agricultural engineering. And so on. The elite regiment commanded by the 8341 Army took over the offices of the old university administration and Communist Party Committee (Hinton, 1972, p. 223). Although there was a certain logic to these assignments, the fact that the average educational level of work-team members did not exceed middle school and the great majority of team members had not previously engaged in any sort of educational work presented obvious obstacles in fulfilling their charge to remake the country's top technology university (Tang, 2015).

3.2.1 Charismatic Mobilization: The Mango Cult

Despite such handicaps, within a week of its occupation of Tsinghua the workers' propaganda team received a powerful psychological boost that more than compensated for its objective shortcomings. On August 3, Mao Zedong had received a box of several dozen mangoes from the foreign minister of Pakistan, who was in Beijing on an official visit. Master of symbolic politics that he was, Mao (whose Hunan peasant palate may not have fancied the unfamiliar taste of mangoes) immediately redirected the exotic fruit as his personal gift to the Tsinghua workers' propaganda team. The gift was accompanied by a statement from Mao indicating that the working class, as China's leading class, should direct the superstructure: henceforth, workers' propaganda teams were to take permanent charge of higher education. As Mao's written instruction put it, "Realizing the proletarian education revolution requires working-class leadership ... Moreover, they will lead the schools forever" (Hinton, 1972, p. 227).

Mao's charismatic intervention had an electrifying impact on the Tsinghua campus that soon reverberated in cultish ceremonies around the country:

> The gift of mangoes and this statement of support had a profound effect. Few people slept at all that night. Everyone wanted to see and touch the mangoes that came directly from Chairman Mao, and everyone wanted to discuss this extraordinary idea that the propaganda teams, far from being a temporary, emergency expedient, were a form of permanent supervision over higher education. If the workers could not contain their joy, most students and staff members were also carried along in the great wave of enthusiasm that Mao's act generated. The original mangoes were preserved, put in glass cases, and displayed in the reception rooms of key factories. [See Figure 3.2.] Later numerous models of these mangoes were made and displayed by all the other factories that had taken part in the pacification of Tsinghua. A veritable cult arose around these mangoes, as if they were some religious relic – a hair of the Buddha, a nail from Christ's cross. (Hinton, 1972, p. 227)

FIGURE 3.2 Workers at Beijing Knitting Mill admire mangoes from Mao Zedong

At the Beijing Textile Factory, for example, "the wax-covered fruit was placed on an altar in the factory auditorium, and workers lined up to file past it, solemnly bowing as they walked by."

When the wax coating proved unable to prevent the revered relic from rotting, members of the factory revolutionary committee peeled the mango and boiled it in a giant cauldron: "Another ceremony was held, equally solemn.... Each worker drank a spoonful of the water in which the sacred mango had been boiled." A wax replica of the original mango was soon placed on the altar, and "workers continued to file by, their veneration for the sacred object in no way diminished." When Mao's personal physician reported this superstitious behavior to the Chairman, "he laughed. He had no problem with the mango worship and seemed delighted by the story" (Li, 1994, p. 503).

Although the Cultural Revolution was supposed to eliminate "feudal superstition" in favor of secular Marxist ideology, the party-state was not above cultivating quasi-religious symbolism for purposes of charismatic mobilization. In addition to the wax and plastic mango replicas displayed on makeshift altars in factories and workers' homes across China, the mango motif appeared in a variety of designs on colorful posters, Mao badges, household enamelware, quilt covers, pencil boxes, candy and cigarette wrappers, mirrors, and other items of daily use (Murck, 2013, pp. 150–233). While most workers may have been unsure about what a mango actually was, they quickly grasped its magical and redemptive potential. Wang Xiaoping, a worker at Beijing's Number One Machine Tool Plant who had long suffered on account of his family's class background, remembered:

Everyone was to receive a mango, a replica of the real fruit originally given to a member of our factory's Workers' Propaganda Team by Chairman Mao. Wax models had already been made, one for every person. What is a "mango"? Nobody knew. Few had ever heard the word, let alone seen one. Knowledgeable people said it was a fruit of extreme rarity, like Mushrooms of Immortality ... To receive such a rare and exotic thing filled people with a surge of excitement ...

That day was indeed a festive one for the factory. People were wild with joy. They shouted "Long Live Chairman Mao!" and "Long Live the Proletarian Cultural Revolution!" A few senior female workers mounted the platform, so excited that they wept ... The next day, wax mangoes were distributed. I got one. It lay in a rectangular glass box, gold colored and kidney shaped. Everyone held their wax model of the sacred fruit solemnly and reverently. Someone was even admonished by senior workers for not holding the fruit securely, which was a sign of disrespect to the Great Leader ... The mangoes were said to have been placed in the most conspicuous place in everyone's home. (Wang, 2013, pp. 37–38, 43)

The mango cult formed part of a quasi-religious craze that was sustained both by the growing veneration of Mao Zedong as revolutionary savior and by general relief at the prospect of replacing callow and impetuous students with more mature and restrained workers as the mainstay of state-mobilized contention (Perry, 2012, chapter 6).

Parades around the country featured mango replicas amidst portraits and statues of Chairman Mao. If anyone failed to grasp the significance of the sacred mission being entrusted to the proletariat by the paramount leader, the October 1 National Day Parade hammered home the point. The central section of the 400,000-person parade, reviewed by Chairman Mao from atop Tiananmen, was composed of worker representatives recruited from all over China marching behind a huge banner inscribed with the slogan "The working class must lead in everything" and carrying aloft gigantic mango replicas to signify Mao's gift to the Tsinghua workers' propaganda team. As Daniel Leese (2013, p. 59) notes, "Read as a political script, the 1968 National Day parade heralded the end of the Red Guard turmoil and a return to Communist Party dictatorship in the name of the working class."

3.2.2 "The Working Class Must Lead in Everything"

That the time had come for Red Guard rampages to give way to a nationwide SMM in the form of orchestrated worker propaganda teams had been made clear less than a month after the Tsinghua occupation in an essay by Shanghai journalist (and later Gang of Four member) Yao Wenyuan entitled "The Working Class Must Lead in Everything." Both the title and much of the content of Yao's highly publicized essay had actually been formulated by Mao himself. Moreover, on the same day that Yao's essay appeared in print (August 24, 1968), a joint proclamation was issued by Party Central, the State Council, the Central Military Commission, and the Central Cultural Revolution Group which called upon the whole country to follow the lead of Beijing's workers' propaganda teams in seizing control of all institutions of education from primary to tertiary (Central Party Office and State Council Secretariat, 1968, pp. 105–106; Tang, 2015). With these authoritative pronouncements, the idea of a "Great Proletarian Cultural Revolution" assumed new meaning: the working class would occupy the superstructure while intellectuals would be relegated to a disparaged category known as "the stinking old ninth" (Li, 2011, p. 35). After Mao's much publicized gift of mangoes to the propaganda team at Tsinghua, similar teams had quickly seized control of other institutions of higher education in Beijing, including the prestigious Peking University (Central Party Office and State Council Secretariat, 1968, p. 120). Following the publication of Yao Wenyuan's celebrated article, the practice spread still further (Xiao, 1997, p. 60).

3.2.3 The Shanghai Scene

Although workers' propaganda teams were a centrally mandated SMM, acting with the blessing of Chairman Mao himself, they operated quite differently in different places. In Beijing, the political capital of the country, the teams were under the command of the 8341 Army. In Yao Wenyuan's home base of Shanghai, the nation's industrial capital, the teams enjoyed greater autonomy and authority, even assuming a major role in municipal governance. The difference was due partly to the more prestigious position of workers in the local society and economy and partly to the particular political circumstances that obtained in the city. A workers' propaganda team from Shanghai's Workers' General Headquarters (a radical faction of mostly factory workers who had seized power in the city) was established to exercise control over the various departments of the municipal Revolutionary Committee (Shanghai

Cultural Revolution Materials Group, 1992, p. 578). Wang Hongwen, a former factory security guard and leader of the Workers' General Headquarters who would also later be named as a member of the infamous Gang of Four, clarified the broad mandate of the workers' propaganda teams in Shanghai: "Not only should they go to universities, middle and elementary schools to turn around and stabilize the 'unbearable chaos' to be found there, but they must also go to all realms of the superstructure ... to replenish all aspects of state agencies and all levels of 'revolutionary committees,' and also to resolve problems at the more than 400 units with serious long-standing issues" (Shanghai Party Committee, 1992, p. 579).

In response to Wang Hongwen's call, more than 90,000 factory workers were mobilized to occupy every Shanghai college campus and school as well as to take charge of municipal cultural, educational, public health, finance, and trade departments and district and county government offices. Eleven thousand workers assumed control of the 26 institutions of higher education in Shanghai; 52,000 workers occupied the middle and elementary schools; 5,800 workers seized control of the more than 400 enterprises marred by "serious long-standing problems"; several thousand workers each were dispatched to the municipal medical and public health, trade and finance, and science and technology administrations; another several thousand apiece took charge of the district, street, and county governments; and more than 500 handpicked workers oversaw the municipal party and government offices. Wang Hongwen emphasized, "Workers' propaganda teams must be leaders, not functionaries" (Shanghai Party Committee, 1992, p. 580; Central Party Office and State Council Secretariat, 1968, p. 93).

On August 24, the day that Yao Wenyuan's essay calling upon the working class to exercise all-round leadership was published, students and faculty at all the Shanghai universities staged massive demonstrations in support. The following day, workers' propaganda teams proceeded to occupy the major universities in the city. Following the Tsinghua precedent, the teams first assembled by columns at designated spots just outside the campus gates. Once in place, team members – sporting Mao badges on their chests and clutching copies of *Quotations from Chairman Mao* (the "Little Red Book") in their hands – separated into units behind flags and marched boldly onto campus. In stark contrast to the hostile reception that the Tsinghua workers' propaganda team had initially encountered in Beijing the month before, however, the Shanghai teams were greeted with the celebratory sounds of cymbals and drums and festive banners inscribed with slogans such as "Learn from the working class; salute the working class!" and "Welcome, Chairman Mao's trusted envoys!" (Li, 2015, pp. 1172–1173).

The warm reception that the workers' teams received on Shanghai campuses was not only a reflection of the high prestige that the proletariat enjoyed in China's industrial capital. During the weeks between the advent of workers' propaganda teams in Beijing and their subsequent introduction to Shanghai,

Mao's personal support for proletarian counterprotest had been made amply manifest. As a result, local authorities and workers – initially slow to take action – now scrambled to emulate and outdo the Beijing model. Thanks to the high proportion of workers in the Shanghai population, it was possible to saturate the universities with propaganda teams comprised of workers (Shanghai Party Committee, 1992, p. 581).[1]

3.2.4 "Education Revolution"

Once campuses across China had been emptied of contentious Red Guards, the workers' propaganda teams recruited a new type of university student, known as worker-peasant-soldier trainees, to take their place. The new students were admitted not on the basis of competitive entrance examinations (as had been the case before the Cultural Revolution) but on the recommendation of their work unit (commune, factory, or military barracks) – supposedly in recognition of their advanced political ideology and activism but often on the basis of personal connections.[2] The workers' propaganda teams proceeded to preside over an "education revolution" (Tang, 2015) in which the teams themselves acted as the university leadership and their newly recruited worker-peasant-soldier trainees served as shock troops for "revolutionary" initiatives directed primarily against faculty members.[3]

During the eight years that workers' propaganda teams held sway over Chinese higher education, public criticism sessions, group political study, and practical labor experience dominated the college curriculum. The propaganda teams also scoured the local environs in search of incriminating evidence for "class education exhibitions" intended to politicize the campus community. At Hangzhou University, for example, the workers' propaganda team fashioned an exhibit from a large, dusty bundle of discarded old clothes that they discovered in a campus dumpster. The tattered items, it turned out, had been thrown away by a recent graduate of the university, originally from a poor working-class family, whose pre–Cultural Revolution "bourgeois" education had apparently made her feel that such unattractive apparel no longer suited her. The entire university was mobilized to view the display of discarded "proletarian"

---

[1] On average, the ratio of work-team members to faculty and students at Shanghai universities varied from 1:2 (at universities deemed friendly to the worker radicals in charge of the city government) to 1:1 (on unfriendly campuses).

[2] The current president of China, Xi Jinping, entered Tsinghua University as a worker-peasant-soldier trainee in 1975. Like many fellow trainees, Xi could claim membership in the "Red aristocracy" thanks to his father's revolutionary credentials.

[3] In the course of the Tsinghua occupation, Workers' Propaganda Teams relied upon the active participation of the worker-peasant-soldier trainees to spearhead a dozen different political campaigns in which more than 1,000 people – about 20 percent of the faculty and staff – were subjected to aggressive interrogation and investigation. Of those investigated, 167 were charged with serious crimes; of these, 20 committed suicide.

clothing, promoting the exhibit as "an indictment of the heinous crimes caused by the revisionist educational line" (*Peking Review*, 1968, pp. 13–16).

The propaganda teams' efforts to revolutionize the faculty and administration were not confined to campus. At Nanjing Teachers' College, instructors and cadres were sent to neighboring factories and villages to conduct social surveys intended to gather ideas for a "new-style socialist university" (Chinese Communist Party Committee at Nanjing Teachers' College, 1974, p. 56). Sometimes the off-campus experiences occurred under remote and harsh conditions. In 1969 the Tsinghua workers' teams established an "experimental farm" in distant Jiangxi Province, to which more than 2,800 instructors and administrators were packed off for labor reform. The farm was located in an area infested with schistosomiasis, and more than 1,000 Tsinghua faculty and staff contracted the disease as a result (Zhu, 2015). Some died; others battled debilitating symptoms for decades (Tang, 2004, 87).[4]

Deng Xiaoping's historic restoration of meritocratic college entrance examinations in 1977 put an abrupt end to Mao's "education revolution." The Cultural Revolution was now roundly denounced for having cost China "ten lost years" in higher education. Political study was reduced, practical labor was phased out, and universities were directed to beef up academic standards in a determined attempt to compensate for lost time. As part of this wholesale reform of higher education, workers' propaganda teams were decommissioned, and regular party and government appointees resumed control of university administration.

3.3 PROLETARIAN PATROLS IN 1989

With the categorical post-Mao repudiation of "ten lost years" of radical educational experimentation during the Cultural Revolution decade, workers' propaganda teams seemed destined for extinction. Twenty years later, however, the tactic of deploying proletarian forces against protesting students made a dramatic reappearance in the spring of 1989 after university campuses had erupted in response to the Tiananmen Democracy Movement. Sensing the grave danger of regime collapse, the state again complemented its strategy of military suppression with a proletarian SMM designed to elicit widespread citizen support. And, as in the Cultural Revolution, Chinese cities responded in markedly different ways that reflected variation in local circumstances.

In Shanghai, factory workers were again confidently called upon in 1989 – under the legacy revolutionary name of "workers' patrols" (*gongren jiuchadui*) – as part of the city's eleventh-hour effort to form a massive counterweight strong enough to quell the student demonstrators. In Beijing, where the Tiananmen protest had been ongoing for weeks, student activists themselves had already forged links with local factories. As a result, the Beijing

---

[4] Even thirty years later, Tsinghua University's medical facilities were still burdened with providing treatment for hundreds of schistosomiasis patients.

government turned to peasants from surrounding suburban counties to mount its "proletarian" offensive.

China's two leading cities differed not only in the composition but also in the scope and objectives of their SMMs. In Beijing, the counterdeployment was a propaganda campaign intended to legitimize the imposition of martial law and the impending military crackdown by the People's Liberation Army. In Shanghai, by contrast, state-mobilized workers' patrols themselves served as the main suppression force. Directed by the municipal police, their role was not limited to propaganda; they were asked to pacify rebellious university campuses, remove roadblocks, end public protests, and return the city to the control of the regime.

Despite their critical importance to the state's suppression effort, the counterprotests in 1989 were less ambitious in ultimate aims than had been the case during the Cultural Revolution. Unlike Mao's day, the proletariat was not tasked with remaking the basic fabric of the nation's politico-ideological superstructure. In neither Beijing nor Shanghai did the countermobilization presage an "education revolution" in institutions of higher learning. This difference points to a sea change in the dynamics of contention in post-Mao China. In contrast to the Red Guards of the Cultural Revolution, the Tiananmen protesters had not been inspired or instigated by the supreme leader of the CCP. And when it came time to demobilize the student protesters, the state could no longer rely on charismatic mobilization but resorted instead to bureaucratic and instrumental means. The "revisionism" of revolutionary purpose warned against by Chairman Mao in the waning years of his life had indeed taken hold.

3.3.1 The Beijing Pattern

By late April 1989, the student movement had spiraled out of control in Beijing. A violent confrontation with security forces protecting the central leadership compound adjacent to Tiananmen Square erupted on the night of April 20. A few days later, *People's Daily* published a strongly worded editorial, accusing demonstrators of having stirred up "political turmoil" and calling upon party members and Communist Youth League members across the country to act in concert to end the political unrest. When protests continued to escalate in both scale and demands, martial law was declared on May 19, and a military operation in the nation's capital seemed all but inevitable.

Two days after the declaration of martial law, Beijing municipal party and government leaders held an emergency meeting at which an organization named the "Mass Task Force to Maintain Order in the Capital" was established (Daxing District Party Committee Military Department, 1989, p. 18). Members of the force represented a composite array of social groups, drawn disproportionately from militias in the countryside surrounding Beijing. With the escalation of political tensions and looming prospect of military intervention, Beijing's propaganda campaign grew more insistent. On May 31, thousands of peasants, workers, staff, and teachers from nearby Shunyi County held a mass rally to "firmly oppose the ongoing political turmoil" (Office of the Beijing Party Committee, 1989, p. 120). That afternoon, similar demonstrations took place in Daxing and Huairou (also suburban counties of Beijing) to voice opposition against "the small group of people who stir up political chaos" (Office of the Beijing Party Committee, 1989, p. 120). The next day, state-mobilized counterprotests reached a peak. According to an official account (written in a hasty style with broken sentences),

> More than 200,000 peasants and township cadres and residents of the five rural counties in the suburbs of Beijing held large-scale rallies and demonstrations in support of the wise decision made by the Central Committee of the CCP and the State Council to halt political turmoil and restore public order. The rallies and demonstrations were also in support of the series of measures adopted by the Communist Party's Municipal Committee and the Municipal Government of Beijing to carry out the decisions made by the central leadership. The numbers of participants in the five suburban counties are as follows: Mengtougou District, 100,000; Tong County, more than 20,000; Fangshan County, more than 10,000; Yanqing County, more than 100,000; and Changping County, 25,000. (Office of the Beijing Party Committee, 1989, p. 121)

A former senior official offered further details of the state-sponsored nature of the June 1 events, revealing that the massive participation had been facilitated by a combination of bureaucratic mobilization and material incentives:

> The large-scale rallies and demonstrations in the suburbs of Beijing were carefully planned and organized by the Municipal Communist Party Committee. They comprised an essential part of the ongoing propaganda war [against the democracy movement]. These officially organized events had to have a large attendance and create high morale. Every district or county was required to mobilize at least 10,000 participants ... Every participating peasant was granted two 'work points' and the government provided transportation. Cadres and workers were each awarded 5–10 RMB in cash for participation; some work units handed out new bath towels or straw hats for free as incentives. (Zhang, 2009, p. 323)

The post-Mao market reforms had brought a welcome rise in household incomes, and cash had replaced charisma as the coin of the realm. These "bath towels or straw hats," not Chairman Mao's Little Red Book or magical mangoes, now served as proletarian protest props. But economic liberalization had not translated into political liberalization, and those who spoke at the state-sponsored demonstrations were careful to mouth the prescribed party line:

> No matter whether cadres or peasants, every speaker at the rallies was required to make three points: first, those who incited the political unrest were only an extremely tiny portion of society; second, the patriotic zeal of the university students was commendable; third, the demands of the anti-government protesters were in line with the Party's own demands. The slogans that participants chanted, such as "firmly oppose political turmoil" and "firmly support the speeches made by Premier Li Peng and President Yang Shangkun," were also determined by the state. (Zhang, 2009, p. 323)

Much like Polish mass rallies in March 1968, in the Beijing rallies of 1989 the language and narrative of these "proletarian" SMMs were supplied by the communist party. The legitimizing function of the series of counterprotests in Beijing was confirmed by the municipal Party Committee's official mouthpiece, which stressed the law-abiding and pro-government import of the state-sponsored demonstrations. One day after the rallies, *Beijing Daily* contained the following account in an article entitled "Please Hear What the Peasants Have to Say":

"Maintain stability and solidarity! Firmly uphold the Four Cardinal Principles! Oppose bourgeois liberalism!" Yesterday, with permission from the Public Security Bureau, more than 200,000 peasants, workers, cadres and teachers from Shunyi, Huairou and Daxing Counties ... held rallies or demonstrations outside the areas that have been declared subject to martial law. The participants supported the wise [martial law] decision and the prompt measures to implement the decision. They also expressed their will to remain at their work posts and commit wholeheartedly to production and a good summer harvest. (*Sichuan Daily* Editorial Department, 1989, pp. 158–159)

The multiple suburban rallies followed a common protocol. Convened in a central sports arena that could accommodate a large crowd, the gatherings featured remarks by local party cadres as well as by peasant, worker, and intellectual representatives. An open letter calling for society-wide endorsement of government policies was read aloud and applauded. In some places, government-sponsored rallies were broadcast live to spillover venues set up outside of the central arena. The rallies were followed by huge street demonstrations in which participants holding pro-government placards marched from the arena to an important political location in town. In some counties, motorcades were organized with participants riding in open vehicles, hoisting banners and shouting slogans. In the spring of 1989 these well-publicized initiatives created a dramatic scene that garnered widespread public attention (Office of the Beijing Party Committee, 1989, p. 159).

Striking as they were, the Beijing counterprotests never went beyond a propaganda offensive. The rallies and marches took place outside of the martial law zone, and participants did not engage directly with anti-regime protesters. The state-mobilized propaganda campaign sought to drum up popular support for the implementation of martial law while encouraging the industrial labor force to maintain its routine work schedule. Beijing authorities did not rely principally on factory workers to halt the escalating political upheaval and curb the unruly youth protesters. When instructed to discredit anti-regime student challengers, municipal authorities in the capital city looked primarily to peasants and rural cadres.

The actual suppression operation in Beijing relied on the People's Liberation Army and state security apparatus (Brook, 1998). In the industrial hub of Shanghai, by contrast, state-mobilized workers played a major role in the suppression campaign. The difference was due in part to the more prominent

3.3.2 The Shanghai Pattern

In Shanghai, the party-state had inherited a rich tradition – dating back to the communists' takeover of the city in 1949 – of deploying the working class as political stabilizer and legitimizer. During the Cultural Revolution, Wang Hongwen's Workers' General Headquarters, composed largely of factory workers, deployed proletarian patrols to exercise control over the municipal government as well as the universities (Perry and Li, 1993). In 1989, factory workers again took center stage as the primary force commissioned to put an end to student unrest on behalf of the beleaguered regime:

After Mayor Zhu Rongji's televised address, more than 5,000 worker patrols at 33 large and medium-sized enterprises throughout the city formed propaganda teams to converge from all directions on three command posts in the city center. By four in the morning on the ninth, more than 5,000 propaganda team members backed by armed police and public security personnel, riding in trucks and holding high banners, took to the streets to clear away all obstructions. At the same time, more than 100,000 worker patrols organized by each district sprang into action. By dawn, the 48 remaining obstructions had all been removed... Zhu Rongji offered praise: "The Shanghai worker patrols took action early this morning, restoring Shanghai's transportation and ending the disorderly situation. You have performed a great service for the people of Shanghai!" (Shanghai Federation of Trade Unions, 1996, p. 514)[5]

As with the suppression of Red Guards during the Cultural Revolution, proletarian counterprotest was deemed more palatable to the general populace than naked military repression. To be sure, in both cases police units provided crucial behind-the-scenes direction and protection for the workers. But the dominant image presented to the Shanghai public was one of unarmed workers parading in open-air trucks and shouting pro-regime slogans through megaphones, rather than of armored tanks and soldiers. The mayor of China's largest industrial city was determined to use his most valuable political resource, the Shanghai working class, as a substitute for a show of state military strength in order to avoid massive bloodshed:

Mayor Zhu Rongji... emphasized that martial law would not be declared in Shanghai. "Many comrades have asked us to call in the People's Armed Police and some have even suggested bringing in the army. As mayor, I solemnly declare that neither the Party Committee nor the Municipal Government has considered calling in the army. We have never envisaged military control or martial law; we seek only to stabilize Shanghai, to

---

[5] This draft version contains much information on sensitive political topics that was omitted from the official published version, which appeared the following year.

steady the situation, to insist on production, and to ensure normal life." That evening tens of thousands of workers were sent out to clear away the roadblocks. (Nathan and Link, 2001, p. 410)

Further replicating the Cultural Revolution pattern, working-class patrols were dispatched to occupy urban districts to reestablish order in restive Shanghai neighborhoods (Zhang, 1991, p. 241). Nationally, more than 2.5 million workers were mobilized to participate in such occupations that spring (Yi and Liu, 1994, p. 195). The official mouthpiece of Shanghai municipality, *Liberation Daily*, reported on June 9:

In the early morning today, about 100,000 workers' patrols from various districts of Shanghai went into the streets with Communist cadres and police to remove the roadblocks that had been set up by a small number of people who intended to paralyze the transportation of Shanghai. The removal of the barriers will ensure the normal flow of traffic and restore public order. (*Liberation Daily*, 1989a)

Thanks to the workers' patrols, roadblocks across Shanghai had been cleared by 4:40 a.m. *Liberation Daily* noted, in a tone reminiscent of reports on Shanghai universities' warm reception of workers' propaganda teams during the Cultural Revolution:

The operation received support from the leaders, teachers and students at Fudan University, Tongji University, Aquatic University and the Institute of Mechanical Engineering. By around 12:45 a.m., protesting students in front of the gates of Fudan and Tongji had all retreated to their respective campuses. Tongji University provided tea and drinking water and offered shelter for members of the operations. After the roadblocks had been cleared, teachers and students at Aquatic University shouted slogans such as "Thank you, working class." (*Liberation Daily*, 1989a)

3.3.3 Beijing and Shanghai Compared

Considering the backlash that the deployment of tanks and troops to suppress student demonstrators in the nation's capital generated at home and abroad, it is tempting to suggest that Shanghai's reliance on counterprotests by unarmed workers was a superior strategy of responding to the national crisis precipitated by the 1989 Democracy Movement. In fact, however, it is hard to gauge the relative efficacy of the contrasting approaches due to very different situations in the two cities. As in the Cultural Revolution, these differences reflected not only distinctive historical legacies and economic circumstances but also the critical matter of sequencing. In both cases, Beijing led (with demobilization that turned violent) and Shanghai followed (with notably less bloodshed). Premier Li Peng, who had advocated for the use of armed force to restore order to Beijing, reacted defensively to suggestions that the Tiananmen massacre might have been averted had proletarian counterprotest been substituted for military might. As Li remarked a few days after the June Fourth crackdown:

Had Beijing not relied on the People's Liberation Army, it would have been difficult to defend this capital of ours. Some democracy activists asked us whether it wouldn't have been better had Beijing been like Shanghai. I told a meeting with democracy activists that Beijing had no choice but to use military force because the capital of the People's Republic was in grave danger. The reason that Shanghai could later restore order with 100,000 workers was because Beijing had already suppressed the rebellion. Had Beijing not already been pacified, even the mobilization of an additional 200,000 workers would not have resolved Shanghai's difficulties. (Li, 1989)

Self-serving though the premier's explanation was, it was not an unreasonable argument. Shanghai benefited from Beijing's prior example, brutal as it was. In this respect, sequencing was crucial.

Differences in levels of political trust also shaped the divergent patterns of state-mobilized counterprotest seen in the two cities' suppression efforts. In the spring of 1989, the Beijing working class was not regarded as a reliable base of support in the eyes of the municipal authorities. Beijing's rogue union, the so-called Autonomous Association of Workers, was established very early on in the Democracy Movement and had gathered a considerable following, particularly among younger workers, when martial law was announced (*Sichuan Daily* Editorial Department, 1989, p. 174; Walder and Gong, 1993). Many of the more rebellious and potentially violent groups among the protesters – the motorcycle brigade known as the "Flying Tigers," for example – were themselves active or former factory workers in state-owned enterprises. Rumors of an imminent general strike had also circulated widely, forcing a refutation from the official All-China Federation of Trade Unions (*Sichuan Daily* Editorial Department, 1989, p. 116).

On May 14, at the height of the student protests, Premier Li Peng paid a well-planned visit to the Capital Iron and Steel Corporation for a discussion session with workers about the mounting crisis. Reading between the lines of the carefully worded coverage by Xinhua News Agency, one could surmise that the conversation did not go quite as party leaders had expected:

During the discussion, workers at the Capital Iron and Steel Corporation offered candid opinions about issues such as regulation of the economy, deepening reform, revitalizing large state-owned enterprises, stabilizing prices, curbing corruption and so on ... After hearing the workers' views on the student protest, the Premier said that the government welcomed criticism and suggestions provided by the workers, students and masses. Some of the opinions of the students – such as the chaotic situation in the economy, the bureaucratism in our state apparatus, and corruption – are indeed problems the Party is seeking to resolve. (*People's Daily*, 1989)

The Xinhua report did not suggest even lukewarm sympathy for the state among the Beijing industrial work force at this critical moment. In fact, just one day after the promulgation of martial law, a "Joint Declaration of Workers and Students in the Capital Region" denounced the martial law and called for the immediate removal of the government leadership (Zhang, 2002, p. 553).

A lack of political trust in its own factory workers convinced authorities in Beijing to resort to peasants to delegitimize the student movement and to call upon the People's Liberation Army to quell it, in sharp contrast to the situation that unfolded a few days later in Shanghai.

On June 1, as the military prepared to clear Tiananmen Square of protesters, *Beijing Daily* published a statement by the managers of six large construction companies in Beijing, the first to issue a patriotic appeal in the name of the working class:

Tiananmen Square is the fruit of the labor of our construction workers and we thus have deep feelings about this revered place. We hope every citizen of the People's Republic cherishes the labor of the builders and voluntarily protects the dignity of the motherland. (*Beijing Daily*, 1989b, p. 1)

Workers were credited for their labor in service to the nation, but in Beijing they were not being hailed as the leading class. The difference with Shanghai, where the working class was understood to be the city's ultimate stabilizer in the midst of widespread social unrest, was reflected in the official newspapers of the two cities. When the central Xinhua News Agency broadcast a report on June 2 about a meeting of the official All-China Federation of Trade Unions held in support of the declaration of martial law in Beijing, *Beijing Daily* published the story under the title "Upholding Social Stability is the Most Urgent Task, Critical to the Overall Situation," whereas Shanghai's *Liberation Daily* chose as its title "The Working Class is the Primary Force in Upholding Social Stability." The alternative framings of the same news item reflected the different status of workers in the two cities.

Differences in timing also contributed to the dissimilar approaches. In the Beijing area, state-mobilized demonstrations occurred only on the two days of June 1 and 2, just prior to the military operation on June 3–4 that forcibly suppressed the student movement. In Shanghai, the Democracy Movement did not create a citywide crisis until after the start of the military offensive in Beijing. On the first day of the crackdown in Beijing, Shanghai authorities announced that final exams would be administered as scheduled on university campuses across the city, seeming to contrast a tranquil Shanghai against the chaotic situation at colleges and universities in the capital city (*Liberation Daily*, 1989b, p. 1). However, after the bloody suppression in Beijing the situation in Shanghai deteriorated dramatically, as students flooded the streets to express sympathy with the Tiananmen victims.

On the evening of June 8, Shanghai Mayor Zhu Rongji delivered a live televised speech calling for a citywide movement aimed at clearing the roads and restoring order. His speech stressed the signal importance of the Shanghai working class:

Shanghai has the highest density of industry of any city in China. We have the strongest working-class contingent with 5.08 million employees among whom 2.3 million are members of the proletariat. If they can be organized to support us, our police and armed police will have sufficient capacity to uphold the rule of law and public order in Shanghai. (*Liberation Daily*, 1989c, p. 1)

Initially the Shanghai government sought to create the impression that the state-mobilized campaign to remove roadblocks was a spontaneous action on the part of individual factories:

In the early morning today, cadres and workers from a number of factories in Shanghai organized themselves and voluntarily removed road blocks. Their action was welcomed by city residents.... Their actions are very valuable. (*Liberation Daily*, 1989d, p. 1)

In reality, the movement against the student protests in Shanghai was methodically organized by municipal authorities through the formal institution of the urban workplace (*danwei*), relying on workers and cadres with clear, hierarchically defined state-owned enterprise affiliations. And soon Mayor Zhu, referencing the historical significance of the Shanghai workers' patrols, dispensed with any pretense that the current mobilization of factory workers was spontaneous rather than state-sponsored:

In the past, workers' patrols assembled by the Shanghai Federation of Trade Unions made great contributions in protecting the factories and upholding public order. Now, they have again been mobilized into action. After three days of preparation, each district of Shanghai municipality organized a force of 10 to 20 thousand people, and 32 major factories in Shanghai organized a back-up force of several tens of thousands of workers. I don't think we should keep this a secret. The workers' patrols are a legal organization whose activities are supported by the municipal government. Their actions to restore order are legitimate. (*Liberation Daily*, 1989c, p. 1)

In turning yet again to its industrial work force, Shanghai in 1989 diverged from the Beijing scenario, where peasants from surrounding rural counties without previous contact with student protesters provided the backbone of the SMMs.

3.3.4 From Charismatic Mobilization to Rational Discourse

The 1989 state-mobilized counterprotests in Beijing and Shanghai, different though they were, both departed in some significant respects from Cultural Revolution precedents. Rational discourse had replaced charismatic mobilization, with concrete material gains now emphasized over symbolic appeals. The death of Mao Zedong in 1976 and subsequent criticisms of the personality cult that had surrounded him undercut the feasibility of charismatic mobilization in the era of market reform. Under Deng Xiaoping, the CCP had been transformed from a vehicle for revolutionary agitation into a routinized bureaucratic machine. In 1989 the party called not for proletarian revolution to restructure the universities and remold the intellectuals but simply for an end to the disorder caused by the student uprising, stressing its negative effects on economic development and citizens' daily lives.

"Order" and "interests," rather than "the working class must lead in everything," were watchwords of the 1989 SMM. Sounding more like a sober statistician than a proletarian polemicist, a speaker at a counterprotest in Beijing's Shunyi County pointed to the economic achievements of the post-Mao market reform in making his pitch for loyalty to the regime:

> During the past ten years of reform, the agricultural production of Shunyi County increased by 71% and the county, town and village enterprise industrial output grew 20 fold ... People's living standards improved greatly. These accomplishments were all realized under the political atmosphere of stability and unity ... thus the people of Shunyi .... must follow the political line of the Party Center. (*Beijing Daily*, 1989a, p. 1)

Similarly, a speaker from Daxing County stressed the need for public order to enable the functioning of daily markets:

> Ordinary people [*laobaixing*] suffer while an extremely tiny portion of society creates social turmoil. These days, our vehicles to transport vegetable and milk into Beijing cannot enter the city ... Now the peasants' watermelons are ripe but they dare not go to Beijing to sell their fruit ... If we allow the turmoil to continue, not only will the peasants not be enriched, I am afraid we won't even have enough food to feed the people. (*Beijing Daily*, 1989a, 1)

The drab, dispassionate language of rational discourse was deployed even with respect to highly charged symbolic matters. An issue specific to Beijing was how to handle the controversial "Goddess of Democracy" statue which had been constructed hastily at the Central Academy of Fine Arts, transported to Tiananmen Square on May 30, and assembled directly in front of the Gate of Heavenly Peace, where it stood defiantly facing the portrait of Mao. Evidently a hybrid between a bodhisattva Goddess of Mercy and the Statue of Liberty, the Goddess of Democracy had captivated the Western media, which hailed it as an iconic reflection of the students' yearning for freedom and democracy.

In discrediting the statue, the Chinese state relied not on charismatic mobilization but on secular, rationalist arguments. On May 31, Beijing Daily (1989b, p. 1) published a series of articles under the title "Restore the Dignified Look of Tiananmen Square as Soon as Possible" and subtitled "Many People Express Strong Disagreement over the Construction of a 'Goddess' Statue." On the same day the paper published public letters and remarks by an assortment of Beijing citizens condemning the statue in Tiananmen Square from various vantage points. For example, the Tiananmen Square Management Office raised legal concerns, noting that the construction of the statue violated official rules regulating the design, construction, and public presentation of sculptures in the city. A letter from the city's street sweepers emphasized the practical difficulties of sanitation work, and attendant public health hazards, if the statue continued to draw throngs of protesters to the Square. An open letter from five university students criticized the statue as antithetical to principles of rationality:

A 'goddess' cannot save China and we do not need a new savior. We and all the people who have a dispassionate mind can see that the CCP is the only realistic force of leadership that will accomplish the historical mission of national revival. Such a statue with a vague theme and poor artistic quality being placed on the square in such a (unserious) manner would not add even a tiny slice of glory to our patriotic democratic movement. It goes directly against the principle of rationality and rule of law that we were trying to promote. (*Beijing Daily*, 1989b, p. 1)

This was a far cry from the "magical mangoes" that had inspired workers during the Cultural Revolution with the conviction that they were the revolutionary elect, specially chosen to carry forth Mao's quasi-religious crusade.

In Shanghai – where, unlike Beijing, continuing trust in the industrial work force cast it in a starring role in the 1989 suppression campaign the rationale for this SMM was nevertheless also presented in prosaic rather than heroic terms. *Liberation Daily* reported on June 6:

Yesterday, a tiny portion of the student population of Shanghai and a few unemployed thugs prowled the streets and intercepted vehicles. This forced all bus lines within the city to terminate service from around 5 a.m. Tens of thousands of workers could not get to work on time. Large amounts of material for production and for daily life could not be transported and delivered ... (*Liberation Daily*, 1989e, p. 1)

We have to organize a strong and capable team, firmly take decisive measures and resolutely stop the increasingly severe destructive activities. Some comrades also think that if we do not organize teams to maintain order and simply rely on education and thought work, the workers' motivation and enthusiasm will be affected. Economic development and social life in Shanghai will become chaotic. (*Liberation Daily*, 1989f, p. 1)

While the SMM in Beijing focused on the crowd in Tiananmen Square, in Shanghai the problem was disruption of the main transportation arteries. On June 7, *Liberation Daily* (1989g) initiated a citywide discussion under the title "Shanghai Must Not Become Anarchic; What Should We Do?"

Due to the sabotage of a very few people, inner-city traffic is totally paralyzed. How many workers cannot go to work as usual? .... The basic needs of all 12 million people in the city face difficulties. A great metropolis stands on the brink of chaos. Our parents and siblings are deeply worried!

Even after municipal authorities had begun preparations to dispatch workers' patrols, the Shanghai media encouraged ordinary people to contribute their own policy suggestions. As in Beijing, the goal was to involve the general public in rational discourse by appealing to a shared interest in social order:

We, the editorial office of Shanghai's newspapers, TV and radio stations, urge our readers and audiences, the owners of the city, to initiate a grand discussion of the theme "Shanghai cannot be chaotic! What should we do?" We urge you to actively contribute your policy suggestions to the government, so as to uncover and smash the minority conspiracy of blocking traffic, hindering production, and destabilizing Shanghai. The prerequisite of loving Shanghai and developing Shanghai is stabilizing Shanghai. All citizens with a conscience and a sense of social responsibility, be active! To maintain Shanghai's social order and material supply, you should contribute what you can! (*Liberation Daily*, 1989g, p. 1)

Although the Shanghai working class was still praised for its exceptional level of ideological and political correctness, its mandate in 1989 was narrow compared to the heady days of the Cultural Revolution when Wang Hongwen had called on workers to be "leaders not functionaries" in "all realms of the superstructure." After the workers' patrols succeeded in removing traffic obstructions and returning students to campus, Shanghai's grateful leaders clarified that their future role would remain circumscribed:

Leaders of Shanghai said, "We thank the Shanghai working class. ... The worker's patrols were the primary force in stabilizing the political situation in Shanghai ... Shanghai's working class has the highest level of ideological enlightenment; it is also the most organized and disciplined class. In this campaign, the workers' patrols displayed a high level of political quality and projected a very good spiritual image" ... The leaders emphasized that the workers' patrols must not be disbanded. They should remove blockades if the roads are blocked again; if there are no road blockades, they should patrol the streets. They should also take action immediately if bad elements are uncovered. (*Liberation Daily*, 1989h, p. 1)

Proletarian patrols would be kept in place for a period after the immediate suppression of the student protest, but merely for the mundane purpose of maintaining social order.

3.4 CONCLUSION

While communist regimes often favor proletarian movements as an antidote to student protests, the resulting SMMs are not all of a piece. SMMs can be vehicles for profound and sustained institutional change (as in the Cultural Revolution) or temporary emergency measures in response to a perceived crisis (as in the Tiananmen Uprising). They can take the form of a quasi-religious crusade for a charismatic supreme leader's utopian vision of revolutionary immortality or of a thinly veiled cover for the tactical maneuvers of an ideology-free party-state clinging to power in the wake of destabilizing economic reform. They may be progressive or reactive. As we have seen in the demobilization of the Red Guard Movement of 1968 and in the Democracy Movement of 1989, arguably the two most politically perilous junctures in the seventy-year history of the PRC, China's party-state mobilized the nation's proletariat in markedly different ways at different times in different places.

In 1968, workers' propaganda teams were initially adopted in Beijing as an emergency measure to stem the spreading Red Guard factional strife and save the Cultural Revolution from alienating the masses. Serious as the armed conflict was, the rival combatants' ultimate loyalty to Chairman Mao afforded the regime considerable latitude for countermeasures. Charismatic mobilization contributed to the workers' speedy success in curtailing campus conflict, offering them an official mandate to serve as the vanguard of a more fundamental restructuring of the nation's institutions of higher learning. "The Working Class must lead in everything ... and forever" was a directive from Chairman Mao himself. State-mobilized contention, energized by Mao's personal gift of "magical" mangoes, was thereby elevated from a makeshift countermeasure against unruly youth to a righteous path toward realizing the charismatic leader's revolutionary utopia. Even so, local manifestations of Mao's proletarian crusade varied widely from one city to another. In Beijing, the workers' propaganda teams concentrated their offensive on the universities; in Shanghai, they tackled the governance structure as well.

Twenty years later, when the post-Mao state faced another tumultuous student movement in the form of the Tiananmen Uprising, proletarian counterprotest remained within the political elite's operational tool kit. This time, however, student protesters were not vying for loyalty to the top leader but were calling for the overthrow of the political system itself. As Mark Beissinger notes in Chapter 6 of this volume, in moments of direct revolutionary challenge to the regime the purposes of SMMs narrow considerably. In 1989 a pragmatic and ideology-free party bureaucracy in Beijing would deploy countermobilization as an instrument to legitimize sending tanks into Tiananmen Square. Despite this narrowing of purpose, different levels of trust in the industrial proletariat, combined with a lag in response time between Beijing and Shanghai, again contributed to notably divergent patterns of counterprotest in China's two most important metropolitan centers. In Beijing, the focus was on justifying the imminent military offensive by the People's Liberation Army; in Shanghai, workers' patrols themselves carried out the pacification.

The shift from charismatic mobilization in the Cultural Revolution to a less personalistic and more pragmatic mode of persuasion in the Tiananmen Uprising, it should be noted, did not signify some unilinear secular evolution toward greater "rationality" on the part of the Chinese state and its citizens. Rather, dissimilarities in the framing of SMMs at different critical junctures reflect differences in general sociopolitical conditions as well as in the particular style and strategy of the leaders in power. Moreover, one cannot draw a stark distinction between "emotional" charisma and "rational" interest. Displaying impassioned devotion to the supreme leader was a perfectly rational response to the political uncertainty and volatility of 1968, just as, in 1989, "dispassionate" calls for social stability and economic prosperity surely struck an emotional chord among a populace that had only recently emerged from the violence and material deprivation of the Cultural Revolution. Convincing elements of society to assist state authorities in suppressing other social actors demands resonant appeals that are highly sensitive to time and place.

SMMs afford a revealing prism through which to view the machinery of the modern state as it interacts with social forces. Previous scholarship on contentious politics, while highlighting significant temporal and regional variation in the composition and character of popular protest, has devoted far less attention and nuance to the question of repression. Yet a regime's survival is not only a function of the severity of the social protests it faces; it also depends on the state's ability to demobilize and delegitimize such challenges. For this purpose, overt military suppression may be less effective than SMMs.

Communist regimes commonly speak and act in the name of the proletariat as a means of asserting authority and authenticity. Successfully marshaling proletarian activism against rampant social protest requires substantial ideational and organizational capacity, however. To be persuasive to the wider public, moreover, the technology and discourse of mobilization must be calibrated to suit the circumstances. In the case of China, the party-state has displayed remarkable versatility in its deployment of proletarian SMMs – from charismatic rhetoric and ritual to rational discourse, from urban factory workers to suburban peasants – in response to the changing national political climate and varied local conditions.

Throughout its eventful history, the Chinese Communist Party has also shown intense interest in learning from developments in other communist countries. One consequence has been a series of SMMs intended as a prophylactic against the sort of threatening popular unrest that occurred in Eastern Europe. In 1956, Mao's Hundred Flowers Campaign was launched to defuse the disaffection among intellectuals that had helped generate revolts in Hungary and Poland. In 1968, at the height of China's Red Guard movement, the Prague Spring offered another warning signal. The rise of the trade union Solidarity in 1980s Poland was taken by the Chinese leadership as evidence of the dangers of autonomous labor unions. The PRC's ability to weather the Tiananmen Uprising of 1989, when most of the rest of the communist world had reached the brink of collapse, is usually attributed to Deng Xiaoping's steely resolve in ordering a military crackdown: In contrast to the weak-kneed Soviets and their client states, the PRC did not shrink from armored tanks to suppress regime-threatening protest. But the willingness of ordinary Chinese citizens to accept the state's ruthless repression as a necessary means of restoring social and economic order was also critical to regime survival. For that purpose, the skillful deployment of proletarian SMMs, tailored to suit the pragmatic post-Mao mood as well as the particulars of different places, proved key.

REFERENCES

Andreas, Joel. 2007. The structure of charismatic mobilization: A case study of rebellion during the Chinese Cultural Revolution. *American Sociological Review* 72(3): 434–458.

Beijing Daily. 1989a (June 1). 请听农民的声音 [Please Hear What the Peasants Have to Say].

Beijing Daily. 1989b (June 1). 尽快恢复天安门广场庄严面貌 [Restoring the Solemn Outlook of the Tiananmen Square As Soon As Possible].

Brook, Timothy. 1998. *Quelling the People: The Military Suppression of the Beijing Democracy Movement*. Stanford, CA: Stanford University Press.

Central Party Office and State Council Secretariat (eds.). 1968. 无产阶级文化大革命有关文件汇集 [Collection of documents concerning the Great Proletarian Cultural Revolution] 7: 105–106.

Chinese Communist Party Committee at Nanjing Teacher's College (ed.). 1974. 在党的一元化领导下充分发挥工人宣传队的政治作用 [Fully develop the political functions of the Workers' Propaganda Teams under the unified leadership of the Party]. 南京师范大学学报 (社会科学版) [Nanjing Normal University Journal (Social Science Edition)]: 55–57.

Daxing District Party Committee Military Department. 1989. 动乱后的反思 [Reflections after the Turmoil]. 中国民兵 [Chinese Militia] 10: 18–19.

Hinton, William. 1972. Hundred Day War: The Cultural Revolution at Tsinghua University. *Monthly Review* 24(3): 185–187.

Leese, Daniel. 2013. Designing Spectacles: The 1968 Beijing National Day Parade. In Alfred Murck (ed.), *Mao's Golden Mangoes and the Cultural Revolution*. Zurich: Scheidegger and Spiess, pp. 46–62.

Li Haiwen 李海文. 2011. 工人阶级必须领导一切' 发表前后 [Before and after the Publication of The Working Class Must Lead in Everything]. 炎黄春秋 [China Through the Ages] 3: 32–38.

Li Peng. 1989. Speech of Li Peng. https://blog.boxun.com/hero/xsj14/, accessed January 16, 2020.

Li Xun 李逊. 2015. 革命造反年代:上海文革运动史稿 [The age of the revolutionary rebels: a history of the Shanghai Cultural Revolution movement]. Hong Kong: Oxford University Press.

Li Zhisui. 1994. *The Private Life of Chairman Mao*. London: Random House.

Liberation Daily. 1989a (June 9). 上海十万工纠队员出动拆除路障 [Shanghai's 100,000 worker patrols sent forth to remove road obstructions].

Liberation Daily. 1989b (June 3). "上海高校将按期考试" [Exams at Shanghai's colleges and universities are to be held as scheduled].

Liberation Daily. 1989c (June 9). "朱镕基市长向全市人民发表电视讲话" [Mayor Zhu Rongji delivers television speech to residents of Shanghai].

Liberation Daily. 1989d (June 7). "坚决维护法制和秩序" [Firmly upholding rule of law and order].

Liberation Daily. 1989e (June 6). 上海交通昨全面瘫痪 [Traffic in Shanghai completely paralyzed yesterday].

Liberation Daily. 1989f (June 6). 清除路障是当务之急 [The top priority is removing road blockers].

Liberation Daily. 1989g (June 7). 上海不能乱 我们怎么办 [Shanghai must not become anarchistic; what should we do?].

Liberation Daily. 1989h (June 10). 感谢你们为上海人民立了一大功 [Thank you for doing such a great thing for the people of Shanghai].

Liu Bing 刘冰. 2010. 风雨岁月: *1964-1976* 年的清华 [Stormy years: Tsinghua in 1964-76]. Beijing: Contemporary China Press.

MacFarquhar, Roderick, and Michael Schoenhals. 2006. *Mao's Last Revolution*. Cambridge, MA: Harvard University Press.

Murck, Alfreda (ed.). 2013. *Mao's Golden Mangoes and the Cultural Revolution*. Zurich: Scheidegger and Spiess.

Nathan, Andrew J., and Perry Link (eds.). 2001. *The Tiananmen Papers*. New York: Perseus.

Office of the Beijing Party Committee. 1989. 北京制止动乱平息反革命暴乱纪事 [1989 annals of Beijing's suppression of turmoil and quelling of counterrevolutionary rebellion]. Beijing: Beijing Daily Press.

Peking Review. 1968. Workers' Mao Tse-tung's thought propaganda teams in colleges and schools. *Peking Review* 11(43): 13–16.

People's Daily. 1989 (May 14). 李鹏与首钢工人座谈对话 [Li Peng's dialogue with the workers at Capital Steel].

Perry, Elizabeth J. 1993. *Shanghai on Strike: The Politics of Chinese Labor*. Stanford, CA: Stanford University Press.

Perry, Elizabeth J. 2006. *Patrolling the Revolution: Worker Militias, Citizenship and the Modern Chinese State*. Lanham, MD: Rowman and Littlefield.

Perry, Elizabeth J. 2012. *Anyuan: Mining China's Revolutionary Tradition*. Berkeley: University of California Press.

Perry, Elizabeth J., and Li Xun. 1993. *Proletarian Power: Shanghai in the Cultural Revolution*. Boulder, CO: Westview Press.

Shanghai Federation of Trade Unions (ed.) 1996. 上海工运志 [Gazetteer of the Shanghai labor movement].

Shanghai Party Committee Cultural Revolution Materials Small Group. 1992. 上海文化大革命史话 [History of the Cultural Revolution in Shanghai]. Shanghai: Shanghai Party Committee.

Sichuan Daily Editorial Department. 1989. 学潮动乱暴乱: 惊心动魄的71天 [The turmoil and disruption of the student movement: 71 harrowing days]. Chengdu: Sichuan People's Press.

Tang Shaojie 唐少杰. 2003. 一叶知秋: 清华大学 *1968* 年"百日大武斗 ["Hundred Days War" at Tsinghua University in 1968]. Hong Kong: Hong Kong Chinese University Press.

Tang Shaojie 唐少杰. 2004. 文化大革命'时期清华工宣队诸问题述评 [Discussion of several issues concerning the Tsinghua Workers' Propaganda Teams during the time of the Cultural Revolution]. 社会科学论坛 [Social Science Forum] 11: 80–88.

Tang Shaojie 唐少杰. 2015. 清华大学工宣队始末 [The Workers' Propaganda Teams at Tsinghua University from start to finish]. 炎黄春秋 [China Through the Ages] 2: 29–35.

Walder, Andrew G. 2012. *Fractured Rebellion: The Beijing Red Guard Movement*. Cambridge, MA: Harvard University Press.

Walder, Andrew G., and Xiaoxia Gong. 1993. Workers in the Tiananmen Protests: The politics of the Beijing Workers' Autonomous Federation. *Australian Journal of Chinese Affairs* 29: 1–29.

Wang Xiaoping. 2013. 1968: My Story of the Mango. In Alfred Murck (ed.), *Mao's Golden Mangoes and the Cultural Revolution*. Zurich: Scheidegger and Spiess, pp. 37-38.

Xiao Jianguo 肖建国. 1997. 我当了一回工宣队 [I joined a round of Workers' Propaganda Teams]. 作家 [Writer] 10: 60-62.

Yi Yuanqiu and Guofu Liu 易元秋刘国福 (eds.). 1994. 民兵纵横谈 [A comprehensive discussion of the militia]. Beijing: National Defense University Press.

Zhang Liang 张良. 2002. 中国"六四"真相 [The true face of China's "June Fourth"]. Hong Kong: Mingjing Press.

Zhang Wanshu 张万舒. 2009. 历史的大爆炸:"六四"事件全景实录 [History's great explosion: A complete account of the June Fourth Incident]. Hong Kong: Tiandi Books.

Zhang Yongkang 张永康. 1991. 中国工人阶级的地位和作用 [The status and function of China's working class]. Beijing: Chinese Communist Party School Press.

Zhu Zucheng 朱祖成. 2015. 工宣队在清华还干了什么 [What else did the Workers' Propaganda Teams at Tsinghua do]. 炎黄春秋 [China Through the Ages] 6: 94-95.

4

State-Mobilized Community Development

The Case of Rural Taiwan

Kristen E. Looney

4.1 INTRODUCTION

In 1950s Taiwan, the defeated Kuomintang regime (KMT or Chinese Nationalist Party) sought to regain control of mainland China by transforming the island into a model province that would legitimize its right to rule. Knowing that the Chinese Communist Party (CCP) had established its rural base in large part through redistributive land reform, the KMT carried out a comprehensive land reform program of its own, which led to the creation of a smallholder farm economy with extremely low levels of inequality. In addition, the Nationalists built up an extensive network of farmers' associations and implemented an agricultural policy that resulted in two decades of accelerated growth. According to former President Lee Teng-hui, agriculture played a textbook role in Taiwan's development, meeting the domestic demand for food, accounting for a significant share of exports, and providing capital and labor for industrialization (Lee, 1971). As one of the first countries in the post–World War II period to achieve industrialized nation status, Taiwan stands out as an exemplary case of successful development.

Taiwan's rapid transformation from a poor agricultural society into a wealthy industrialized nation has received much scholarly attention. Robert Wade's research, for example, reveals how the state in Taiwan, like Japan, was able to effectively "govern the market" and promote development through well-formulated institutions and industrial policy (Wade, 1990; on Japan, see Johnson, 1982). To explain the rural side of Taiwan's success, scholars have similarly emphasized the importance of institutions – the presence of a land tenure system dominated by owner-cultivators with secure private property rights, an effective rural extension system maintained by a technocratic bureaucracy and robust farmers' associations, and firm state control over

State-Mobilized Community Development: The Case of Rural Taiwan 87

rice production.[1] Not only in Taiwan but also in Japan and South Korea, this combination of institutions was powerful. It led to widely dispersed, long-term gains in agricultural production, enabled the back-and-forth transfer of resources between the industrial and agricultural sectors, and mitigated against rural policy decisions that were purely extractive (Franks, 1999). These convergences suggest a rural counterpart to the East Asian model of development that is grounded in a common set of institutions. However, in this chapter I depart from the existing literature to focus on the phenomenon of rural modernization campaigns as a distinctive, extra-institutional approach to development.

The case of Taiwan illustrates a broader regional pattern; by the late 1960s, the countryside was in a state of decline, having suffered from policies that privileged the industrial sector, and the KMT's solution was to launch a modernization campaign, mobilizing society to collectively tackle rural poverty and backwardness. Official policy documents describe the Community Development Campaign as a state-mobilized movement (SMM), which was initiated and executed by the state in partnership with society. It focused heavily on village improvement projects such as replacing thatched roofs with tiled roofs, installing flush toilets and water taps, paving village roads, and building community centers.

In this way, the Community Development Campaign clearly followed the logic of *infrastructural mobilization*, with the state harnessing the power of non-state collective actors to accomplish particular development goals. Taiwan's leaders believed that, compared to other drivers of development such as changing market conditions or more routine adjustments to rural policy, the campaign would deliver greater change to more places in a shorter period time. The campaign also exemplified *spoiler mobilization*, as it was intended to preemptively counter potential challenges to the regime by defusing social tensions and crowding out rural oppositional forces, namely local factions and communist sympathizers. The campaign's success can be attributed to the strength of the central government and the quality of societal participation, which provided critical checks on local officials who otherwise might have been tempted to ignore campaign directives or, conversely, carry them to extremes.

The analysis showcases the Taiwanese state as a proactive agent of social mobilization. Unlike some of the other cases in this volume, the state's role was direct and transparent, and the target of mobilization was a relatively cohesive social class – that is, all Taiwanese farmers – rather than disparate social elements. These features are consistent with mass campaigns traditionally carried out by communist, fascist, and populist authoritarian regimes. The KMT's Leninist organization and its own past experience with campaigns as an approach to state-building partially explain why it decided on such an

---

[1] See, for example, Ho (1978).

approach. Yet, the case is still somewhat puzzling because it occurred twenty years after the KMT had taken over Taiwan, at which point the regime had already transitioned into a post-revolutionary, more institutionalized mode of governance. Furthermore, the campaign is surprising in light of the developmental state literature, which portrays Taiwanese politics and policy in terms of technocratic rule, the suppression of social forces, and strategic state intervention in the market aimed at promoting certain industries. The implication of my analysis is that these modes of politics – bureaucratic and mobilizational – are distinct but not mutually exclusive.

The chapter is organized as follows. Section 4.2 elaborates the concept of rural modernization campaigns. Section 4.3 presents the main case of Taiwan. Section 4.4 addresses the use of campaigns throughout East Asia. Whereas most scholars dismiss the region's campaigns as illiberal and misguided deviations from a more successful, technocratic approach to development, I suggest that they had a major impact on the countryside, especially in terms of changing the village environment, and that variation in development outcomes may be explained by the interaction of bureaucratic and mobilizational politics. Looking at this dynamic, rather than bureaucratic or institutional factors alone, provides a more complete understanding of how rural development occurred.

4.2 RURAL MODERNIZATION CAMPAIGNS

State-mobilized movements (SMMs) rely on high levels of mobilization to achieve dramatic change. They may have broad or specific goals, but in general they are meant to be transformative policies and are often dressed up in revolutionary language. They employ mobilization – efforts to activate and involve a population in pursuit of certain goals – as the dominant mode of policy implementation. While the extent of popular or mass mobilization varies significantly based on campaign goals and targets, bureaucratic mobilization is a central feature of all campaigns.[2]

This type of politics has long captured the attention of scholars such as Robert Tucker (1961), who put forward the idea of movement regimes to describe communism in the Soviet Union, fascism in Europe, and nationalist revolutionary movements in Asia, Africa, and other parts of the postcolonial world. Mobilization is also a defining characteristic of totalitarian regimes. As

---

[2] My understanding of campaigns was developed with reference to the classic literature on Mao-era China. Gordon Bennett (1976, p. 18) defines a campaign as "a government sponsored effort to storm and eventually overwhelm strong but vulnerable barriers to the progress of socialism through intensive mass mobilization and active personal commitment." Similarly, Charles Cell (1977, p. 7) defines it as "an organized mobilization of collective action aimed at transforming thought patterns, class/power relationships and/or economic institutions and productivity." The definition of mobilization comes from J. P. Nettl (1967), as cited in Cell (1977), pp. 92–93, 104–105.

Juan Linz (1975, pp. 191–192) explains: "Citizen participation in and active mobilization for political and collective social tasks are encouraged, demanded, rewarded, and channeled through a single party and many monopolistic secondary groups. Passive obedience and apathy, retreat into the role of 'parochials' and 'subjects,' characteristic of many authoritarian regimes, are considered undesirable by the rulers." Though anathema to liberal democratic principles, mobilized participation is absolutely critical for understanding politics and policy implementation in much of the world.

Campaigns are more likely to occur when political leaders determine there is an urgent need for change, normally in response to a challenge or crisis, and when the change envisioned is considered so great that it cannot be accomplished through routine practices. In launching campaigns, the state draws on latent power resources, including traditions and cultures of mobilization rooted in the legacies of revolution, war, and militarism. Examining the historical origins of campaigns in China, scholars have noted the Soviet Union's influence and, more importantly, Mao's penchant for mass mobilization developed during the Jiangxi Soviet and Yan'an periods when the CCP had to rely on the peasantry for survival and guerrilla warfare. According to Tyrene White (2006, p. 2), campaigns were used under Mao as a means of advancing collectivist goals and "instilling a revolutionary ethic deep within society," and this heritage helps to explain the persistence of campaign politics in the reform era.

Through campaigns, the state can circumvent institutional constraints to change by reordering existing power structures or creating new ones. Depending on campaign objectives, these ad hoc structures may include traditional bureaucratic actors and extra-institutional actors, such as social activists, grassroots organizations, and interest or pressure groups. Campaigns thus resemble social movements and may, in fact, try to co-opt existing social movements. Campaigns also resemble informal institutions in the sense of being grounded in particular norms, traditions, and cultures rather than formal organizations and laws.

To be more specific, rural modernization campaigns are policies that aim to transform the countryside through the mobilization of bureaucratic and societal actors. This kind of campaign is not just a legitimation strategy designed to shore up support for the regime but also a development strategy that seeks to overcome resource barriers and institutional constraints to change. East Asian governments adopted this strategy in place of a routine legislative process because they viewed the rural situation with political urgency. Campaigns were considered a viable solution to the rural problem, capable of producing quick results and minimizing policy resistance from groups representing the urban-industrial sector or other actors inclined to support the status quo. Although rural modernization campaigns can have many different goals, the campaigns analyzed in this chapter were launched primarily to achieve breakthroughs in rural economic and infrastructure development. Specific goals included stimulating agricultural production, raising rural incomes, and improving access to quality roads, electricity, water, sanitation, and housing.

There are surely many reasons to question the state's role in these activities. Government officials may benefit politically from the creation of scientifically designed, beautifully manicured villages, which in reality amount to nothing more than vanity projects. Or worse, the state's reorganization of rural society into carefully planned villages may result in economic disaster, as was the case with Tanzania's Ujamaa village campaign of the 1970s.[3] To give another extreme example of failure, China's Great Leap Forward of the late 1950s resulted in tens of millions of famine deaths, not to mention a whole range of campaign excesses – production failures, political persecution, social alienation, and violence.

Yet, not all campaigns have turned out like the Great Leap Forward. Gordon Bennett (1976, p. 15) argues that, except for the Leap, Maoist economic campaigns spurred economic development by involving the population to overcome managerial and resource bottlenecks: "in balance, they contribute more to economic growth than they take away."[4] Indeed, popular mobilization may lead to a greater commitment of local resources, thus reducing the cost of central policy implementation. Mass involvement can also lead to more flexible adaptations of national policy and provide a check against overzealous local officials. Additionally, campaigns can be more effective than other policies at bringing social groups into contact with the state and inculcating a sense of political loyalty among the population.

Despite these benefits, infrastructural mobilization, which tends to have explicit and concrete targets, requires a lot of effort to sustain, and state control over society, or even over its own bureaucratic agents, is not guaranteed. Campaigns create a highly politicized environment, which can result in false compliance on the one hand and excessive compliance on the other – the erection of Potemkin villages to deceive inspecting officials, or an all-out effort to achieve results and exceed the central government's expectations through grandiose applications of the policy. It is therefore necessary to have oversight and feedback mechanisms to address these potential problems. So while campaigns represent an alternative, mobilizational approach to development, their success still depends on the strength of formal bureaucratic institutions.

4.3 THE CASE OF TAIWAN

Most accounts of rural Taiwan focus on how the KMT successfully developed agriculture after the war. For reasons related to the legacy of Japanese colonialism and the nature of US assistance, the regime was able to rehabilitate preexisting technologies and institutions rather than build them

---

[3] See Scott (1998), chapter 7. [4] See also Cell (1977), pp. 32–34, 153–154, 174–175.

from scratch, and it was careful to protect the interests of small farmers. Production was restored to prewar peak levels by 1951 and then entered a fifteen-year period of accelerated growth, averaging 4.6 percent annually (almost twice the global average). Between 1952 and 1967, staple crop production increased 82 percent, and livestock production increased 186 percent. Output of fruits and vegetables grew 476 percent and 107 percent, respectively, providing the basis for a large-scale food processing industry. Agricultural exports grew 128 percent and comprised the majority of total exports until 1966. Agriculture was also a key source of domestic capital formation until about 1970.[5]

Although farmers benefited from agriculture's strong performance, urban bias was nevertheless a fundamental characteristic of rural policy. To extract the surplus from producers, the government established monopoly control over the fertilizer and rice markets. Under the rice–fertilizer barter system (1948–1972), Taiwanese farmers were paid only 70 percent of world market prices for rice and were forced to pay about 40 percent more for fertilizer than Japanese, Dutch, American, or Indian farmers.[6] Such price distortions had a negative effect on farm incomes, which increased slightly after land reform and then remained constant until the barter system was phased out. In fact, virtually all gains in rural incomes during this period can be traced to the rise of off-farm employment opportunities (Stavis, 1974, pp. 11–14).

Besides unfavorable pricing policies, another problem facing rural households was the declining size of Taiwan's farms. Land reform had drastically reduced tenancy rates and created a more equal society, but it also resulted in very small landholdings, made even smaller by the postwar population boom. In 1952, the average farm size was 1.29 hectares (3.19 acres); by 1976, it was only 1.06 hectares (2.62 acres) (Hsiao, 1981, p. 61). Significantly, about 42 percent of farmers actually cultivated less than 0.5 hectares (1.24 acres), an amount too small to support a typical family.[7]

By the late 1960s, the relative decline of agriculture had become apparent. Due to fast-paced industrialization, agriculture's share of GDP, exports, and employment had all dropped significantly, and the rate of out-migration increased. The rural–urban income gap, which stood at 25 percent in 1953, had increased to 42 percent in 1968, meaning rural households earned that much less than urban households (Hsiao, 1981, p. 63). Moreover, despite the diversification of rural incomes, most households perceived that their overall welfare was slow to improve. In 1964, sociologist Martin M. C. Yang conducted a survey of rural living conditions, collecting data on nutrition, water, housing, clothing, transportation, communication, and health care for

---

[5] See Yager (1988), pp. 2–3, 51–52, 61–62, 254–255. On the structure of exports, see *Taiwan Statistical Data Book* (1982), p. 189.

[6] See Amsden (1985), p. 86; Francks (1999), p. 173.

[7] See Francks (1999), 29; Stavis (1974), 18.

a sample of 3,075 households. To assess the impact of land reform on different types of households, the survey targeted six groups: former tenants, tenants, original owner cultivators, hired farm laborers, former landlords, and non-farmers. With the exception of former tenants and non-farmers, the majority of households from all other groups reported no improvement or even a deterioration of living conditions since land reform. In addition, over 38 percent of former tenants reported no improvement in living conditions, a surprising finding given that they had the most to gain from land ownership (Yang, 1970).

These structural changes in the economy coincided with political liberalization measures intended to increase the number of Taiwanese serving in government. Since the early 1950s, regular elections had been held for leadership positions in local governments and the farmers' associations. In 1969, elections were expanded to include a small portion of seats in the parliament. As Thomas Gold (1986) explains, the "Taiwanization" of politics was a way to create buy-in from the local population and to fill vacancies created by the KMT's aging political elite. One consequence of this political opening at the top was the emergence of a small but vocal group of agricultural advocates. They altered public discourse about the countryside, from one focused on "agriculture" and "production" for the sake of "government revenue" to one more concerned with "farmers" and "welfare." The barter system in particular came under fire for depressing rural incomes, and passionate appeals were made to address rural poverty. Even those politicians without a background in agriculture were sensitive to these issues because of Taiwan's highly organized rural electorate (Hsiao, 1981; Liao et al., 1986).

The time was ripe for policy change. In 1972, the government adopted the Accelerated Rural Development Program (ARDP). It was a rather ordinary agricultural adjustment policy, calling for reduced taxes, increased spending, low-interest credit, better services, and scale agriculture. The government allocated a minimum of 2 billion yuan to the ARDP annually between 1973 and 1979. This was a small percentage of total government spending (1–3 percent, depending on the year) but marked an important break from the past.[8] Due to the elimination of the barter system and supplementary policy measures like subsidies and import restrictions, the rural–urban income gap was reduced, eventually falling below 30 percent in the early 1980s (Hsiao, 1981, p. 63; Liao et al., 1986, p. 36). By itself, however, the ARDP was regarded as an insufficient solution to the rural problem. To achieve more immediate and visible results, and to increase state control over the countryside, the government turned to mass mobilization.

---

[8] For details on the ARDP, see Yager (1988), pp. 95–98. Government spending figures come from *Statistical Yearbook of the Republic of China* (1982), p. 467; Joint Commission on Rural Reconstruction (1978), p. 33.

The Community Development Campaign cannot be understood without reference to past campaigns. In China, the Mass Education and Rural Reconstruction Movements of the 1920s and 1930s focused on improving rural conditions through the development of autonomous village organizations. Led by Y. C. James Yen, Liang Shuming, and other activist intellectuals, these movements sought to provide an alternative to communism. Yen later served as a commissioner for the Joint Commission on Rural Reconstruction (part of the US aid mission to the Republic of China) and moved to Taiwan, where his ideas about grassroots community-building influenced the top leadership.[9]

The New Life Movement was another campaign that took place in the 1930s and 1940s to counter the influence of communism. Some scholars view it as linked to global fascism, whereas others emphasize that it was closely intertwined with state-building and civilian relief during the war period. Importantly, because KMT leader Chiang Kai-shek and his son Chiang Ching-kuo personally led the campaign, it provides a window into how they thought about the countryside. The main objective was to create an orderly and civilized society by using ideological education to reform the most basic aspects of rural life: clothing, food, housing, and behavior. Although thousands of new life community organizations were established across the country, the campaign's momentum ultimately fizzled out because the communists proved more capable of providing people with real economic and security benefits.[10] Taiwan's countryside was similarly viewed as backward, but now the leadership understood that any campaign to reform it needed to deliver tangible change to be successful.

In 1955, the government launched the People's Livelihood Construction Campaign, which drew inspiration from KMT founder Sun Yat-sen's ideology. It stressed ensuring equal access to land resources, sustaining high levels of production, and satisfying villagers' basic needs (similar to the New Life Movement, these were defined as clothing, food, housing, transportation, education, and recreation). Taiwanese sources state that the campaign was intended to pick up where land reform had left off, and, given the timing, it is possible the campaign was launched in response to China's collectivization drive.

Even though Taiwanese farmers maintained control over their own land and production practices, laws on compulsory labor were invoked to push forward village improvement projects. An earlier law requiring men ages eighteen to fifty to take part in roadbuilding, irrigation, production, and defense work was revised to incorporate more projects related to village infrastructure. Campaign coordination committees were formed to bring together leaders

---

[9] For recent work on these campaigns, see Merkel-Hess (2016).
[10] On the New Life Movement's fascist qualities, see Dirlik (1975). For the state-building perspective, see Ferlanti (2010).

from government, schools, the police, and the farmers' associations. In addition, the government initiated a formal competition among local jurisdictions to mobilize labor and other resources. The campaign, which lasted for ten years, affected less than 10 percent of all villages (there were 515 experimental sites in total), but its impact was nonetheless significant. Hundreds of miles of roads, irrigation canals, and drainage pipes were added to existing infrastructure. Other improvements included the installation or construction of embankments, water towers, pumps, bridges, rice drying areas, toilets, bathhouses, animal pens, compost sheds, streetlights, televisions, radios, childcare centers, community centers, and gardens.[11]

The success of local experiments, combined with international development trends, eventually paved the way for a more comprehensive campaign. In the 1960s, when the United Nations was supporting community development programs worldwide, UN consultant Chang Hung-chun introduced the concept to Taiwan. It quickly gained currency among officials who were eager to raise their government's status internationally. This became even more pressing after Taiwan lost its UN seat to China in 1971. Earlier experiments were scaled up and repackaged as community development in a series of national policy documents that served as the foundation for the Community Development Campaign: the People's Livelihood Social Policy (1965), the Community Development Eight-Year-Plan (1969), and the Community Development Ten-Year-Plan (1972).[12] The Chinese names of these policies are listed in Table 4.1. Taiwan likely also took notice of Japan's New Life Campaign (which incidentally took its name from Chiang Kai-shek's earlier campaign) and South Korea's New Village Movement, modeling certain aspects of its approach after those countries, such as the intensive training of village activists in order to change rural culture.[13]

Compared to Korea, Taiwan's bureaucracy was more inclined to support rural development, and groups representing urban-industrial interests were not as strong politically. This difference had to do with historically close ties between agriculture and industry and the fact that many local officials had started their careers by working for the farmers' associations. The bigger barrier to change, from the perspective of the leadership, was rural culture itself. They believed that land reform had created a society that was simultaneously more egalitarian and more individualistic. Furthermore, if rural backwardness stemmed from a lack

---

[11] For a detailed account of the campaign, see Central Committee of the Kuomintang (1961); Lee (1965). For English, see Joint Commission on Rural Reconstruction (1960).
[12] On the evolution of community development policies and UN involvement, see Tan (1969); Hung (1978).
[13] On Japan, see Garon (1997), pp. 162–172. For a Taiwanese take on the Korean case, see Lee (1979).

TABLE 4.1 *Community development policies in Taiwan, 1955–1981*[1]

Campaigns and Supporting Policies	Chinese Name	Years
People's Livelihood Construction Campaign	基層民生建設運動	1955–1965
Compulsory Labor	國民義務勞動	1947
Community Development Campaign	社區發展運動	1965–1981
People's Livelihood Social Policy	民生主義現階段社會政策	1965
Community Development Eight-Year-Plan	社區發展八年計畫	1969
Community Development Ten-Year-Plan	社區發展十年計畫	1972

[1] The Ten-Year-Plan, which was supposed to conclude in 1978, was extended through the year 1981. Single years indicate the first year that a policy became effective.

of community spirit, then a campaign would be more effective than a normal piece of legislation (like the ARDP) at delivering spiritual or moral change. Mass mobilization would not only advance the material well-being of the village but would foster a public ethos as well.

Taking this historical context into account, it is clear that the KMT's favorable view of campaigns was driven by competition with the Chinese communists and attendant political insecurity. Chiang Kai-shek had been fearful of an underground communist movement since arriving in Taiwan and viewed the countryside through the lens of his failed policies on the mainland. As virtually any rural policy document from this period shows, the regime was fixated on the question of how it had lost the Chinese peasantry.

In Taiwan, the KMT was given a second chance. It successfully executed land reform and penetrated the farmers' associations, recruiting the majority of association leaders to join the party. Yet, it was never fully confident it could hold on to its rural base. By the late 1960s, farmers had become a powerful interest group. There were no significant protests against the state or direct challenges to Chiang's authority, but reports of rural decline and popular discontent deeply concerned him. Having experienced some success with infrastructural mobilization in the past, there was strong reason to believe that this approach could deliver greater change to the countryside than market forces alone could produce. The campaign also promised to change rural culture and reassert state control over the countryside at a time when elections were expanding. Local factions, whose ties to society ran deeper than any allegiances to the party, had always tried to use elections to gain power. And it was an important moment for Chiang Ching-kuo, who wanted to create a popular base of support as he prepared to take over from his father.[14]

Regarding the KMT's political development, Bruce Dickson (1993) has noted that the regime was in fact more Leninist in Taiwan than it had been on the mainland, reorganizing itself in the early 1950s based on the communists' example of elevating the party above the state and the military. Julia Strauss (2017) has similarly observed that the KMT and the CCP both deployed campaigns as a mode of state-building and policy implementation, as evidenced by broad similarities in their land reform programs. My research further demonstrates that the KMT's use of mobilization persisted as the regime matured. This finding is consistent with Kenneth Jowitt's (1975) analysis of Leninist regimes in Europe, where – even with greater, more systematic social inclusion in political decision-making – mobilization continued to serve the purpose of expanding state control over society and addressing political challenges. The case of Taiwan shows how an increasingly technocratic and inclusive regime relied not only on bureaucratic and representative institutions but also on mass mobilization to achieve its goals.

In short, campaigns were seen as a means of development and legitimation. They could overcome barriers to change, accomplish concrete tasks, and engender loyalty among the population. The framework of community development in particular was also a way of signaling certain messages about the regime to international actors – that it was progressive and open compared to China, and that it cared about helping those left behind by industrialization. As one might expect, scholars critical of the campaign lament the state's heavy involvement as running counter to international norms concerning community development.[15] However, viewed as an SMM rather than in terms of the ideals of community development per se, it was actually very successful.

The Community Development Campaign succeeded at producing policy compliance and positive outcomes because its overarching goal was rural development, rather than extraction, and because of the political-institutional context in which it was implemented. Taiwan's centralized political system and technocratic leadership facilitated bureaucratic monitoring, and, although the farmers' associations were just one of several groups responsible for campaign implementation, their strong presence in the villages prior to the campaign helped to normalize participation in the policy process.

In terms of goals, the Community Development Eight-Year-Plan (1969–1976) described the policy as a "social movement" aimed at "eliminating dirt, disorder, and poverty, increasing production and welfare, and promoting a new morality." Accordingly, in this document and the revised

---

[14] On the government's concern about rural discontent and factions, see Francks (1999), pp. 193–194, 220. For more on factions and elections, see Bosco (1992). The point about Chiang Ching-kuo's rural populism comes from Moore (1988), pp. 139–141.
[15] For a negative assessment, see Hsueh (1987).

Ten-Year-Plan (1969–1978), specific projects were divided into three categories: basic infrastructure; production and social welfare; and spiritual and moral construction. This last category called for community organizations and activities that would promote healthy living and a collective consciousness – for example, the formation of Boy Scout troops and Chinese musical orchestras. "Life basics" courses on civilized behavior – standing in line, wearing clean clothes, eating at a table, etc. – were also commonly conducted during the campaign.[16] By most accounts, these projects were less successful than those focused on infrastructure and production, but the emotional appeal of making the community better was still a powerful call to action.

The elimination of taxes and disbursement of grants further bolstered popular enthusiasm for the campaign, though it was not without costs. Initially, the government allocated 250,000 yuan to each community. This money covered roughly half of the cost of community development, and residents were expected to provide matching funds to make up the difference. The poorest households had to borrow money or donate more of their labor to meet this requirement. To reduce their burden, the government later revised the policy so that it would contribute a greater percentage of funds for every site (about 52 percent of the cost), with even higher levels of support for poverty areas (about 84 percent). The Ten-Year-Plan also stated that poorer villages should be developed first, so that local governments would not be tempted to channel funds to the easiest cases, i.e. those villages near the township with a better baseline of development.[17]

To facilitate local compliance, campaign coordination committees were formed at the provincial, county, and township levels. These were comprised of leading officials from nearly every institution, including the military and the police. The committees were charged with developing plans, disbursing funds, and overseeing implementation. During the planning stage, village assemblies were held to solicit ideas from residents. Villages were legally defined as an extension of the township government and considered to be separate from communities, which were conceptualized as autonomous, service-oriented units. But in practice, the functions of these units overlapped.

The creation of communities gave rise to two changes in the local leadership structure. First, some villages were amalgamated so that each community was roughly the same size, about 350 households. When mergers occurred – the Eight-Year-Plan organized all of Taiwan's 6,215 villages into 4,893 communities – leaders from different villages had to negotiate the location of community projects, a contentious process that was subject to the influence of

---

[16] For a thorough elaboration of government policy, see Republic of China Community Development Research and Training Center (1972); Tan (1972); Wu (1986). For English, see Taiwan Provincial Government (1970).
[17] In 1972, government support amounted to 330,000 yuan for regular sites and 530,000 yuan for poverty sites; see Hung (1978), pp. 106–108.

local factions. In these cases, the coordination committee was expected to play the role of mediator. Second, a younger generation of activists gained power through the establishment of community development councils. These were elected bodies of roughly ten people representing a mix of traditional and new elites. The empowerment of individuals in their twenties, thirties, and forties, who otherwise might consider leaving the countryside, added to the campaign's momentum.

The community development councils operated at the village (or community) level. They were responsible for mobilizing residents and managing the day-to-day activities of the campaign. They were also in charge of community center operations and infrastructure maintenance. The village "small agricultural unit" leader (the lowest branch of the farmers' association) usually held a spot on the council and took the lead on production-related projects. The township coordination committee frequently dispatched officials to consult with council members and check on the campaign's progress. In addition, the provincial government arranged for outside inspection teams to evaluate and rank local governments based on the quality of the communities in their jurisdiction. Places that performed better were rewarded with media attention, medals, and other benefits. Taiwan's small size and centralized political system contributed to policy coherence among different levels of government.

In conjunction with education and training, as well as fiscal and administrative regulations, all of these mechanisms – the campaign coordination committees, community development councils, and competitive evaluations – were used to exert central control over local authorities and increase compliance. Stated differently, these policy tools effectively brought local actors into an implementing coalition with the central government.

On the issues of rural participation and accountability to village residents, scholarly assessments are mixed. Several ethnographic case studies assert that the community development councils were weak. They point out that projects were mostly passed down from the township and that the campaign relied on compulsory labor.[18] Still other studies reach the opposite conclusion, showing that the councils crafted and adjusted development plans based on local needs and feedback and that people were eager to contribute to projects that directly benefited the village (this was not necessarily true of other compulsory labor projects).[19] This discrepancy in the literature likely stems from real variation in local campaign experiences.

Nevertheless, there are good reasons to believe that, on the whole, the campaign was implemented in a relatively flexible and participatory manner. First, the example of the farmers' associations demonstrates that villagers regularly voted in elections and treated them seriously.[20] Council elections

---

[18] See, for example, Chuang (1972); Chen (1973); Hsueh (1987). [19] See Huang (1978); (1979).
[20] Elections for farmers' association leaders began in the mid-1950s. On the competitiveness of elections, see Bosco (1992).

were probably treated the same way, especially given the influx of new resources tied to community development. There was an expectation that council members would advocate for villagers to higher levels of the state, which was reinforced by villagers' own ability to communicate their preferences to the farmers' associations or outside inspection teams.

Second, despite government claims to the contrary, the countryside already had a rich associational life. Besides the farmers' associations, there were irrigation associations, credit cooperatives, labor exchange groups, temple associations, and a myriad of groups organized around lineage, neighborhood, gender, age, and profession.[21] These organizations surely had their own views on how to improve the community and wanted to see those reflected in the campaign. So even if the community development councils were weak, there were other groups that sought out partnerships with the government and offered their contacts and resources in exchange for influence.

Third, Taiwanese sources are filled with references to Western examples of community development and translations of phrases that evoke democratic norms of participation: civic organization, community action, inclusion of the poor in decision-making, sense of belonging, and felt needs, to name just a few.[22] Since the intended audience of these materials was local officials and campaign activists, it seems the regime's embrace of these norms was not just about international posturing. It reflected a real commitment to grassroots engagement.

With regard to outcomes, the campaign had a moderate effect on the agricultural economy. While, on the one hand, production-related infrastructure was successfully upgraded and expanded, on the other hand, efforts to develop new rural sidelines and scale up production fell flat. In fact, between 1960 and 1990, the number of households with farms smaller than 1 hectare (2.47 acres) increased from about 67 to 75 percent, and the number of farms larger than 3 hectares (7.41 acres) decreased from 3.3 to 2.5 percent (Huang, 1993, pp. 50, 60). The difficulty of scaling up agriculture in Taiwan, like the rest of East Asia, was not only a product of land reform but also the farmers' associations, which protected and entrenched the position of small farmers in Taiwanese society.[23]

The Community Development Campaign's greatest impact was to change the village environment. It led to dramatic improvements in public infrastructure, sanitation, and housing. Most if not all of Taiwan's villages were affected, and the sheer scope of the campaign in terms of the number of projects implemented was impressive (see Table 4.2). Official statistics also reveal an unevenness to project implementation, meaning that different communities experienced

---

[21] See Yang (1970).   [22] See, for example, Hsiung (1973); Wang (1974).
[23] Taiwan's Second Stage Land Reform of 1980 tried to resolve this problem but was only moderately successful. For a discussion of this policy and comparison among East Asian countries, see Bramall (2004).

TABLE 4.2 *Results of the Community Development Campaign in Taiwan, 1969–1981*

Total number of communities	**4,025**
Total number of community residents	7,328,074 (about 1.3 million households)
Total cost of community development	6,082,449,911 yuan
Government expenditures	3,687,463,819 yuan (about 61%)
Community expenditures	2,394,986,092 yuan (about 39%)
Basic Infrastructure Projects	
1. Water towers	9,274
2. Toilets	172,307
3. Showers	37,107
4. Drainage pipes	10,395,456 meters
5. Pathways	21,055,140 square meters
6. Parks	1,520
7. Playgrounds	913
8. Athletic fields	1,016
9. Activities centers	3,531
10. Home sanitation improvement	335,307 households
11. Township roads	71,023 kilometers
12. Village roads	57,132 kilometers
Production and social welfare projects	
1. Rice drying areas	2,101,259 square meters
2. Animal pens	55,831
3. Compost sheds	39,478
4. Technology training classes	3,898
5. Farm improvement stations	1,577
6. Childcare centers	1,725
7. Agricultural cooperatives	122
8. Home renovation for the poor	20,262 households
9. Home construction for the poor	25,481 households
10. Employment assistance	33,405 people
11. Community production funds	1,063
12. Cooperative farms	49
Spiritual and moral construction projects	
1. "Life basics" courses	12,706
2. Cultural and athletic activities	20,383

(continued)

TABLE 4.2 (*continued*)

Total number of communities	4,025
3. Recognizing good people/deeds	4,343
4. Elderly associations	1,909
5. Boy Scout troops	389
6. Classes for mothers	2,945
7. Sports tournaments	494

Source: Taiwan Provincial Government Social Affairs Department, cited in Liu (1991), pp. 69–72.

different kinds of change. Apart from variation in resources, which certainly existed across communities, another explanation for this unevenness is that the campaign did not impose a one-size-fits-all vision of modernity on the countryside. Villagers had some degree of choice over which projects to implement, and there were fewer negative outcomes as a result. For instance, older homes were preserved and renovated instead of torn down and rebuilt, so there was very little displacement, and the government, rather than villagers, shouldered the majority of campaign expenses.

To summarize, the use of infrastructural mobilization to spur development stands out as quite different from the conventional wisdom. The developmental state model is correct in its portrayal of Taiwan's institutions, but it does not fully account for what happened in the countryside. The state did not "pick winners" and let the market do the rest. Instead, it launched a modernization campaign to speed up the pace of rural transformation, a decision that had more in common with Maoism or Leninism than Japanese industrial policy. At the same time, this portrait of the campaign as a top-down policy with genuine societal participation distinguishes the Taiwanese case from a purely Leninist system. Similar to other SMMs, the boundaries between state and society were fuzzy and permeable, conforming neither to the image of a traditional mass campaign nor to that of a standard social movement.

The Community Development Campaign succeeded at improving rural conditions because it occurred in a particular context that prevented the campaign from working against farmers' interests. It was meticulously planned and implemented by a technocratic bureaucracy operating in a highly centralized political system. Frequent inspections and crosscutting coordination agencies stopped government support from being diverted to other purposes. Taiwan's strong rural organizations also provided a critical check against campaign excesses. The community development councils and farmers' associations, with their extensive organizational reach and politically influential leadership, were crucial for shaping local plans and generating mass participation. Without them, the use of compulsory labor alone would have likely failed to sustain the campaign. It was these various checks on local governments from above and below which contributed to campaign success.

As for how the campaign ended, it seems that, after the more concrete infrastructure-related goals were achieved, it began to lose momentum and eventually petered out. By the late 1970s, the state had retreated from playing an activist role in community affairs, and rural policy had returned to normal. The agricultural bureaucracy resumed its regular work, as did leaders of other departments and institutions who had been mobilized during the campaign. Although the state intended for the community development councils to exist indefinitely, its withdrawal had the effect of demobilizing them. These organizations, while comprised of non-state collective actors, had been created and managed by the state. Their mission was to promote development, not to advance a broader political agenda, and they rarely if ever acted independently. Taiwan had a strong state, and the leadership knew that, as long as rural conditions were improving, there was little chance the councils or any other organizations would present a challenge. The campaign had served the purpose of stabilizing the countryside, and once Chiang Ching-kuo had consolidated power, the state's strategy shifted from mobilization to less interventionist policy measures, namely supporting farmers through protective tariffs and subsidies.

Following Taiwan's transition to democracy in the 1980s and 1990s, President Lee Teng-hui resurrected the idea of community development. The new program was different from the old in that it targeted urban areas and did not take the form of a campaign. Still, one point of continuity was that the state supported the creation of community development associations as an alternative to what Lee saw as an overly bureaucratic approach to neighborhood governance. State-sponsored activism, or what Benjamin Read has called administrative grassroots engagement, in which the state creates, sponsors, and manages organizations at the most local level, thus continued under democracy and represents a long-standing feature of governance in Taiwan (Read, 2012).

4.4 THE BROADER EAST ASIAN REGION

Situating Taiwan's rural policies within a broader regional context reveals that they are part of a long tradition of rural modernization campaigns dating back to Meiji-era Japan. There are in fact several examples of such campaigns in Japan, beginning with the Local Improvement Movement at the turn of the twentieth century, continuing with the Rural Revitalization Campaign in the wake of the Great Depression, and then resuming after World War II with the New Village and New Life Campaigns. At each of these moments, the government's response to rural decline and unrest was to mobilize the bureaucracy and rural society for collective village improvement.[24] The Rural Revitalization Campaign (1932–1941) was the largest in scope and was intended to co-opt two streams of social protest – a tenant union movement that erupted in the 1920s and an agrarianist movement, which produced a generation of rural spokespersons who successfully lobbied the government for relief after the Great Depression devastated Japan's silk and rice markets, the mainstays of the rural economy. According to Kerry Smith (2001), the campaign led to the successful upgrading of infrastructure in 80 percent of Japan's villages and brought disaffected groups into closer alignment with the state.[25]

In South Korea, Park Chung-hee decided to adopt protective policies for agriculture after being seriously challenged in the 1967 and 1971 presidential elections by opposition candidates who successfully used the issue of low rice prices to capture much of the rural vote. The New Village Movement (1970–1979), also known as the New Community Movement or Saemaul Undong, attempted to raise farm output and income levels in at least two ways. First, the state orchestrated a green revolution by distributing a high-yield variety of rice called Tong'il (unification). Rice procurement prices were also adjusted such that rural incomes actually surpassed urban incomes in 1974. However, by the late 1970s the government could no longer afford its price support policy, and Tong'il production was abandoned after several failed harvests.[26] Second, the state promoted the development of rural industry as an avenue for off-farm employment, but this effort, known as Factory Saemaul, failed to curb a rural exodus to the cities. Between 1970 and 1990, more than half of the rural population (7.7 million out of 14.4 million people) migrated to urban areas.[27]

Neither Tong'il nor Factory Saemaul was very successful, but, in the area of rural infrastructure, the campaign produced enormous changes. Villagers were mobilized for the construction of roads, bridges, irrigation channels, sewage systems, warehouses, and community centers. Village homes were renovated with the installation of water taps, electricity, telephones, and blue tiled roofs. Whereas some observers lamented these changes as damaging to traditional aesthetic values, for many people the new roofs became a welcome symbol of modernity, since the old thatched roofs made of rice straw had to be replaced every year.[28] And among the Korean public today, the campaign is remembered

---

[24] Sheldon Garon describes these movements as "moral suasion campaigns," which were used by the Japanese state as a tool for "social management" in both the pre- and postwar periods; see Garon (1997).
[25] See also Waswo (1988).
[26] For Korean government data on incomes in the 1970s, see National Council of Saemaul Undong (1999), 50. On Korea's green revolution, see Burmeister (1988).
[27] With migration data being spotty and inconsistent, the decline of the rural population is being used as a proxy measure; see Park (1998), p. 212.
[28] For a critical view, see Steinberg (1982), pp. 17–18.

as a kind of golden age. In 2008, to mark the sixtieth anniversary of the Republic of Korea, *The Chosun Ilbo* published the results of a Korean Gallup poll about the country's most important achievements. The New Village Movement topped the list for over 40 percent of respondents, receiving more votes than any other event.[29]

Similar to Taiwan, Korean officials operated within a highly centralized system. Frequent inspections and mass supervision, facilitated by public radio announcements about villages that would be receiving funding, worked to ensure that government assistance was not diverted. Rural participation in the policy process was not the norm, but significantly, most campaign decisions were made at the village level with clear input from village activists. By organizing local "Saemaul councils," focusing on village improvement projects, and supporting a large number of villages (not just a few models), the government succeeded at generating widespread approval for the campaign and for Park.

Finally, the case of China suggests that rural modernization campaigns continue to be an important tool of the state in East Asia, although they do not always (or even usually) result in positive outcomes. In 2005, following a period of escalating rural protest, the Hu Jintao government adopted a comprehensive rural modernization program called Building a New Socialist Countryside. It aimed to reduce the rural–urban income gap, stimulate agricultural production, and improve rural public goods provision. The central government never called the New Socialist Countryside a campaign because of the Maoist connotations of that term, but many officials nonetheless understood and implemented it as a campaign. Local plans were drawn up that emphasized speed and hard targets, and policy coordination committees were formed to realign the interests of various departments. Cadre work teams were sent down to the villages, where they recruited activists and, in some cases, organized residents for collective action. Images of model villages and propaganda slogans about a better life appeared in newspapers, on billboards, and along the sides of buildings and fences. Even the phrase "building a new socialist countryside" originated in the 1950s when Maoism as a development ideology was at its peak.

Although China's shift away from urban bias was successful in some ways, it was also extremely problematic. Early in the Hu administration, a consensus was reached that rural society was in crisis and something needed to be done. Yet, there was much disagreement about the ultimate purpose of the policy.

---

[29] The top ten achievements were 1) the New Village Movement 2) the Olympics 3) the five-year economic plans, especially the 1970s heavy and chemical industrialization drive 4) completion of the Seoul–Pusan highway 5) the World Cup 6) the Gwangju prodemocracy movement 7) development of the semiconductor industry 8) per capita gross income surpassing US$20,000 9) the South–North (inter-Korean) summits 10) the 1987 democracy movement; see Hong (2008). The New Village Movement was also ranked first in a survey conducted ten years earlier for the fiftieth anniversary; see National Council of Saemaul Undong (1999), p. 50.

Was it to speed up the process of urbanization, to stimulate domestic consumption, or to promote rural development as an end in itself? This debate had the effect of expanding local discretion over the campaign, and it went unresolved until the leadership transition from Hu Jintao to Xi Jinping, whose policies represented a clear victory for those advocating urbanization.

This level of discretionary local authority over how and what to implement did not exist in Taiwan and Korea. In those cases, the center achieved controlled decentralization. There were strong checks on local officials from above, combined with some checks from below, due to the mobilization of rural organizations and village activists. In contrast, China's Building a New Socialist Countryside is better described as co-opted decentralization, with weak checks on local officials from above and virtually no checks from below. In many places, local officials blocked central efforts to promote balanced rural development by prioritizing only those goals that benefited the urban-industrial sector, such as housing and land consolidation. In addition, the fact that rural citizens were, for the most part, left out of the policy process made the aggressive pursuit of those goals that much easier. The result was a continuation of rural resource extraction. In the name of village modernization, millions of people were moved into apartments, and their former housing plots were sold off for urban-industrial development (Looney, 2015).

This overview of the region, though certainly incomplete, is suggestive of the larger argument I am making that bureaucratic and mobilizational politics were simultaneously used to achieve development and address rural unrest. On a basic level, it highlights the centrality of campaigns in an unexpected context – countries that are not in a state of perpetual revolution and, to the contrary, are known for their more technical, bureaucratic approach to policymaking. It also provides preliminary support for the contention that campaigns can have a positive or negative effect on development, depending on institutional context and especially on whether they are carried out in partnership with rural citizens.

REFERENCES

Amsden, Alice. 1985. The state and Taiwan's economic development. In Peter B. Evans, Dietrich Rueschemeyer, and Theda Skocpol (eds.), *Bringing the State Back In*. New York: Cambridge University Press, pp. 78–106.

Bennett, Gordon A. 1976. *Yundong: Mass Campaigns in Chinese Communist Leadership*. Berkeley: University of California, Berkeley, Center for Chinese Studies.

Bosco, Joseph. 1992. Taiwan factions: Guanxi, patronage, and the state in local politics. *Ethnology* 31(2): 157–183.

Bramall, Chris. 2004. Chinese land reform in long-run perspective and in the wider East Asian context. *Journal of Agrarian Change* 4(1–2): 107–141.

Burmeister, Larry L. 1988. *Research, Realpolitik, and Development in Korea: The State and the Green Revolution*. Boulder, CO: Westview Press.

Cell, Charles P. 1977. *Revolution at Work: Mobilization Campaigns in China*. New York: Academic Press.

Central Committee of the Kuomintang. 1961. *Jiceng minsheng jianshe shiyan yundong zhuanji (zai ban)* [The People's Livelihood Construction Experimental Campaign (2nd edition)]. Taipei, Taiwan: Central Committee of the Kuomintang, Fifth Division.

Chen Wen-huang (Chen Wenhuang). 1973. Taiwan sheng zhengfu tuixing shequ fazhan gongzuo zhi jiantao yanjiu [Assessment of the Taiwan Provincial Government's implementation of community development work]. M.A. Thesis, National Chengchi University.

Chuang Chao-ming (Zhuang Zhaoming). 1972. Yilan xian shequ fazhan zhi yanjiu [Research on community development in Yilan County]. M.A. Thesis, National Chengchi University.

Dickson, Bruce J. 1993. The lessons of defeat: The reorganization of the Kuomintang on Taiwan, 1950–52. *The China Quarterly* 133: 56–84.

Dirlik, Arif. 1975. The ideological foundations of the New Life Movement: A study in counterrevolution. *The Journal of Asian Studies* 34(4): 945–980.

Ferlanti, Federica. 2010. The New Life Movement in Jiangxi Province, 1934–1938. *Modern Asian Studies* 44(5): 961–1000.

Francks, Penelope (with Johanna Boestel and Choo Hyop Kim). 1999. *Agriculture and Economic Development in East Asia: From Growth to Protectionism in Japan, Korea, and Taiwan*. New York: Routledge.

Garon, Sheldon. *Molding Japanese Minds: The State in Everyday Life*. Princeton, NJ: Princeton University Press.

Gold, Thomas B. 1986. *State and Society in the Taiwan Miracle*. Armonk, NY: M. E. Sharpe.

Ho, Samuel P. S. 1978. *Economic Development of Taiwan, 1860–1970*. New Haven, CT: Yale University Press.

Hong Young-lim. 2008 (March 5). Saemaul Undong, 1988 Olympics, Five-Year Economic Development Plans top the list: The people's greatest achievements. *Chosun Daily*.

Hsiao, Michael Hsin-huang. 1981. *Government Agricultural Strategies in Taiwan and South Korea: A Macrosociological Assessment*. Taipei, Taiwan: Institute of Ethnology, Academia Sinica.

Hsiung Li-sheng (Xiong Lisheng). 1973. *Shequ fazhan yu minzhong canyu* [Community development and public participation]. Taipei, Taiwan: Republic of China Community Development Research and Training Center.

Hsueh, Wen-liang (Xue Wenliang). 1987. *Wo guo shequ fazhan de lilun yu shiji* [The Theory and Practice of Community Development in Taiwan]. Taipei, Taiwan: Xiaoyuan chubanshe [Hsiao Yuan Publication Company].

Huang, Sophia Wu. 1993. Structural Change in Taiwan's Agricultural Economy. *Economic Development and Cultural Change* 42(1): 43–65.

Huang Ta-chou (Huang Dazhou). 1978. *Lun shequ fazhan he xiangcun jiceng jianshe* [On community development and grassroots rural construction]. Taipei, Taiwan: Ministry of Education, Department of Social Education.

Huang Ta-chou (Huang Dazhou). 1979. *Xiangcun jianshe wenji* [Rural construction anthology]. Taipei, Taiwan: Huanqiu shushe [Global Books].

Hung Yu-kun (Hong Yukun). 1978. *Guofu difang zizhi tizhi yu Taiwan shequ fazhan zhi yanjiu* [Research on Sun Yat-sen's local self-governance system and taiwanese community development]. Taipei, Taiwan: Zhongyang wenwu gongyingshe [Central Supply Agency of Cultural Relics].

Johnson, Chalmers. 1982. *MITI and the Japanese Miracle: The Growth of Industrial Policy, 1925–1975*. Stanford, CA: Stanford University Press.

Joint Commission on Rural Reconstruction. 1960. *Intensive Village Improvement in Taiwan*. Taipei, Taiwan: Joint Commission on Rural Reconstruction.

Joint Commission on Rural Reconstruction. 1978. *Nongfuhui sanshi nian jishi: Zhongguo nongcun fuxing lianhe weiyuanhui chengli sanshi zhou nian jinian tekan* [JCRR and agricultural development in Taiwan, 1948–1978: A thirtieth anniversary publication of the Joint Commission on Rural Reconstruction]. Taipei, Taiwan: Joint Commission on Rural Reconstruction.

Jowitt, Kenneth. 1975. Inclusion and Mobilization in European Leninist Regime. *World Politics* 28(1): 69–96.

Lee Chung-yan (Li Zhongyuan). 1979. Hanguo de Saemaul Undong xin shequ yundong [The Saemaul New Community Movement in Korea]. *Shequ fazhan jikan* [Community Development Journal] 6: 107–112.

Lee Shou-lian (Li Shoulian). 1965. *Jiceng minsheng jianshe zai Taiwan* [People's livelihood construction in Taiwan]. Taipei, Taiwan: Provincial People's Livelihood Construction Steering Committee.

Lee, Teng-hui. 1971. *Intersectoral Capital Flows in the Economic Development of Taiwan, 1895–1960*. Ithaca, NY: Cornell University Press.

Liao, Cheng-hung, Chun-chieh Huang, and Michael Hsin-huang Hsiao. 1986. *Guangfuhou Taiwan nongye zhengce de yanbian: lishi yu shehui de fenxi* [The development of agricultural policies in postwar Taiwan: Historical and sociological perspectives]. Taipei, Taiwan: Institute of Ethnology, Academia Sinica.

Linz, Juan J. 1975. Totalitarian and Authoritarian Regimes. In Fred I. Greenstein and Nelson W. Polsby (eds.), *Handbook of Political Science, Vol. 3. Macropolitical Theory*. Reading, MA: Addison-Wesley, pp. 175–411.

Liu Jui-chung (Liu Ruizhong). 1991. *Sanminzhuyi shehui jianshe de linian yu shijian: Taiwan diqu shequ fazhan zhi yanjiu* [Theory and practice of building a society based on the three principles of the people: Research on community development in the Taiwan Region]. Taipei, Taiwan: Zhengzhong shuju [Cheng Chung Book Company].

Looney, Kristen E. 2015. China's campaign to build a new socialist countryside: Village modernization, peasant councils, and the Ganzhou model of rural development. *The China Quarterly* 224: 909–932.

Merkel-Hess, Kate. 2016. *The Rural Modern: Reconstructing the Self and State in Republican China*. Chicago, IL: The University of Chicago Press.

Moore, Mick. 1988. Economic growth and the rise of civil society: Agriculture in Taiwan and South Korea. In Gordon White (eds.), *Developmental States in East Asia*. New York: Saint Martin's Press, pp. 113–152.

National Council of Saemaul Undong. 1999. *Saemaul Undong in Korea*. Seoul: The National Council of Saemaul Undong Movement in Korea.

Park, Jin-hwan. 1998. *The Saemaul Movement: Korea's Approach to Rural Modernization in the 1970s*. Seoul: Korea Rural Economic Institute.

Read, Benjamin L. 2012. *Roots of the State: Neighborhood Organization and Social Networks in Beijing and Taipei*. Stanford, CA: Stanford University Press.

Republic of China Community Development Research and Training Center. 1972. *Zhonghua minguo shequ fazhan gongzuo yantao hui zong baogao*. [Republic of China Community Development Work Conference general report]. Taipei, Taiwan: Republic of China Community Development Research and Training Center.

Scott, James C. 1998. *Seeing Like a State: How Certain Schemes to Improve the Human Condition Have Failed*. New Haven, CT: Yale University Press.

Smith, Kerry. 2001. *A Time of Crisis: Japan, the Great Depression, and Rural Revitalization*. Cambridge, MA: Harvard University Press.

Statistical Yearbook of the Republic of China. 1982. Taipei, Taiwan: Directorate-General of Budget, Accounting and Statistics, Executive Yuan.

Stavis, Benedict. 1974. *Rural Local Governance and Agricultural Development in Taiwan*. Ithaca, NY: Rural Development Committee, Center for International Studies at Cornell University.

Steinberg, David. 1982. *The Economic Development of Korea, Sui Generis or Generic? Reflections on the Harvard University Press Studies of the Modernization of the Republic of Korea, 1974–75*. Washington, DC: US Agency for International Development.

Strauss, Julia C. 2017. Campaigns of Redistribution: Land Reform and State Building in China and Taiwan, 1950–1953. In Miguel A. Centeno, Atul Kohli, and Deborah J. Yashar (with Dinsha Mistree) (eds.), *States in the Developing World*. New York, NY: Cambridge University Press, pp. 339–632.

Taiwan Provincial Government. 1970. *A Brief Account of Community Development in Taiwan, Republic of China*. Taipei, Taiwan: Taiwan Provincial Government, Department of Social Affairs.

Taiwan Statistical Data Book. 1982. Taipei, Taiwan: Council for International Economic Cooperation and Development.

Tan, Chin-hsi (Tan Zhenxi). 1972. *Shequ fazhan de yanjiu*. [A study of community development]. Taipei, Taiwan: Republic of China Community Development Research and Training Center.

Tan Yi-min (Tan Yimin). 1969. *Shequ fazhan gailun* [Introduction to community development]. Yangmingshan, Taiwan: Guofang yanjiuyuan [Institute for National Defense Research].

Tucker, Robert C. 1961. Towards a comparative politics of movement-regimes. *The American Political Science Review* 55(2): 281–289.

Wade, Robert. 1990. *Governing the Market: Economic Theory and the Role of Government in East Asian Industrialization*. Princeton, NJ: Princeton University Press.

Wang Pei-hsun (Wang Peixun), ed. 1974. *Shequ fazhan wenda* [Community development questions and answers]. Taipei, Taiwan: Republic of China Community Development Research and Training Center.

Waswo, Ann. 1988. The transformation of rural society, 1900–1950. In Peter Duus (ed.), *The Cambridge History of Japan, Vol. 6, The Twentieth Century*. New York: Cambridge University Press, pp. 541–605.

White, Tyrene. 2006. *China's Longest Campaign: Birth Planning in the People's Republic, 1949–2005*. Ithaca, NY: Cornell University Press.

Wu Po-hsiung (Wu Boxiong). 1986. *Shequ fazhan de huigu yu zhanwang*. [Community development reflections and future prospects]. Taipei, Taiwan: Republic of China Community Development Research and Training Center.

Yager, Joseph A. 1988. *Transforming Agriculture in Taiwan: The Experience of the Joint Commission on Rural Reconstruction*. Ithaca, NY: Cornell University Press.

Yang, Martin M. C. 1970. *Socio-economic Results of Land Reform in Taiwan*. Honolulu, HI: East-West Center Press.

5

Enforcement Networks and Racial Contention in Civil Rights–Era Mississippi

David Cunningham and Peter B. Owens

5.1 INTRODUCTION

Early in the fall of 1964, the governor of Mississippi, Paul B. Johnson, embarked on an unusual journey. His destination was the small railroad city of McComb, located halfway between Jackson, the state's capitol, and New Orleans. Awaiting him at the end of the 80-mile drive were the area's two top policing officials: McComb Police Chief George Guy and Pike County Sheriff R. W. Warren. The situation was urgent for all concerned, as McComb had become a steady presence in the national news for its charged racial situation – a series of vicious bombings had targeted supporters of a voter registration campaign mounted by a coalition of civil rights organizations. Local residents and national reporters alike were in on the open secret: the bombings had been perpetrated by members of local chapters of the Ku Klux Klan (KKK), a violent vigilante outfit that had mobilized extensively in McComb over the past year.

Governor Johnson's concern with the continuing violence was closely bound to what he referred to obliquely as the "difficulty down here in the complete enforcement of the law." But he was not motivated by a desire to protect the civil rights workers, whose efforts he strongly opposed, or even the KKK bombers, whom he viewed as well-intended but misguided in their methods. Instead, he sought to avoid the looming threat of federal government intervention, which in his view could lead to the declaration of "martial law" in McComb and beyond:

[O]nce they do it in this county, they're going to do it in Greenwood. They're going to do it in Natchez and in many other counties of this state, and it's going to be like a cancer that's going to eat up the whole state and eventually mean that they will come in here and usurp the prerogatives of the state government. (Mississippi Department of Archives and History, 1964)

Johnson's role in this meeting was as a buffer of sorts, mediating the efforts of local police to enforce Mississippi's segregationist status quo and the federal officials who sought to force the state's compliance with recent national legislation outlawing legalized forms of segregation. As such, he was seeking to recalibrate Mississippi officials' campaign to, as the editors describe it in their Introduction to this volume, expand opportunities "to permit societal actors to engage in contestation that serves state interests ... [as] a conscious technology of rule." This aim to open space for local contentious action had served as Mississippi officials' predominant approach to staving off the threat posed to the region-specific Jim Crow legal system that – in seeming contradiction with the nation's democratic foundation – undergirded racial segregation and Black disenfranchisement in the US South. This threat had emerged both from below – through burgeoning grassroots campaigns initiated by civil rights activists – and from above, via legal efforts by the federal government to dismantle Jim Crow practices. As such, it serves as an instructive, and perhaps signal, case of the complexities associated with a modern democratic state seeking to "rule by other means" through the mobilization of contentious action.

Such struggles speak to broader questions of how, and to what extent, we should account for state-mobilized movements (SMMs) as a feature of democratic regimes. Alongside the valuable studies here that engage primarily with authoritarian cases, in conversation with a developing literature that views SMMs as especially salient in nondemocratic settings (Radnitz, 2010, p. 16), key questions remain about how such dynamics extend across the political spectrum. To assert – as we do here – that SMMs do not align exclusively with authoritarianism leads as well to questions of how this broadened analytic lens informs our overall understanding of the phenomenon. While contributions to this volume complicate a simple top-down conception of centralized state action in authoritarian settings, considering such dynamics in democratic regimes opens up new questions about how SMMs are both enabled and constrained by state process and organization. In particular, we emphasize how federalist arrangements spanning national, regional, and local governing bodies can create opportunities for multiple configurations of blended state and civic action. Considering such processes, and why they might vary across localities, provides a vantage from which to consider SMMs in democratic contexts, in particular, and to engage more expansively general questions of how states shape contention.

5.2 STATE-MOBILIZED MOVEMENT IN MODERN DEMOCRATIC REGIMES

Toward such ends, we examine the Civil Rights-era US South, a case that starkly demonstrates the nested character of modern democratic regimes. Observing the antebellum United States, Tocqueville famously noted the "premodern" aspects of certain democratic institutions, underscoring the feudal character of the southern plantation system in particular, rooted in a decentralized politics and the aristocratic values of judges and other legal administrators (Wolin, 2003). These blurred political distinctions remained evident a century later (Key, 1984, p. 4) and provide a basis to assess the complex orientation of the federal state to local and regional political struggles. Beginning in the 1950s, spurred by new opportunities stemming from federal pressures to break down regional sectional divisions surrounding legally enforced racial segregation, a burgeoning Civil Rights Movement successfully sparked the dissolution of the "Jim Crow" system that enabled the state-sanctioned denial of equal access to African Americans. While the movement itself has attained canonical status among scholars – serving as the core case for the development of predominant political process approaches to the study of social movements (see, e.g., McAdam, 1988, 1999; Meyer and Minkoff, 1996; Morris, 1984) – we know considerably less about the forces that civil rights activists confronted. Here, we shift the typical lens on the struggle to examine the configuration of actors that maintained, and later fought to preserve, racial segregation in Mississippi, the Deep South state with the most elaborate, entrenched, and brutal commitment to Jim Crow.

Doing so calls into sharp relief a number of considerations associated with SMMs. First, the Western democratic context inverts the typical dynamic associated with authoritarian regimes, which – as the studies in this volume demonstrate – often center on hierarchical national efforts to build counterrevolutionary or otherwise reactionary infrastructures. As Hemment (Chapter 7) notes, mobilization in such cases often takes on a top-down "astroturf" character, with national state actors working to build collectives – either coalitional or composite in character (Beissinger, Chapter 6) – that permeate local and regional politics. Even when decentralized, as in the Nashi (Hemment, Chapter 7) and Polish (Kruszewska and Ekiert, Chapter 2) cases considered in this volume, the bottom-up character of reactionary mobilization frequently remains "manufactured" (Ekiert and Kruszewska), driven by national efforts to suppress the vitality of challenges to the state.

As with these cases, southern efforts to resist civil rights reform possessed a strong defensive or reactive character, developed in response to the challenge posed by burgeoning protest movements. As the editors note in their Introduction, the state's motivation in this sense was at least partly "to maintain the appearance of popular legitimacy and social support" that the deployment of overtly coercive state measures could have undermined.

But at the same time, the Western democratic setting we explore complicates such understandings, as the state-centered anti–civil rights countermovement arose at the regional level, in response not only to a grassroots challenge but also to federal pressures to alter a sectional political apparatus that – as a formal system at least – was confined to the South. As such, the deployment of resources and emergence of rearticulated state bodies to resist civil rights reform centered on officials governing Mississippi and other southern states. Such efforts were reproduced, reinforced, and sometimes transformed at the local level, but in all cases such instantiations emerged in oppositional reaction to national state efforts to construct and, later, to guarantee civil rights protections. As such, the struggle took on a distinctly *nested* character, with federal bodies viewed largely as threats to subnational autonomy – articulated most commonly as struggles over "states' rights" and local sovereignty.

The resulting regional efforts to resist civil rights challenges thus targeted both activists and state actors. The latter were embodied by federal agencies such as the US Civil Rights Commission, which held hearings in Jackson, Mississippi's capital city, in 1965 that featured testimony and exhibits intended to demonstrate illegal local resistance to federal civil rights legislation. The adversarial character of the proceedings were underscored, on the one hand, by federal commissioners' direct challenges to local officials' discriminatory treatment of African Americans attempting to exercise voting rights, and, on the other, by Mississippi Governor Johnson, who noted in his opening remarks that "law and order will be maintained in Mississippi *by Mississippians*" (emphasis added), imploring the national audience to "get off of our back and get on our side" (Library of Congress, n.d.).

More pervasive was the increased presence of the nation's preeminent national criminal justice agency, the Federal Bureau of Investigation (FBI), in the state beginning in 1964. As a result of the killings of three civil rights workers in Mississippi's Neshoba County, perpetrated as part of a conspiracy involving both the vigilantist Ku Klux Klan (KKK) and local police officials, FBI Director J. Edgar Hoover – unsympathetic to the civil rights cause but under pressure from Attorney General Robert Kennedy – established a new FBI field office in Jackson, transferring 153 agents to the state to work primarily on the investigation of anti–civil rights crimes (Cunningham, 2004). Both efforts were emblematic of federal action to oppose the state-sanctioned maintenance of now-illegal racial segregation in the state.

Second, as these federalist antagonisms indicate, Mississippi's campaign to maintain segregation took the form of a particular kind of intra-state conflict. Motivated by a dual desire to defensively stem the civil rights tide while also avoiding federal intervention that would trump efforts to suppress activist campaigns, Mississippi officials eschewed overt mobilization and instead favored a form of *state engagement* – providing resources that would counter civil rights reform efforts by opening space for "autonomous" locally rooted action. By tolerating existing anti–civil rights initiatives, and encouraging similarly oriented incipient efforts, state actors provided a favorable environment for the expansion of such local activities, akin to social movement theorists' conceptions of a conducive "political opportunity structure" (McAdam, 1999; Tarrow, 2011).

As we will see, such action had a pronounced blended character, involving both local officials and civic initiatives, and built upon an established and durable infrastructure that had long ensured the routine maintenance of Jim Crow. A variety of fiscal, legal, and legislative resources comprised this foundation, enabling proactive measures centered on the wide discretion provided to both local officials and private citizens for their sanctioning of perceived breaches of racial etiquette (Luckett, 2015; McMillen, 1989). The mobilization of those resources also furthered programmatic efforts to build and maintain white (supremacist) identities and to transmit related messages to audiences outside of the state and region, via public relations efforts spearheaded by state and civil organizations such as the Citizens' Councils and Mississippi State Sovereignty Commission (MSSC) (Irons, 2010; McMillen, 1994). Such blending of state and civic spheres underscores social movement analysts' longstanding difficulties in differentiating between authorities and countermovements (Irons, 2006; Zald and Useem, 1987).

Finally, while the state's overarching motivation was defined by its need to enable local anti–civil rights action in a manner that also insulated local bodies from federal intervention, state engagement in Mississippi was characterized by significant local variation. As we note in this chapter, both the relevant state actors and the repertoire of tactics employed to suppress challenges to Jim Crow differed significantly across regions and communities within the state. As such, we conceptualize distinct configurations of anti–civil rights actors as *enforcement networks* comprised of both state and civil bodies. Akin to Dolenec and Širinić's invocation of Fishman's (1990) state/regime distinction in their Croatian case (Chapter 10), where the transitional character of that nation's post-conflict period ensured that political power resided within formal state networks as well as in civil bodies and party agents that possessed the capacity to shape modes of state repression, state/civil enforcement networks in Mississippi were characterized by varying degrees of active and "ambiguous" collaboration. Associated enforcement efforts were catalyzed actively through overt partnerships and, especially, via less direct efforts by state officials to open spaces for autonomous vigilantist action by civil actors. The emphasis on the latter speaks to Governor Johnson's dilemma during his 1964 visit to McComb – centered on the importance of identifying alternative means to quell local challenges to segregation without provoking the sort of federal intervention that would result from a full and open state-sponsored campaign.

In the sections that follow, we focus on these enforcement networks, comprised of state and civil actors invested in ensuring stability around specific social arrangements predicated on unequal access to political, economic, and/or social resources. Engaging with the differing network configurations organized to enforce Jim Crow racial segregation in Civil Rights–era Mississippi, we emphasize: (1) the field of actors that comprised the enforcement network (i.e. those active in maintaining status quo arrangements surrounding racial segregation and/or mobilizing to counter challenges to those prevailing arrangements); (2) the synergistic (and, in some cases, competitive) dynamics that enabled or prohibited coordination between state and civil actors within the field; and (3) predictable patterns of variation in the composition and organization of these enforcement networks, rooted jointly in localized political economic factors and the contours of challenges posed by local civil rights campaigns. Through a general discussion of the organizations and other institutions associated with the enforcement field, we highlight the ways in which the state intersects with, and at times enables, mobilization among civil actors. Then, we present case studies of two Mississippi communities, in order to think comparatively about the logic of local variation in enforcement networks.

5.3 STATE AND CIVIL PILLARS OF JIM CROW SEGREGATION IN THE US SOUTH

As a means of economic, political, and social dominance extending through the Civil Rights era, the system of legalized racial segregation known as "Jim Crow" dominated the southern landscape in the United States for decades. Enabled primarily by the disenfranchisement of Black citizens in the late nineteenth century, Jim Crow emerged as a coordinated set of laws and customs intended to ensure unequal access to social, economic, and political resources and spaces, to insulate whites from Black residents.

Formal segregation was engineered most visibly through institutional separation – via the creation of dual (and unequal) racially exclusive educational, health, commercial, and religious spaces. In other cases, however, racial insulation was maintained through often-elaborate routines associated with particular spaces that provided differential access to both white and Black patrons in a manner that precluded interracial contact as "equals." Many movie theaters across the South, for instance, were outfitted with separate ticket windows and entrances, typically maintaining whites-only lobby and orchestra seating areas while channeling Black patrons up an external staircase to segregated balcony seating. Similarly, "whites-only" restaurants might be outfitted with an outside window to serve take-out orders for an exclusively Black clientele. Though local patterns varied, segregation within these public spaces was reinforced residentially, with "indigenous" Black institutions typically forming within neighborhoods restricted to African Americans (McMillen, 1989).

Though a colloquialism, "Jim Crow" encompassed both the legal strictures that mandated racial separation and the informal customs through which such insulation was enforced. While most accounts of segregation focus primarily on formal statutes that prohibited many forms of racial contact, the uncodified "rules" associated with Jim Crow were much more pervasive. This was especially true in Mississippi, where entrenched racist practices and cultural routines – and attendant tolerance for violent enforcement of associated breaches of such understandings – rendered many legal mandates redundant (to illustrate this distinction, in 1950 Mississippi had 20 percent fewer Jim Crow laws on its books than North Carolina, the state widely considered the South's most progressive [see Murray, 1950]). Racialized norms pervaded daily routines, ensuring, for instance, that Black residents would subserviently step aside on sidewalks to cede space to passing whites, remove hats while in the presence of whites in elevators and other intimate spaces, and be denied the respect of courtesy titles (Berrey, 2015). In all cases, the aim was to preserve and reinforce a strict racialized hierarchy, which precluded any social interaction predicated on an equal plane (McMillen, 1989).

Crucially, economic interdependence undergirded such social distinctions. The organization of Jim Crow enabled the maintenance of a strict dual labor market, defined by white control over Black labor. In most areas, jobs were coded as strictly reserved either for white or Black workers. As historian Tim Tyson puts it, "to say 'black maid' or 'black janitor' would have been entirely redundant; there were no other kinds" (Tyson, 2004, p. 17). Larger firms might hire both Black and white workers but reserve particular positions only for one or the other, with whites always maintaining access to valued high-status work. Such divisions would then be maintained within fully segregated common spaces such as cafeterias and restrooms.

As the logic of Jim Crow developed in large part to ensure and accommodate such economic advantage, the system's contours varied according to local and regional distinctions. In Mississippi, the startlingly flat agricultural Delta region spanned the state's northwest quadrant and was distinguished by its rich soil and abundantly profitable cotton crops. The region also possessed the nation's highest concentration of African-American residents. These factors were of course intertwined, with an elite white planter class overseeing a Black agricultural labor force. African Americans outnumbered whites overall in many communities across the Delta, giving rise to an elaborate system of social mores that ensured both racial separation and political control by the white minority. Such customs hinged on a strict disenfranchisement of Black voters, a condition regulated predominantly via the acute economic vulnerability faced by most Black Deltans, whose livelihood was dependent upon landowning employers who often controlled access to both work and shelter. Exploiting such vulnerabilities reduced (but of course did not eliminate) the need for organized violence as a means of maintaining the racial status quo. As sociologist Charles Payne (1995, pp. 113–114) explains: "[S]ocial distance between Blacks and whites was so great that no one ever needed to be reminded of it, rendering the Klan less necessary and lynchings less common." In contrast, other areas of the state, in particular the "piney woods" region stretching across southern Mississippi, employed a racially mixed labor force in logging and industry. As such, a more stringent admixture of policing and unsanctioned civil violence developed as a means of enforcing perceived transgressions of the Jim Crow system.

Thus, in the absence of a collective, organized civil rights challenge, baseline modes of regulation combined – to regionally differing degrees – (1) informal control by white employers and landlords; (2) enforcement of Jim Crow statutes by police, who also frequently employed an array of trumped-up accusations to stretch the formal legal means at their disposal to repress any perceived disruptions of racial customs; and (3) intimidation and physical violence by members of the white citizenry, who typically carried out such vigilantist acts with virtual impunity.

Beginning in the mid-1950s, however, the landmark *Brown v. Board* legal decision and the subsequent rise of organized civil rights campaigns intended to challenge racial segregation's legal and moral foundations provided a trigger for fresh modes of state involvement in efforts to enforce local breaches of Jim Crow. The presence of these dual challenges to the sustained legal and political viability of Jim Crow set the broad terms of SMMs, centered on efforts by the state of Mississippi and local officials and civil bodies within its borders to maintain a sectionally distinct system of racial segregation in the face of federal pressures to align with national politics. Such pressures were embodied by the presence of FBI agents and investigators from the US Civil Rights Commission within Mississippi's borders, but they took on a diffuse character oriented around opposition to any perceived federal infringement on "states' rights."

The intensified enforcement campaign that resulted emerged through a number of modes, including:

- *Statewide legislation*, expressly designed to restrict the ability of civil rights activists to operate. Such statutes frequently expanded local authorities' control over public space, by empowering municipal officials to enforce curfews, widen the purview of "breach of peace" violations, and increase sentencing guidelines surrounding virtually any form of public protests. By 1967, with the need for Black agricultural labor sharply reduced due to mechanization advances, Delta legislators even sought – but ultimately were not able to pass – a bill proposing a plan to relocate Black residents to other states (Dittmer, 1995; Hughes, 1964).
- *Local ordinances*, enabling officials to exploit their enhanced legislative purview surrounding the suppression of civil rights protest. Common ordinances included prohibitions on the distribution of leaflets, expanded discretion around applying blue laws and other restrictive statutes against civil rights adherents, and severe restrictions on picketing or obstructing public and commercial spaces (Dittmer, 1995; McAdam, 1988). To demonstrate the clear pattern of abuse of such ordinances against civil rights workers, a US Civil Rights Commission (1965, p. 486) study found that, in the Delta city of Greenwood, fines levied against activists ranged from two to twenty times larger than those for equivalent offenses against other local citizens.

- *Broadened police capacity and purview*, through an increase in the size of the State Highway Patrol, the deputization of large numbers of county and city auxiliary officers to assist with civil rights "unrest," and the purchase of militarized equipment. For instance, in anticipation of the 1964 Freedom Summer campaign, the Jackson police department acquired searchlight trucks, trailers to transport large numbers of protesters to local and state jails, gas masks and other riot gear, and – most infamously – a 23-foot armored van, dubbed "Thompson's tank" after the city's mayor, Allen Thompson (Asch, 2011; McAdam, 1988; Murphree, 2006; Spofford, 1988).
- A *dedicated statewide agency*, the Mississippi State Sovereignty Commission (MSSC). Formed in 1956, the MSSC was primarily an investigative and information-gathering organization, focused on the preservation of Jim Crow in the state through resistance to the supposed "encroachment" by the federal government and civil rights forces (Luckett, 2015). Its agents sought to uncover intelligence associated with threats to the segregationist status quo, share information to support the anti–civil rights actions of a range of local officials, and develop public relations campaigns to defend Mississippi's racial practices (Irons, 2010). As such, it served as an official state organ with connections to a range of institutional and civic segregationist interests.

As the MSSC's actions and orientation indicate, such initiatives not only increased state capacity to address challenges to Jim Crow but also strengthened the efforts of a range of civil bodies as they worked to hinder the progress of the Civil Rights Movement and federal intervention efforts, in an effort to maintain the segregationist status quo.

A spectrum of civil organizations and initiatives emerged to fill the space created or enabled by these state initiatives, in some cases benefiting from direct government support. Most prominently, the Citizens' Councils, a network of local associations comprised largely of local business and civic leaders, were organized to exact economic pressure and retribution on those suspected of civil rights advocacy. Founded by Robert "Tut" Patterson in the Delta town of Indianola shortly following the 1954 *Brown* decision, Council chapters exerted an especially large influence throughout the Delta, exploiting Black workers' economic vulnerability. The Council movement also quickly spread across the state – most pronouncedly in counties with significant African-American presence – with local chapters sometimes forming in direct reaction to school desegregation petitions filed by the NAACP and local black families.

Following Mississippi Senator James O. Eastland's call to expand the Councils' model nationwide, to fight a range of civil rights organizations and "all the conscienceless pressure groups who are attempting our destruction," the subtly rebranded Citizens' Councils of America (CCA) formed as an "association of associations" spanning much of the South (McMillen, 1994,

p. 116). Eschewing the early Councils' penchant for secrecy, the CCA trumpeted its public face, hosting speakers and rallies to accompany its official newspaper, the "The Citizens' Council" (later shortened to "The Citizen"), which was printed at the organization's national headquarters in Jackson. The association's governmental connections were clear as well, with powerful elected officials from Mississippi, Georgia, and South Carolina gracing the advisory board of the temporary federation that preceded the CCA. By 1956, reporters and other observers increasingly considered the Councils as Mississippi's de facto government, a point underscored by its cozy relationship with the MSSC and, by the early 1960s, with Mississippi Governor Ross Barnett (Irons, 2010; Luckett, 2015; McMillen, 1994; Rolph, 2018).

Such connections also enabled the organization's more nefarious underside. Council members emphasized intimidation to suppress any threats to the segregationist status quo, through the active "application of economic pressure" (a phrasing featured prominently in an influential Council recording, intended for recruitment purposes) alongside tacit support for more aggressive modes of harassment. In 1968, well past the CCA's period of peak influence, an estimated 15 percent of participants in the Southern Christian Leadership Conference–sponsored Poor People's Campaign subsequently were evicted from their homes by white landlords (Wright, 2011), demonstrating the broad reach of such Council campaigns. In its effort to form an "impregnable front," the CCA sought also to regulate its own core constituency, ostracizing and often ruining any member of the white business class accused of a "disloyal" break from segregationist orthodoxy (McMillen, 1994).

Throughout this period, and tellingly for our purposes, the Councils received support from state bodies for their enforcement efforts. The MSSC funneled resources to the Councils to support some of its activities, and its agents consulted with Council leaders about various aspects of "the racial situation in Mississippi." Similarly, the state's two longstanding US congressmen, James O. Eastland and John Bell Williams, aided Council efforts to produce and distribute its own *Forum* radio and television shows (Irons, 2010). Such support peaked in the early 1960s, when – under the watch of Council member and booster Governor Ross Barnett – nearly $200,000 of public funds moved into the Councils' coffers (McMillen, 1994). Nearly a decade later, with the state facing the prospects of court-enforced school desegregation, many communities with strong Council infrastructures were able to rapidly construct private "seg" academies for white students, in part by illegally securing a range of public educational resources to facilitate the process (Andrews, 2002; Crespino, 2007).

While the Citizens' Councils formally eschewed violence, all the while spearheading a range of enforcement actions with similar ends, other groups endorsed more active forms of intimidation. The Americans for the Preservation of the White Race (APWR) was formed in Natchez in 1963 and quickly spread to Jackson the following year. Speaking to a *Newsweek* reporter in 1964, APWR President W. Arsene Dick Sr., an electrician from the state's southwest piney woods region, characterized the group as "appeal[ing] to the man with hands like mine." Showing his "gnarled callused palms," he underscored that the APWR attracts "working-type people who can operate at the grass-roots level," a euphemism for adherents' willingness to undertake a range of harassment actions against local targets. While the APWR did not actively promote physical violence, its members sought to pressure local businesses and other community leaders to maintain uncompromising support of segregation. One Mississippi newspaper tellingly referred to the group as a "semi-secret society," underscoring its role as a sort of bridge between the Citizens' Councils and the state's most powerful extremist organ: the Ku Klux Klan (Crespino, 2007; Cunningham, 2013a; *Delta Democrat Times*, May 11, 1964).

The KKK in Mississippi arrived relatively late to the anti–civil rights party, first moving into the state near the end of 1963. By the following year, however, two powerful Klan organizations enjoyed a significant presence throughout the state. The Sam Bowers–led White Knights of the KKK operated as an underground paramilitary outfit, relying on secrecy and strong hierarchical leadership to engineer hundreds of bombings, beatings, and acts of intimidation. Most tragically, a cadre of White Knights collaborated with local police to carry out the 1964 murders of three civil rights workers in Neshoba County, and Bowers was open about his advocacy of violence "when considered necessary" (Cunningham, 2013a; Huie, 2000).

Soon after the White Knights' 1963 rise, however, Bowers faced competition for his members' allegiance. The Alabama-based United Klans of America (UKA), headed by Imperial Wizard Robert Shelton, asserted itself by the mid-1960s as the South's preeminent KKK organization. Possessing upward of 25,000 members region-wide, Shelton sought to move into Mississippi to promote his admixture of open public presence – centered on frequent rallies and Klan parades – and underground terror. This approach allowed Shelton to publicly disavow violence while providing local membership with a longer leash to intimidate and harass under the cover of darkness. This combination appealed both to White Knights members, who felt that Bowers' militancy was not matched by his willingness and ability to provide legal support to members implicated in terroristic plots, and to those frustrated by the limits imposed by his elaborate systems of authorization for violent acts (Cunningham, 2013a, 2013b). As a result, the UKA attracted an unwieldy mix of Klan adherents who felt that the White Knights were too dangerously violent and those who felt they were not militant enough.

Mississippi Klan leader E. L. McDaniel epitomized the palpable tension between these two groups and their respective orientations to maintaining white supremacy. Originally a member of the White Knights, McDaniel's move to the UKA followed his secretive campaign to partner with Shelton to siphon members to his outfit. While, distinct from Bowers' approach with the White Knights, McDaniel didn't regularly engineer terror campaigns against civil rights targets, he also did little to discourage rank-and-file members from such actions. This tacit support enabled, among dozens of other acts of violence statewide, UKA members to embark in an extended bombing campaign in McComb (discussed in more detail in Section 5.5) and a similarly gruesome campaign of violence in McDaniel's home base in Natchez.

While understanding the KKK's organizational landscape – and particularly these struggles over Klan turf – is important, an emphasis on intra-KKK competition shouldn't obscure the fact that both the White Knights and the UKA's Mississippi membership engaged in violence to a degree unsurpassed elsewhere in the South during this period. In addition to the large number of tragic bombings and murder plots, excerpts from a surreptitiously recorded conversation among UKA members in Natchez (Crane and Young, 1968) underscores the range of intimidation tactics that Mississippi Klansmen employed throughout this period:

"We had a nigger down in Natchez tried to send his boy to a white school. His cornfield kept disappearing on him, stalks and all."

"That's right, and then his car caught the Sugar Diabetes – that's the disease get in the oil."

"We taught him to sleep in a raincoat, we had so many damn holes in that nigger's roof that buckshot wouldn't bounce off no more."

Klan adherents' ability to engage in such acts for extended periods also highlights the tacit or active support that the KKK received from law enforcement. In many communities, sheriffs, police chiefs, and rank-and-file officers could be counted among the Klan's membership, and – even if not – exhibited sympathy and tolerance for the KKK's brand of terrorism, enabling Klansmen to undertake violence with impunity. At the state level, the Mississippi Highway Patrol was dogged by accusations of Klansmen in their ranks. While the MSSC publicly spoke out against Klan violence, its agents did nothing to prevent KKK mobilization in general or overt alliances between Klansmen and local police officials in particular (Cunningham, 2013a, 2013b; Irons, 2010; Watson, 2010). A 1966 interaction between these parties clearly illustrated these connections. After one particularly notorious Natchez-area Klansman was arrested for the bombing of a local jewelry store in December of that year, Sovereignty Commission investigator L. E. Cole Jr. arrived at the county jail to find the perpetrator outside of his cell, "telling jokes" with Sheriff Odell Anders, UKA leader McDaniel, and two other well-known Klan officers. Cole, for his part, seemed less troubled by this apparent miscarriage of justice than by the fact that several of the jokes "made light of the Sovereignty Commission and our work in front of these KKK officials" (MSSC file # 2-36-2-69-1-1-1).

Such close associations were characteristic of the broader anti–civil rights field. According to federal investigators, despite claims by APWR leaders that "[w]e are not secret. We are not part of the Klan. We are not nightriders. We don't front for no organization," typical APWR chapters "encompass[ed] all Klansmen in the area, plus a few non-Klansmen," often disgruntled Citizens' Council members. Similarly, as McDaniel noted: "You had a lot of people that belonged to the Citizens' Council that was members of the Klan. A lot of Citizen's Council, a lot of them were members of the ... Americans for the Preservation of the White Race, and so on." Police also openly affiliated with their local APWR chapters; describing a typical Jackson chapter meeting, one report noted a city officer – his police department patch displayed openly on his jacket – seated front and center among the collection of 75 to 100 APWR adherents present (*Christian Science Monitor*, July 3, 1964; Cunningham, 2013a).

In many larger Mississippi communities, a range of more traditional segregationist associations augmented the resistance campaigns mobilized through this collection of militant civil efforts. Groups promoting white supremacy under the guise of "constitutional government" or "religious integrity" abounded, and such mainstream outlets attracted more moderate adherents of the CCA and APWR alongside a broader swath of the white community. This spectrum of organizations remained quite fluid; as one contemporaneous news account put it:

Assorted women's and youth organizations also exist for the purpose of battling integration and 'commie agitators' ... As civil rights pressures build and these organizations react, it becomes harder and harder to delineate between them. Some people are members of two or more at a time. Other people are known to be shifting from one group to another either because politicians and practices are either too extreme or not extreme enough. (*Christian Science Monitor*, July 3, 1964)

Such characterizations of proliferating segregationist efforts lent a strong degree of credibility to civil rights activist Bob Moses's conclusion that, throughout the mid-1960s, "the full resources of the state will continue to be at the disposal of local authorities to fight civil rights gains.... The entire white population will continue to be the Klan" (quoted in Dittmer, 1995, pp. 198–199). More generally, the efflorescence of these segregationist initiatives across the political and civic spectrum underscored a complex duality: these bodies were both expressions of the US democratic constitutional system and also reflections of the endemic federalist tensions within that system. In this sense, an organization promoting "constitutional government" simultaneously promoted local political freedom in the white community, negated parallel Black political expression, and resisted intervention by supra-local bodies that would threaten the prevailing Jim Crow system.

Mirroring such tensions, instances of conflict and competition also at times percolated within segregationist campaigns, both locally and statewide. In particular, the KKK's flouting of law and order was frequently cited as counterproductive to the broader white supremacist cause and often painted in opposition to the professionalized efforts of police forces. "No officer in this state or anywhere needs the help of the Ku Klux Klan in enforcing the law," proclaimed Mississippi Attorney General Joe T. Patterson in 1965. "The good people of each community and city should band together to enforce and obey the law and demand assistance from their law officers" (MSSC file # 6-53-0-12-1-1-1). Speaking more generally against vigilantism – but, tellingly, not against segregationist resistance generally – Governor Paul Johnson offered a public appeal to allow police to address civil rights activity, warning that he would "not tolerate anyone taking the law into his own hands" (NARA, HUAC Box 49[23], folder: APWR). Such logics also held within certain communities as segregationist outfits sought to maintain their turf. In Yazoo City, at the boundary of the Delta, the Citizens' Council issued a statement that obliquely addressed the looming threat posed by the KKK: "your Citizens' Council was formed to preserve separation of the races, and believes that it can best serve the county where it is the only organization operating in the field" (quoted in Dittmer, 1995, p. 218).

In the sections that follow, we grapple with such distinctions, to focus on the interplay within this segregationist field and in particular the orientation of state bodies to civic efforts such as the Citizens' Councils, the APWR, and the KKK. To gain leverage over such relationships, we focus on two local communities – McComb in southwest Mississippi and Clarksdale in the Delta – highlighting in each case local demographic and economic climates, the nature and extent of the civil rights threat, and the organization of local enforcement networks. These two cases are themselves situated within the broader milieu of repressive anti–civil rights mobilization in Mississippi, characterized by state and state-sponsored actors operating within the logic of a collective action field (Fligstein and McAdam, 2012). This conceptualization implies that these repressive agents, although working toward nominally shared ends (i.e. the maintenance of de jure racial segregation in the state), had differing orientations to the proper means to confront civil rights challenges. Thus, these agents organized their actions relative not only to the contours of perceived challenges and the contextual factors that enabled differing degrees of reactive mobilization but also to the actions of other enforcement agents who competed for legitimacy within this field.

Within the context of Civil Rights-era Mississippi, the dual cases we discuss in Sections 5.4 and 5.5 demonstrate differing configurations of state-mobilized segregationist movements, which we see as broadly organized within three distinct regional logics (Cunningham et al., 2019). First, in Clarksdale and its surrounding Delta region, the relatively limited and tentative nature of insurgent civil rights actions and corresponding reactions by segregation enforcers were broadly conditioned by the overwhelming vulnerability of African Americans to targeted economic sanctioning by white elites. This acute vulnerability increased the viability of "legitimate" segregationist organizations, such as the Citizens' Councils and local police units and auxiliaries, and correspondingly decreased the appeal of vigilante organizations, such as the Klan. Second, in the southwest and south-central region of the state around McComb and Natchez, desegregated factories run by northern industrialists enabled the growth of a relatively independent Black working class that was less vulnerable to such sanctioning and thus enabled civil rights insurgents to mobilize more pronounced challenges to segregation and voter suppression. Because of the more extreme nature of these perceived challenges, state and local law enforcement efforts often competed for legitimacy with various vigilante forces (in particular the KKK), with both engaging in comparatively high levels of violence against insurgents; such actions were comparatively much less frequent in the Delta. Third, for the largely rural counties in the state's Northeast and East-Central regions, relative isolation – in terms of both their inaccessibility by road and rail travel and the lack of attention they received from federal agents and national journalists – enabled local law enforcement to operate with relative impunity in preventing significant civil rights challenges from being organized.

Across these regional configurations, the state's motive – i.e. to preserve Jim Crow segregation in the face of challenges from grassroots activists and federal governmental officials – remained uniform. That its modes differed so sharply demonstrated the degree to which state bodies were attuned to local conditions, both distinguishing and strategizing around rising racial competition in southwest Mississippi and pronounced white resource control in the Delta. Such adaptive approaches shaped the contours of enforcement. State agents, for instance, conveyed to Clarksdale's planter elites the urgent need to impose economic sanctions while, alternately, tacitly encouraging (and, later, reining in) vigilantism in McComb. By examining this local variation in the organization and operation of enforcement networks, we aim to underscore the baseline point that enforcement unfolded differently across locales and that such differences were associated with the capacities and orientations of particular state actors. In short, the contours of the segregationist responses to the civil rights struggle in Clarksdale and McComb enable us to elaborate on how the logic of state engagement impacted the progression of mobilization on all sides of the struggle.

5.4 CLARKSDALE

Located in the heart of the Mississippi Delta in the state's northwest region, our interest in Clarksdale relates to its historical rootedness in the cotton planting economy, the resulting disproportionate level of economic and social power that whites accumulated and consolidated over African-American tenant farmers, and the ways in which this accumulation and consolidation made African Americans acutely vulnerable to economic and social sanctions for perceived infractions against the racial caste system. The racially segmented labor force associated with the cotton economy harked directly back to arrangements associated with enslavement – namely, an entrenched paternalistic culture in which white planters emphasized ostensible goodwill between racial groups while accumulating great wealth through the violent exploitation of Black labor. As such, the preservation of racism was rooted in a structurally unequal partnership, with white landowners frequently advocating for "their" workers when it met their interests to do so. Such arrangements created seemingly paradoxical political possibilities. As civil rights activists battled across the state to enfranchise Black citizens, Clarksdale's voter rolls included several hundred African Americans, a practice designed to produce additional votes in support of their employers' preferred candidates or positions on bond issues (MSSC file # 2-62-1-21-3-1-1).

The maintenance of this paternalistic system thus served as both the motive and the means for enforcing the status quo in the face of civil rights challenge. Ultimately, such enforcement efforts centered on African Americans' vulnerability to economic forms of social control, which created challenges for civil rights organizers in mobilizing change efforts in the region, increased the effectiveness and salience of "legitimate" Jim Crow enforcers (best exemplified through the close interactions among local Citizens Councils, the State Sovereignty Commission, and local law enforcement), and correspondingly decreased the perceived need for and appeal of violent vigilante groups such as the KKK relative to other areas of the state.

Organized civil rights challenges to Jim Crow in Clarksdale, the Coahoma County seat, began in 1952 with the founding of the county's first NAACP chapter. Civil rights organizers faced particular hurdles in trying to organize for social change in the Delta, due to the dispersed nature of Black settlement and the specific vulnerability of its Black population to economic reprisals from white elites and business owners who felt threatened by local challenges to segregation. NAACP leaders, in noting the specific vulnerability of African Americans in the Delta, wrote that "most of the economy of Clarksdale and Coahoma County is built around agriculture with many Negroes humbly abiding on plantations .... Many rigidly deprived Negroes work on the plantations from eight to ten hours per day for a rate of thirty cents per hour. Most of the housing for Negroes is rental housing by White real estate companies and individuals" (quoted in Dirks, 2007, p. 77).

The linkage of the Delta's specific economy of racial domination and the emerging national civil rights struggle, represented locally by Clarksdale's NAACP chapter founding, drew both from indigenous Black organizing and important triggering events that demonstrated the shortcomings of more traditional accommodationist organizations to local residents. First, NAACP regional organizers like Ruby Hurley, dispatched from New York to oversee recruitment efforts in the Southeast in the 1950s, benefited from the substantial strength of existing Black political organizations in Coahoma and in the Delta more generally, including the Regional Council of Negro Leadership (RCNL) and the Mississippi Progressive Voters League (MPVL). The former, founded in 1951, had been focused more squarely on issues of Black communal self-help and civic engagement, with some attention to voter registration; the latter, founded in 1946, had focused relatively exclusively on voter registration efforts while acquiescing to poll taxes and other segregationist impediments to Black political franchise (Hamlin, 2012). Such organizations had managed to coexist relatively well within the particular white power structure of the county, whose residents prided themselves on their paternalistic "tolerance" and willingness to promote a veneer of interracial cooperation in civic affairs. Even so, as local business-owner and NAACP leader Aaron Henry noted, whites "held a tight grip, and we knew that our fight for equality would be long and difficult" (quoted in Hamlin, 2012, p. 25).

Second, the transition – symbolized by the growth of the NAACP – from a local organizing focus on Black communal aid and self-help to increasing involvement in challenges to Jim Crow also seems to have been triggered by critical local events in the early 1950s, which encouraged local Black residents toward more organized and insurgent resistance. One event began with the rape of two Black women, 35-year-old Leola Tates and 22-year-old Erline Mills, by a local white truck driver, E. L. Roach, in 1951; the charges were quickly dropped over alleged conflicts in victim testimonies, despite the open admissions of the perpetrator to having done so. The MPVL protested this outcome, despite its relative normalcy within Jim Crow, by collecting money from residents to hire a special counsel and by pushing for the convening of a grand jury to secure further indictments. A second pivotal event was the 1952 murder by Clarksdale police of Denzill Turner, an epileptic who had experienced a seizure on the street and was shot multiple times by police responding to a "drunk man on the loose," despite the officers having been informed of Turner's medical condition by his father. All three officers involved were later exonerated. This exoneration, occurring only months after the Roach verdict, led Aaron Henry to organize local Black residents to protest the killing to the mayor (Hamlin, 2012).

These critical events and the subsequent collective actions by local residents had important effects, revealing "subtle crack[s] in the Delta's seemingly impenetrable Jim Crow façade" by demonstrating the collective ability of local residents to resist local enforcement of these norms (Hamlin, 2012, p. 26). The MPVL ran a voter registration drive in 1953 that promised to register 1,200 new Black voters by 1954; the RCNL began to increasingly adopt the anti–Jim Crow framework of the NAACP; and the NAACP's regional organizing efforts, coordinated by Ruby Hurley under the slogan "Let's Do More in '54 Because We Want to Be Free in '63," ran consecutive membership drives throughout the 1950s that increased its ties with RCNL and MPVL (Hamlin, 2012). Together, these efforts helped to solidify the foundation for challenging Jim Crow in the Delta's seemingly impervious web of white economic, political, and legal controls.

These efforts also punctured the "selective tolerance" of the local white power governance structure, leading to increasing reactive efforts by local white elites, officials, and residents to utilize their economic and political leverage against Black insurgents. These efforts were largely coordinated under the auspices of the Citizens' Councils, which endeavored to use economic tactics to stamp out progressive activism – as Aaron Henry saw it, targeting activists "for extinction." For their part, Delta-based Council leaders emphasized their ostensibly nonviolent orientation, with Clarksdale native Tut Patterson arguing that "we felt that our position could be defended without hurting anyone, on purely legal and constitutional grounds" (quoted in Hamlin, 2012, p. 33). By 1956, in response to local activism and the broader threat of desegregation from the Supreme Court's *Brown v. Board* decisions, the Coahoma Citizens' Council had grown to a membership of 1,130, and its efforts were augmented by regular intelligence on the activities of local civil rights proponents provided by the MSSC. Clarksdale police largely acted as the out-front enforcers of these organizations by utilizing physical harassment and intimidation when economic reprisals failed to achieve desired results.

The specific role of the local police as official agents of intimidation and violence, alongside the high capacity for economic intimidation, largely obviated the need for extra-legal vigilantist groups such as the APWR and KKK (Dirks, 2007; Hill, 2004). Neither of those groups enjoyed widespread support in Coahoma, despite organizing efforts that extended through late 1965. In November of that year, UKA organizers sought to solidify a membership drive by electing officers, but – according to an FBI informant – they could not even attract enough members to the meeting to proceed with the election (FBI Memo from SA James W. Sammon to SAC, Jackson, November 13, 1965). Sporadic vigilante violence, however, did supplement the official force wielded by the police in the region, though the unorganized nature of such acts meant that they never reached the terroristic proportions that KKK-perpetrated action did in other regions of the state.

State officials in Mississippi instead aided the mobilization of Clarksdale's more aboveboard bodies, by opening space for them to operate as well as providing support to enhance the effectiveness of their efforts. Doing so at times entailed regular visits by MSSC agents to "teach" local officials to deviate from paternalistic traditions to exert more aggressive sanctions on suspected civil rights adherents. In meetings with local officials, MSSC agents encouraged Citizens' Council leaders to undertake intelligence operations on NAACP activities and also to remove family members of "agitators" from city employment. Following a 1960 meeting with local Clarksdale officials, the MSSC's Tom Scarbrough expressed frustration around the Councils' readiness to act:

[T]hose who are in authority are not ready to use economic pressure against the Negro agitators which are causing the trouble in Coahoma County, as it has been pointed out to these people the agitators' wives are teaching school in Coahoma County and should be disposed of as teachers, yet they are unwilling to take any action on the grounds the teachers themselves have done nothing to justify the school board in letting them out.... Until those in authority make up their minds to dispose of any member of the family services who are wives or brothers and sisters of these agitators and advocates of desegregation it appears to me there is not much the Sovereignty Commission can do to help them solve their problem. (MSSC file # 2–62–1–8–2–1–1)

Over time, such prodding bore fruit. In sharp contrast with Scarbrough's lament about Clarksdale officials' laissez-faire orientation, by 1962 Aaron Henry's wife Noelle had been fired by the Coahoma County School Board, and her husband was being surveilled "very closely" by local police, in hopes of catching him in a "dope racket" run out of his pharmacy. Both acts had been strongly encouraged during meetings that city officials and civic leaders had called with Citizens' Council head Tut Patterson and MSSC Agent Scarbrough (MSSC files # 2–62–2–8–1–1–1, 2–62–2–10–1–1–1, 2–62–1–21–4–1–1).

Given such pronounced pressure and the broader pattern of racial economic vulnerability in Clarksdale, the relative economic independence of local movement organizers became central. Aaron Henry, who bridged membership in both local organizations such as the RCNL and MPVL and extra-regional groups such as the NAACP, owned a drug store in downtown Clarksdale that served as an important meeting and safe space for local activists. Similarly, Vera Pigee, a central NAACP organizer in Clarksdale from the late 1950s on, owned a beauty salon where African Americans could discuss local politics openly without fear of reprisal. Reflecting the mode of front-line enforcement that predominated in Clarksdale, Pigee featured a large poster in her shop encouraging voter registration with an aim to "stop police brutality" (Hamlin, 2012, p. 66). Focusing on economic impediments to involvement in the movement, local organizers also convened efforts such as clothing and food drives throughout the late 1950s and early 1960s that sought to alleviate the vulnerability of local residents to economic sanctioning.

Such networks and spaces remained key as the regional movement's focus shifted away from the NAACP – whose membership in the Delta had declined under consistent onslaughts from the Citizens Councils, MSSC, and local law enforcement by the early 1960s – and toward the increasing dynamism of youth activists in the Student Nonviolent Coordinating Committee (SNCC) and the SCLC. These younger activists focused more closely on direct-action challenges to Jim Crow rather than the NAACP's more deliberate legal challenges and thus were able to position themselves as more effectively resisting established Jim Crow social structures. This increasing direct action focus was best instantiated through the organization of an economic boycott of white businesses in downtown Clarksdale throughout 1961 and 1962, continued voter registration efforts such as the Council of Federated Organizations' (COFO) Freedom Vote campaign in 1963, and the Freedom Summer voter registration and outreach campaigns during the summer of 1964. These efforts, in turn, drew increasingly violent reactions from local police, driven largely by the perception that existing economic and legal structures could no longer be counted on to stymie civil rights agitation.

Through the mid-1960s, then, enforcement via a tightly interconnected network of local political figures and economic elites, along with the use of law enforcement to provide legalized intimidation and violence when these backroom tactics failed to quell support for change, limited civil rights advances in the Mississippi Delta, where almost all major public institutions remained completely segregated. While that would ultimately change, anti–civil rights enforcement in Clarksdale gained temporary traction based on its exploitation of historical arrangements that rendered the majority of the African-American population vulnerable to economic sanction. Officials' efforts to exert effective pressure in the face of a growing civil rights challenge were directly enabled by the state, which opened space and utilized personnel to "train" locals to develop effective enforcement strategies. Given the relative absence of organized vigilantism, Clarksdale's coordinated response to grassroots challenges was marshaled in a manner that largely avoided federal intervention.

5.5 MCCOMB

Such efforts became considerably more complex in communities like McComb, where vigilante violence undergirded enforcement campaigns. Located in Pike County in the heart of southwest Mississippi, McComb's strategic location midway between New Orleans and Jackson aided its growth as an early rail center. The community's small-city industrial character intersected with the presence of early sustained SNCC organizing campaigns to shape the contours of an enforcement network centered on pronounced institutional overlap between local officials and a range of organized militant, and frequently vigilantist, organizations.

In sharp contrast with the Delta, Mississippi's southwestern region lacked a lucrative agricultural base, and thus McComb's economy centered primarily on the railroad, oil, and manufacturing rather than on anything resembling Coahoma County's racially segmented plantation system. By the early 1960s, more than a dozen industrial firms – the Illinois Central railroad and a lingerie factory the largest among them – employed 5,000 workers in the city and surrounding areas of Pike County, and hundreds of others worked in the many active sawmills around the county. By the 1960s, African Americans comprised approximately a third of McComb's 13,000 residents, with the railroad tracks that bisected the community strictly separating the white and Black sides of town.

McComb's reputation as a rough blue-collar town was cemented early; civil violence as a means of activating and settling conflicts looms large in the community's popular memory. Famed Mississippi journalist Hodding Carter

(1965) dates the area's predilection for vigilantism to the early nineteenth century, and throughout the Jim Crow era such acts were frequently directed toward the enforcement of racial norms. Indeed, at the outset of the 1960s more known acts of racial violence had occurred in McComb than in any other Mississippi community (Ward, 2019; see also Peterson and Ward, 2015). Such vigilantism only intensified when the city became an early beachhead of the Mississippi Movement, sparked by SNCC worker Bob Moses's arrival in the community in 1961.

With the support of longtime local NAACP leader C. C. Bryant and other veteran local NAACP adherents, Moses built a grassroots voter registration drive that extended through the latter half of that summer (Carson, 1981, p. 26). Some of the local young people energized by that work also engaged in a parallel campaign, staging sit-ins at the local Woolworth's and the Greyhound Bus Terminal. Direct action of this sort had long been considered prohibitively dangerous in Mississippi, but more than 100 students at McComb's African-American high school, Burglund High, upped the ante that fall by staging a mass walkout and march to city hall in protest of the supposed expulsion of two of the teens participating in the earlier Greyhound sit-in. Framing that incident as symptomatic of broader issues, student leaders released a statement noting that "[i]n school we are taught democracy, but the rights that democracy has to offer have been denied to us by our oppressor" (FBI, 1961, p. 28).

Police and school board officials responded harshly, arresting all of the students involved in the walkout, forcing them to sign a pledge not to participate in further civil rights activity as a condition of their return to school (dozens of students refused to sign and eventually enrolled in Campbell College in Jackson to complete their high school coursework), and also engaging in physical retribution against adult SNCC workers. As part of the latter campaign, Bob Moses was badly beaten by a cousin of the Pike County sheriff, with other SNCC adherents facing similar violence at the hands of the registrar and police officers in Pike and nearby Amite County. Violent repression crested in late September when Amite County NAACP leader and SNCC ally Herbert Lee was shot and killed in cold blood by state legislator E. H. Hurst, an act that effectively halted SNCC's 1961 McComb campaign (Dittmer, 1995).

In the face of such severe hostility – which Martin Luther King Jr. described as an "apparent reign of terror" – McComb maintained a large and active NAACP branch; in 1966, local membership still exceeded 150 (Andrews, 2004; UPI, 1961). SNCC's organizational resilience and deep roots in the community also enabled a renewed McComb campaign in 1964, augmented by a group of Freedom Summer project volunteers who arrived that July, to continue voter registration work and open a freedom school. The dynamics of this second campaign were forged by the strong official reaction to the perceived threat posed by this civil rights challenge, once again cementing McComb's status as the most viciously contentious community in the Civil Rights–era South (Carson, 1981; Dittmer, 1995).

Indeed, the 1964 drive to suppress civil rights actions was notable for its broad-based reactionary militance, with both official and civil actors playing significant roles in the progression of conflict that summer and fall. Prior to the start of the Freedom Summer campaign, an editorial in the local McComb *Enterprise-Journal* noted preparations for a coordinated official response, with "Gov. Paul Johnson at the state level, Sheriff R. R. Warren at the county level and Mayor Gordon Burt and Police Chief George Guy at the city level ... all in agreement as to the procedures to pursue." While public pronouncements of those procedures predictably opposed civil rights activity, they also emphasized a measured approach to maintain order. Police officials stressed that they were prepared to handle any conflicts and that, in their efforts to enforce the law, they would "see to it that we ourselves observe the law." The county circuit clerk added that he would fairly assess any applicants for voter registration: "My responsibility is to apply the law and I will apply it to white and colored people alike and with no distinction because of race" (quoted in Carter, 1965, p. 63). During a mid-July meeting with a representative of the incipient Freedom Summer campaign, arranged by *Enterprise-Journal* editor Oliver Emmerich, Sheriff Warren reiterated similar themes, pledging full police cooperation so long as the civil rights workers conducted voter registration efforts "in an orderly manner" and ensured that any other activities remained "purely educational" (Carter, 1965).

In practice, however, officials' response to the civil rights campaign unfolded quite differently. One of the two Black officers hired onto McComb's eighteen-person police force in 1964 quit after refusing orders to plant an informant among the cadre of local civil rights activists and initiate a petition to force them to leave McComb (Dittmer, 1995). To increase police capacity, Chief Guy augmented his force with auxiliary deputies, including several known (and later indicted) KKK members (Pearson, 1964). Such actions aligned with his purposeful laissez-faire approach to – and thus tacit support for – rising vigilantist countermobilization.

This countermobilization campaign took a variety of intersecting forms. By late 1964, eight separate chapters of the UKA had organized in Pike County, marking the area in and around McComb as the most active Klan region in the South (US House of Representatives, 1966, 1967). The APWR also built a sizable local following, with at least some of its members also active in the Klan (Cummings, 1964). These groups were joined by the local neighborhood "self-protection" association Help Inc., which mobilized residents of two of McComb's most prominent subdivisions under the guise of "protection of one's family, home and property." Employing an elaborate network of officers and block captains, the organization developed a hyperbolic protocol for securing fellow residents against home invasion and assault by encroaching civil rights forces. On at least three occasions, Help Inc. mobilized car caravans to encircle the house of one resident with supposed ties to civil rights activists (based on his hosting of an impromptu dinner with a minister and Freedom Summer worker), and engineered a subsequent harassment campaign that resulted in more than 350 threatening phone calls and the poisoning of the target's family dog (Carter, 1965, pp. 68–71).

Contrary to the claims of goodwill offered by Sheriff Warren, the rise of the KKK, APWR, and Help Inc. was supported by their close connections to his office and other local and state officials. Help Inc.'s 1964 coming-out party, a potluck supper for more than 200 residents of its subdivisions, featured an invocation by Warren. When, later that summer, McComb Mayor Gordon Burt agreed to a rather delicate interview with Chicago *Daily News* reporter Nicholas Van Hoffman, he brought along two of Help Inc.'s vice presidents for support (Carter, 1965). Likewise, Chief Guy, an avowed APWR member, actively encouraged that group's activities. Sheriff Warren spoke to the group as well, pledging to "recruit" APWR adherents as auxiliary officers to deal with the upcoming "long hot summer" of 1964 (Dittmer, 1995). When the KKK held a public rally in Pike County in the spring of 1964, McComb Selectman Philip Bailey introduced Imperial Wizard Robert Shelton (Carter, 1965). For his part, Mayor Burt served as Pike County chairman of the CCA, though the limited economic vulnerability of the local Black population meant that the Councils' strength in southwestern Mississippi never approached that of their Delta counterparts.

While, through such connections, vigilantist forces gained valuable resources and strategic advantage, perhaps the most significant impact of this pattern of official complicity was the opening of space within which they could act with impunity. During the summer and fall of 1964, McComb UKA units embarked on an extensive bombing campaign, selecting targets from a hat filled with the names of those deemed threatening to the segregationist status quo (Mississippi Bureau of Investigation, 1964). With the support of local oil baron J. E. Thornhill – whose success in the industry made him one of McComb's wealthiest citizens and also provided easy access to dynamite – Klansmen perpetrated at least two dozen bombings, along with a handful of arson attempts, beatings, and cross burnings (US House of Representatives, 1965). Throughout, as McComb attorney and then-Chamber of Commerce president Robert Brumfield recalled, "a lot of people sat back and enjoyed what was going on" (quoted in Dittmer, 1995, p. 267).

Indeed, as a motivating prelude to Gov. Johnson's fateful McComb visit described at the outset of the chapter, Chief Guy, Sheriff Warren, and their respective forces seemed befuddled by the wave of terror, claiming not to have any leads and on several occasions accusing movement allies of staging the bombings themselves (see, e.g., McComb *Enterprise-Journal*, September 23, 1964). While the FBI noted that certain local officers were themselves active KKK members, police also conducted parallel harassment efforts against local civil rights activists, threatening pretext arrests of campaign workers for violating a new anti-leafleting ordinance and carrying out a midnight raid on the movement's headquarters, ostensibly to search for illegal whiskey and proof of interracial cohabitation (Carter, 1965; Dittmer, 1995; FBI, 1964, p. 47). The police's lack of veracity with their bombing investigations soon became evident, as – once under pressure to do so – they would quickly apprehend eleven Klansmen involved in one or more terrorist acts. During the subsequent trial, the plaintiffs put Sheriff Warren on the stand, considering him an adverse (i.e. hostile) witness to the state's case against the Klan bombers (Gordon, 1964a).

The escalating pressure placed on local police to halt the bombing campaign stemmed from increased national scrutiny and criticism of McComb, which produced a looming fear of state and federal intervention to restore order along with mounting anxiety among the business class that vigilantism was doing irreparable harm to the city's economic prospects. Beginning in late September, *Enterprise-Journal* editor Oliver Emmerich penned a series of editorials that condemned the bombings and associated acts of terror and harassment, culminating in the full-page "Statement of Principles" published in the newspaper and backed by the signatures of a large swath of local business leaders. Notably, while far from progressive, the statement criticized a full range of official and private efforts to thwart civil rights efforts, calling for an end to harassment arrests, economic threats, and unequal treatment under the law along with vigilante violence (Dittmer, 1995).

The KKK bombing trial underscored a similar point about the spectrum of forces mobilized to contest civil rights advances, demonstrating that conflicts among white officials resided with means rather than ends. Following guilty pleas lodged by the defendants, the judge in the case, W. H. Watkins Jr., controversially handed out astoundingly light punishments. To explain his rationale for ruling that the guilty parties would receive only suspended sentences and parole, he noted how the court "understands and appreciates" that these crimes were to some extent caused by "unnecessary and unwanted ... outside influences" whose "presence has provoked a lot of people." His closing admonition to the Klan defendants clearly underscored the synergistic nature of the enforcement network aligned against civil rights forces:

Now what you have done is to hurt your white friends, your family, and your responsible friends, and it has been to hurt the law. You have placed the law enforcement officers in jeopardy .... You have caused riot, almost riot and civil commotion, and you have caused these officers to go out and expose themselves to dangers where they shouldn't be required to go. Now, *when the law is on your side* there's no use and there is no excuse whatever for you doing anything or any act that's contrary to the law, *you are both working for the same end, for the same goal, you and the law.* But you were not doing it the right way. You should have been cooperating with the law instead of placing your law enforcement officers in jeopardy and in a dangerous situation. We have Civil Defense, we need auxiliary officers to take care of these explosive situations when they arise .... I am sure if this situation gets bad enough the sheriff will need auxiliary deputies. Any number of situations might arise where the law enforcement officers need you. They sure don't need you to be combating them, to be fighting for them. (Gordon, 1964b; emphasis added)

5.6 CONFIGURING ENFORCEMENT: STATE-MOBILIZED MOVEMENTS IN COMPARATIVE RELIEF

Though McComb's configuration of state–civil connections differed from those in Clarksdale, these dual cases underscore both the clear alignment and coordination of actors within enforcement networks and the manner in which state support for civil efforts maps locally onto the contours of the civil rights challenge and perceived vulnerabilities within the Black community. Given the pronounced racialized patterns of economic dependence throughout the Delta, segregationist forces in Clarksdale benefited most from support imparted to Citizens' Councils and other economic pressure points to reinforce police action and sporadic violence. Correspondingly, organized vigilantism from the KKK or other militant bodies held less appeal, and these groups were relatively minor players in Clarksdale's enforcement network.

In contrast, support for the KKK, APWR, and residentially based civil efforts were central to the field of enforcement in McComb, with significant overlap between city and county officials and organized vigilantism. Such distinctions reflected both the differing character of local civil rights mobilization – with the NAACP's capacity for multi-pronged negotiation and action driving tactical exchanges between activists and Clarksdale's white power structure, and SNCC's grassroots organizing campaigns in McComb posing a more acute threat less easily addressed via official channels – and vulnerabilities rooted in localized political economies. Such contrasts underscore both the *constancy* of state efforts to enable and sustain contention rooted in broad countermobilization against challenges to Jim Crow and the logic of pronounced *variation* across local fields of enforcement within a state often treated as unitary in its resistance to civil rights challenges.

Emanating from dissimilar political-economic environments, such configurations also had distinct consequences. Clarksdale officials' predilection for proximate control of the city's Black population – rooted in long-standing paternalistic patterns – continued after federal legislation banned most forms of Jim Crow segregation in 1965. With the support of the MSSC, the city's white leadership quickly adopted a management orientation that allowed them to access and control various federal resources made available to support civil rights and racial equity programs. While white elites were clear that they were not in favor of such federal "Community Action" initiatives, they soon realized that biracial participation would provide a means to maintain control over associated resources. As a visiting MSSC agent put it, "unless they did take some hand in administering the affairs of the program, ... thousands and thousands of dollars would go down the drain by the bungling of incompetent

Negroes" (MSSC file # 2-62-2-35-1-1-1). Similarly, rather than abandoning public schools in the face of desegregation mandates later in the 1960s, the white-controlled School Board established a number of ostensibly nonracial criteria – including rigged residential zoning plans and biased standardized tests – that would in fact maintain strictly segregated schools (MSSC files # 2-62-2-48-1-1-1, 2-62-2-66-1-1-1). Such approaches were emblematic of Clarksdale's orientation to federal civil rights pressures, centered on the development of race-neutral policy to preserve the racist status quo.

In contrast, McComb's long-standing reliance on vigilantist violence came at the expense of strategic bridge-building that could have provided a basis for white city leaders to manage civil rights reform as in Clarksdale. MSSC collaboration toward these ends was entirely lacking, and the 1964 bombing campaign undercut McComb's efforts to attract industry and other capital to the city, diminishing the business community's ability to redefine segregation in softer terms in the name of civic "progress." Instead, white officials adopted a separatist model, "detaching" from its borders 350 acres of land that the city had annexed in 1961, a decision that served to remove the predominantly-Black population in those areas from the local political process (MSSC file # 2-36-2-110-1-1-1). And white families abandoned the city's public school system en masse, in many cases in favor of Parklane Academy, founded in 1970 as part of a campaign to establish private "seg" academies for white families seeking to circumvent the court-mandated desegregation of public schools (Andrews, 2002; McMillen, 1994).

Most generally, these divergent trajectories and the distinct enforcement configurations that laid the groundwork for Clarksdale and McComb's contentious resistance to civil rights challenges are instructive for considering how state-mobilized movements unfold in a democratic context. In the Civil Rights-era United States, such contention was reactionary and defensive in posture. It also was marshaled regionally and enacted locally, in opposition to federal pressures to expand the contours of democracy in the South by more fully incorporating and accommodating African Americans as citizens. As such, both the motive and form of such campaigns differ from those typically associated with authoritarian cases. Rather than a top-down effort to manufacture or otherwise support grassroots campaigns to enhance the legitimacy of a centralized state, such contention provides one outlet for furthering sectional disputes within a federalist system. We thus pay attention to the manner in which states like Mississippi mediate the federal and local, opening space for action in the latter free from intervention by the former. Thus, far from strengthening a centralized state, such processes serve to undermine coordinated state action and retain a degree of autonomy that can, as in Mississippi, run counter to the democratic values at the heart of the federalist system.

To interrogate how such nested processes operate, we have highlighted the broad institutional locus through which the state of Mississippi engaged contention in the face of federal challenges. During this period of heightened conflict over the nature of democratic governance, the scope and scale of state action expanded, to incorporate a range of state and civil actors. While this baseline character has been well documented, its trajectory often obscures the pronounced local variation in the composition of enforcement networks. The Clarksdale and McComb cases demonstrate how officials located within police departments, school boards, and City Council chambers did not operate equivalently across communities, nor was the presence and predominance of civil bodies such as Citizens' Councils or vigilantist KKK outfits given or constant. Instead, enforcement networks differed in their configuration, each possessing an identifiable logic determined in large part by the degree and form of vulnerability associated with local challengers. Our aim here has been to recognize that variation and to elucidate these logics, to provide a basis for better understanding how states maintain and extend their power, not only through direct demonstration but also by engaging governmental and civil sectors to prod the contours of contention toward their own interests and ends.

REFERENCES

Andrews, Kenneth T. 2002. Movement-countermovement dynamics and the emergence of new institutions: the Case of "white flight" schools in Mississippi. *Social Forces* 80: 911–936.

Andrews, Kenneth T. 2004. *Freedom Is a Constant Struggle*. Chicago, IL: University of Chicago Press.

Asch, Chris Myers. 2011. *The Senator and the Sharecropper: The Freedom Struggles of James O. Eastland and Fannie Lou Hamer*. Chapel Hill, NC: University of North Carolina Press.

Berrey, Stephen A. 2015. *The Jim Crow Routine: Everyday Performances of Race, Civil Rights, and Segregation in Mississippi*. Chapel Hill, NC: University of North Carolina Press.

Carson, Clayborne. 1981. *In Struggle: SNCC and the Black Awakening of the 1960s*. Cambridge, MA: Harvard University Press.

Carter, Hodding. 1965. *So the Heffners Left McComb*. New York: Doubleday.

Christian Science Monitor. 1964 (July 3). "McComb: 'Never' Mood Strong."

Crane, Tony, and Pete Young. 1968. *Voices from the White Ghetto*. Unpublished. Accessed through the Lyndon Baines Johnson Presidential Library, Record Group 283, Task Force I, Series 12 (2 of 2).

Crespino, Joseph. 2007. *In Search of Another Country: Mississippi and the Conservative Counterrevolution*. Princeton, NJ: Princeton University Press.

Cummings, Peter. 1964 (October 2). Three arrested For Miss. bombings; others suspected says police chief. *Harvard Crimson*.

Cunningham, David. 2004. *There's Something Happening Here: The New Left, the Klan, and FBI Counterintelligence*. Berkeley, CA: University of California Press.

Cunningham, David. 2013a. Shades of anti-civil rights violence: reconsidering the Ku Klux Klan in Mississippi. In Ted Ownby (ed.), *The Civil Rights Movement in Mississippi*. Oxford: University Press of Mississippi, pp. 180–203.

Cunningham, David. 2013b. *Klansville, USA: The Rise and Fall of the Civil Rights-Era Ku Klux Klan*. New York: Oxford University Press.

Cunningham, David, Geoff Ward, and Peter B. Owens. 2019. Configuring political repression: anti-civil rights enforcement in Mississippi. *Mobilization: An International Journal* 24 (3): 319–343.

Delta Democrat Times. 1964 (May 11). New racist organization terrorizes several south Mississippi counties.

Dirks, Annelieke. 2007. Between threat and reality: the National Association for the Advancement of Colored People and the emergence of armed self-defense in Clarksdale and Natchez, Mississippi, 1960–1965. *Journal for the Study of Radicalism* 1: 71–98.

Dittmer, J. 1995. *Local People: The Struggle for Civil Rights in Mississippi*. Urbana: University of Illinois Press.

Federal Bureau of Investigation. 1964. White Knights of the Ku Klux Klan of MS, https://archive.org/details/WKKKKOM/page/n47, accessed March 4, 2019.

Federal Bureau of Investigation. 1961. A statement from the Burglund High School students. Case File 157-JN-5, Demonstration of Negro High School Students in McComb, Mississippi, Volume 1, p. 28.

Fishman, Robert M. 1990. Rethinking state and regime: southern Europe's transition to democracy. *World Politics* 42 (3): 422–440.

Fligstein, Neil, and Doug McAdam. 2012. *A Theory of Fields*. New York: Oxford University Press.

Gordon, Charles B. 1964a (November 19). Court hears Pike sheriff. *McComb Enterprise-Journal*.

Gordon, Charles B. 1964b (October 28). Text of judge's sentence for bombers. *McComb Enterprise-Journal*.

Hamlin, Francoise N. 2012. *Crossroads at Clarksdale: The Black Freedom Struggle in the Mississippi Delta after World War II*. Chapel Hill, NC: University of North Carolina Press.

Hill, Lance. 2004. *The Deacons for Defense: Armed Resistance and the Civil Rights Movement*. Chapel Hill, NC: University of North Carolina Press.

Hughes, Everett C. 1964. Meeting of sociologists of the State of Mississippi, Tougaloo College, March 13–14, 1964. Unpublished notes, Everett Cherrington Hughes Papers, University of Chicago, Box 97, Folder 20.

Huie, William Bradford. 2000 [1965]. *Three Lives for Mississippi*. Oxford: University Press of Mississippi.

Irons, Jenny. 2006. Who rules the social control of protest? Variability in the state-countermovement relationship. *Mobilization* 11 (2): 165–180.

Irons, Jenny. 2010. *Reconstituting Whiteness: The Mississippi State Sovereignty Commission*. Nashville, TN: Vanderbilt University Press.

Key, V. O., Jr. 1984 [1949]. *Southern Politics in State and Nation*. Knoxville: University of Tennessee Press.

Library of Congress, Motion Picture, Broadcasting and Recorded Sound Division. n.d. The U.S. Commission on Civil Rights in Jackson, Mississippi. Exhibit on *The Civil Rights Act of 1964: A Long Struggle for Freedom*, www.loc.gov/exhibits/civil-rights-act/multimedia/commission-on-civil-rights.html, accessed December 22, 2016.

Luckett, Robert E., Jr. 2015. *Joe T. Patterson and the White South's Dilemma: Evolving Resistance to Black Advancement*. Jackson: University Press of Mississippi.

McAdam, Doug. 1988. *Freedom Summer*. New York: Oxford University Press.
McAdam, Doug. 1999. *Political Process and the Development of Black Insurgency, 1930–1970*. Chicago, IL: University of Chicago Press.
McComb Enterprise-Journal. 1964 (September 23). COFO blasts the E-J's bombing, riot account.
McMillen, Neil. 1989. *Dark Journey: Black Mississippians in the Age of Jim Crow*. Urbana: University of Illinois Press.
McMillen, Neil R. 1994 [1971]. *The Citizens' Council: Organized Resistance to the Second Reconstruction, 1954–64*. Urbana: University of Illinois Press.
Meyer, David S., and Debra Minkoff. 1996. Conceptualizing political opportunity. *Social Forces* 82 (4): 1457–1492.
Mississippi Bureau of Investigation. 1964. Unlawful use of explosives and conspiracy, Pike and Lincoln Counties, Mississippi. House Un-American Activities Committee Investigation of the Ku Klux Klan (accessed at the National Archives, April 13, 2012).
Mississippi Department of Archives and History. 1964. Governor Paul B. Johnson speaking at a meeting in McComb with chief of police, George Guy, Mayor Gordon Burt, Jr. and Sheriff Warren, September 19, 1964, www.mdah.ms.gov/arrec/digital_archives/vault/projects/ohtranscripts/au071_096107.pdf, accessed October 3, 2017.
Mississippi State Sovereignty Commission. Various dates and files, http://mdah.state.ms.us/arrec/digital_archives/sovcom/.
Mississippi State Sovereignty Commission. 1966 (December 6). Investigation report by L. E. Cole Jr., File # 2-36-2-69-1-1-1.
Morris, Aldon D. 1984. *The Origins of the Civil Rights Movement: Black Communities Organizing for Change*. New York: Free Press.
Murphree, Vanessa. 2006. *The Selling of Civil Rights: The Student Nonviolent Coordinating Committee and the Use of Public Relations*. New York: Routledge.
Murray, Pauli (ed.). 1997 [1950]. *States' Laws on Race and Color*. Athens: University of Georgia Press.
Payne, Charles M. 1995. *I've Got the Light of Freedom: The Organizing Tradition and the Mississippi Freedom Struggle*. Berkeley: University of California Press.
Pearson, Drew. 1964 (November 21). Lone Mississippi editor wins battle for moderation. *McComb Enterprise-Journal*.
Petersen, Nick, and Geoff Ward. 2015. The transmission of historical racial biolence: lynching, civil rights era terror, and contemporary interracial homicide. *Race and Justice* 5 (2): 114–143.
Radnitz, Scott. 2010. *Weapons of the Wealthy: Predatory Regimes and Elite-Led Protests in Central Asia*. Ithaca, NY: Cornell University Press.
Rolph, Stephanie B. 2018. *Resisting Equality: The Citizens' Council, 1954–1989*. Baton Rouge: Louisiana State University Press.
Spofford, Tim. 1988. *Lynch Street: The May 1970 Slayings at Jackson State College*. Kent, OH: Kent State University Press.
Tarrow, Sidney. 2011. *Power in Movement: Social Movements and Contentious Politics*. New York and Cambridge: Cambridge University Press.
Tyson, Timothy B. 2004. *Blood Done Sign My Name: A True Story*. New York: Crown.
UPI. 1961 (October 6). Mayor says King wrong. *Jackson Clarion-Ledger*.
US Commission on Civil Rights. 1965. *Hearings Held in Jackson, Miss., February 16–20, 1965*. Washington, DC: US Government Printing Office.

US House of Representatives, Committee on Un-American Activities. 1965. Violence 1964 – McComb, Miss. Accessed at the National Archives, May 15, 2009.
US House of Representatives, Committee on Un-American Activities. 1966. *Activities of Ku Klux Klan Organizations in the United States, Parts I–V*. Washington, DC: US Government Printing Office.
US House of Representatives, Committee on Un-American Activities. 1967. *The Present Day Ku Klux Klan Movement*. Washington, DC: US Government Printing Office.
Ward, Geoff. 2019. Racial violence archive. Online database, www.racialviolencearchive.com/, accessed March 7, 2019.
Watson, Bruce. 2010. *Freedom Summer: The Savage Season of 1964 That Made Mississippi Burn and Made America a Democracy*. New York: Penguin.
Wolin, Sheldon S. 2003. *Tocqueville between Two Worlds: The Making of a Political and Theoretical Life*. Princeton, NJ: Princeton University Press.
Wright, Amy Nathan. 2011. The 1968 Poor People's Campaign: Marks, Mississippi, and the mule train. In Emilye Crosby, ed., *Building Civil Rights History from the Ground Up: Local Struggles, a National Movement*. Athens: University of Georgia Press, pp. 110–143.
Zald, Mayer N., and Bert Useem. 1987. Movement and countermovement interaction: mobilization, tactics and state involvement. In Mayer N. Zald and John D. McCarthy (eds.), *Social Movements in an Organizational Society*, New Brunswick, NJ: Transaction Books, pp. 247–272.

6

Social Sources of Counterrevolution
State-Sponsored Contention during Revolutionary Episodes

Mark R. Beissinger

> While supporters of Viktor Yushchenko maintained their grip on the capital, Kiev, at the weekend, in the east of Ukraine the mood against the "orange revolution" hardened. Politicians and officials in the pro-Yanukovich east and south yesterday voted for a referendum on autonomy for a breakaway "South-East Republic" with its capital in Kharkov ... In Donetsk, the mining capital of the east, some 150,000 Yanukovich backers filled the central square on Saturday. The city's mayor ... branded the opposition a "nationalist junta," and the regional governor ... attacked the "extremists in Kiev" and demanded that Ukraine become a federal state with autonomy for the east. The mood of the crowd was angry and defensive.
>
> David Crouch, correspondent for *The Guardian*, reporting from Donetsk on November 29, 2004

6.1 INTRODUCTION

The Orange Revolution from November 21, 2004, through January 10, 2005, is widely considered one of the most spectacular displays of revolutionary protest on the European continent since the end of the Cold War. Over a two-week span, up to a million citizens turned out on Maidan, the main square of Kiev, in temperatures as cold as minus 12 degrees centigrade to demand the annulment of falsified elections and an end to the incumbent regime of Leonid Kuchma and his chosen successor, Viktor Yanukovych.[1] On November 23, Orange candidate Viktor Yushchenko was sworn in as president on Maidan in front of a large crowd of onlookers – even before the fraudulent electoral results

---

[1] In all somewhere between 4.9 and 6.7 million people are estimated to have participated in Orange Revolution protests in support of Viktor Yushchenko throughout Ukraine (Beissinger, 2013, 580). For detailed accounts, see Wilson (2005); Way (2005); Åslund and McFaul (2006); Bunce and Wolchik (2011).

declaring pro-incumbent candidate Viktor Yanukovych as winner were announced. There were several key turning points in the revolution: the defection of pro-Kuchma legislators in voting no-confidence in the Electoral Commission on November 27 (and later their dismissal of Yanukovych as prime minister on December 1); the abandoned effort on November 28 to use force to gain back control over the situation; and the remarkable display of independence on December 3 by members of the Ukrainian Supreme Court to invalidate the election, leading to new elections on December 26 in which Yushchenko won with 52 percent of the vote, resolving the situation of dual power in favor of the opposition.

But as the journalist account at the beginning of this chapter makes clear, the Orange Revolution did not consist only of protests aimed at overturning the Kuchma regime. There were also numerous pro-incumbent demonstrations organized by the Yanukovych campaign. Moreover, as the final vote on December 26 showed, a large portion of the Ukrainian population – 48 percent of the participating electorate – opposed the Orange Revolution, failing to vote for Yushchenko. As political processes, revolutions are much more complex than simplistic narratives about elites versus the masses make them out to be. This significant degree of opposition to the revolution was not reflected in mobilizations in support of Yanukovych, which were intermittent and mostly concentrated in the east and south of the country. The weakness of counterrevolutionary mobilization (despite the starkly divided preferences over revolution within society at large) needs to be considered an essential element of any robust explanation of why the opposition succeeded in the Orange Revolution.

This chapter addresses a serious lacuna in the literature on revolutions: the failure to attend to the role and character of civilian counterrevolutionary mobilization in revolutionary processes.[2] We know considerably more about the networks, identities, and organizational structures that sustain revolutionary mobilization than we do about the political and social sources of those who mobilize against revolution. Why do regimes facing revolutionary threats foster counterrevolutionary mass mobilizations as a tactic for undermining challenges rather than deal directly with challengers through their own bureaucratic or police agencies? When counterrevolution is examined, the tendency in much of the literature has been to treat individual participation as motivated primarily by material concerns (as a result of either cash payments, hierarchical authority, or threats to jobs) and subject to strong selective incentives from bureaucratic agencies and the police. But is this always true, and to what extent does counterrevolutionary mobilization also tap into autonomous sources of support within society? What makes for effective

---

[2] For exceptions, see Tilly (1964); Mayer (1971, 2000); Sutherland (1986); Gould (1995); Weyland (2016); Slater and Smith (2016).

counterrevolutionary mobilization (i.e. counterrevolutionary mobilization that successfully defends an incumbent regime)?

In this chapter I make four related arguments. First, though its role is often overlooked, counterrevolutionary mobilization has always been an integral part of revolutionary processes going back to the origins of modern revolution in the seventeenth and eighteenth centuries. Second, like social movement coalitions, there is a segmented character to counterrevolutionary mobilization consisting of both those mobilized through selective incentives and a more autonomous element that mobilizes in support of the status quo. This autonomous element is often motivated less by enthusiasm for the incumbent regime than by fear of the social forces represented by revolutionary movements and the potential consequences should they attain power. Third, these disparate hierarchical and autonomous constituencies are pieced together in an ad hoc manner by agents of the state in the context of revolutionary challenge, often with little integration across them. Counterrevolutionary mobilization tends to be "composite" rather than coalitional in character; whereas elements of a party or social movement coalition negotiate about their representation, their obligations, and the distribution of spoils (Riker, 1962; Laver and Schofield, 1998; Staggenborg, 2010), no such negotiation takes place among counterrevolutionaries, largely because they participate at the calling of the state and its agents and in support of existing authority. Finally, I argue that the ability of regimes to mobilize autonomous social forces and not rely simply on selective incentives is a critical part of what makes for effective counterrevolutionary mobilization. Particularly in an age in which revolutionary success has come to depend heavily on the power of numbers, effective civilian counterrevolutionary mobilization has also increasingly come to rely on generating numbers, and these can only be achieved by tapping into autonomous social and cultural cleavages. I illustrate these arguments through a variety of historical examples and through unusual survey data from the Orange Revolution.

6.2 THE ORIGINS AND PURPOSES OF CIVILIAN COUNTERREVOLUTIONARY MOBILIZATION

As the editors to this volume detail in their introductory chapter, State-Mobilized Movements serve multiple purposes. In times of hegemonic state dominance, states may sponsor mass mobilization to intimidate opponents (Atwal and Bacon, 2012), reinforce belief in the power of the state (Scott, 1990), aid implementation of policy or hold bureaucrats accountable (Heurlin, 2016), or demonstrate displeasure over the policies of other states (Weiss, 2013). But in unusual times of intensified challenge, the purposes of state-sponsored mobilization narrow considerably, growing increasingly defensive in character. Slater and Smith utilize the term counterrevolution to refer to "collective and reactive efforts to defend the status quo and its varied range of dominant elites against a credible threat to overturn them from below" (Slater and Smith, 2016, p. 1472). I define a revolution as a mass siege aimed at displacing an incumbent regime and substantially altering the political or social order.³ In this respect, counterrevolutionary mobilization is civilian mobilization aimed at countering a credible revolutionary threat. The obvious paradox of counterrevolutionary mobilization is that, while it is ostensibly civilian in composition, it enjoys the support, encouragement, close affiliation with, or direction from the regime that it seeks to defend. This raises the deeper question of why some regimes resort to counterrevolutionary mobilization at all in order to carry out repressive functions normally performed by the police or the military. It also raises questions about how independent counterrevolutionary mobilization ever is from the regime that launches it. In some cases counterrevolutionary mobilizations may be more encouraged than directly orchestrated, and counterrevolutionaries may be motivated less by support for the incumbent regime than by opposition to the social forces represented by revolutionary movements. All this creates ambiguities and tensions within counterrevolutionary mobilizations that merit deeper analysis.⁴

Civilian counterrevolutionary mobilization has been an integral part of modern revolution since its invention. In the so-called Glorious Revolution of 1688, for example, Irish Catholics and Scottish Highlander clans put up significant violent resistance to the new Williamite order, providing a social base for counterrevolutionary efforts aimed at restoring King James V to the throne (Pincus, 2009, pp. 267–277). Similarly, in the American Revolution (1775–1783) between 30,000 and 50,000 Loyalists fought on the side of the British, with up to 20 percent of the white population of the colonies openly supporting the Crown and with Loyalists participating in approximately three-quarters of the battles and skirmishes of the revolution (Brown, 1965, p. 249; Allen, 2010, pp. xix–xx). Loyalism in the American Revolution was a distinctly urban and coastal phenomenon. Its most significant social sources were officeholders and appointees of the Crown, wealthy landlords and owners of landed estates, merchants with strong British interests, urban professionals, recent immigrants from England and Scotland, ethnic and religious minorities who feared the implications of a power shift for their personal security, freed or

---

³ This definition bears similarity to Goodwin's (2001, p. 9) definition: "any and all instances in which a state or political regime is overthrown and thereby transformed by a popular movement in an irregular, extraconstitutional, and/or violent fashion."
⁴ Revolutionary regimes have at times institutionalized mobilization as a means of consolidating control or preventing revolutionary challenges from materializing – so that the divide between mobilization within and outside of periods of heightened contention may be less clear-cut than implied here. Administered mass organizations like the Basij in contemporary Iran – created as a mass movement by a revolutionary regime to defend the revolution against internal enemies and functioning as an arm of the regime for attacking the regime's opponents – illustrate how the line between revolution and counterrevolution can easily grow blurred. See Golkar (2015). On the Chinese case, see also Perry (2006).

runaway slaves hoping for British support against slavery, and Indian tribes opposed to farmers and settlers.[5] Still, as Brown (among others) has noted, "the British government was generally woefully negligent in rallying and making use of the Loyalists" (Brown, 1965, p. 251), and the weakness of Loyalist mobilization in support of the Crown is considered an important factor leading to British defeat.

In the French Revolution an anti-revolutionary majority in the countryside confronted a pro-revolutionary minority in cities – a gap that widened in particular as the new revolutionary regime moved against the power of the clergy and local aristocracy and imposed mass conscription on the population. The result was a civil war in the countryside, leading to mass repressions by republican armies. As Tilly noted, "Contrary to the old image of a unitary people welcoming the arrival of long-awaited reform, local histories of the revolution make clear that France's revolutionaries established their power through struggle, and frequently over stubborn popular resistance ... Counterrevolution occurred not where everyone opposed the revolution, but where irreconcilable differences divided well-defined blocs of supporters and opponents" (Tilly, 1989, p. 86).

French counterrevolution began as insurrectionary plots by aristocrats connected to the Crown who hoped to capitalize on support from foreign powers. It quickly came to encompass a variety of social actors drawn from the old regime's privileged orders – clergy, rural gentry, country squires, disgruntled army officers. In Sutherland's words, "[t]he combination of hurt pride, ancient loyalties, fear of disorder, loss of income, and the prospect of unemployment propelled many of these men into careers of conspiracy and exile" (Sutherland, 1986, p. 112). But counterrevolution also tapped into deeper societal cleavages in France. Religion was a major factor that mobilized large numbers against the revolution, splitting the third estate across class and occupational lines and pitting parishioners against supporters of the new regime. As Sutherland notes, one could find merchants, silk and textile workers, artisans, and peasants on both sides of the political divide depending on local economic conditions, the loyalties of local elites, and the contours of religious belief.[6] Nor was counterrevolution confined to a particular region of France (despite the notoriety of the uprising in the Vendée). As Tilly emphasizes, the urban/rural divide was one of the key cleavages separating revolutionary from counterrevolutionary – though again, activity varied according to local circumstances (Tilly, 1964).

Above all, counterrevolution in France was deeply decentralized and reactive, with units operating more or less autonomously and without central

---

[5] Calhoon, 1973, 431–435; Brown, 1965. Only in New York and New Jersey were farmers well-represented in Loyalist ranks.

[6] Sutherland, 1986, pp. 107–114. A similar point is made by Tilly (1964, pp. 323–325), who cites figures showing that a large portion of the participants in the Vendée were non-peasants.

coordination. Indeed, Arno Mayer distinguished between what he called the "composite and organized *counter*-revolution from the top and the spontaneous and irregular *anti*-revolution from the ground up" that characterized opposition to the French Revolution. As he noted, anti-revolution took the form of peasant revolts that materialized against measures introduced by the newly established urban revolutionary regime – but often remained unconnected with the elite-driven counterrevolution directed by agents of the old regime. Mayer argued that counterrevolution could only be effective if it were coordinated across localities and connected with this more autonomous anti-revolution from below (Mayer, 2000, pp. 7, 57). Throughout much of the nineteenth century this gap between elite-based and mass-based opposition to revolution remained. For instance, as Weyland has documented, in the Revolutions of 1848 the strategies of Prussian and Austrian monarchs for defeating revolutionary threats were oriented primarily toward isolation and repression of revolutionary elites rather than generating mass-based counterrevolutionary mobilization from below. He notes that "in a hierarchical society with a strong, coercion-wielding state, reactionaries' careful evaluations of the domestic opportunity structure were distinctly top-heavy, focused on middle and elite sectors more than the popular masses" (Weyland, 2016, p. 223).

Over time state agents began to learn new forms of mass mobilization as ways of thwarting revolution. In Paris in 1848, a novel twist on counterrevolution was introduced by the new revolutionary regime in order to prevent a second revolution: the use of organized paramilitaries recruited from the population. The Provisional Government brought to power through the revolutionary overthrow of Louis Phillippe in February 1848 was threatened by a second, more radical, insurrection in June led by the National Workshops and fueled in significant part by the new regime's tax and social policies. The force used to put down the June Uprising was a Mobile Guard – a paid, 20,000-person civilian militia organized by the Provisional Government. Ironically, it took a revolutionary government to invent the practice of using civilian paramilitaries for the purpose of countering revolutionary threats.

Marx claimed that these paramilitary groups consisted primarily of hired lumpenproletariat ("thieves and criminals of all kinds, living on the crumbs of society, people without definite trade, vagabonds") (Marx, 1978, p. 62). It was Marx who first gave voice to what we might call the "thuggish" theory of counterrevolutionary mobilization: the idea that civilians participating in counterrevolutionary efforts are paid criminals hired by the regime to beat heads. As we will see in the case of Ukraine, for a portion of the civilians participating in counterrevolutionary efforts, this may in fact hold true. However, there has always been a greater complexity to civilian-based counterrevolution. Research by Traugott uncovered that those recruited into the Mobile Guard in 1848 differed little in occupational background from the insurgents that they were charged with suppressing. They were not predominantly criminals but rather were disproportionately recruited from the same artisanal classes out of which revolutionaries emerged (though Mobile Guard members were younger than their revolutionary counterparts, suggesting greater economic vulnerability) (Traugott, 1980, 1985). Gould (1995) also observed a spatial and network dimension differentiating those who mobilized as revolutionaries and counterrevolutionaries in 1848, pointing to the key role played by personal networks in shaping counterrevolutionary recruitment.

By the early twentieth century, autocratic regimes had begun experimenting with still more coordinated models of civilian counterrevolutionary mobilization: the use of mass movements and parties. During the Revolution of 1905 in Russia, for instance, a series of counterrevolutionary mass movements burst onto the political scene, the most infamous of which was the Union of Russian People (URP) and its affiliate organization, the Black Hundred. These movements organized demonstrations, street fights, pogroms, assassinations, and vigilante actions aimed at defending tsarist autocracy, defeating revolutionary threats, and preserving aristocratic privilege and Russian ethnic dominance throughout the empire. While the leadership of the movement was drawn from the upper and middle classes, the rank-and-file were recruited largely from workers, peasants, shopkeepers, priests, and professionals, as well as criminals and the unemployed – exemplifying the composite character of modern counterrevolutionary movements. The police actively abetted the movement, even printing leaflets calling for pogroms in some instances. Langer (2007, pp. 77–79), describing the attractions for joining, states that motives were mixed:

Many undeniably believed in the organization's stated goals of fighting the revolutionaries and protecting the autocracy ... But there was more to URP recruitment than pure political conviction ... Some people clearly joined the organization thanks to the prospect of jobs, money-making opportunities, and power associated with membership in a movement that had the tsar's blessing ... Some rank-and-file members viewed the organization as a means to drum up customers for their businesses, even using their speeches during URP meetings as opportunities to hawk their wares ... [And some] members of the URP's various paramilitary groups exploited their positions to earn money through robberies and extortion schemes, particularly aimed at Jews ... The prospect of engaging in organized violence represented a final incentive for joining the URP.

At its height, the URP encompassed over 400,000 members. But once the threat of revolution receded, the organization declined – due in part to its leadership's habit of large-scale skimming from state subsidies. Nevertheless, the URP played an important role in the reconsolidation of tsarist authority over the empire and the rollback of political reforms in the wake of the 1905 Revolution.

There are a number of reasons why regimes countering revolutionary threats might be attracted to using civilian mobilization alongside or in place of their own police or military forces. For one thing, it can relieve pressure from the police or military. The cohesion of state institutions (and particularly the cohesion of those institutions called upon to carry out repression – the police and the army) is critical for the ability of regimes to survive revolutionary crises (Trotsky, 1932; Skocpol, 1979; Barany, 2016). Defections from the military or police are much more likely when they are in direct contact with opposition forces or repeatedly suffer casualties as a result of being deployed against crowds. For example, declining morale within the military and police as a result of their constant deployment to put down nationalist unrest was a key element in the refusal of many military and KGB officers to defend the Soviet regime at the time of its collapse in 1991 (Beissinger, 2002). Also, for a variety of reasons, the police or military may not be fully reliable or may have network connections with the revolutionary opposition. Revolutionaries have long advocated fraternization with the military and the police as a strategy for undermining the coherence of a regime's forces of order (Barany, 2016; Ketchley, 2014). For all these reasons, using civilians to carry out repressions can help a regime avoid elite defections from the military or the police.

Moreover, crowds can aid regime control over the streets by engaging in the kind of ruthless acts of violence against opposition protesters that the police or military may be reticent to adopt due to the restrictions of organizational discipline, divisions within a regime, or fear of public backlash. Street fights, pogroms, and acts of vigilantism against the opposition or its supporters are controversial and often difficult for the military or police to carry out, as they turn the military or police into a mob and can sharpen divisions within the regime. Using civilians to repress oppositions may also make it more difficult for the public to attribute blame for repression, lowering the chances of backlash mobilizations. Such calculations are not always correct. In the infamous Battle of the Camel in Tahrir Square on February 2, 2011, for instance, hired thugs armed with swords and cudgels riding camels and horses attacked revolutionary protesters. Others threw Molotov cocktails at protesters while police snipers shot from higher locations, killing and injuring hundreds. Broadcast live on Al-Jazeera and other media, the barbaric scenes of thugs attacking protesters with swords backfired, undermining whatever remained of the regime's domestic and international legitimacy and ultimately sealing its fate (Ketchley, 2014, p. 174).

Civilian counterrevolutionary mobilization can also demonstrate the continuing power of the regime to command popular resources, raising the perceived costs of elite defection. As Graeme Robertson has observed, "[m]aintaining the incumbent advantage ... depends to a significant extent on maintaining an air of invincibility or permanence, and convincing other potential leaders and elites that their best hopes for advancement lie in continuing to work together with the ruling group rather than organizing against it" (Robertson, 2009, p. 530). If sufficiently large, counterrevolutionary mobilization can demonstrate the limits of public support for revolution, undermining revolutionary claims to popular legitimacy. In the 2011 Pearl Revolution in Bahrain, after a week of large-scale demonstrations by predominantly Shiite protesters, the monarchy mobilized its own Sunni counterdemonstration of 120,000 on February 21, 2011 (billed by the government as the largest demonstration in Bahraini history) as a way of shoring up support (Bahrain Independent Commission of Inquiry, 2011, p. 96; Youssef, 2011). Of course, the flip side of this is that, if visibly small relative to revolutionary crowds, counterrevolutionary mobilizations can display a lack of public support for the regime and further undermine its legitimacy and coherence. Particularly in an age of television and social media, numbers matter in the politics of counterrevolution, for they relay signals about where popular sentiments lie.

Violent clashes between revolutionary and counterrevolutionary civilians can also be used to justify emergency rule and the imposition of political order, legitimating harsher and more systematic government repression. In its attempts to halt their drives to independence, for example, Moscow consciously precipitated a crisis in the Baltic republics in 1991 in order to pave the way for imposing martial law. In Lithuania this was done by mobilizing demonstrations by local Russians and Poles, who demanded the resignation of the Lithuanian government over price increases and tried to storm the parliament. In Latvia, after a series of mysterious bombings carried out by the Soviet army to make it appear as if the situation had gotten out of control, pro-Moscow organizations within the Russian-speaking community were directed to organize demonstrations and attempted to seize control over the parliament. Kremlin-controlled media portrayed the region as having slipped into chaos, and in both republics civilian National Salvation Committees were formed demanding that emergency rule be introduced (see Senn, 1995; Jundzis, 2009). In both instances, the strategy failed, largely because of weak commitment to Moscow within local Russian-speaking communities and the appearance of widespread civilian opposition to imposing martial law in Moscow (Beissinger, 2002).

Examples such as these reveal how more than simply selective incentives are at play in civilian counterrevolutionary mobilization. Certainly, civilian counterrevolutionary mobilization has typically relied on diffuse networks of local brokers tied to the regime who utilize their resources, authority, and connections to mobilize individuals in support of the regime. The nature of those brokered networks has changed tremendously over time. In contrast to the late eighteenth century, when local gentry and clerics fulfilled this role, today organizational settings such as government offices and factories have grown increasingly central to the politics of counterrevolution. Whereas village, local parish, and neighborhood networks were once critical to counterrevolutionary mobilizations, today sports clubs, organized criminal groups, and the workplace are more often sites for recruitment – particularly for the enlistment of muscle.

Social Sources of Counterrevolution 149

But counterrevolution capable of mobilizing significant numbers requires more than just selective incentives. Rather, a social base is needed to generate the commitment necessary to fuel large-scale counterrevolutionary participation. That social base might form for programmatic reasons (i.e. for belief in the issues championed by the incumbent regime). But it is often based in fear – and often in cultural difference. In pro-regime demonstrations during the Pearl Revolution, for instance, most of the participants were Sunni citizens frightened by the implications of Shia majority rule in a country in which Sunni constituted only 30 percent of the population. Similar use of minorities as a base for pro-regime mobilization occurred during the Soviet collapse. Cultural groups that have relied on a regime for favored treatment or safety are likely candidates to serve as bases of support for counterrevolution due to fear of the harm that successful revolution might do to their interests or the retribution that might accompany a shift in power.

Usually, some mix of incentivized and autonomous elements is pulled together by regime brokers in counterrevolutionary mobilization. While coordinated by businessmen close to the regime and members of Mubarak's government (including his son Gamal), participants in the Battle of the Camel in Egypt had a variety of motives for participation. Some were recruited by stable owners in the district of El-Haram (where the Great Pyramids are located), believing that the protests were taking a toll on their livelihood of tourism. Others were simply paid to participate. But there were also some who attacked protesters out of their personal belief (formed largely through pro-regime messages broadcast on state-run media) that the protesters represented "enemies of the nation" (Tarek, 2011). In short, most civilian counterrevolutionary mobilizations are composite in character, involving a mix of participation based on material incentives and societal divisions. The nature of the mix varies across cases. But as the cited examples suggest, those who are autonomously mobilized can be motivated more by fear of the power of the social forces represented in the revolutionary opposition than by loyalty to the incumbent regime per se.

6.3 COUNTERREVOLUTION IN THE ORANGE REVOLUTION: EVIDENCE FROM TWO SURVEYS

While we have a great deal of anecdotal information about civilian counterrevolutionary mobilization, we have generally lacked the kind of systematic data on who participates that would allow us to know much about the types of individuals mobilized and how they compare with others in society. Two highly unusual nationally representative surveys conducted during and after the Orange Revolution in Ukraine help remedy this gap.

The first is a nationally representative survey of 2,044 adults (aged eighteen or older) carried out by the Kyiv International Institute of Sociology (KIIS) on December 10–14, 2004 – in the immediate wake of the protests but prior to the

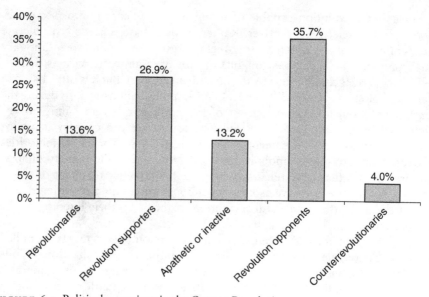

FIGURE 6.1 Political groupings in the Orange Revolution (KIIS survey)

third and final round of the presidential vote (i.e. in the midst of the revolutionary crisis and before its outcome was fully known). The survey asked respondents not only whether they had participated in demonstrations after the second round of voting but also for whom they intended to vote in the upcoming third round of the election, which was to take place on December 26, 2004.[7] Assuming that those who intended to vote for Yanukovych did not demonstrate for Yushchenko (and vice versa), in essence these questions allow one to identify five distinct groups with respect to the revolution (as depicted in Figure 6.1): 1) revolutionaries (those who intended to vote for Yushchenko in the third round of voting and who also participated in protests during the Orange Revolution – 13.6 percent of respondents); 2) revolution supporters (those who intended to vote for Yushchenko in the third round but did not participate in any demonstrations – 26.9 percent of respondents); 3) revolution opponents (those who intended to vote for pro-incumbent candidate Viktor Yanukovych or against all candidates in the third round but did not participate in protests – 35.7 percent of respondents); 4) counterrevolutionaries (those who participated in protest demonstrations but intended to vote for Yanukovych, against all candidates, or intended not to vote – 4.0 percent of respondents); and 5) the inactive or apathetic (those who did not participate in any protests

---

[7] This third round of voting was the clearest expression of whether an individual supported or did not support the Yushchenko candidacy. The first round included numerous other candidates, and the second round occurred prior to the onset of the revolutionary events.

and were undecided about their electoral preference – 18.6 percent of respondents).[8] Of course, given that the survey was taken prior to the third round of the presidential election, it may be a more accurate expression of who participated in the protests than of actual voting behavior (12.2 percent of the sample did not know at the time for whom they would vote or indicated no electoral preference). However, only 2.4 percent of those who said that they participated in protests during the revolution indicated that they did not know for whom they would vote in the upcoming election.

The KIIS survey was a bare-bones survey focused on voting and protest behavior during the revolution; it provides us with some basic demographics on voters and protesters and a few questions about attitudes toward the revolution. Its main advantage is that it occurred in the midst of the revolution and therefore is unlikely to suffer from problems of preference falsification, but it lacks the texture necessary to unpack civilian counterrevolutionary mobilization in much detail. A second survey taken in March 2005, only two months after the conclusion of the revolution, provides a more nuanced picture. The 2005 Monitoring survey was not designed specifically as a study of Orange Revolution participation. Monitoring surveys had been conducted by the Institute of Sociology of the Ukrainian Academy of Sciences every year since 1994 as a means for analyzing trends within Ukrainian society (Panina, 2005). The survey consisted of two parts: a battery of questions, repeated annually; and one-time questions designed to probe particular issues of the day.[9] In the 2005 Monitoring survey, a series of one-time questions was added on the 2004 Ukrainian presidential election and the Orange Revolution. Respondents were asked to identify the candidate for whom they voted in each of the three rounds of the 2004 presidential election and whether they had participated in any demonstrations during the Orange Revolution and in what manner. Again assuming that those who voted for Yanukovych did not demonstrate for Yushchenko (and vice versa), the questions allow one to identify five distinct groups with respect to the revolution (as depicted in Figure 6.2): 1) revolutionaries (those who reported voting for Yushchenko in the third round of the elections and reported participating in protests during the Orange Revolution – 18.6 percent of respondents); 2) revolution supporters (those who voted for Yushchenko in the third round but did not participate in any demonstrations – 36.3 percent of respondents); 3) revolution opponents (those who voted for pro-incumbent candidate Viktor Yanukovych or voted against all candidates in the third round but did not participate in protests – 31.5 percent of respondents); 4) counterrevolutionaries

---

[8] A small portion (0.9 percent) of the sample refused to answer the question of whether they or their relatives had participated in any demonstrations, and another 5.4 percent refused to answer the question about their electoral preference. These respondents were dropped from the analysis.
[9] The March 2005 Monitoring survey was based on a representative sample of 1,801 adult Ukrainians (eighteen years or older) using a combination of stratified, random, and quota sampling and was conducted March 2–30, 2005, in all provinces of Ukraine. For details on sampling procedures, see Panina (2005), pp. 17–18.

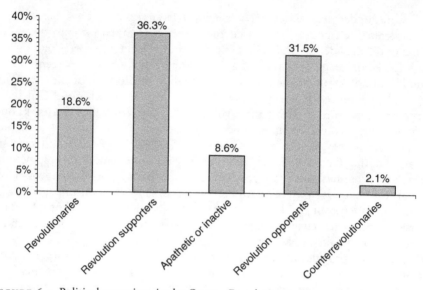

FIGURE 6.2 Political groupings in the Orange Revolution (Monitoring survey)

(those who participated in protest demonstrations but voted for Yanukovych, voted against all candidates, or willingly chose not vote – 2.0 percent of respondents); and 5) the inactive or apathetic (those who neither voted nor participated in any protests – 8.6 percent of respondents).[10]

The main advantage of the Monitoring survey over the KIIS survey is the level of detail about respondents that it provides. In all, the survey asked a total of 357 questions covering a wide variety of topics. In addition to questions about the respondent's age, gender, marital and family status, level of education, place of residence, religion, nationality, language use, and economic and material situation, the survey asked respondents about their attitudes toward privatization, Ukraine's geopolitical orientation, citizenship and language policy, and political institutions. It asked about respondents' political self-identification, participation in civil society associations, trust in other people and in institutions, evaluations of political leaders, interactions with the state over the previous twelve months, attitudes toward various nationalities, their biggest fears and what they desired more in their lives, health and drinking habits, height and weight, the size of their living space and how well it was

---

[10] A small portion (1.4 percent of the sample) refused to indicate whether they had voted in the presidential election or whether they had participated in any demonstrations. These respondents were dropped from the analysis. Another 1.7 percent was disqualified from voting and was also dropped from the analysis (Only two of these respondents indicated that they had participated in the Orange Revolution protests).

Social Sources of Counterrevolution

heated, how they spent their free time and what consumer goods they owned, thoughts of migration within Ukraine or abroad, access to the Internet and cell-phone ownership, and numerous other questions.

But there are obvious issues with using any retrospective survey of participation in a revolution. Attitudes and beliefs may be affected by the experience of revolution, and bandwagoning and preference falsification are inherent parts of the revolutionary process. The issues are magnified in particular for those on the losing side. The KIIS survey largely avoids these problems, given that it was taken in the middle of the revolution. Not surprisingly, the KIIS sample identified a larger number of counterrevolutionaries (4.0 percent of the sample, or eighty-two individuals) compared with the Monitoring sample (only 2.0 percent of the sample, or thirty-eight individuals). Clearly, one should feel more comfortable about findings based on the KIIS sample than the Monitoring sample, as generalizations based on a sample of only thirty-eight individuals are suspect. Given these trade-offs, my strategy is to compare the results of the two samples, see if they demonstrate similar patterns in those areas in which they overlap, and only then look to the broader range of questions represented in the Monitoring survey.

If one were to project the results of both surveys on Ukraine's adult population of 36 million, they would indicate that somewhere between 700,000 and 1.4 million people participated in counterrevolutionary protests in support of Yanukovych and the incumbent regime across various parts of Ukraine. That represents a fairly robust level of counterrevolutionary mobilization, even though it was only a fraction of the revolutionary mobilization against which it was oriented. Both surveys show, however, that while more Ukrainians supported the revolution than opposed it, Ukrainian society was much more closely divided over regime-change than the differences in turnout between revolutionaries and counterrevolutionaries suggested. The official electoral results of the third round of voting indicated that Yushchenko supporters outnumbered Yushchenko opponents on the order of about 6 to 5; the Monitoring survey records a margin of 8 to 5, while the KIIS survey showed a narrow margin of 11 to 10 among likely voters. Nevertheless, protest mobilization among revolution supporters far outnumbered mobilization by revolution opponents (by a factor of almost 9 to 1 in the Monitoring survey and in the KIIS survey by a factor of almost 4 to 1). According to the KIIS survey, 51 percent of Yushchenko voters who did not participate in protests themselves knew someone (a friend, relative, or acquaintance) who participated in a protest during the revolution; by contrast, only 18 percent of Yanukovych voters who did not participate themselves knew someone who participated. Thus, even in successful revolutions like the Orange Revolution (i.e. revolutions in which the opposition is able to attain power), preferences toward the incumbent regime are usually much more deeply divided than visible patterns of collective action suggest. Furthermore, the outcomes of successful revolutions may be due as much to the relative passivity of potential regime supporters as to the effective mobilization of regime opponents.

6.4 SOCIAL SOURCES OF UKRAINIAN COUNTERREVOLUTION

What do the two samples tell us about the nature of counterrevolutionary mobilization? Table 6.1 shows a number of demographic features of counterrevolutionary participants across the two samples, placing them into comparative perspective relative to the Ukrainian population as a whole, to the Yanukovych supporters from which they were recruited, and to the Orange revolutionaries against whom they mobilized. A number of interesting patterns stand out. For one thing, in terms of gender, both samples show that counterrevolutionaries were more male than the Ukrainian population or Yanukovych voters as a whole, though the differences are more apparent in the Monitoring sample than in the KIIS sample (where gender differences are not statistically significant). In terms of age, both surveys show that counterrevolutionaries tended to be older and more middle-aged than revolutionaries but nevertheless younger than either the Ukrainian population or Yanukovych voters as a whole (the differences are statistically significant in the larger KIIS sample). Surprisingly, according to the KIIS survey, 31 percent of counterrevolutionaries had a higher education – considerably more than Yanukovych voters as a whole (14 percent) and about the same level as those who participated in the pro-Yushchenko protests in Orange Revolution (33 percent).[11] Similar patterns appear in the smaller but less reliable Monitoring survey. Thus, the notion that counterrevolutionaries were uneducated or consisted only of "thugs" is clearly contradicted by the surveys. Rather, both revolutionaries and counterrevolutionaries consisted disproportionately of those with higher education. Given that education is often associated with the cognitive skills necessary for mobilization (Inglehart, 1990) and that, in most societies, the educated participate disproportionately in protest, the fact that education is associated with participation in both revolution and counterrevolution makes sense, though it defies stereotypes.

At the same time, it is also clear from the surveys that there were multiple dimensions – programmatic, cultural, and clientelistic – to the recruitment of Orange Revolution counterrevolutionaries. For example, in the KIIS survey 42 percent of counterrevolutionaries (as opposed to only 11 percent of Yanukovych voters as a whole) fully agreed with the statement that it was necessary to protest in order to defend their vote for president. Indeed, counterrevolutionaries were much more committed to Yanukovych as a candidate than Yanukovych voters more generally. When asked in the KIIS

---

[11] Even controlling for gender, age, and nationality, counterrevolutionaries were more than twice as likely as either Yanukovych supporters or the Ukrainian population as a whole to have had a higher education.

TABLE 6.1 *The demography of counterrevolution in Ukraine, 2004*

	KIIS Survey (December 2004)				Monitoring Survey (March 2005)			
	Sample as a whole	Counter revolutionaries	Yanukovych supporters	Orange revolutionaries	Sample as a whole	Counter revolutionaries	Yanukovych supporters	Orange revolutionaries
n	2,044	82	729	277	1,800	38	567	335
Male	44.7%	45.7%	42.6%	48.4%	44.3%	63.2%	41.3%	54.3%
Ages 35 or younger	31.1%	34.2%	28.3	41.9%	33.8%	39.5%	33.0%	42.4%
Ages 36–55	36.4%	42.7%	33.5%	44.0%	36.8%	34.2%	34.2%	37.3%
Ages 56 or older	32.5%	23.2%	38.3%	14.1%	29.4%	26.3%	32.8%	20.3%
Median age	46	44	49	39	45	40.5	47	40
Higher education	18.7%	30.5%	14.1%	33.2%	11.2%	15.8%	9.5%	16.1%
Russian nationality	17.5%	35.4%	30.7%	4.7%	17.4%	34.2%	31.5%	3.9%
Claims Russian as native language	26.4%	59.2%	45.1%	7.4%	–	–	–	–
Speaks only Russian at home	–	–	–	–	36.4%	65.8%	64.3%	10.2%
Donetsk province	10.7%	58.5%	20.6%	0.4%	10.4%	36.8%	24.3%	0%
Other Eastern provinces	11.6%	18.3%	22.1%	1.8%	11.9%	18.4%	23.1%	3.3%
Southern provinces	26.5%	17.1%	39.9%	8.7%	26.8%	7.9%	39.0%	6.3%

survey for whom they would vote if Yanukovych dropped out of the race, 77 percent of counterrevolutionaries indicated that they would vote against all the other candidates or not vote at all, as opposed to only 58 percent of Yanukovych voters as a whole.[12] In addition to being more educated than Yanukovych voters or the Ukrainian population, for the most part counterrevolutionaries were not one-time activists; 51 percent indicated that they had participated in earlier political meetings or demonstrations during the past twelve months (as opposed to 14 percent of the Ukrainian population and only 2 percent of Yanukovych voters as a whole). In fact, counterrevolutionaries were about as politically active in the year leading up to the revolution as were revolutionaries participating in pro-Yushchenko protests – 68 percent of whom had participated in political meetings or demonstrations during the previous year. Counterrevolutionaries also had clearer opinions on a number of public policy issues relative to other groupings. They were more likely to say that they supported socialism over capitalism (47 percent) compared to either Yanukovych supporters (30 percent) or the Ukrainian population as a whole (25 percent), more likely to oppose the privatization of land (71 percent) compared to Yanukovych supporters (55 percent) or the Ukrainian population as a whole (57 percent), and more likely to identify themselves as communists (21 percent) than either Yanukovych supporters (13 percent) or the Ukrainian population as a whole (7 percent).[13] Again, this hardly fits the image of a politically apathetic mass manipulated by selective incentives and points to at least an element of counterrevolutionary mobilization bearing a programmatic character.

At the same time, the KIIS and the Monitoring surveys provide some highly suggestive evidence of a patronage basis among a significant number of counterrevolutionaries. According to the KIIS survey, 59 percent of counterrevolutionaries came from a single province: Donetsk. Donetsk province is Yanukovych's home base, where he was born, where he built his political career, and where he received the second-highest level of electoral support (after neighboring Luhansk province).[14] By contrast, only 21 percent of Yanukovych voters as a whole came from Donetsk province.[15] The Monitoring data provide additional insights into the personalities and lifestyles of counterrevolutionaries that suggest that selective incentives may have played an important role in mobilizing substantial portion of counterrevolutionaries. Thus, controlling for gender and age (and holding their effects constant at their means), there was a .42 probability that

---

[12] These differences are statistically significant at the .05 level.
[13] All these differences are statistically significant at the .05 level or better.
[14] Indeed, 71 percent of counterrevolutionaries came from the Donbas provinces of Donetsk and Luhansk (with another 9 percent from Crimea and 5 percent from Kharkiv). In short, counter-revolutionaries were almost entirely recruited from four out of Ukraine's twenty-five provinces.
[15] The difference is statistically significant at the .001 level.

a counterrevolutionary had exercised in the last seven days (as opposed to .22 for other Yanukovych voters, and .17 for all others in Ukrainian society). There was also a .16 probability that counterrevolutionaries had visited a lawyer sometime in the last twelve months (compared to only .05 for other Yanukovych voters and .05 for all others), a .18 probability that they had experienced a crime (robbery, attack, theft, or swindle) in the last twelve months (compared to .08 for other Yanukovych supporters and .08 for all others),[16] and a .26 probability that they believed the militia and state security played an important role in the life of Ukrainian society (compared to .13 for other revolution opponents and .12 for all others – even though no counterrevolutionaries reported being a police employee). Moreover, controlling for gender and age, there was a .80 probability that counterrevolutionaries were dissatisfied with the amenities and sanitary conditions of their home (as opposed to .64 for other Yanukovych voters and .39 for all others).[17] Surprisingly, controlling for gender and age, there also was a .31 probability that counterrevolutionaries belonged to some civil society association (versus .17 for other revolution opponents and .16 for others).[18] As it turned out, most of these groups were sports clubs and professional associations. They also drank alcohol more regularly than other Yanukovych supporters and the rest of the Ukrainian population.[19] Counterrevolutionaries were significantly more likely to say that they were in good health, to believe that people are fundamentally dishonest, to lack trust in religious authority, and to believe themselves to be decisive than Yanukovych supporters as a whole or the rest of Ukrainian society. In short, a significant portion of counterrevolutionaries fit the profile one would expect from the thuggish theory of counterrevolution; they were more physically fit (disproportionately belonging to sports clubs), more likely to have had run-ins with the law and legal institutions, and more likely to be dissatisfied with their material situation than either other Yanukovych voters or the rest of the Ukrainian population.

At the same time, there were also significant cultural differences between counterrevolutionaries and the rest of the Ukrainian population. In all, 35 percent of counterrevolutionaries were ethnic Russians (compared to 31 percent of Yanukovych supporters more generally but only 17 percent of the rest of the Ukrainian population and 5 percent of pro-Yushchenko Orange Revolution participants). Only 7 percent of counterrevolutionaries considered

---

[16] Ironically, though they claimed more frequently to be victims of crime, they were also less likely than other revolution opponents or the rest of Ukrainian society to agree that organized crime and criminals played an important role in Ukrainian life.
[17] For instance, counterrevolutionaries were less likely to own a refrigerator or a washing machine than Yanukovych voters more generally.
[18] All differences were statistically significant at the .001 level.
[19] Thus, 63 percent reported drinking several times a month or more frequently, as opposed to only 45 percent of other Yanukovych supporters and 47 percent of the rest of Ukrainian society. These differences were statistically significant at the .05 level or better.

Ukrainian their native language (as opposed to 23 percent of Yanukovych supporters as a whole, 65 percent of the rest of the population, and 83 percent of pro-Yushchenko Orange Revolution participants). Controlling for age and gender, counterrevolutionaries were much less likely to consider Ukraine their motherland (a .68 probability) compared to other Yanukovych voters as a whole (.84) or the rest of the Ukrainian population (.95). And controlling for nationality, counterrevolutionaries were more likely to claim that they had encountered discrimination against Russians over the previous year (a .21 probability) than either other Yanukovych voters as a whole (.09) or the rest of Ukrainian society (.03).[20] In short, given these attitudes, it seems likely that, for some counterrevolutionaries, fears of what a change in power might mean for Russians and Russian-speakers fueled their activism – a pattern evident in many other counterrevolutionary mobilizations over the last two centuries.

6.5 THE COMPOSITE CHARACTER OF UKRAINIAN COUNTERREVOLUTION

To examine further the composite nature of counterrevolutionary mobilization in the Orange Revolution, I performed a latent class cluster analysis on the KIIS sample of counterrevolutionaries. Latent class cluster analysis is a finite mixture approach used to identify groupings of individuals who share similar interests, values, characteristics, or behaviors. Individuals are classified into clusters based on the probabilities of their membership, which (unlike traditional k-means cluster analysis) are estimated directly from the model. Moreover, unlike traditional k-means clustering, latent class cluster variables can be continuous, nominal, or ordinal.[21] My expectation was to find that the social sources of counterrevolution in the Orange Revolution clustered into a few key groupings that were also associated with different attitudes and relationships to the incumbent regime.

Although the Monitoring sample provided a richer array of potential clustering variables, the small sample size (n=38) inhibited any credible attempt at clustering. The KIIS sample, by contrast, contained a limited number of variables but a sample size of counterrevolutionaries (n=82) large enough to have some confidence in the results. My strategy was to identify clusters of counterrevolutionaries in the KIIS sample according to the region from which they hailed and self-ascribed cultural characteristics (specifically, ethnicity and language use) and then to test to see whether these clusters corresponded with different attitudinal orientations to the extent that these were measured in the KIIS survey. Luckily, there were several questions in the KIIS survey asking respondents about their attitudes toward current events that

---

[20] These findings are statistically significant to at least the .05 level or better.
[21] See Vermunt and Magidson (2002). Latent Gold 4.5.0 was used to perform the analyses.

allow us to test whether clusters of counterrevolutionaries differed in more than just a demographic sense. Respondents were asked, for example, why they thought people were protesting (respondents could choose up to two reasons from a set list); whether they believed that electoral fraud had taken place in the second round of presidential voting and whether Yanukovych should be considered the legitimate president; and whether they supported preserving public order at any price (this latter question in essence measured a respondent's willingness to support a violent crackdown against Orange revolution participants). For the question on why people were protesting, two of the responses frequently chosen by Orange revolutionaries received practically no support from counterrevolutionaries: that people were protesting because of electoral fraud; and that people were protesting in support of Viktor Yushchenko. Rather, counterrevolutionaries believed that people were protesting either because they were paid money to do so (35 percent), because they supported Viktor Yanukovych (23 percent), to express their attitudes toward the authorities (12 percent), or to support a just democratic society (12 percent). While we cannot be certain, these answers seemed to imply that respondents were describing their own motivations for participation rather than the motivations of other groupings, though, given the way the question is worded, one cannot be certain. I used the answers to these questions to test whether counterrevolutionaries were divided in their opinions about the revolution and, if so, whether these divisions corresponded with specific demographic clusters.

An initial 5-variable model based on a combination of region, ethnicity, and language performed a reasonable job fitting the data into clusters, producing an R-square value of .93.[22] I used the Bayesian Information Criterion (BIC) to adjudicate between models with different numbers of clusters (Fonseca, 2008; Andrews and Currim, 2003), with the lowest BIC (439.03) suggesting a three-cluster model over the two-cluster or four-cluster alternatives. I have labeled the three clusters: 1) the "Donbas Russian-language-only" contingent (comprising 50 percent of counterrevolutionaries); 2) the "Donbas dual-language" contingent (comprising 30 percent of counterrevolutionaries); and 3) the "Southern" contingent (comprising 20 percent of counterrevolutionaries).[23] Not

---

[22] The bootstrapped p-value of L-squared (.526) and the dissimilarity index (.84) also suggest a reasonable fit. See Vermunt and Magidson (2002). All of the five variables included in the model were statistically significant at the .05 level, with the exception of the dummy variable for southern regions, which was statistically significant at the .10 level. Out of the eighty-two counterrevolutionaries in the KIIS sample, there were four counterrevolutionaries who came from central Ukraine, and four who came from Kharkov province – groups that were too small to constitute separate clusters but that nevertheless weakened the statistical significance of the southern dummy.

[23] Southern provinces in this analysis consist of Crimea, Dnipro, Zaporizhia, Mikolaiv, Odesa, and Kherson. Half of Southern counterrevolutionaries came from Crimea. As the profile plot

unexpectedly, these also happened to be the regions that, a decade later in the wake of the Euromaidan Revolution, seceded from Ukraine. The fact that in 2004 counterrevolutionaries also attempted to create a separate republic (though without the support of the Russian state at the time) not only speaks to the deeper cultural divisions underpinning Ukrainian counterrevolution but also suggests the existence of particular scripts of counterrevolution that were repeatedly relied upon in acting out counterrevolution. The Russian-language-only contingent of counterrevolutionaries from the Donbas and the counterrevolutionaries from the south included among them a large number of ethnic Russians, though the southern contingent was the most diverse of the three clusters in terms of language usage. As this breakdown suggests, one of the reasons for the failure of counterrevolution during the Orange Revolution was its limited regional reach: the regime was simply unable to mobilize large numbers outside the Donbas region. In 2014 the regional distribution of counterrevolutionary mobilization was similarly limited, but external Russian state support for separation substituted for this limited regional reach.

As can be seen in Figure 6.3, the two Donbas clusters of counterrevolutionaries demonstrated some sharply different attitudes toward the ongoing events in the Orange Revolution compared to the Southern cluster. When asked why people were protesting in the revolution, Donbas counterrevolutionaries, irrespective of whether they spoke Russian only or had dual-language capability, overwhelmingly replied that they were protesting in order to support Yanukovych, while Southern counterrevolutionaries disproportionately responded that people were protesting in order to defend the values of a just democratic society (though they were also slightly more likely than the Russian-speaking Donbas contingent to indicate that people were protesting because they were paid money). The two Donbas clusters refused to recognize that any electoral fraud had occurred in the second round of the presidential vote and believed that Yanukovych was the legitimate president of Ukraine. By contrast, the Southern counterrevolutionaries by and large did not support this position. The Donbas clusters also were much more supportive of preserving public order at any cost (i.e. supporting a crackdown against revolutionaries) than were the Southern counterrevolutionaries. In short, as one might expect, counterrevolutionaries from the Donbas, where local patronage ties were more evident, were overwhelmingly committed to Yanukovych personally and were willing to accept a violent crackdown against opponents in order to ensure his power, whereas the bases for Southern counterrevolution were more diverse, more policy-driven, and less committed to Yanukovych personally.

indicates, 80 percent of the Southern cluster came from southern Ukrainian provinces; the remainder consisted of the scattered counterrevolutionaries located elsewhere in Ukraine outside the Donbas.

Social Sources of Counterrevolution

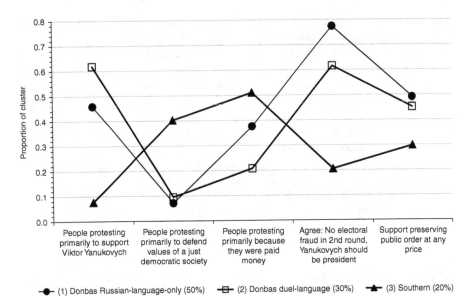

FIGURE 6.3 Attitudinal profile plot for three clusters of counterrevolutionaries in the Orange Revolution

6.6 CONCLUSION

As we have seen, civilian counterrevolutionary mobilization is an integral part of revolutionary processes and has been since the invention of modern revolution in the seventeenth century. It has served a variety of purposes. It can demonstrate the continuing power of an incumbent regime to control institutions and command popular support, raising the costs of defection. It can be used as a tool of repression in place of the police or the military, thereby preserving the morale of the regime's institutions of order, masking responsibility for repression, providing an avenue for more ruthless violence, and justifying a deeper crackdown through the imposition of a state of emergency. And it can visibly demonstrate the degree of popular support for the incumbent regime within society, undermining revolutionary claims to popular legitimacy.

Counterrevolutionary mobilization has evolved over time much as revolution itself has evolved. It has become much more integrated into the state and into bureaucratic institutions, more urban and less rural, and (as was evident during the Orange Revolution) more educated. But certain features of counterrevolution seem to persist. Counterrevolutionary mobilization has tended to be composite, consisting of a variety of societal segments who are pulled together on an ad hoc basis by state agents (usually, local brokers) and are mobilized along programmatic, cultural, and patronage lines. It often remains relatively decentralized and not well integrated across localities. Selective incentives usually play some important role, especially in recruiting muscle. But larger and more persistent counterrevolutionary mobilizations require tapping into deeper societal cleavages that can provide a basis for more autonomous mobilization. Clearly, those privileged under an incumbent regime or who share its ideology have particular reason to mobilize in its support. But we have also seen repeatedly that counterrevolutionary mobilizations often tap regional, sectoral, or cultural groups who fear the consequences that a shift of power resulting from revolutionary change might have for their safety and position in society. Such divisions serve as a more reliable base of support for counterrevolution than selective incentives, for they render defection more difficult.

As we have seen, societies experiencing revolutions are much more deeply divided over the fate of the incumbent regime than revolutionary narratives typically admit. Nevertheless, much counterrevolutionary mobilization fails in its purpose of regime defense, in large part because it is limited in scope, reach, and commitment. Such was the case, for instance, in the Orange Revolution, in which counterrevolutionary mobilization was predominantly confined to the Donbas region, relied significantly on patronage relations for mobilization, and had difficulty projecting itself outside of Yanukovych's home base. Part of the explanation for the success of the Orange Revolution in capturing power was the weakness of the counterrevolutionary forces that it encountered. In this sense, successful revolution involves not merely the effective mobilization of regime opponents but the relative passivity and demobilization of regime supporters as well.

REFERENCES

Allen, Thomas B. 2010. *Tories: Fighting for the King in America's First Civil War*. New York: Harper.

Andrews, Rick L., and Imran S. Currim. 2003. Retention of latent segments in regression based marketing models. *International Journal of Research in Marketing* 20 (4): 315–321.

Åslund, Anders, and Michael McFaul (eds.). 2006. *Revolution in Orange: The Origins of Ukraine's Democratic Breakthrough*. Washington, DC: Carnegie Endowment for International Peace.

Atwal, M., and Edwin Bacon. 2012. The youth movement Nashi: contentious politics, civil society, and party politics. *East European Politics* 28 (3): 256–266.

Bahrain Independent Commission of Inquiry. 2011. Report of the Bahrain Independent Commission of Inquiry, December 10, 2011. Manama, Bahrain. http://files.bici.org.bh/BICIreportEN.pdf.

Barany, Zoltan. 2016. *How Armies Respond to Revolutions and Why*. Princeton, NJ: Princeton University Press.

Beissinger, Mark R. 2002. *Nationalist Mobilization and the Collapse of the Soviet State*. Cambridge: Cambridge University Press.

Beissinger, Mark R. 2013. The semblance of democratic revolution: coalitions in Ukraine's Orange Revolution. *American Political Science Review* 107 (3): 574–592.

Brown, Wallace. 1965. *The King's Friends: The Composition and Motives of the American Loyalist Claimants*. Providence, RI: Brown University Press.

Bunce, Valerie J., and Sharon L. Wolchik. 2011. *Defeating Authoritarian Leaders in Postcommunist Countries*. Cambridge: Cambridge University Press.

Calhoon, R. M. 1973. *The Loyalists in Revolutionary America, 1760–1781*. New York: Harcourt Brace Jovanovich.

Crouch, David. 2004. East Ukraine threatens autonomy. *The Guardian*, November 29. www.theguardian.com/world/2004/nov/29/ukraine.

Fonseca, Jaime R. S. 2008. The application of mixture modeling and information criteria for discovering patterns of coronary heart disease. *Journal of Applied Quantitative Methods* 3 (4): 292–303.

Golkar, Saeid. 2015. *Captive Society: The Basij Militia and Social Control in Iran*. Washington, DC: Woodrow Wilson Center Press.

Goodwin, Jeff. 2001. *No Other Way Out: States and Revolutionary Movements, 1945–1991*. Cambridge: Cambridge University Press.

Gould, Roger V. 1995. *Insurgent Identities: Class, Community, and Protest in Paris from 1848 to the Commune*. Chicago, IL: University of Chicago Press.

Heurlin, Christopher. 2016. *Responsive Authoritarianism in China*. Cambridge: Cambridge University Press.

Inglehart, Ronald. 1990. Values, ideology and cognitive mobilization in new social movements. In Russell J. Dalton and Manfred Kuechler (eds.), *Challenging the Political Order: New Social and Political Movements in Western Democracies*. Cambridge, MA: Polity Press, pp. 43–66.

Jundzis, Tālavs. 2009. The role of non-violent resistance in the struggle to achieve full independence (4 May 1990–21 August 1991). In Valdis Blūzma, Tālavs Jundzis, Jānis Riekstiņš, Gene Sharp, and Heinrihs Strods (eds.), *Regaining Independence: Non-Violent Resistance in Latvia, 1945–1991*. Riga, Latvia: Latvian Academy of Sciences: 532–598.

Ketchley, Neil. 2014. "The army and the people are one hand!" Fraternization and the 25th January Egyptian Revolution. *Comparative Studies in Society and History* 56 (1): 155–186.

Langer, Jacob. 2007. Corruption and the counterrevolution: the rise and fall of the Black Hundred. Ph.D. Dissertation, Department of History, Duke University, http://dukespace.lib.duke.edu/dspace/bitstream/handle/10161/438/D_Langer_Jacob_a_200712.pdf?sequence=1.

Laver, Michael, and Norman Schofield. 1998. *Multiparty Government: The Politics of Coalition in Europe*. Ann Arbor: University of Michigan Press.

Marx, Karl, 1978. The class struggles in France: 1848 to 1850. In Karl Marx and Frederick Engels, *Collected Works*, vol. 10. New York: International Publishers, pp. 45–145.

Mayer, Arno J. 1971. *Dynamics of Counterrevolution in Europe, 1870–1956: An Analytic Framework*. New York: Harper and Row.

Mayer, Arno J. 2000. *The Furies: Violence and Terror in the French and Russian Revolutions.* Princeton, NJ: Princeton University Press.

Panina, Natalya. 2005. *Ukrainian Society 1994–2005: Sociological Monitoring.* Kiev: International Center for Policy Studies.

Perry, Elizabeth J. 2006. *Patrolling the Revolution: Worker Militias, Citizenship, and the Modern Chinese State.* Lanham, MD: Rowman & Littlefield.

Pincus, Steven. 2009. *1688: The First Modern Revolution.* New Haven, CT: Yale University Press.

Riker, William H. 1962. *The Theory of Political Coalitions.* New Haven, CT: Yale University Press.

Robertson, Graeme B. 2009. Managing society: protest, civil society, and regime in Putin's Russia. *Slavic Review* 68 (3): 528–547.

Scott, James C. 1990. *Domination and the Arts of Resistance: Hidden Transcripts.* New Haven, CT: Yale University Press.

Senn, Alfred Erich. 1995. *Gorbachev's Failure in Lithuania.* New York: St. Martin's Press.

Skocpol, Theda. 1979. *States and Social Revolutions: A Comparative Analysis of France, Russia, and China.* Cambridge: Cambridge University Press.

Slater, Dan, and Nicholas Rush Smith. 2016. "The power of counterrevolution: elitist origins of political order in postcolonial Asia and Africa 1." *American Journal of Sociology* 121 (5): 1472–1516.

Staggenborg, Suzanne. 2010. Conclusion: research on social movement coalitions. In Nella Van Dyke and Holly J. McCammon (eds.), *Strategic Alliances: Coalition Building and Social Movements.* Minneapolis: University of Minnesota Press, pp. 316–330.

Sutherland, D. M. G. 1986. *France 1789–1815: Revolution and Counterrevolution.* Oxford: Oxford University Press.

Tarek, Sharif. 2011. Bosses, enforcers and thugs in Egypt's Battle of the Camel to see harsh retribution. *Ahramonline,* April 19. http://english.ahram.org.eg/NewsContent/1/64/10293/Egypt/Politics-/Bosses,-enforcers-and-thugs-in-Egypts-Battle-of-th.aspx.

Tilly, Charles. 1989. State and counterrevolution in France. *Social Research* 56 (1): 71–97.

Tilly, Charles. 1964. *The Vendée.* Cambridge, MA: Harvard University Press.

Traugott, Mark. 1980. Determinants of political orientation: class and organization in the Parisian Insurrection of June 1848. *American Journal of Sociology* 86 (1): 32–49.

Traugott, Mark. 1985. *Armies of the Poor: Determinants of Working-Class Participation in the Parisian Insurrection of June 1848.* New Brunswick, NJ: Transaction Publishers.

Trotsky, Leon. 1932. *The History of the Russian Revolution,* Vols. 1–3. New York: Simon and Schuster.

Vermunt, Jeroen K., and Jay Magidson. 2002. Latent class cluster analysis. In J. A. Hagenaars and A. L. McCutcheon (eds.), *Applied Latent Class Analysis.* Cambridge: Cambridge University Press: 88–106.

Way, Lucan. 2005. Kuchma's failed authoritarianism. *Journal of Democracy* 16 (2): 131–145.

Weiss, Jessica Chen. 2013. Authoritarian signaling, mass audiences, and nationalist protest in China. *International Organization* 67 (1): 1–35.

Weyland, Kurt. 2016. Crafting counterrevolution: how reactionaries learned to combat change in 1848. *American Political Science Review* 110 (2): 215–231.
Wilson, Andrew. 2005. *Ukraine's Orange Revolution*. New Haven, CT: Yale University Press.
Youssef, Nancy A. 2011. Huge Bahraini counter-protest reflects rising sectarian strife. *McClatchyDC*, February 21. www.mcclatchydc.com/news/nation-world/world/article24612922.html.

7

Occupy Youth!

State-Mobilized Movements in the Putin Era (or, What Was Nashi and What Comes Next?)

Julie Hemment

7.1 TVER', RUSSIA, DECEMBER 16, 2006

One frigid December morning, I struggled out of bed at 5 am to join several hundred local youth at the Tver' railway station. I was joining a campaign organized by the pro-Kremlin youth movement Nashi (Ours). We were traveling to Moscow to meet with World War II veterans, bearing gifts and best wishes for the New Year. Our train was one of many traveling from the provinces to Moscow that morning. Kirill, my Nashi activist contact (a "komissar" in the movement who had participated in our research project), explained that the campaign, entitled "A Holiday Returned," was timed to coincide with the sixty-fifth anniversary of the Battle of Moscow – to give back to surviving veterans the New Year's holiday celebration that had been cruelly snatched from them by the Nazis during the winter of 1941. Kirill had explained that the campaign would bring 100,000 young people from across the Russian Federation to the capital in specially commissioned trains. Each group of 100 was to meet with a group of veterans and present them with a New Year's gift.

At the station, I joined a seething mass of young people; as I shuffled through the crowds to find Kirill, I marveled at the complexity of the organization. Komissar-organizers ushered us into numbered cohort groups, signaled by large placards or signs. They then began to load big plastic sacks of what looked like food onto the train, after which we were told to move onboard. I spilled into a wagon with the others who had amassed under Kirill's sign.

As the train pulled out of the station, Kirill and his fellow komissars paced up and down the wagon, barking instructions (there was to be no smoking, no

---

For their support and encouragement of this piece as well as their helpful feedback, I thank editors Liz Perry and Grzegorz Ekiert. This piece benefited from dialogue with other volume contributors, particularly Graeme Robertson and David Palmer. It draws on research undertaken between 2006 and 2011 in Tver', Russia, with the support of the National Science Foundation, IREX and the National Council for Eurasian and East European Research. I am grateful for the support of my research colleagues, faculty and students associated with the Center for Women's History and Gender Studies, Tver' State University, led by Dr. Valentina Uspenskaya.

State-Mobilized Movements in the Putin Era

drinking; we shouldn't come to the organizers with any complaints) and handing out supplies. They passed out box lunches, return tickets and costumes for us to wear as we distributed gifts – Grandfather Frost (*Ded Moroz*) suits for the boys, Snow Maiden (*Snegurochka*) suits for the girls.[1] "These are gifts for you," Kirill called out. "You may keep them, but don't give them to anyone else."

In Moscow, the excitement mounted. We poured out of the train in the half-light to join crowds of young people – who had arrived on trains from other cities – and lined up in our cohorts. As I took my place in line, I saw Kirill sneaking a cigarette. From the front of our line (other groups from Tver'), a chant began – "Happy New Year!" (*S novym godom*) – and we began to pick it up.

At last, all assembled, we shuffled forth. As we rounded the corner and approached the square where the rally was to take place I saw that the streets were eerily empty. The wide boulevards of central Moscow – usually jam-packed with cars – were blocked off to traffic by scores of police. As we cleared the security checkpoints, the space opened up and the crowd behind me let out a cheer. The scene was startling: thousands of young people dressed in costumes, snapping pictures of each other with their cell phones, as sound systems pumped out Soviet wartime songs mixed to a techno beat. The words appeared karaoke-like on a large screen, against a backdrop of black and white World War II combat scenes, presumably excerpted from a Soviet-era movie I did not recognize. On stage in the foreground, young people breakdanced and sang along.

Nashi (Ours), the "Independent Youth Democratic Antifascist Movement," burst onto the Russian political scene in the spring of 2005. Until 2012, when it was disbanded, Nashi was highly controversial, both domestically and internationally, because, with its mass actions and youth in uniforms, it resembled prior Soviet forms (the Komsomol) and because it was taken to signal Russia's authoritarian turn and rejection of liberal democracy. Indeed, the movement came to symbolize Putin-era authoritarianism. This "independent youth movement" was state-run, founded and funded by top Kremlin aides; Nashi's administrative founder was Putin's chief ideologist, Vladislav Surkov. Its public meetings – always pro-state, nationalist-patriotic in hue, often with a pronounced anti-Western or anti-liberal orientation – were permitted at a time when oppositional meetings were not, frequently blocking them. The young people who colorfully, loudly occupied the streets on that frosty day in December wittingly or unwittingly signaled this displacement.

Nashi is most commonly cited as a straightforward case of "astro-turfism." Dominant media and scholarly accounts have depicted it as a top-down project that seeks to dupe innocent young people and divert their energies away from "real" and independent forms of civic engagement and activism, as the cynical

---

[1] Grandfather Frost, the mythical character of fairy tales, was "unmasked as an ally of the priest and the kulak" by the Bolsheviks as part of their assault upon religion (Stites, 1988, p. 231). He was subsequently rehabilitated and was a beloved figure for children during later Soviet periods.

output of Russia's nefarious *polittechnologi* (political technologists), spin-doctors and advisers like Surkov who have played such an important role in the Putin era (Wilson, 2005; Baker and Glasser, 2005; Pomerantsev, 2014).[2] However, the categories of state, grassroots and civil society are highly unstable in the post-Soviet context as my ethnographic research revealed. Moreover, political identification in Russia is complex and does not necessarily align with Western social science expectations (Klumbytė, 2011; Yurchak, 2006).

In this chapter, I examine Nashi as an iconic instance of the state-mobilized movements (SMMs) this volume examines. It was forged at – and responded to – a distinctive and very urgently felt local crisis when the Putin administration grappled with both roiling discontents at home and the threat of external "meddling" (at a time when political elites worried that contention would diffuse to Russia from Ukraine). I view it as a defensive, or spoiler, mobilization, with global signaling elements also. Nashi's campaigns sternly signaled, often satirically, their displeasure at the actions of Western states. While prevailing accounts frame it as a uniquely post-Soviet (or "neo-Bolshevik") phenomenon, I thus emphasize its location within global trends and processes, including international democracy promotion, global protest cycles and the authoritarian recalibration of governance that is taking place within and beyond the postsocialist context and across different regime types. Indeed, as is increasingly clear at the time of writing, Nashi is exotic no more; it shares traits with forms of SMMs on the rise globally.

Nashi was a trailblazer of the innovative mobilizational techniques this volume examines and which have been associated with "hybrid regimes" (Robertson, 2010). Indeed, it was a complex political technology project in motion. The product of a distinctively reflexive, highly self-conscious political culture, the Nashi project skillfully mobilized existing discontents to captivate youth and their energies. While unmistakably state-emanating, it engaged multiple actors. Self-aware, it was constantly rebranding and recalibrating its message in line with both shifting state priorities and the interests of the youth it sought to engage (Lassila, 2014). It drew on a diverse range of repertoires and mobilizing technologies as it did so,[3] including the liberal democracy promotion tool kit, the "orange" technologies associated with Ukraine's color revolution and global protest repertoires as well as Western management techniques. Nashi was bound up in the digital revolution also as Russian state actors, witnessing the powerfully catalyzing effect of new

---

[2] The Russian term for the analysts and political advisers who work behind the scenes of post-socialist political life.

[3] I should stress that "technology" was an emic term, used widely in Nashi materials and by those who participated in it, as well as in other state-run youth projects (the session on voluntarism at the Lake Seliger 2009 educational summer camp was called "Technologies of Kindness," for example). The term – less jarring in Russian than in English – is particularly apt and bears reflecting upon. Unlike the classical "repertoire," it signals dynamic, bricolage-like situations, where actors borrow in context-sensitive ways.

communication technologies for uprisings and protest movements, turned their attention to the Internet and social media. This chapter's title – "Occupy Youth!" – is a provocative borrowing that intends to signal both this circulation of tactics and the mutually constituting relationship between state-run and oppositional movements – and to emphasize this global vector also. The adoption of these techniques lent it significant volatility; its outcomes were unstable and complex, its results unanticipated and sometimes unintended.

In this paper, I first account for Nashi by contextualizing it and examining the historical, geopolitical and political economic factors that prompted it. I trace Nashi's trajectory through two distinctive phases – its early "contentious politics" phase (2005–2008) and its more civil (or formal politics) rendition during the Putin-Medvedev administration (2008–2012) – showing how it changed substantially in the course of its existence in response to different political moments and agendas. Second, drawing on ethnographic data collected in the course of a collaborative research project, I examine some of the distinctive technologies it harnessed. These are: (1) "street technologies" (associated with international democracy promotion and the countercultural and protest repertoires it interacted with);[4] and (2) "project design" technologies (associated with both global repertoires of corporate capitalism and management consultancy, manifest in the NGO world also). Profiling several Nashi activists, I track the way they encountered the Nashi project and these technologies. I provide a "thick" description to emphasize the heterogeneity of perspectives, internal tensions and politics within (c.f. Urla and Helepololei, 2014), as well as what *else* the Nashi project mobilized. Beyond sheer youthful biomass, Nashi mobilized loyalties, affect and idealism as well. My ethnographic account of these komissars reveals their agency and the improvised and multifaceted characteristic of their activities. Finally, I turn to consider the implications of the Nashi case and the lessons we can draw from it about state mobilization strategies and state power.

7.2 NASHI THUMBNAIL

Nashi (Ours) was founded by Vasily Yakemenko, a hitherto little-known political operative who found favor with Surkov, in the spring of 2005. Building on the youth organization he had founded in 2001, Moving Together (Idushchie Vmeste),[5] Nashi started out as a patriotic movement to provide ideological support for the Kremlin at a sensitive time: the roiling

---

[4] Anthropological scholarship has revealed international democracy promotion to be a highly dynamic field that picks up resources across the trajectory of its emplotment, with actors moving in and out of NGO work, to participate in "uncivil" mobilizations such as the alterglobalization movement. See for example Jessica Greenberg (2014) and Maple Razsa (2015) on the disenchantments it has engendered amongst former participants.

political aftermath of Ukraine's "Orange Revolution" when "nonsystemic" oppositional movements burgeoned.[6] It was a (controversial) cornerstone of the second Putin administration's efforts to achieve legitimacy and articulate a "national idea." Between 2005 and 2008, Nashi grew; at its peak, during the 2007–2008 election cycle, it claimed several tens of thousands of members (and many more supporters) and had approximately fifty regional branches across the Russian Federation. Nashi's hallmark activity was the high-profile mass event – pro-Kremlin campaigns that brought tens of thousands of young people onto Moscow's streets and plazas. Many of these, like the A Holiday Returned rally I attended, had a nationalist-patriotic hue and frequently invoked World War II.[7] Nashi summer educational camps – held at the popular resort Lake Seliger – also attracted tens of thousands of participants and were attended by high-ranking politicians and Kremlin aides. These rallies, as well as the more militant and contentious actions Nashi engaged in (harassing political opponents; rumored thuggish acts of violent retribution) won it the most press (and notoriety) and surely drew some youth to the movement.[8] However, Nashi activists also engaged in a wide range of socially focused activities that received less media coverage but were prominent and valued at the local level. Some of these bore strong resemblance to prior Komsomol campaigns, for example events for orphans and programs for local veterans, sessions on cultural tolerance and friendship with international students, and campaigns against littering, graffiti, and the sale of cigarettes and alcohol to minors. Like the Komsomol, Nashi had a reward structure and promised forms of social mobility for its participants. Nashi activists took classes and seminars in Moscow as well as at Lake Seliger. Komissars, the activist-leaders of the movement, were rewarded with the opportunity to study at Nashi's own Moscow-based higher-education institute – the Natsionalnyi Institut Vyshaia Shkola Upravleniia.

---

[5] This Nashi precursor project (described as a "pilot project" by many of the Nashi activists I spoke with) was founded by Vasily Yakemenko in 2001. For a comparison between IM and Nashi and the relationship between them, see Lassila (2014).

[6] Squeezed out of formal political space after the 2003–2004 election cycle, the opposition proved adaptive and began to form horizontal coalitions. The Other Russia coalition (founded 2006) brought together an ideologically diverse set of opponents; Solidarity was later founded in 2008 by some of the same actors; Oborona, the leaderless horizontal youth movement, was founded in 2005.

[7] Nashi's inaugural rally brought 60,000 youth from all over Moscow to march in commemoration of the sixtieth anniversary of the Soviet victory over the Nazis (or "fascists," as they are more commonly recalled).

[8] Some of the most controversial of these were the campaigns against international diplomats – against the British ambassador Tony Brenton (2006) and against the Estonian ambassador (2007) in protest against the Estonian decision to relocate the Bronze Soldier war memorial in Talinn, which depicted Soviet losses in World War II. These "militant" acts led to condemnation by representatives of the EU and NATO (Mijnssen, 2014, p. 117). Nashi was also blamed for other more serious actions, most notably the savage beating of liberal journalist Oleg Kashin in 2011.

Despite its proximity to the state and to the President himself – Putin attended Nashi events and addressed Nashi activists, and his image featured prominently in the movement's promotional materials – Nashi had a rogue energy and uncertain status. Some Nashi campaigns irritated its Kremlin backers, leading to periodic reorganization and "rebooting" attempts. The 2007–2008 period was a turbulent one for Nashi; the presidential administration distanced itself from the organization following a number of controversial campaigns, and it was restructured after the December 2007 federal elections, resulting in the closing of the majority of the regional branches. While leading Nashi komissars were kicked upstairs and rewarded with federal positions (and as Nashi founder Vasily Yakemenko was appointed leader of the newly founded Federal Youth Affairs Agency, or Rosmolodezh), rank and file participants found themselves cut adrift. Liberal newspapers jubilantly reported Nashi's demise; however, it reemerged later that year as a number of regionally based "directions" (*napravleniia* – themed projects or sub-organizations).[9] The scholarly consensus is that this moment marked a distinctive shift. In the post-2008 period (with the "Orange" problem resolved and the Medvedev presidency secured), Nashi retooled its activities and campaigns, largely abandoning street politics to engage in more formal political activities and youth development programs (Atwal and Bacon, 2012; Robertson, 2010). In line with the Medvedev administration's policy focus on "modernization," many post-2008 projects focused on entrepreneurship and innovation. Indeed, the summer youth camp Seliger 2009 was rebranded and its Nashi connection energetically denied. It advertised itself as a competitive forum open to all "talented" youth across the federation, organized by Rosmolodezh in partnership with the Ministry of Sports, Tourism, and Youth Policy. However, elements of the earlier "contentious" mode persisted, as manifest in the decentralized directions or offshoot splinter projects such as Stal (Steel), which continued to run aggressive anti-liberal provocations. Until 2012, when it finally disappeared, Nashi engaged in a constant rebranding and respinning, updating and rebooting itself in response to the changing times and to keep its young constituents interested and/or lure them from other youth organizations that competed for their attention.

This tendency to fragment and splinter made Nashi a slippery object to track. So too did its uncertain center of gravity. Nashi offshoot projects that took form after 2009 – such as Run With Me (promoting fitness); Piggies Against (which campaigned against the sale of expired products in food stores); and StopKham! (a campaign against traffic infractions), were "semi-autonomous movements" that denied their Nashi connection (Krivonos and Fedorova, 2014). Meanwhile, Nashi founder Yakemenko continued to spin Nashi-like projects,

---

[9] Lassila attributes this dynamism in part to the movement's inevitable propensity to "fail" communicatively – that is, it was successful only for as long as it looked to be a movement of and by youth: when its "state-ness" became manifest, people moved away.

many of them digital, under the auspices of Rosmolodezh and mobilized former-Nashi activists – as well as third party entrepreneurs (Fedor and Fredheim, 2017) – beyond the organization's final dismantling.

But what prompted Nashi? What kind of mobilization was this?

7.3 "THE STREETS ARE WITH US!" CONTEXTUALIZING NASHI/ RUSSIA ON THE BRINK

I first became aware of Nashi during the spring of 2005 when I heard rumors of a pro- Kremlin youth summer camp to be held at Lake Seliger, about 200 miles from my field site in Tver' oblast. Browsing the newspapers in a kiosk at Sheremetevo airport, one front-page story caught my eye: "OUR millions (*Nashe Milliony*): both the Kremlin, and the opposition are looking at youth as a political resource." A large photo depicted a thirty-something-year-old man in a white shirt, with the Nashi logo emblazoned on it, against a backdrop of thousands of youth supporters, similarly clad, holding red flags with a white cross. It was a bold image, its fascist suggestion unmistakable. On the plane ride home, I read the article, gripped. "The 'orange revolution' [in Ukraine] is becoming a brand [*brend*] before our eyes," the article stated, "one that brings together two opposing [*nachala*] assumptions – hope for some, a threat for others." The article reported that political parties and groups of diverse ideological persuasion were mobilizing youth via summer camps.[10] The man in the photo was Vasily Yakemenko, Surkov confidante and architect of prior state-run youth projects, now founder and leader of Nashi.

Nashi was born of a time of crisis. The mood in the spring of 2005 was polarized and edgy. Nashi's most proximate cause was Ukraine's "Orange Revolution" of late 2004, a largely youth-led prodemocracy movement, prompted by the perception of rigged elections. Like the other "color" revolutions that took place in the former Soviet Union between 2003 and 2005, it was celebrated in the West as a triumph of democracy, an analogue to the prodemocracy "velvet revolutions" of 1989; the youthful bodies on streets that *New York Times* articles portrayed were framed in heroic, civil terms, as a "civilizing force" that swept away authoritarian incumbents. However, this color revolution was highly controversial in Russia, and opinions were polarized. While liberal activists and journalists drew inspiration from it, other newspaper commentators, following the state line,

---

[10] In part due to the squeeze on formal political space in 2003–2004, youth movements burgeoned. These included nationalist-oriented groups such as the Eurasian Union of Youth (headed by Alexander Dugin), the youth organization of the Liberal Democratic Party of Russia (led by Vladimir Zhirinovsky), and leftist groups such as the Union of Communist Youth, the National Bolshevik Party and the Vanguard of Red Youth, as well as liberal-oriented ones. The National Bolshevik Party was the most prominent oppositional youth movement. Founded in 1994, it had an extensive network that extended to many provincial Russian cities. For discussion of this period, see Robertson (2009, 2011).

drew attention to the large amounts of foreign money, especially from the United States, expended in supporting it and expressed concern about foreign meddling in postsocialist space. I found these skeptical views to be surprisingly widespread. As "orange" imagery and aesthetics spread amongst youth oppositional movements (Horvath, 2015, pp. 6–7),[11] consternation and a sense of crisis amongst Russia's political establishment grew. Nashi emerged a few short months later to articulate a firm retort. An important part of Nashi's "work" was to sternly articulate (or "signal") to foreigners – and the domestic actors (especially liberal oppositionists) who would support them – what was no longer permissible. Its materials explicitly invoked the Orange Revolution, pitching itself as a counterinsurgency operation to prevent similar foreign interventions from taking place and to guarantee Russia's sovereignty. Signaling its objection to another unpopular foreign-sponsored initiative (the 1990s-era project of democratization), the Nashi Manifesto named a second goal – to create an "active" civil society that would uphold Russian sovereignty.

Important as this geopolitical context was, there were other, domestic factors at play also. A series of unpopular social welfare reforms introduced in 2004 led to a wave of protests in January and February 2005. Underreported in the international media, they represented a major political crisis for the Putin administration. Tens of thousands of protesters came out in demonstrations to contest the "monetization" of social benefits. While the majority of protesters were pensioners, the group most seriously disadvantaged by the reforms, youth were also involved. Young people, mostly students, joined retirees bearing communist banners and placards. Radical student groups (including antiglobalist leftist ones) emerged on campuses, and some young people formed online communities of protest, such as Skazhi-Net (Say No); Liudi v Kurse (People in the Know); Idushchiye Bez Putina (Walking Without Putin). To the authorities' dismay, these loosely coordinated protests began to spread, from St. Petersburg and Moscow to cities all across the Russian Federation, joining forces with existing oppositional groups – groups which, squeezed out of formal electoral politics, had begun to proliferate and form coalitions after 2004. These groups used social media to issue powerful slogans, denouncing the reform and the administration that enacted it (Hemment, 2012) and giving rise to a perception of "imminent revolutionary threat" (Horvath, 2011).[12]

I was in Tver' in March 2005, two months after law 122 took effect. People spoke about nothing but the reforms and their antisocial, or anti-people

---

[11] For example, the oppositional youth coalition Oborona (Defense), which was inspired by the Orange Revolution and founded by youth activists from Yabloko, SPS and others, adopted the symbolism of the color revolutions that were controversially spreading through postsocialist space (the raised fist symbol used by the Serbian and Ukrainian prodemocracy movements Otpor! and Pora!) See Lyytikäinen (2016).

[12] Horvath (2011) characterizes the mood of this moment. While the opposition issued a vote of no confidence in the administration, erstwhile Kremlin allies (including conservative

(*antinarodnyi*), character. This term suggested continuities with the unpopular liberalizing reforms of the 1990s, upsetting a major component of Putin's legitimacy – his distinctiveness from the "*antinarodyni*" Yeltsin administration and reformers. Youth politicization was already a touchy subject; youth groups – including ultranationalist formations – had begun to proliferate between 2003 and 2005, some engaging in forms of street protest (Robertson, 2009, p. 535; Horvath, 2011). The National Bolshevik Party in particular, with its provocative countercultural appeal and proclivity to direct action and unsanctioned assemblies in public spaces, caused alarm.[13] These new mobilizations – foreign- sponsored, domestically fomented, with the potential to join forces with existing oppositional groups and coalitions – represented a crisis for the Putin administration.[14]

Zakhar Prilepin's novel *Sankya* (2006) gives a rich account of some of the kinds of youth mobilizations Russian state actors most feared. The book, published to great acclaim one year after the anti-monetization protests, was a shocking – and loosely autobiographical – account of youth involvement in a radical anti-establishment oppositional movement, "the Founders," a fictional group based on the National Bolshevik Party he belonged to. Prilepin's "new realist" novel captured the energy of a generation's discontents. Members of the Founders were young provincial men, on fire with fury about the dispossessions of the 1990s. Some of the most moving and evocative sections discuss the ire of the provincial subject confronting new Russia's obscene inequalities – the luxury stores and unaffordable goods. They powerfully invoke the sense of outrage young Russians (especially young Russian men) experience at generational wrongs: depopulated villages where isolated elders (members of Russia's Last Great Generation) lie on their deathbeds, alcoholic, prematurely deceased fathers. Founder members are highly disciplined and fiercely motivated to right these wrongs – and smash the state as they do so. Their ire is directed equally at the West, the domestic liberals who support it and the new (Putin-era) Russian political elites, between which they appear to draw little distinction.

Greeted with acclaim in Moscow literary circles, *Sankya* must have caused consternation in the political establishment (anti-corruption and oppositional

---

Senator Valentina Matvienko and Patriarch Aleksei II) joined their critique of law 122. Rodina party leader Rogozin went on hunger strike and released an open letter to Putin warning of the reform's revolutionary consequences (2011, p. 8).

[13] The NBP played a crucial role here, as Robertson (2010) notes. See also Horvath (2015). See Fenghi (2017) for a rich account of NBP's "anarcho-militaristic" aesthetics and ideology and its origins in the work of countercultural poet (and NBP founding father) Eduard Limonov.

[14] Horvath (2011, p. 16) draws attention to contention about Nashi among Russian political elites, some of whom were deeply skeptical about the risks it presented. For example, Federation Council Chairman Sergei Mironov likened Nashi to the Maoist "Red Guards." Indeed, the Nashi project only gained political currency and support after the Orange Revolution; it took this sense of crisis for the project to gain political favor.

activist Alexei Navalny retrospectively referred to Prelepin as "an active politician with influence over the hearts and minds of young Russians").[15] Indeed, the Putin administration took swift steps to contain the National Bolshevik Party Prilepin drew inspiration from – and which was playing a key role in the new creative non-systemic opposition that was taking shape – outlawing the party in 2007, arresting (once again) its founder Eduard Limonov and, coopting some of its ideologists.[16] It quickly moved to demobilize the protests, via "a combination of coercion, channeling and concessions" (Robertson, 2010, p. 183), which discredited the opposition (drawing a distinction between legitimate economic concerns of pensioners and the illegitimate "extremists" manipulating them in pursuit of their political agenda).

To invoke this volume's typology, Nashi was a classic "spoiler" mobilization, born at the crucible of this "revolutionary" energy and at this moment of experimentation and improvisation as the administration desperately sought to deal with the new and urgent problem of "the streets." Its formation marked a new phase of Russian politics and state–opposition interactions, one of frequent skirmishes and "dueling protests" (Robertson, 2010, p. 12).[17] As should be clear, however, Nashi was not only a counterinsurgency project directed toward foreign meddlers and the oppositionists they sought to encourage but a domestic project of prevention also, one that addressed deeply rooted social issues and targeted a specific youth constituency. Although never made explicit, there was clearly a politics of class afoot here.[18] The Nashi project directed itself toward provincial youth, potential NBP recruits – the students of colleges and institutes who did not have the same connections and opportunities as their urban peers.[19] Answering long-term policy concerns – addressing domestic audiences worried about the state's neglect of youth since the Soviet Union's dissolution – Nashi sought to occupy these youth, direct their energies and provide them with the chance of upward mobility (or "social lift," as policy documents called it). It did so in

---

[15] In his preface to the 2013 English language publication of *Sankya* (Prilepin, 2014). Prilepin's "new realism" (*Novyi Realizm*) is a genre that seeks to challenge the predominantly postmodernist aesthetic of the Moscow literary establishment (regarded as complacent and politically ineffectual, complicit with the political administration it disparages).

[16] Notably, NBP co-founder and Eurasian ideologist Aleksandr Dugin drew close to the Putin administration at this time and has played a key role since then as a consultant for the political establishment.

[17] Beyond Nashi, youth were mobilized to participate in pro-state rallies by other means. University administrators called upon students to participate in Edinaia Rossiia events in Tver' and other cities, for example.

[18] On the status of class as a category in postsocialist state, see Salmenniemi (2012); Kalb (2009); Ost (2005). Indeed, as Salmenniemi has noted, Putin-era political parties downplay class to emphasize Russian "unity" (see Salmenniemi, 2012).

[19] While the NBP began as an urban countercultural project that aimed to create a radical intellectual elite (Fenghi, 2017, p. 190), its demographics changed over the course of its existence.

ways that conformed to the period's most prominent youth policy goals – "patriotic education" and "modernization."[20]

7.4 MOBILIZATION CHALLENGES AND STRATEGIES

Nashi's challenge was to appeal to apolitical youth, to young people who were sick of "politics" and who would be repelled by anything official or conformist (Lassila, 2014). In Russia and other postsocialist states, young people are disillusioned and cynical about formal politics and politicians. Indeed, youth "apoliticism" has long been a Russian governmental policy concern.[21] In this, Russia is on trend with global tendencies; however, this apoliticism and disenchantment bears specific postsocialist inflection. It is both a legacy of state socialism and has more proximate cause, infused with specific disgust at the processes of the 1990s.[22] Nashi was cleverly crafted to hook youth who were deeply skeptical about formal politics and about politicians also. It catered to the "apolitical" orientation the Russian government identified as problematic – and dangerous, insofar as it renders youth vulnerable to "political manipulation" – yet it pandered to it as well.

To make its pitch, Nashi architects undertook a curious blend and set of fusions. Nashi proclaimed itself to be a movement of and by youth (an "Independent youth movement"), yet it was state-initiated. It was pro-Kremlin (above all, pro-Putin) yet not affiliated with any formal political party; indeed I found that many of the komissars I spoke with were highly skeptical even of the "party of power," Edinaiia Rossiia. Nashi skillfully mobilized the discontents of the 1990s and appealed to the sense of dispossession and outrage many provincial young people feel (Oushakine, 2009) about politics, the tight relationship between political and economic elites, and enduring systems of bureaucratic privilege. In sum, despite its

---

[20] The State Patriotic Education Program, founded in 2001, engaged several ministries in a project to increase patriotic feeling among young people. "Modernization" goals are most clearly expressed in a 2002 order: *Prikaz: O Kontseptsii modernizatsii rossiiskogo obrazovaniia na period do 2010 goda*. As Doug Blum notes, Russia's youth policy of this period manifested a tension between the demand for modernity and normalcy (civil society and democratic legitimacy) and a unique national path ("control, stability and a guaranteed normative order" (2006, p. 96)). These two programs are expressive of this tension.

[21] A 2005 policy document (*Strategy of State Youth Policy in the Russian Federation*) names the following issues as most pressing youth problems: ethnic intolerance; unemployment/social marginalization; low marriage rate; housing crisis; demographic situation (low birthrate); and, crucially, "the danger of an apolitical orientation [apolitichnost']," "which leaves young people vulnerable to political manipulation."

[22] Yurchak discusses how, during late socialism, the figure of the "activist" was regarded as pathological (2006, p. 103), frequently contrasted with "normal" people who kept away from politics. Exploring the topic of political mobilization in the 2005–2011 period from another angle, Karine Clément examines how this sentiment still prevails. Indeed, she classifies "ordinary people" as those who avoid public, collective action and find it distasteful (2015, p. 213).

proximity to the Kremlin, Nashi had a pronounced populist kind of "antiestablishment" energy as well.

True to other state-sponsored projects of this period – the Patriotic Education project directed at schoolchildren, patriotic films ("historical blockbusters") and TV programming – a prominent tactic was memory work. As other elements of the Putin administration's "state memory project" (Norris, 2012, p. 6), Nashi campaigns made strategic use of the Soviet past, most frequently the Great Patriotic War (World War II). Mass campaigns like "Our Victory" and "A Holiday Returned" invited young people to identify with Russia's "Last Great Generation" which saved Europe from fascism. This memory work indexed more recent history also, invoking the decade of the 1990s as a period of shame and national humiliation. Campaigns drew a heroic link between Nashi youth and World War II veterans whilst disparaging the Gorbachev generation – the "defeatists" who allowed the collapse of the Soviet Union and Russia's geopolitical decline to occur and who were thus responsible for the dislocations of the 1990s. As the Nashi Manifesto puts it, "Our generation must take the wheel [*smenit' u rulia*] from the defeatist generation who rule this country. Those people who believe neither in Russia's future, nor in themselves." In this way, it both pointed to the agents of this dispossession, the liberals it deemed responsible for the nineties-era affronts and delegitimized the contemporary protests these liberals were engaged in, characterizing the "nesystemni" oppositional coalition as an "unnatural union ... between pseudoliberals and fascists, Westernizers and ultranationalists."[23]

7.5 MOBILIZING MECHANISMS AND SPECIFIC TECHNOLOGIES

While Nashi drew on the Soviet playbook (busing in youth, mass rallies), it did not stick to it. Largely eschewing the old-school transmission-belt tactics other state-run projects were still engaging in, it – rather controversially[24] – embraced new methods and technologies of recruitment and mobilization. I draw on my ethnographic research to discuss some of the distinctive mobilizing technologies it adopted, as well as the ways they were received by youth participants: (1) "street technologies"; and (2) "project design" technologies. Although these technologies overlapped to some extent, they correspond roughly to different chronological periods, where the street technologies and mass mobilizational strategies were a hallmark of the early "contentious politics" phase of Nashi (2005–2008), and project design was associated prominently with the "civil

---

[23] Manifest molodezhnogo demokraticheskogo antifashistskogo dvizheniia "Nashi" (Manifesto of the youth democratic antifascist movement "Nashi"), also available at http://nashi.su/manifest.

[24] Nashi's upstart energy, propensity to bypass the usual channels and jarring violations of institutional norms – placing komissars within the offices of state administration via internships or leadership roles – caused some state actors to bristle; I found to my surprise that many local state officials expressed disapproval or impatience with it.

turn" the organization took during the latter phase of its existence, in line with the "modernization" goals of the Medvedev administration (2008–2012).[25]

7.5.1 Street Technologies

As we've seen, Nashi's hallmark mobilizing strategy was the mass rally. Its first phase task was to undertake this new "politics of the street" I have described. While the form bears a Soviet ideological hallmark and while uniformed Nashi activists (wearing branded T-shirts, baseball caps and bandanas) visually recalled Soviet-era youth organizations, this was not your mother's Komsomol.

Nashi offered young people distinctive technologies (themselves borrowed from oppositional movements both domestic and foreign: the radical oppositional National Bolshevik Party, the "Orange" technologies deployed in the Ukraine) to occupy or take control of the streets. While Nashi rallies were pro-state and nationalist-patriotic, they frequently embraced a playful register. Borrowing from the NBP playbook (as well as global subcultural repertoires), Nashi campaigns and flash mobs included theatrical, surrealist elements. As the opening vignette indicated, these involved curious juxtapositions and bewildering fusions (Soviet wartime iconography, combined with techno music). Here, as in alter-globalization movements, we see the privileging of the ludic and the performative. At the same time as it was playful and fun, this campaign was elaborately choreographed and scripted – as I realized from my participation in the event. The brochure komissars distributed to us on the train read like a precise script for the event that was to unfold ("Ten thousand young people will present veterans with gifts," it proclaimed). The stage where we assembled was adorned with enormous cartoonlike drawings depicting the exchange that was to take place (a beaming, crinkly-eyed elder, surrounded by young people in Grandfather Frost costumes). It was highly mass-mediated as well. TV cameras zoomed down, intruding on the view, capturing signs and snatches of youth enthusiasm, which were beamed back to us on the giant screens before us.

This description appears to confirm the skeptical accounts I've outlined – Nashi as "astroturf," or a cynical project that duped youth and diverted their energies from "authentic" forms of civic engagement (Wilson, 2005). However, my ethnographic research and participation in some of these mass events caused me to question this characterization (as well as the state/society binary it rests upon). I learned that these carefully staged events allowed space for agency as well. Indeed, there was frequently a curious disconnect between the campaigns' espoused goals and participants' experience of them. Many participants – thrilled to be in Moscow or at Lake Seliger – casually disregarded the

---

[25] Not to say that the political challenge was over. The opposition continued to morph during the Medvedev administration, as exemplified in the Strategy 31 initiative (another broad coalition, which NBP leader Limonov played a leading role in establishing).

overbearing images of state power (the Putin posters) and were often oblivious about campaigns' stated purpose and intent. A Holiday Returned campaign participants I observed were less focused on the central stage than they were absorbed in their immediate social circles, sharing photos and excitement via their cell phones. Indeed, I discovered many participants were oblivious of the rally's stated goals. Few in my wagon bore gifts; the Indian dentistry students I traveled up with (recruited in a "friendship" outreach initiative) had no idea we were to meet with veterans at all. Even komissar organizers were sometimes unable to enlighten me about the purpose of specific events or campaigns. This instability and carelessness about content did not mean they were empty or not meaningful. Rather, it opened space for youth to experience them in unique and different ways – that did not always coincide with what the state intended (Klumbytė, 2011; Yurchak, 2006).

7.5.1.1 Kirill: Mobilizing Sovereign Democracy

Kirill, the komissar who invited me to the Holiday Returned campaign that day, joined Nashi at the very beginning in 2005. He became interested in our project after learning about it from his teachers and peers and offered to join our research team as a "consultant." Absorbed as he was by Nashi's innovative use of "soft power" technologies (which he understood to be a necessary defense against malign foreign-emanating projects), he made for an interesting interlocutor, and I learned a great deal from him. Notably, he drew my attention to the peculiar transparency with which Nashi signaled its embrace of these technologies and ambition to govern. One of Kirill's first Nashi events was a conference in Moscow. He submitted an abstract on "technologies of the Orange Revolution," which I learned was one of the main themes (Nashi activists explicitly studied this, along with techniques of "political communication"). At the 2006 summer camp at Lake Seliger he had attended lectures by Nashi's leading ideologues, including Nashi founder Vassily Yakemenko's session on mass campaigns – "how to create them, how to disperse them ... how to properly plan a mass campaign." The ability to do this, he told me neutrally, "is nowadays one of the leading, one might say, stages of human development. Because if a person can bring people onto the street, it means he must be pretty strong. And these are the people who declare [*provozglasiat*] public opinion."

I interviewed Kirill in December 2006. Reflecting on the early phase of Nashi's work, he explained that the priority was to work with the masses, on the streets (*s massami, na ulitsakh*). Insufficiently attuned to Nashi terminologies, I thought at first that he was referring to the social discontents that brought people (the masses) out onto the street – the dissatisfaction and concern around social benefits reform, for example, or roiling forms of political contestation. "No," he corrected me, "I meant something different – control of street technology. Campaigns on the streets, a street format [*aktsii na ulitsakh*, *format ulichnyi*]." This was the time of the color revolutions and the Orange technologies, he reminded me. He had led a bunch of these kinds of actions, he said; one time he brought a train full of young people to Moscow from North Ossetia. Since 2008, priorities had changed, he explained, "but we don't forget about the street. The streets are with us [*ulitsy s namy*]."

I was struck by this formulation. Here, "the street" was a kind of political resource, a site to be managed and an opportunity to demonstrate strength in numbers and the ability to amass crowds. It was curiously disassociated from any social or political issues and from ideology as well. Kirill confirmed this. When I quizzed him about the meaning of the Holiday Returned campaign, he told me that it didn't have any ideological significance and that the veterans were beside the point. If they'd wanted to do nice things for veterans, they could have stayed in Tver'. Growing impatient with my obtuseness, he shouted, "The point was that we could pull people together! One hundred thousand people – there's been nothing like it since [the Russian Revolution of] 1905! The point was – the very fact that *we could do it*!"

As I have argued elsewhere (2012a; 2015), Russia's political technologists drew on the tool kit of the democracy promotion project they disparaged as they mobilized youth. They rebranded "revolution" as something dangerous, dire and bloody (rather than the civilizing, democratizing force it was presented as in Western newspapers) and oppositional activists as "extremists," emphasizing the undesirability of the political use of the streets or politicized youth on streets (c.f. Greenberg, 2014; Manning, 2007). This rebranding had historical reach, as Kirill's remark about 1905 reveals. Nashi materials invoked the revolutionary turbulence of the early 1900s as a dangerous historical precedent (Horvath, 2011, p. 11). They repackaged "civil society" (the cornerstone concept of 1990s-era democratizing interventions) as something that presented a "solution" to the "problem" of the crowd, invoking it as something that would deflect and contain this energy.

Kirill's use of the term "technologies" signaled an analytic orientation as well, a kind of "counterinsurgency subjectivity" that was encouraged by his Nashi training. As should be clear, he did not see the liberal democratic tool kit (or the Internet technology it harnessed) as neutral, let alone inherently democratic and progressive.[26] In our conversations, he signaled that he was not only wise to Western-emanating soft power but well equipped to subvert it. Indeed, he spoke explicitly about the technologies of control that were part of his training, presenting them as an unfortunate necessity, a response to the nefarious methods of social control that were part and parcel of the liberal

---

[26] Kirill, as with many young people I spoke with, did not view PR, opinion polling or other "electoral technologies" as neutral or technocratic. I can add, though, that although the term "political technology" is understood by Western commentators to refer to quintessentially post-Soviet Bolshevik practices, it first emerged to describe the electoral technologies embraced by Yeltsin's "young reformers," in collaboration with US advisers.

governing project which had contributed to undermining Russia during the 1990s (he mentioned the "velvet strategy" of fomenting revolution undertaken by George Soros, for example). Nashi's street technologies, as other things ("political communication" and "political PR") were hybrid technologies that drew on these resources. They were offered up as resources that would protect young people and equip them to withstand the political manipulation they would inevitably encounter, both from malign foreigners (Soros, agents associated with the US State Department) and from domestic "enemies within" (oligarchs who had offshore accounts, servants of capital).

During our last interview in June 2007, Kirill told me that Nashi had served its purpose: it was over, he said, "because it has outlived its usefulness from within. Not because it is successful or not successful. It is successful as long as everything is done well. And when it has played itself out, even if it is successful in principle, behold, it falls like a skeleton." He was confident that there would be a successor project. "They'll change the name and there'll be a new movement like the old one," he told me neutrally. "It's PR, it's marketing, it's all technologies. It's all just smart technologies." This insight didn't repel him, however. Despite his critique, he was poised to join another Kremlin project, "League of Equality" (*Liga Spravedlivosti*).

Nashi campaigns deployed other "street technologies" also – technologies of "direct action" and flash mob events. These varied in ideological hue and content. I learned something about them from Kirill as well.

Kirill participated in some of Nashi's early "antifascist" forms of direct action (here, signaling action against ethnic intolerance). He was the leader (*rukovoditel'*) of the Tver' branch's antifascist direction and led "lessons of friendship" in schools and colleges. When I spoke with him in 2006, he had recently returned from the Russian republic of Karelia where he had been on a kind of fact-finding mission to investigate a well-publicized incident of ethnic violence. A fight had broken out in a bar in a small town, he told me, and it had resulted in sustained conflict between Chechens and ethnic Russians. Nashi bused in young people to see the consequences firsthand.

Kirill had returned to the university on fire with the "truth" he'd discovered. All was not what it seemed, he told me. The TV reports (which had referred to the violence that followed as a "pogrom" against ethnic Chechens) had shown footage of sunny weather; however, it was raining when they arrived. "It was all a lie!" he told me. He had concluded that the resulting ethnic conflict had been stage-managed; it was a plot, the work of malign outsiders. "Someone's gaining from it," he said knowingly. While he didn't know who was responsible, there was a European magnate, he told me, whose interests would be served by the expulsion of the Chechen community.

His accounts helped me better understand the place of Nashi in the "functioning civil society" Nashi's Manifesto pledged to create. Nashi activists are furious cells, tracing leads, following threads, and trusting nobody. Beyond the opportunity to travel for advancement and study, the movement offered a distinctive kind of mobility: travel for a kind of investigative purpose. In a pro-state appropriation of flash mob technologies, Nashi bused its activists around the country to take direct action – in this case to serve as citizen-investigators.

Other forms of direct action involved opposition baiting, focused on the much-derided National Bolshevik Party (Nashi's "Other") or liberal groups. Employing NBP-like tactics, Nashi activists went head to head with liberal youth groups, engaging in provocative campaigns that mocked and subverted liberal positions, identities and commitments, including gender and sexual politics (Hemment, 2015, p. 193).[27] Also prominent among these provocations were the bawdy and sometimes scatological run-ins with the liberal newspaper *Kommersant,* with which it had a long-running feud. In a protest action in 2008, Nashi activists posing as *Kommersant* employees distributed toilet paper featuring the newspaper's logo, including to parliamentarians; billboards around the city announced the paper's new toilet paper format. An even more grotesque act was captured on film by the 2012 documentary *Putin's Kiss*: a Nashi activist defecating on liberal oppositionist Ilya Yashin's car.

These forms of direct action were animated by what Svetlana Stephenson (2015) calls a "lad's logic," a rough, tough, nativist energy that we might see as a form of what Douglas Holmes (2010) has called "integralism" – homegrown, determinedly illiberal, or counter to the effete, Western-emanating mode of discourse and politics that was associated with the liberal opposition. This same street energy was manifest in forms of direct action undertaken by later Nashi and Nashi splinter campaigns, such as Piggies Against and StopKham ("Stop the Boorishness!"), launched in 2009–2010. Here, a second generation of less "politically" inclined young people took to the streets to campaign against other kinds of "street" infractions.[28] Moving in small groups, participants of these campaigns sought out and challenged individual violators – private vendors who sold spoiled goods or who sold alcohol and cigarettes to minors, motorists who violated traffic rules by parking or driving on sidewalks – digitally documenting their infractions to later post on social media sites. Their campaigns had some social resonance – both Piggies and StopKham tapped widespread anger about unscrupulous vendors, roadhogs or rule breakers. They coexisted with oppositional initiatives to contest corruption and citizen direct action such as anti-corruption blogger Alexei Navalny came to represent. But they intersected with and mobilized forms of xenophobic

---

[27] See also Lyytkäinen (2016) and Sperling (2014) for textured accounts of these stand-offs.
[28] Recent research confirms that participants of Nashi offshoot projects (Piggies Against, StopKham) saw themselves as apolitical actors, engaged in diverse forms of civic activity. The documentary film (associated with the MYPLACE research project, Hilary Pilkington PI and directed by Dmitry Omel'chenko) *"Our Former Ours"* confirms and illustrates this well (https://myplaceresearch.wordpress.com/documentary-our-former-ours-the-nashi-youth-movement/). See also Krivonos and Fedorova (2014).

State-Mobilized Movements in the Putin Era 183

populism also and spilled over into a disconcerting form of vigilantism.[29] Recent research suggests that StopKham and Piggies often played out in racialized ways – the MYPLACE documentary captures uncomfortable standoffs between righteous ethnic Russian youth and linguistically or ethnically marked others – taxi drivers, shop store assistants and managers. Once again, there was a specific dynamic of appropriation here; StopKham undercut and took the edge off more oppositional protests that contested state actors' traffic violations, appropriating the protest technology formulated by the Blue Bucket Brigade.[30]

7.5.1.2 *Masha: Mobilizing Affect*

Masha, a twenty-year-old student and former Nashi activist, had a rather different vantage point on the early phase of mobilization. While Kirill spoke predominantly about the technologies, in a knowing, managerial register (the "soft power smarts" that the movement offered him), Masha chose to speak about specific local events and the face-to-face encounters they had entailed. Her narrative brought another kind of mobilization into view for me – the mobilization of affect and the intra-movement effect of affective solidarity that was an outcome of her participation (see also Juris, 2008). Speaking to me in 2009, she told me that, when she joined the movement, "mass actions" was one of the largest campaigns. The focus of this early campaign was to teach activists how to organize patriotic social events. One of the earliest local campaigns she'd engaged in was "Day after Day." Young people invited veterans to a social event in the city park, she explained: "there was a dance floor, boat rides, food. And every young person was paired with a veteran; he had to spend the whole evening with them, to talk with him, etc. And because they were all together sometimes they even got a little drunk [laughs] – well, our veterans are ... soulful," she added, with a wry smile. "They played on the harmonica, they sang. It was a "concert for them. So, it was pleasant to do such interesting things."

Masha spoke frequently of the relationships that propelled her – with the elders, veterans and especially the disadvantaged children she had encountered via her socially oriented Nashi work. Like Kirill, she had been involved in the December 2006 "A Holiday Returned" campaign. However, for her, the veterans were definitely not beside the point. Indeed, she told me regretfully that she felt bad that some of them had gone home disappointed; there had not been enough gifts.

Masha spoke movingly about the emotional experience of participation in Nashi's mass campaigns. For her, participation in this SMM had clearly had

---

[29] See Atwal and March (2012) for discussion of Nashi's ambivalent relationship to nationalism.
[30] Balmforth reported that Stopkham received grants from the Kremlin of 4 million rubles in 2013 and 6 million rubles in 2014 (www.rferl.org/content/nashi-stopkham-kremlin-traffic-violators /26857904.html).

a transformative effect. "Well," she explained, "each campaign was such a boost, a shot of adrenaline for the young people who found themselves in [it] – and if [the campaign] was extreme, well, you were left with such intense emotions! It was ... so positive, it left you feeling so warm because you'd gone through it, not alone but with your comrades. It was great," she told me. "There was nothing like it. Well," she added, in a wry aside that brought new valence to the rehabbed revolutionary rhetoric and technologies Kirill had earlier drawn on: "probably *revolutionaries* experience something similar when they unite and do something like this together. Even if it's absolute nonsense [*chepukha*], just a regular flash mob, where people just stand in lines and clap their hands ... but they like it ... [because there are so many of them]." Recalling her younger self a little ironically, her face still glowed as she recalled the experience. Indeed, although she drifted away from Nashi (she didn't quit, she explained; rather, she just stopped attending, as she felt she'd grown out of it), she maintained her commitment to the issues and spoke with appreciation of the tools Nashi had bequeathed her.

Masha was exceptional in many respects and moreover a leader within the organization; however, my research suggested that rank and file members found similar meaning in it as well. I found that many were drawn by Nashi's projects to "do good" – to work with orphans, veterans or on interethnic tolerance campaign. Beyond that, the organization, or "*dvizhuka*," offered young people an attractive combination of work, fun and activism that was particularly appealing to those who came from impoverished and socially desolate rural and provincial regions (see also Arutunyan, 2014; Krivonos and Fedorova, 2014).[31]

Our expectation of SMMs is that they – as opposed to "grassroots" mobilizations – are somehow inauthentic; Masha's narrative throws this binary into question. Her words make it clear that she experienced Nashi campaigns as venues for expression of her authentic self (Klumbytė, 2011; Yurchak, 2006). Moreover, her narrative reveals further unexpected outcomes associated with the form her mobilization took: in all our discussions, she emphasized the experience of solidarity through belonging. Her participation in Nashi's mass actions was transformative insofar as it generated a form of affective solidarity rather than ideologically based sense of belonging. Her participation resulted in a form of affective excess or overspill energy that was not contained by Nashi.

---

[31] Krivonos and Fedorova (2014) also note the affective dimension of belonging in Nashi. They report that Nashi activists asserted the category "dvizhukha" to describe their activities, defined as "an active and interesting pastime in the company of other young people." The term also often implies civic motivation.

7.5.2 Project Design

A second set of technologies derive more clearly from the NGO and business worlds and reveal how the Russian state harnessed tools of management consultancy and Silicon Valley–style entrepreneurship. Most prominent amongst these was project design. This new technology of governance became prominent during the Medvedev era (2008–2011) and partially displaced the "patriotic education" focus of earlier work. The streets secured, the administration turned its attention to tackling youth issues by other means. Linked to "modernization" objectives of the Medvedev administration (2008–2011), the move to embrace these technologies may have been stimulated by concerns about the 2008 global economic crisis also – as all over Europe, concerns about social instability in its aftermath were intense.[32]

Project design technology (*upravleniia proektami*) was most prominent at Seliger 2009, the IT-saturated federal youth education forum that I attended with several of my Russian colleagues. This Nashi-originating but Rosmolodezh-organized event energetically denied any Nashi affiliation, with materials emphasizing it was open to all "talented" youth. Echoing the logic of the international agencies that channeled funding to NGOs during the 1990s, projects were central both to the application process and to activities at Seliger. Participants needed to have one to register on the Rosmolodezh website, and they were supposed to develop it while there. As one organizer explained to me, project design had a "special place in the program" as the key technology; it was the core of the educational program offered to participants in each eight-day thematic session. It was usually taught during the morning of each day. After that, participants could select among different "master classes" and lectures. They then had the option to compete; events culminated in a project fair, where they presented their projects to potential sponsors.

"Project Design: Create Your Tomorrow," the glossy booklet distributed to all participants at Seliger who were coming without their own projects, offered practical steps and skills. It walked the reader through four main stages, from project development to formal presentation – four stages derived from the US management consultancy models it drew The on. But "project" represented more; the "project approach" (*proektnyi podkhod*) Seliger promotional materials promised was an enticingly new approach to life and work. It emphasized new qualities and skills for which it offered new terms – a strategic way of thinking (*proektnoe myshlenie*) – and a life stance of appealing agility and flexibility. "The person who develops his ability to

---

[32] Horvath notes that there was great anxiety about the potential fallout and the potential mobilizations that might ensue (2015, p. 585). Indeed, this period saw a renewed round of "dueling protests," as Edinaiia Rossiia (prompted by calls from Surkov) held pro-state rallies to counteract oppositional assemblies e.g. the communist party announced a "Day of Protest" on January 31, 2009, in response to the government's anti-crisis measures; the first Strategy 31 demonstration took place in January 2009.

effectively manage projects will lay a solid foundation for success in life!" promised Evgenii Sokolov in the lecture on project design he delivered at Seliger 2009.

Materials like this were shared via both the official Rosmolodezh website and social media (I became aware that Nashi organizers harnessed YouTube to "virally" circulate them during the spring of 2009; see also Fedor and Fredheim, 2017).[33] They delivered a message of choice and mobility and made a specific empowerment pledge. As one Seliger 2009 promotional video put it, "Your approach to life will completely change .... You'll forget the concept of work, work as a boring necessity that begins in school and ends in the grave, along with the fear of losing work or not being able to find it. The grandiose and precise word 'project' will now define the rhythm of your life. Your social mobility will increase. You'll easily be able to move from project to project, from town to town, from country to country." At this point, the video switched to an image of a young man with his laptop on the beach. "Your connections will cause envy. Your diplomas and workbook [*trudovaia kniga*] will recede into the past ... and you'll ask yourself – *do I really like what I am doing?*" Neither wage slave nor *sovok* (the disparaging slang term for passive, dependent Homo Sovieticus), the new subject invoked here was self-directing and dynamic and experienced work as an aesthetic experience, as creative play. Indeed, in the image of the beach bum with his laptop, work and play blended in an intoxicating fusion.

Contra the expectations of "patriotic education" that predominated in Nashi's early phase, project design technology contained an individualizing logic. It placed emphasis squarely on the individual self and on individual performance. Indeed, I learned that at Seliger 2009 winning projects were selected by teams of psychologists, who were dispatched by the organizers to observe some of the most promising volunteers in action and to examine their skills, behavior, and conduct. Providing evidence of the wide influence of discourses and practices of individual self-improvement in Russia (Lerner, 2015; Salmenniemi, 2012), their evaluation focused as much on the person and their comportment as it did on the substance of the projects themselves.

Igor was a komissar active in Nashi since 2005. He was hired as an organizer (*organizator*) at Seliger 2009. When I spoke with him in 2009 he told me he had encountered this project-based way of thinking via Nashi and spoke with appreciation of the tools it had provided. "You need a system or logistics. The movement taught me how to think about this systematically and to be able to analyze situations," he said. Igor explained to me how this training was enacted at Camp Seliger: "You need to understand that people are given an opportunity," he told me, "to sit for half an hour in front of the campfire and

---

[33] These authors discuss how the production and circulation of digital materials became central to the Russian state's post-2011 "informational management" strategies, emphasizing the central role Nashi activists played in developing these during the 2008–2011 period.

think: What don't I like about my environment? What can I do to change it? That's easy. And it becomes your project on which you can work. It may be, I don't know, the lack of sandboxes.... For example, you see children in your neighborhood climbing in construction sites or poking around in the trash or something. And you are concerned that there's no sandbox in the yard. This is also a project! This is something you can ask for money for." Here, Igor launched into a distinctive empowerment narrative (one I recognized as a script originating in Nashi campaigns) – in which, if only young people are bold enough to approach them, the representatives of the state are enlightened enough to listen and open to persuasion: "Lots of governors come to Seliger," he told me. "You can go up to them and say, 'You know, look...' Then you can go on the Internet and see how much a playground for kids would cost, how much it would cost to build... and go to that person and say, 'You know, this really bothers me.... It's necessary.' That is a project. It is an idea you want to realize."

I was captivated by Igor's narrative and his version of project design. It was a participatory rendition that acknowledged and addressed some of Russia's serious social problems in a practical way and suggested local, community-based solutions. For the problem of isolated *babushki* who can't get to the shops, for instance, he proposed a project designed to put them in touch with their neighbors; and for the problem of derelict buildings and poor infrastructure for children, a project of building sandboxes or playgrounds in courtyards. Significantly, for Igor, project design was an IT-enabled tactic. Many of the projects he named – including the one oriented to isolated *babushki* – used IT and social media to good effect (connecting young people with their elderly neighbors; putting would-be travelers in touch with other drivers).

For young people like him, project design promised a captivating path to the future. However, what of the dangers of disappointment? Young people were urged to be impactful and innovate. More precisely, they were trained to embrace a self-directed and aesthetic form of self-making and to *perform* innovation. Yet they were dissuaded from doing anything very direct or that would actually involve (certainly mobilize) people. Moreover, they had little chance of ever seeing their projects enacted; I found that very few Seliger participants received sponsorship or were able to enact their projects and that the vast majority returned home empty-handed. Indeed, I discovered that at Seliger 2009 prizes were awarded less frequently to projects than to *products* that could be marketed or sold.[34]

Igor's narrative reveals Nashi to be a more diffuse and uncertain project of governing than critical accounts suggested. Seliger 2009's emphasis on "innovation" gave rise to a proliferation of projects, some only loosely

---

[34] Winning projects at Seliger 2009 included a dog-waste disposal system, sponsored by a dog food company; a nicotine-free cigarette; and a biodegradable bag.

associated with state goals. The "project approach" spawned not only multiple projects but new agents with multiple and complex motivations as well (c.f. Rogers, 2015). Indeed, Nashi's greatest legacy (one of the unintended consequences of this form of SMMs) may have been the mode of agency it instilled in the individuals who participated in it – an individualized agency that exceeded Nashi the movement, as Igor's case illustrates. During our interview, and although we had ostensibly gotten together to talk about Nashi, Igor barely made mention of the movement. Rather, his emphasis was on the confidence and sense of agency it had fostered in him and the process of self-actualization that it had permitted. When I noted this and asked him about the role of Nashi and his relationship to it, he said, "You understand, the movement is a tool [*instrument*] that helps me; it's like a car that takes me somewhere." Like Kirill, he subordinated Nashi to his own needs.

7.6 CONCLUSION

My account should make plain that Nashi was an iconic instance of the SMMs this volume examines and served as a prime innovation lab for the kinds of technologies and strategies they are associated with. At a time of consternation about the Russian state's technologies and their transnational reach, it is especially instructive to return to this case. What are the lessons we can draw?

This ethnographically informed account reveals a more diffuse and uncertain project of governing than many critical accounts suggest. While indisputably state-emanating, and in sync with state policy discussions, Nashi (and Yakemenko-era youth projects more broadly) were a site of chaotic productions and improvisations, revealing a "highly dynamic field of state-societal interactions" (Chapter 1 in this volume) and contingent borrowings.

I have drawn attention to Nashi's instabilities at the levels of both design and reception. To some extent, these instabilities were hardwired. Nashi emerged at a time when the Kremlin had acknowledged one-size-fits-all youth strategies to be out of step with the times;[35] we can thus view Nashi's dynamism as a form of product diversification. But Nashi's instabilities were also the result of the technologies it harnessed, together with the diverse actors it empowered to use them, as we've seen. Indeed, the "project design" technology I have described partially accounts for the logic manifest in Nashi over time – the dynamic of moving from big bold mass rallies to individualized campaigns, splinter projects or "autonomous movements" that deny or obfuscate their origins in Nashi. Digital technology has played a role here too. Nashi's trajectory – as other social movements – was bound up with the informational

---

[35] The 2005 Youth Policy document, the Strategy, recognized the impossibility of returning to "the model of a single and unitary children and youth organization" that existed in the Soviet period (Blum, 2006).

and technological revolution that accompanied it and which has transformed political engagement into a more individualized form of activity (Gabowitsch, 2016, p. 3).

But what do these instabilities signal in terms of state power and governance? Is this intentional, calculated ambiguity suggestive of a new, "postmodern" form of authoritarian rule? The "postmodern dictatorship" (Pomerantsev, 2014) thesis has gained traction since 2011 and is widely held in US policy circles.[36] However, suggestive as it is and as much as it captures, it obscures certain things, assuming a level of intentionality and coherence that I don't find in this case – or in what came next (Chapter 8 in this volume).

Against the old/new consensus – that state-run projects like Nashi derive from a uniquely Soviet legacy of political cynicism and dissembling tactics (Pomerantsev, 2014; Wilson, 2005) – I insist on emphasizing the global context that gave Nashi shape. I have shown how the Nashi project emerged at a specific juncture. Born of a moment of crisis (concern about Western meddling, anxiety about Russia's geopolitical positioning), the project took form as it encountered both domestic political currents and global shifts. At the same time as it drew energy, tactics and tools from domestic oppositional movements (the "non-systemic" coalitions and groups that it dueled with), it coincided and interacted with the novel and creative forms of protest and political activism that circulated globally between 2005 and 2012. There was thus a global element to the movement/countermovement dynamic. Launched in response to the color revolutions, the Nashi project coincided with other global protest cycles as well – Arab Spring and Occupy. Russian state actors were paying close attention, both to these revolutions and to the technologies they harnessed, as well as to the soft power strategies adopted to contain them, refining their own tactics accordingly.[37] Nashi morphed over time as its precipitants and participants became enmeshed in this fast-paced, fast-moving terrain.

Russia made for a particularly innovative laboratory in terms of these mobilizational technologies, but the Russian state's preoccupations are hardly unique. Both its anxieties about youth and the tactics it has adopted are widely shared. In crafting the Nashi project, the Russian state was not merely seeking to control the domestic political field but grappling with broader currents and issues also, responding to twenty-first-century disenchantments: cycles of

---

[36] I refer here to the work of the Soviet-born British journalist and TV producer Peter Pomerantsev, whose policy papers (2013) and book (2014) have proven quite influential in the United States as well as the United Kingdom.

[37] Fedor and Fredheim's (2017) discussion reveals the extent to which Russian state information policy was propelled by a sense of having lost prior Western-led "information wars" (notably, the 2008 Georgian conflict). They track statements regarding state Internet policy, noting Nashi founder Surkov's use of the term *osvoenie* to explain the defensive nature of the state's goals: this key term was "used as a euphemism for colonial conquest and invasion; literally, to make one's own, or to master" (2017, p. 5).

economic crisis, disillusion about political liberalism, and the ever-widening gap between the affluent and the precarious under globalizing neoliberalism (Hemment, 2015). It's important to situate these Putin-era political developments within this broader context and to see Russia within the context of comparative authoritarianisms or managed democracies (Penzin, 2014, p. 165; see also Chapter 8 in this volume).

REFERENCES

Arutunyan, A. 2014. *The Putin Mystique: Inside Russia's Power Cult*. Northampton, MA: Interlink Publishing.
Atwal, Maya, and Edwin Bacon. 2012. The youth movement Nashi: contentious politics, civil society, and party politics. *East European Politics* 28 (3): 256–266.
Baker, Peter, and Susan Glasser. 2005. *Kremlin Rising: Vladimir Putin's Russia and the End of Revolution*. New York: Simon and Schuster.
Blum, Douglas W. 2006. Russian youth policy: shaping the nation-state's future. *SAIS Review* 26 (2): 95–108.
Clément, Karine. 2015. Unlikely mobilisations: how ordinary Russian people become involved in collective action. *European Journal of Cultural and Political Sociology* 2: 3–4: 211–240.
Colton, Timothy J., and Henry E. Hale, Luke March and Graeme B. Robertson. 2009. Responses: political science, democracy, and authoritarianism. *Slavic Review* 68 (3): 552–556.
Fedor, J., and Fredheim, R. 2017. "We need more clips about Putin, and lots of them": Russia's state-commissioned online visual culture. *Nationalities Papers* 45 (2): 161–181.
Fenghi, Fabrizio. 2017. Making post-Soviet counterpublics: the aesthetics of Limonka and the National-Bolshevik Party. *Nationalities Papers* 45 (2): 182–205.
Gabowitsch, M. 2016. Are copycats subversive? Strategy-31, the Russian Runs, the Immortal Regiment, and the transformative potential of non-hierarchical movements. *Problems of Post-Communism* 65 (5): 1–18.
Greenberg, Jessica. 2014. *After the Revolution: Youth, Democracy, and the Politics of Disappointment in Serbia*. Stanford, CA: Stanford University Press.
Hemment, Julie. 2009. Soviet-style neoliberalism? Nashi, youth voluntarism, and the restructuring of social welfare in Russia. *Problems of Post-Communism* 56 (6): 36–50.
Hemment, Julie. 2012a. Nashi, youth voluntarism, and Potemkin NGOs: Making sense of civil society in post-Soviet Russia. *Slavic Review* 71 (2): 234–260.
Hemment, Julie. 2012b. Redefining need, reconfiguring expectations: the rise of state-run youth voluntarism programs in Russia. *Anthropological Quarterly* 85 (2): 519–554.
Hemment, Julie. 2015. *Youth Politics in Putin's Russia: Producing Patriots and Entrepreneurs*. Bloomington: Indiana University Press.
Holmes, Douglas R. 2010. *Integral Europe: Fast-Capitalism, Multiculturalism, Neofascism*. Princeton, NJ: Princeton University Press.
Horvath, Robert. 2011. Putin's "preventive counter-revolution": Post-Soviet authoritarianism and the spectre of Velvet revolution. *Europe-Asia Studies* 63 (1): 1–25.

Horvath, Robert. 2015. "Sakharov would be with us": Limonov, Strategy-31, and the Dissident Legacy. *Russian Review* 74 (4): 581–598.
Juris, Jeffrey S. 2008. Performing politics: image, embodiment, and affective solidarity during anti-corporate globalization protests. *Ethnography* 9 (1): 61–97.
Kalb, Don. 2009. Conversations with a Polish populist: Tracing hidden histories of globalization, class, and dispossession in postsocialism (and beyond). *American Ethnologist* 36 (2): 207–223.
Klumbytė, Neringa. 2011. Political intimacy: power, laughter, and coexistence in late Soviet Lithuania. *East European Politics and Societies* 25 (4): 658–677.
Krivonos, Daria, and Natalia Fedorova. 2014. MYPLACE (Memory, Youth, Political Legacy And Civic Engagement) Grant agreement no: FP7-266831 WP7: Interpreting Activism (Ethnographies) Deliverable 7.1: Ethnographic Case Studies of Youth Activism Vse Doma Russia.
Lassila, Jussi. 2014. *The Quest for an Ideal Youth in Putin's Russia II: The Search for Distinctive Conformism in the Political Communication of Nashi, 2005–2009*. Vol. 115. New York: Columbia University Press.
Lerner, Julia. 2015. The changing meanings of Russian love: emotional Socialism and therapeutic culture on the post-Soviet screen. *Sexuality & Culture* 19 (2): 349–368.
Lyytikäinen, Laura. 2016. *Performing political opposition in Russia*. London: Routledge.
Manning, Paul. 2007. Rose-colored glasses? Color revolutions and cartoon chaos in postsocialist Georgia. *Cultural Anthropology* 22 (2): 171–213.
Matveev, I. 2014. The "two Russias" culture war: constructions of the "people" during the 2011–2013 protests. *South Atlantic Quarterly* 113 (1): 186–195.
Mijnssen, Ivo. 2014. *The Quest for an Ideal Youth in Putin's Russia I: Back to Our Future! History, Modernity, and Patriotism According to Nashi, 2005-2013*. New York: Columbia University Press.
Norris, Stephen M. 2012. *Blockbuster History in the New Russia: Movies, Memory, and Patriotism*. Bloomington: Indiana University Press.
Ost, David. 2005. *The Defeat of Solidarity: Anger and Politics in Postcommunist Europe*. Ithaca, NY: Cornell University Press.
Oushakin, Sergeĭ. 2009. *The Patriotism of Despair: Nation, War, and Loss in Russia*. Ithaca, NY: Cornell University Press.
Penzin, Alexei. 2014. Tumult in the Land of Managed Democracy: An Introduction. *South Atlantic Quarterly* 113 (1): 162–168.
Pilkington, Hilary, and Gary Polluck. 2015. *Radical Futures? Youth, Politics and Activism in Contemporary Europe*. Hoboken, NJ: Wiley Blackwell.
Pomerantsev, Peter. 2013. *Russia: A Postmodern Dictatorship?* London: Legatum Institute.
Pomerantsev, P. 2014. *Nothing Is True and Everything Is Possible: The Surreal Heart of the New Russia*. New York: PublicAffairs.
Prilepin, Zakhar. 2014. *Sankya*. New York: Open Road Media.
Razsa, Maple. 2015. *Bastards of Utopia: Living Radical Politics after Socialism*. Bloomington: Indiana University Press.
Robertson, Graeme B. 2009. Managing society: protest, civil society, and regime in Putin's Russia. *Slavic Review* 68 (3): 528–547.
Robertson, Graeme B. 2010. *The Politics of Protest in Hybrid Regimes: Managing Dissent in Post-communist Russia*. Cambridge: Cambridge University Press.

Rogers, D. 2015. *The Depths of Russia: Oil, Power, and Culture after Socialism.* Ithaca, NY: Cornell University Press.
Salmenniemi, S. (ed.). 2012. *Rethinking Class in Russia.* Farnham: Ashgate Publishing.
Sperling, V. 2014. *Sex, Politics, and Putin: Political Legitimacy in Russia.* Oxford: Oxford University Press.
Stephenson, S. 2015. *Gangs of Russia: From the Streets to the Corridors of Power.* Ithaca, NY: Cornell University Press.
Stites, Richard. 1988. *Revolutionary Dreams: Utopian Vision and Experimental Life in the Russian Revolution.* Oxford: Oxford University Press.
Urla, Jacqueline, and Justin Helepololei. 2014. The ethnography of resistance then and now: On thickness and activist engagement in the twenty-first century. *History and Anthropology* 25 (4): 431–451.
Wilson, Andrew. 2005. *Virtual Politics: Faking Democracy in the Post-Soviet World.* New Haven, CT: Yale University Press.
Yurchak, Alexei. 2006. *Everything Was Forever, until It Was No More: The Last Soviet Generation.* Princeton, NJ: Princeton University Press.

8

State-Mobilized Movements after Annexation of Crimea

The Construction of Novorossiya

Samuel A. Greene and Graeme B. Robertson

8.1 INTRODUCTION

During and after the Crimean annexation in March 2014, Russia witnessed a huge increase in support for President Vladimir Putin (Hale, 2018). More importantly for events on the ground, however, this rally was not limited to changes in political approval: it extended to the mobilization of large numbers of volunteers, donors and sympathizers in support of military action outside the country's borders. Both online and offline, a surge of activism was unleashed to strengthen, militarily and ideologically, the claim that Crimea and eastern Ukraine were somehow a natural part of Russia that had been accidentally and wrongly alienated by the idiosyncrasies of the collapse of the USSR (Matveeva, 2018). Two names that came to be adopted by the movement, "Russian Spring"/"Novorossiya," reflect the intertwined ideas of a revival of ethnic Russian consciousness, the return of a previously dormant Russia back onto the international stage, and the tsarist-era basis of the Russian claim to much of what is today southern and eastern Ukraine.

The conventional wisdom on the "Russian Spring"/"Novorossiya" movement holds that it was brought into existence by a combination of propaganda and "astro-turf" organizing, heavily directed from the Kremlin. While there is undoubtedly some truth to both of these claims, we argue here that much of the groundswell of support for the Kremlin and its intervention in Ukraine came through the engagement of existing nationalist ideas and constituencies that had previously been either neglected or actively suppressed by the state. Thus, rather than reorienting loyal citizens toward a new cause sewn out of whole cloth, Russia's Novorossiya movement drew on existing ideas and networks to spur disaffected but politically available constituencies to rally to the flag, bringing on board a motivated following who had previously seen little reason to support whoever was occupying the post-Soviet Kremlin.

In this chapter, we take advantage of the fact that much of the organizational and ideological work behind this movement took place online. This allows us to examine in detail patterns of pro-Russian contention and how it changed over time. We can see how events on the ground drove levels of engagement and shifted the aspirations and goals of activists over time. We look at patterns in the content and framing of claims made by members of the movement, illustrate the proliferation over time of the different groups involved in pro-Russian contention and demonstrate shifts in patterns of influence or authority among those groups. In the process, we describe the construction of a cross-border community of action in support of Russian state goals.

Our analysis sheds new light on this crucial period in Russian and Ukrainian politics, but it also has implications for scholars thinking about the nature of contemporary authoritarianism more broadly. For this was more than just a "small victorious war" and that generated a "rally around the flag." The war mobilized an active constituency of partisans, willing to contribute not just their sentiment but also their actions and, in some cases, their lives, with consequences that both strengthened the Russian state and limited the leadership's freedom of action. The citizens we describe are not just passive recipients of mobilizational stimuli produced by their leaders but also active participants in the construction of the legitimacy that makes it possible for autocrats to rule – in much the same way that voters in democracies provide the electoral, ideational and organizational resources on which their own leaders rely for power.

To the extent that the Russian experience can be generalized, it suggests a rethinking of how authoritarianism works in the contemporary world. Since the foundational work of Juan Linz, scholars have thought of authoritarianism primarily as a demobilizing system that channels citizens' energies away from politics (Linz, 2000). While this is often true, this view obscures the fact that some of the most successful authoritarian projects actually rely on active and autonomous participation from below. However, as we will see, when contemporary authoritarians benefit from the added strength of vigorous citizen engagement, they also encounter new kinds of limits and constraints that such engagement imposes.

8.2 MOBILIZING CONTENTION IN DEMOCRACY AND DICTATORSHIP

The dominant image in most media accounts of social movements, especially in authoritarian contexts, is of a set of weak or politically marginalized actors attempting to break into the public sphere and achieve change in ways that could not be achieved without transgressive forms of contentious political action. However, students of social movements have long recognized that things are more complicated than this simple David and Goliath model would suggest. In reality, mobilization takes place in an interactive field, with the dynamics of political contestation depending heavily on the interaction between movements, state structures and other organizations. As we show in this section, scholars of mobilization in both democracies and autocracies have increasingly adopted this interactive view of mobilization.

In the literature on contention in democratic states, much of the recent focus has been on the role political and economic elites play in the organizational work behind movements and campaigns. It has long been understood that political organizing is a highly specialized activity, and over time such work has become increasingly professionalized (McCarthy and Zald, 1977). Moreover, the repertoire of actions of mass social movement organizations has increasingly been integrated into interest group politics, with private, often corporate, interests adopting the same techniques used by grassroots organizations. This has led to the emergence of a phenomenon known as "astroturfing," whereby the real initiators or sponsors of a campaign are hidden behind an artificially constructed facade of grassroots organizing. Front and center in this discussion is the role of public affairs consultancies, for-profit professional organizations dedicated to the management of political and issue campaigns. Unsurprisingly, given the importance placed on civic activism in contemporary theories of democratic politics and democratization, the emergence of the professionalized campaign and so-called memberless organizations has led to concerns about the impact on the nature of public policymaking, on civil society and on what Howard calls the "managed citizen" (McNutt and Boland, 2007; Howard, 2006).

Other scholars have taken a less top-down view of the role of professional consultants. Walker, while still alert to the acute normative issues at stake, sees advocacy professionals not so much as generating a fake or controlled citizenry but rather as creating "subsidized publics" where a select of group of citizens have their participation facilitated by the money and expertise of professional organizers (Walker, 2014). This term does not have quite the negative connotations of "astroturf," and citizens are treated not as dupes so much as activists who genuinely care about the issues at stake. Nevertheless, the role of political consultancies in mobilizing selected groups still puts a rather heavy thumb on the political scales.

The evolution of notions of contention and mobilized contention in the literature on long-standing democracies has fascinating parallels in work on the question of mobilization in authoritarian regimes. Early research that interpreted approved or supportive political action in autocracies as predominantly top-down and heavily (and usually clumsily) managed is starting to be challenged by analyses that take a more nuanced and coproduced view of pro-regime political action in contemporary nondemocratic regimes.

The degree to which a regime seeks to either mobilize or demobilize its citizenry was one of the key distinguishing features between different kinds of nondemocratic regimes, according to Juan Linz's classic analysis (Linz, 2000).

For Linz, totalitarian regimes were defined by deliberate and intensive efforts to mobilize citizens into pro-regime political action. By contrast, authoritarian regimes were those that actively sought to demobilize citizens and keep them away from political participation.

However, even non-totalitarian leaders need to mobilize citizens on occasion, particularly if the practices of the regime involve an electoral component. In post-Yugoslav Serbia, for example, nationalist mobilization formed part of a broader regime strategy designed to "make alternatives to its rule unavailable," by marginalizing and fatiguing opponents and enforcing passivity among the bulk of the citizenry (Gordy, 1999, p. 2). In addition, a large literature on clientelism was developed in which participation in authoritarian political institutions, and in particular elections, was explained by a trade of votes and participation for patronage and transfers (Stokes, Dunning and Nazareno, 2013). Magaloni referred to this system as a "punishment regime," in which costs could be imposed upon voters who attempted to defect from the regime (Magaloni, 2006). This largely economistic approach to rewards and punishments shaping political mobilization in authoritarian regimes continues to be influential. Specifically in the postcommunist context, scholars have looked to political and economic incentives to explain patterns of labor protest and voting (Robertson, 2007; Frye, Reuter and Szakonyi, 2014).

However, recent work on pro-regime mobilization is changing the emphasis of the conversation in important ways. For example, Chen Weiss argues for much more autonomy and efficacy on the part of pro-regime protesters in China than is usually assumed (Weiss, 2014). In her book, nationalist protests are driven largely from below and are tolerated or repressed depending upon the relationship between the protests and the particular foreign policy goals of the government. Indeed, nationalist street protest in China – when allowed by Beijing for reasons mostly to do with foreign policy signaling – is often critical of the regime itself, which is seen by protesters as insufficiently robust in the protection and projection of China's national (and nationalist) interests (Weiss, 2013).

The issue of state-mobilized movement (SMM) has been particularly extensively engaged in recent literature on contemporary authoritarianism in Russia, with a number of new strands being added to the conversation as the Putin regime has stepped up its efforts to engage supportive forces in society. Some scholars have emphasized the top-down element in pro-state mobilization, particularly of young people, in state-organized and -supported "ersatz social movements" (Balzar, 2003; Petrov, Lipman and Hale, 2013; Robertson, 2009, 2011). Others have focused more on the agency of the societal actors themselves. Cheskin and March, for example, focus on what they call "consentful" contention, by which they mean autonomous protest that, nevertheless, pursues regime-sanctioned goals (Cheskin and March, 2015). Others still look at less visible forms of sanctioned contention such as

Public Monitoring Commissions or the promotion of social and economic rights (Owen, 2015; Bindman, 2015; Tarasenko, 2015). Julie Hemment has taken the idea of citizen agency in the context of SMMs in Russia the farthest, arguing that, from the very moment the idea of a movement is out of the minds of the politicians and into the world, it takes on a life of its own as interpreted, developed, adopted or rejected by citizens in the light of their own ideas and prevailing trends in the world (Hemment, 2015). In the rest of this paper, we build upon the idea that both the state and protesters enjoy agency even in the context of intensive SMMs.

8.3 STATE-MOBILIZED MOVEMENT IN POST-SOVIET RUSSIA

Active efforts to mobilize elements of society in support of the regime have been a key characteristic of Russian politics in recent years. This represents a sharp contrast to the first two terms of Putin's presidency when, buoyed by high oil and gas prices, the regime was largely able to leave society to its own devices, as the administration focused on neoliberal economic reforms and reestablishing control over media and natural resource companies. However, with the end of relatively easy economic times and increasing pressure from the international environment, the Kremlin has become active in its mobilization efforts and, in doing so, has resorted to ever more nationalist and imperialist ideas.

The post-Soviet Russian state began to become interested in mobilization in a concerted way in reaction to the wave of popular uprisings that helped topple authoritarian rulers in Serbia, Georgia, Ukraine and Kyrgyzstan in 2000–2005. The Kremlin saw (and publicly portrayed) what came to be known as the "color revolutions" as part of a Western-led effort to install friendly governments in the region. While authoritarian rulers in various countries responded to this wave of regime changes in different ways, Vladimir Putin's Russia settled on a strategy that included aspects of coercion, co-optation and preemptive occupation of mobilizational spaces but focused primarily on persuasion, as the Kremlin sought to convince Russians – particularly young Russians – that its policies and ideas were more attractive than anything that might come from the West (Finkel and Brudny, 2012). While consolidating control over television and the party system, the leadership created an ecosystem of pro-Putin youth movements and loyal "GONGOs," or government-organized nongovernment organizations, to take the president's case to the public and to harass Putin's opponents. For example, participants in Nashi, the largest of the resulting youth movements, were frequently found protesting outside the US, UK and Estonian embassies and shouting down opposition protesters.

Throughout most of the 2000s, however, and until the end of President Dmitry Medvedev's term in office, the Kremlin was content to rely on a largely "technocratic" arsenal of managerial (as opposed to ideological) weapons to defend its positions. Relatively favorable economic conditions in the country backed up its popular legitimacy – most Russians, after all, had never had it so good – and created space for the administration to experiment with new techniques for cementing the leadership's power. These included repeated changes in the party system, reforms of the electoral system and manipulation of the rules covering candidate registration, a switch from elected to appointed regional governors and back again, changes to the management of regional politics and tighter state control over "strategic industries" in natural resources, high finance and the media.

The Kremlin's first cut at shaping civil society was similarly "technocratic" and focused on adapting Soviet-era technologies to the new competitive authoritarian context. Key elements involved creating a system for licensing nongovernmental organizations that would give the state extensive tools to harass and marginalize groups officials did not like. Groups the state did like were invited into new institutions called Public Chambers, which provided a talking shop and financing for state-sanctioned voluntary and charitable organizations. In addition, there was the creation/support of a variety of ersatz social movements that were directly funded by the Kremlin and operated in close cooperation with leading Kremlin officials – groups such as Nashi (Ours) or Molodaya Gvardia (Young Guard). These social movements were designed to capture the energies of ambitious young people who might otherwise become disaffected.

Nevertheless, the system failed to prevent major anti-Putin protests in a number of big cities, most prominently in Moscow, sparked by allegations of widespread fraud in the parliamentary elections of December 2011. These protests, which initially seemed to catch the Kremlin off guard, eventually provoked an increased reliance on repression, but they also led the Kremlin to double down on its ideational appeal. In the face of its first major crisis of legitimacy, the Putin administration set out to draw a thick line between supportive "healthy" elements in society and dangerous, immoral, Western-backed forces seeking to overthrow the regime. The strategy had domestic and international components that portrayed Russian civilization as a holdout and bulwark against the decadence of the West. Internally, laws against offending Orthodox believers and anti-gay legislation were part of an effort to drive a sharp wedge between Russian and "Western" values (Greene and Robertson, 2019). Internationally, the Kremlin sought to expand its view of Russian civilization beyond the borders of the Russian Federation to include a broader "Russian world" (*russkii mir*) of mostly Russian-speaking Slavic people living around the former USSR.

At the heart of the Kremlin's ideological strategy was nationalism and, in particular, a related set of imperialist ideas commonly known as Eurasianism. Related to nationalism, but with its own baroque elements, Eurasianism draws on late-nineteenth- and early-twentieth-century thinking about Russia's particular place in the world. Eurasianism explicitly rejects the possibility of Russia participating in processes of European integration and instead asserts

Russia's essence as a land empire exercising dominance over the territories lost in the Soviet collapse (Clover, 2016).

This discourse was important in the Soviet foreign policy establishment and retained its attractions in the post-Soviet era as Moscow protested over NATO expansion (quietly) and involvement in Yugoslavia (loudly) (Kerr, 1995; Bassin, 2003). Moreover, parties and movements expressing ideas of this kind have long had a significant popular appeal. In the 1993 parliamentary elections, Vladimir Zhirinovsky's nationalist Liberal Democratic Party of Russia won a surprise victory and presented a credible challenge to Boris Yeltsin in the 1996 presidential election. From time to time, too, establishment politicians would pick up on these and other "nationalist" grievances for their own purposes; throughout the 1990s, for example, the populist Moscow mayor Yury Luzhkov harped on the issue of Crimea, both to boost his visibility and to bolster his own presidential ambitions (Colton, 1999).

Although it retained some popular appeal, nationalism was not central to either domestic or foreign policymaking in the first Putin administration. Rodina, a new party created in 2003 in part at the Kremlin's instigation to soak up nationalist votes, had to be shut down after threatening to become too successful. In fact, until Putin's return to the presidency in 2012, Russia neither pursued regional integration projects with anything that might be mistaken for vigor nor sought consistently to intervene on behalf of Russian-speaking minorities in the "near abroad" (though there were notable exceptions in Estonia and Georgia).

Even as it failed to consolidate as an organized movement or a structural part of the Russian foreign policy establishment, however, nationalism as a loose ideological community (and its disparate correlates and variations, including Eurasianism) persisted, both prodding the Kremlin from the sidelines and serving as an occasional resource (Laruelle, 2004; Tsygankov, 1998). Locked out of mainstream politics, nationalist ideas found sway in a large "illiberal" civil society, which soaked up most of the fervor that might otherwise have gone into robust right-wing parties (Umland, 2002; Verkhovsky, 2000). A central claim of "Eurasianists" in particular is that the Kremlin has been consistently both insufficiently "Russian" and insufficiently strong (Ingram, 1999). For these movements' adherents – both among elites and masses – the "loss" of Ukraine and the sight of that country's own nation-building process was always an open and festering wound (Kuzio, 1997).

8.4 STATE-MOBILIZED MOVEMENT AND SOCIETY IN THE RUSSO-UKRAINIAN CRISIS

It was in this context that the Euromaidan Revolution in Ukraine, the annexation of Crimea and the beginnings of uprisings in eastern Ukraine took place in February–March 2014. Pro-Russian organizations from the *russkii mir* constellation and elsewhere quickly sprung into action, both online and on the streets of Russia. Major demonstrations in support of Russian military action in Crimea took place on March 2, 2014, in Moscow, with some 27,000 people in attendance (much smaller anti-war demonstrations took place at the same time).[1] A Kremlin-supported motorcycle club, the Night Wolves, also joined the demonstrations and organized similar events in eastern Ukraine.[2] Other demonstrations, typically involving students, public sector workers, veterans, Cossack organizations and members of political parties, also took place around the country, particularly in southern Russia.[3] These participants joined existing far-right groups but tended to crowd them out, as national-patriotic rhetoric and support for Russian speakers in Ukraine displaced the existing anti-immigrant message of the far right. Moreover, nationalist groups that were formerly opposed to the Kremlin, such as Eduard Limonov's "Other Russia" movement, now rallied to the cause.[4]

In addition to organizing support amongst activists, the Kremlin's state television propaganda machine went into overdrive. Night after night, Russian state television bombarded its enormous viewership with images and stories of the plight of Russian speakers in eastern Ukraine and on the new "fascist junta" that had taken power in Kiev. This blanket coverage interacted with pre-existing patriotic sentiment in Russia to create a huge wave of popular support (Greene and Robertson, 2016). According to polls, more than three-quarters of Russians used television as their primary source of information on the conflict in Ukraine, a proportion that increased to nearly 90 percent by August 2014. Moreover, more than 70 percent of national survey respondents thought that the relentless coverage on television was "objective."[5] The result was enormous support for action to protect Russians in eastern Ukraine. According to the polling company Levada Center, some 67 percent of Russians blamed radical Ukrainian nationalists for the crisis in Crimea, and some 58 percent supported the introduction of Russian troops to Crimea. President Putin's personal popularity ratings also rose dramatically to almost 90 percent, as measured by Levada.

The Russian annexation of Crimea was popular, but it was not a popular movement. When protests erupted in Sebastopol, the regional capital Simferopol and other parts of the peninsula after Yanukovych's flight from Kiev, the decision to mobilize "little green men" – a combination of regular troops and "volunteers," well trained and well equipped but without insignia – in order to wrest Crimea from Ukrainian control was made quietly (Higgens and Erlanger, 2014; Raibman, 2014; Agence France Press, 2015). In no real sense were

---

[1] See www.forbes.ru/sobytiya-photogallery/obshchestvo/251576-voina-i-mir-kak-mitingovali-v-moskve-storonniki-i-protivnik/photo/1. Some 361 people were arrested at the anti-war demonstration (http://grani.ru/Politics/Russia/m.225936.html). There were no reports of arrest at the pro-government action.
[2] See https://lenta.ru/news/2014/03/02/wolfes/.
[3] See http://ria.ru/society/20140304/998132179.html#ixzz48yB2PciC.
[4] See http://polit.ru/article/2015/03/25/xeno/.   [5] See http://fom.ru/Mir/11731.

Russians themselves asked before the move to acquire Crimea was made, but the response was nevertheless positive. The "return" of Crimea to the Russian Federation – a historic moment that was publicly justified by the Kremlin in syncretic terms of defending Russian-speaking civilians, resisting Western advances on strategic Russian positions, regaining a supposed cradle of Orthodox Christianity, restoring the acquisitions of Russian tsars and righting the wrongs of Soviet leaders (Putin, 2014) – brought almost immediate dividends. Putin's popularity, which had been foundering since before his reelection, and which had not been significantly boosted by the spectacle of the Sochi Olympics, rose dramatically (Gudkov, 2015; Greene and Robertson, 2014).

What Putin would later describe as a carefully planned special operation became the model for a conflict that would be considerably more fraught. By late spring, "little green men" – who had been referred to by Russian officials as "polite people" – began popping up in eastern Ukraine, occupying government buildings in scenes that looked to be a carbon copy of what had transpired in Crimea. The Russian government has maintained that it has no direct command-and-control relationship with any of the Russian citizens – many of them active-duty troops – who arrived to take part in what turned into a long and bloody military conflict; the government has allegedly gone to great lengths to hide the resulting casualties from its own population (Petlianova, 2014). Nonetheless, the image of "little green men" and "polite people" – ridiculed in the West as a symbol of Russian state subterfuge – became a point of pride for many Russian citizens (Oliphant, 2014; Kashin, 2014). Tents began popping up in Moscow and other cities, outside metro stations and other public places, bearing the black, blue and red flag of the Donetsk People's Republic, with agitators seeking recruits and donations. As the war in Ukraine stretched into 2015, some 7 percent of Russians reported knowing someone who had volunteered to fight in Donbas, while 65 percent of respondents had a favorable opinion of the volunteers (against 22 percent who thought negatively of them) (BBC Russian Service, 2014).

The relationship between the Russian government and the fighters themselves remains unclear, even if most observers have little doubt that many of the fighters are regular Russian troops, and all of them rely on Russian supplies of arms and money (ICG, 2016). While much of the recruitment evidently operated through military channels (even if informally), a lot also appears to have happened online. For that purpose, the site www.dobrovolec.org was registered on February 22, 2014, the day after Yanukovych fled Ukraine, abandoning power to the leaders of the Euromaidan, although it remained dormant until the summer of that year, when it began advertising for experienced soldiers only, particularly those capable of driving tanks and flying helicopters.[6]

---

[6] ICANN WHOIS: dobrovolec.org (https://whois.icann.org/en/lookup?name=dobrovolec.org, accessed May 22, 2016); Kostiuchenko (2014).

By late in the summer of 2015, official reports estimated between 30,000 and 50,000 Russian volunteers serving in the Donbas, and leaders from the region spent considerable time in Russia building up networks to recruit more (TASS, 2015). Separatist leaders, meanwhile, made no bones about their ties to Russian officialdom. Igor Girkin, who became the Donetsk People's Republic's defense minister under the nom de guerre of Strelkov, publicly claimed to be a serving colonel in the FSB, Russia's state security service (Strelkov, 2014). In making those claims, and in building their online and off-line presences in Russia and on Russian-language social media, Girkin, Aleksandr Zakharchenko, Denis Pushilin and other separatist leaders – alongside their ideological comrades in Russia and Ukraine – built a cross-border community of action, even as that action itself ran the gamut from "liking" a post on VKontakte to volunteering to fight in Donbas.

For the Novorossiya/Russian Spring leaders and activists, claiming ties to the Russian state, even if the state did not reciprocate those claims, evidently served to boost the internal legitimacy of the community and its actions. In broadening their appeal to the point where they could generate millions of "likes" a month, however, they had help from ideational frames that had been present in Russia for years. One such frame was "Eurasianism," which has provided something of an intellectual justification for both territorial acquisition and conflict with the West, but there are other frames too (Laruelle, 2004). The Russian political observer Sergei Medvedev has pointed to an emerging ideology of *ressentiment*, beginning with Putin's now-famous line about the fall of the USSR being the twentieth century's "greatest geopolitical catastrophe" (Medvedev, 2014). Svetlana Alexievich, the Russian-speaking winner of the 2015 Nobel Prize for literature, argues that this *ressentiment* is embedded in the Russian population at large: "There is a collective Putin, consisting of some millions of people who do not want to be humiliated by the West. There is a little piece of Putin in everyone" (Donadio, 2016). To this, other observers add an increasingly dichotomous politics, which creates stark divides between "us" and "them," and a more emotion-laden, aggressive and sometimes hateful language that has come to dominate both social media interaction and, at times, the nightly news (Baunov, 2016; Sorkin, 2014).

The availability of a fertile discursive field and a constituency inclined to nationalist sentiment did not make pro-regime nationalist or patriotic mobilization inevitable, however. In his investigation of the ways in which nationalist mobilization has been used to support the legitimacy of post-Soviet regimes, Goode points in particular to the ability of leaders to "seek legitimacy by echoing nationalist stances and repertoires inherited and refashioned from the cycle of anti-Soviet mobilization" (Goode, 2012). This presented a problem for would-be patriotic mobilizers in the Kremlin. Post-Soviet Russia had not been born out of a drive for independence and nation-building, and the Russian ethnic movements that had emerged under glasnost and perestroika had an adversarial relationship with both the Yeltsin and Putin

Kremlins. In fact, Russia's most prominent ethno-nationalist movement – motivated by antipathy toward labor migrants from the Caucasus and Central Asia – has found more common cause of late with the anti-regime opposition than with Putin (Laruelle, 2014). By contrast, when the overtly Kremlin-sponsored "anti-Maidan" protests marched through Moscow and other major cities, they carried portraits of Putin and Chechen leader Ramzan Kadyrov, as if to demonstrate the breadth of the regime's ethnic tent (Azar, 2015). Thus, it is perhaps no surprise that most of the pre-Donbas content in the VKontakte groups that would later evolve into the network we studied here displayed an attachment primarily to the past: to the memory of victory in World War II, to nostalgia for all things Soviet, and to the old dream of pan-Slavic and Orthodox unity.

The Novorossiya/Russian Spring mobilization created something new: a connection for Russian patriotic nationalists to the here and now and to the state. In the Donbas, the Kremlin pursued a war against an enemy that could be framed in the comfortable tropes of the past: ostensibly fascist and anti-Soviet, Western-backed and anti-Russian. What's more, the Kremlin seemed to be fighting on behalf of an ostensible victim whose Russianness transcended national borders and harked back to a shared history, both Soviet and pre-Soviet. In providing images of heroic participation – the "little green men" and "polite people" – and by allowing separatist leaders to boast (with a wink and a nod) of their ties to Moscow, the regime gave patriots a pathway of participation that could be as real or as virtual as each individual's biography allowed. In doing all of this, the Kremlin provided a discursive and mobilizational field on which it could find common ground with a constituency it had previously failed to motivate.

8.5 NOVOROSSIYA ONLINE

In the rest of this chapter, we review an original data set of activity and content from sixteen public VKontakte communities, involving more than 500,000 posts made between December 13, 2011 and May 2, 2016. We employed a "saturating snowball" sampling technique, whereby we began with the largest groups on VKontakte found by searching for content including "Donbas," "Novorossiia" and "Russkaia Vesna" (Russian Spring) and then following VKontakte's built-in affinity algorithm – "if you like this group, you'll also like … " – until the sample had exhausted all relevant groups with at least 25,000 followers.[7] Counts of activity were plotted across the network over time, "authorities" (the most influential sources of text across the network) were identified and a random sample of 100 texts were human coded for content. Figure 8.1 shows activity on the network over the period, beginning to gather steam as the Euromaidan captured headlines in late 2013, reaching an

---

[7] Data collected using Romanov (2016).

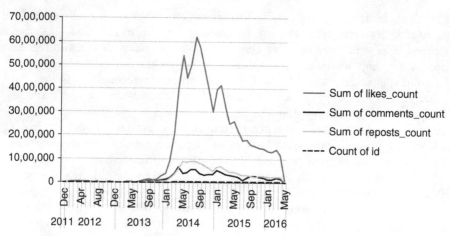

FIGURE 8.1 Donbas–Russian Spring network activity, 2011–2016

initial peak of some 5.5 million "likes" per month during the annexation of Crimea in April 2014 and then hitting an all-time high of more than 6 million likes per month later that summer, during the war in Donbas and following the downing of a Malaysian airliner, flight MH-17, over separatist-controlled territory.

In the months and years before the Euromaidan, the online network that would emerge as the core Novorossiya/Russian Spring community was quiet but not dormant. Topics prominent in 2012–2013 included news on the state of the Russian military, nostalgia for the Soviet Union and victory in World War II, the "problem" of non-Slavic labor migrants in Russia and the wedge issues that the Kremlin deployed against the opposition, including LGBT rights and the role of religion (particularly Russian Orthodoxy) in society. Putin was mentioned only once in the sample, in relation to laws he had signed banning "gay propaganda" and offending the sensibilities of religious observers. An overriding theme was what might be called "Slavic nationalism," strongly identifying with ethnic Russianness (often in a very expansive sense, which would include Belarusians and Ukrainians, as well as affinities with Serbs), rather than with the Russian state or its leadership. Amongst nationalistic poems and vignettes were sentiments along the following lines:

The historical truth is that it was the Russian people who blocked the path for German fascism to world domination, who carried on their shoulders the greatest weight of the second world war and who made the decisive contribution to achieving Victory.[8]

---

[8] http://vk.com/public33066465, "Respublika Novorossiia I Velikaia Rus'," October 1, 2013.

State-Mobilized Movements after Crimea

In the period prior to the Euromaidan, only two of the sixteen groups in the data set had any activity – one titled "The Republic of Novorossiya | Great Rus'" and another titled "For Russia, Novorossiya, DNR, LNR and A.V. Zakharchenko." (It is likely that both of these groups, which have held these titles since the summer of 2014 at the least, carried different titles prior to that, but those titles have sadly been lost to history.) Prior to the Euromaidan, these groups' discourse was unsurprisingly focused on Russia, which was mentioned directly in approximately 60 percent of the early posts in the data set – but not on the Kremlin. Until the very end of 2013, the Russian president figured in approximately 5 percent of the posts and comments made on these nationalist community pages. For all the expected emphasis on nostalgia, the USSR was only mentioned in about 10 percent of posts. The word "revenge," however, figured in some 20 percent of pre-Euromaidan posts, pointing to an aggrieved constituency, if one as yet lacking an outlet for their grievances. (A graph of major topics over time is presented in Figure 8.2.)

As the geography shifts, so do both the content and the framing. General philosophizing about Russia and Russians gives way to analysis of the situation in Ukraine, criticism of the Euromaidan and, somewhat later, war reporting. By the second quarter of 2014 – when the Donbas has fallen into full-scale warfare and many online "partisans" are eagerly predicting the spread of violence further afield, to Mariupol, Kharkiv and Odessa – reports from the front lines in eastern Ukraine dominate the sample. Meanwhile, pan-Slavic nationalism gives way to Russian state-linked patriotism; Putin himself figures in more than 20 percent of posts by the time of the Crimean annexation in March 2014. While the language of revenge remains, the military conflict is couched first and foremost in terms of the fight against fascism – picking up on earlier tropes – and then in terms of outright separatism.

Separatism itself, however, does not appear to have been the immediate reaction to events in Kiev. Thus, as the Euromaidan gathered steam, posts were focused not on breaking away but, pragmatically, on the place eastern Ukraine could occupy in a new Ukrainian political landscape. While some in the network – particularly, of course, those who lived in eastern Ukraine – argued for increased autonomy, safeguards for the Russian language and so on, most of the dialogue concerned how best to press these agendas in Kiev; as Yanukovych's rule began to crumble, this often meant looking for avenues of representation outside the president's Party of Regions power base. In late 2013 and very early 2014, it is difficult to find anything in the movement community pages that signaled preparations for war.

As "little green men" began appearing in eastern Ukraine, however, occupying government buildings and declaring the breakaway people's republics of Donetsk and Lugansk, the tone and purpose of

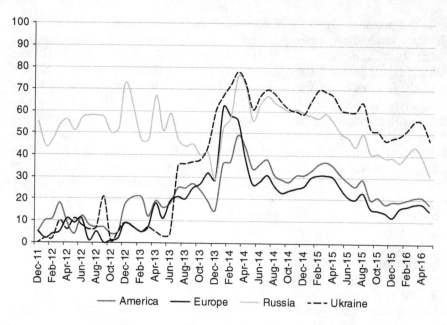
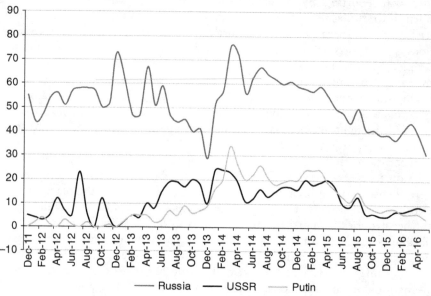

FIGURE 8.2 Topics over time

communication shifted: language became more emotional, particularly as the "fascism" tag emerged, and the talk shifted to war. Moreover, while the bulk of the networks' participants seem to be in Russia, at least in the

State-Mobilized Movements after Crimea

initial year of the conflict there was a clear link between the online communication and events on the ground, suggesting that the VKontakte groups themselves were being used to coordinate efforts in Donbas and elsewhere in Ukraine, mobilizing both virtual and physical support networks. Thus:

Urgent, Lugansk, tell the guys!!!!!! NEWS !!!!!!!!!!! I just watched [Ukrainian news broadcaster Savik] Shuster. There's a journalist on the barricades in the SBU building. Her name is Irina (that's how she presented herself). She's leaking all the info about [what's going on at] the SBU. She's wearing a red sweater with a hood. Guys!! Block that beast!!! [9]

In Odessa last night, someone set fire to two branches of Igor Kolomoisky's Privatbank. Hello from our Odessa cell to that bastard. [10]

Over time, new themes emerged, including the state of the Ukrainian and Russian economies, the role of the United States in the conflict, and the Minsk Agreements, which were negotiated (in vain) to end the fighting. The number of posts that talked about Donbas without mentioning Ukraine also grew, including reports on separatist leaders like Zakharchenko visiting hospitals, opening new schools and trying to get the lights back on. The steady drumbeat of war reporting continued unabated, however, through into 2016, even as the fighting itself died down. Writers often tried to convey a sense of urgency, even when there was not much to report:

There has never been such a glut of munitions. The shipments keep us up at night. And this is happening on both sides. Strafing and battles – every day and every night. This is what "the prolonged Minsk Agreements, to which there is no alternative" look like in reality. By the way, what were [separatist leader] "Pushilin and co." going on about, about "agreements to ban exercises, so as not to provoke the sides" and other idiocies? Hypocrisy! [11]

As activity on the network increased, so did diversity. The explosion of participation – from a few hundred thousand to more than 5 million "likes" per month in the spring of 2014 – was accompanied by new entries into the online field. Thus, the network was dominated by two groups in the fall of 2013 and still only four in February 2014 (when the Euromaidan came to a head and Yanukovych fled the country), but all sixteen groups in our data set were represented by that summer.

The network, of course, is not a closed system and is not entirely self-sufficient in terms of content. Of the more than half a million posts in the network from 2011 through April 2016, some 59,000 – or about 12 percent – were "reposts," texts that users or community moderators

---

[9] http://vk.com/public62241455, "Russkie Online," April 9, 2014.
[10] http://vk.com/public68578180, "Partizany Novorossii/DNR/LNR," June 18, 2014.
[11] http://vk.com/public57424472, "Svodki ot opolcheniia Novorossii," October 7, 2015.

found on other VKontakte pages and shared with their own community's followers.[12] Reviewing these "shares" or "reposts" allows us to identify "authorities" in the network – those, whether part of the network or brought into it from outside, whose contribution to the discourse is particularly influential.

The structure of authority is not stable over time, however. As activity on the network increases, "authorities" rise and fall in rapid succession; only a very small number of contributors manage to remain authoritative for more than four or five months, and once authority is lost it is not generally regained. There are, however, patterns in the apparent chaos, and they mirror the shifts in framing and content reviewed earlier. As shown in Table 8.1, in the early months of mobilization the chief authorities were long-standing groups characterized by a mixture of Slavic pride, nostalgia and generalized patriotism, as well as a bit of humor (see Figures 8.3, 8.4 and 8.5 for indicative examples). Among these was a group currently known as "The Republic of Novorossiya | Great Rus," which was present in the network from mid-2013, though it may initially have been known by a different name.

TABLE 8.1 *Authorities at peak periods of activity*

	May 2014	August 2014	January 2015	February 2015
1	Red Way Красный Путь https://vk.com/club39902460	This country can't be beaten! Эту страну не победить! https://vk.com/public53474	Russians Online Русские Онлайн https://vk.com/public62241455	Russians Online Русские Онлайн https://vk.com/public62241455
2	Republic of Novorossia	Great Rus' Республика Новороссия	Великая Русь https://vk.com/the_republic_of_new_russia	Russian Patriots ‖ Union of Slavs Русские Патриоты ‖ Союз Славян https://vk.com/russian_patriots_union_of_slavs	News Front Новостной Фронт https://vk.com/public7020 4174	Putin Путин https://vk.com/public76835213
3	This country can't be beaten! Russian motivators, humor Эту страну не победить! Русские мотиваторы Юмор https://vk.com/public69786071	Red Way Красный Путь https://vk.com/club39902460	Putin Путин https://vk.com/public76835213	Army Армия https://vk.com/public32356181

[12] This figure does not include text that is "copied and pasted" from another page, only those "reposts" where direct links to other VKontakte pages are present, similar to the "share" function on Facebook.

State-Mobilized Movements after Crimea

FIGURE 8.3 This country can't be beaten!

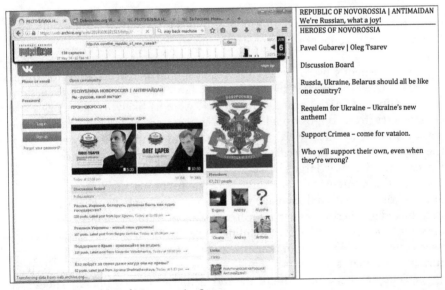

FIGURE 8.4 Republic of Novorossia, June 2014

By 2015, however, the initial authorities had faded, and the network was dominated by groups and content much more focused on the "here and now" of the conflict. These included groups like "Russians Online," whose symbolism

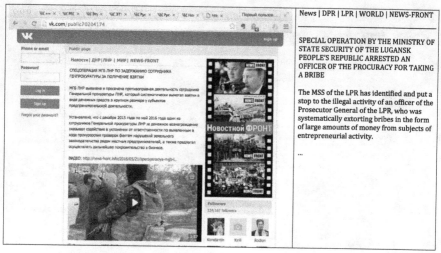

FIGURE 8.5 News front

draws together emblems of both Russia and the Donetsk People's Republic, and "News Front" (see Figure 8.5), providing up-to-the-minute reporting from the front lines.

The movement's use of media sources is similarly instructive. Prior to the "centripetal" force exerted by the Euromaidan and the Kremlin's excursions into Ukraine, the nationalist groups on VK were as likely to share news and commentary from oppositional media sources – such as lenta.ru, RBC and newsru.com – as they were to quote Kremlin-controlled or government-friendly media. As the conflict heated up and became a wedge issue for Russian politics writ large, however, the nationalists would find more and more of the content on state-linked media to be to their liking, and the obverse for oppositional media; thus, as shown in Table 8.2 there were four state-linked media sources in the top 10 cited by movement members on VK. At the same time, rhetoric that the Kremlin had deployed powerfully to fuel wedge-issue counter-mobilization in domestic politics found its way into the Russian Spring movement's discourse. Thus, use of anti-LGBT rhetoric peaked at 37 percent of posts and comments and denigration of "liberal values" at 18 percent, despite not having been part of the movement's discourse prior to Crimea.

The focus on both state-controlled media and the rhetorical content of the state's messaging, however, faded rapidly as the movement itself began to lose faith in the Kremlin's commitment to the war. After the signing of the first Minsk Protocol in September 2014 involved

TABLE 8.2 Top ten media – Russian Spring movement

2012	2013	2014	2015	2016
news.rambler.ru	livejournal.com@	rusvesna.su	rusvesna.su	rusvesna.su
vz.ru†	russiapost.su	newrussiannews.ru	news-front.info	news-front.info
lenta.ru*	regnum.ru	rt.com†	city-today.ru	novorosinform.org
pn14.info	segodnya.ua	ria.ru†	novo-russia.su	free-news.su
rbc.ru*	news.mail.ru	itar-tass.com†	newrussiannews.ru	city-today.ru
ria.ru†	rt.com†	lifenews.ru†	molotpravdu.su	nahnews.org
newsru.com*	telegrafist.org	x-time.info	vesti-ukr.com	riafan.ru
news.mail.ru	ria.ru†	zmej-gorynich.ru	russiapost.su	inforeactor.ru
itar-tass.com†	rosbalt.ru†	russiapost.su	rt.com†	voskhodinfo.su
vk.com@	odnako.org	info-patriot.com	nahnews.org	katehon.com
Opposition Media (*)		Kremlin-Loyal Media (†)		Online Social Media (@)

compromises with Kiev that many of the nationalists found to be unpalatable, Kremlin-linked media disappeared from the movement's VK community pages almost entirely, as did the values-laden rhetoric that had earlier served to link the movement to the broader Russian political discourse.

What the online record shows, then, is a movement that builds on a small number of preexisting groups which explode into action and draw many new participants in response to events on the ground in Ukraine. The network is transnational, seems to grow largely spontaneously and is not dominated for long by any one set of actors. The ideology of participants seems diffuse, sentimental and nostalgic at first but becomes more coherent given a shared and highly resonant analysis of the political context in Ukraine. As the conflict intensifies, the trend is away from broad political messaging and toward specific and operational messages focused on events on the ground and the conduct of the war. The Kremlin, which is initially seen as an opponent of the activists, has its values and narrative embraced by the movement as the war ramps up and then is dropped again as people start to sense a coming betrayal.

8.6 CONCLUSIONS

This volume as a whole posits a range of reasons why autocratic rulers such as those currently in charge of Russia might want to mobilize parts of their own populations. These reasons include a "defensive or reactive" impulse, to guard against grassroots challenges; "proactive" or "spoiler" mobilization through which a regime might seek to "dominate the battlefield" of politics; the exploitation of factional conflicts within the state for purposes of control or leverage; the use of managed mobilization as a "signaling device" to shape broader public behavior; a desire to use mobilized citizens to help accomplish developmental tasks; and cross-border mobilization, as a weapon of influence or war. This chapter, if anything, both demonstrates and challenges the insights of this kind of typology. In the Russian Spring – as, indeed, in Julie Hemment's study of the Kremlin-backed youth movement Nashi in Chapter 7 – we can certainly discern several of these motivations at work. The state's initial use of wedge-issue mobilization to counteract the 2011–2012 "Bolotnaya" protests might be seen as initially a defensive mobilization aimed at preventing the opposition from gaining traction. This strategy then looks like a spoiler mobilization in the Russian Spring, where nationalists were deployed as part of the "Anti-Maidan" drive to prevent any democratizing contagion after Ukraine's revolution. The movement's emotional and violent content were also clearly expected to shape action in Russia itself by suppressing opposition. The cross-border element is also clearly visible.

However, the chapter also suggests that these categories are anything but rigid and exclusive. While we can discern these various motivations and effects in the Russian Spring case, the mobilization itself does not fit easily into any of these categories but rather spans them, both over time and, often, at the same time.

Moreover, our analysis of the Russian Spring indicates that it goes beyond these categories too. What we find on VKontakte is a vibrant, fluid and evidently genuine community of energized partisans, whose loyalty to the Russian state and willingness to expend time, emotion and, in some cases, blood on that state's behalf was procured by the Kremlin through real-world action rather than rhetoric or direct co-optation. Within this community, which includes important local and transnational elements, mobilization is heavily driven by events on the ground, while there is little indication of strong, central authority – something we would have expected to find if what we were observing was a largely state-controlled phenomenon.

To say that the Novorossiya/Russian Spring movement is not truly state-controlled, however, is not to say that it isn't state-led. The Russian state clearly exercises quite significant power over and through the movement, largely because of its ability to command and control events on the ground. As noted, once the outbreak of war draws larger numbers of VKontakte users into the relevant communities, the online mobilization remains largely event-focused and event-driven; when things on the battlefield go quiet, activity in the network eventually fades. The agenda for mobilization is thus set by the state, rather than by the movement, which reacts enthusiastically to "facts on the ground" and helps to escalate them but does not create them. When the activists we observe online do become involved in events on the ground – such as through the collection and distribution of information, some of which may then have been used by actual combatants – their role is tactical rather than strategic. The movement is not itself prosecuting the war in eastern Ukraine, but to a very real extent the Kremlin would find it much more difficult to prosecute that war – or to manage its domestic political consequences – without the movement's involvement.

There is, thus, power in the movement, too. The meaning of the Russian state's actions in Donbas and Crimea is refracted through the preexisting ideational prisms of long-established communities, and it is apparently because the state's actions have finally come in line with these citizens' orientations that they are willingly drawn into mobilization – including, for people like the volunteer fighters, high-risk mobilization. While the decision-making mechanisms through which the war in Donbas is prosecuted remain opaque – and while there are always a multiplicity of actors in war – if the maintenance of a mobilized constituency such as the one observed on VKontakte is among the Kremlin's objectives then the Kremlin cannot easily ignore how its actions (and inactions) are received. Prior to Crimea and Donbas, the constituencies that make up the Russian Spring/Novorossiya movement were not friendly to Russia's rulers, due largely to what they perceived as those rulers' abdication of Russia's and Russians' interests. This understanding may thus encourage the Kremlin to press forward with the campaign in Donbas, less it risk being seen as abandoning the cause. Similarly, the lack of a preexisting constituency may partly explain why Russia's intervention in Syria provoked a much less robust popular response. This suggests that there are limits to the state's ability to lead mobilization and that these limits are set in large part by the availability of ideologically committed constituencies in society.

REFERENCES

Azar, I. (2015) Rasserzhennye patrioty. *Meduza*, February 21. https://meduza.io/feature/2015/02/21/rasserzhennye-patrioty (accessed May 22, 2016).

Balzer, Harley. 2003. Managed pluralism: Vladimir Putin's emerging regime. *Post-Soviet Affairs* 19 (3): 189–227.

Bassin, Mark. 2003. "Classical" Eurasianism and the Geopolitics of Russian Identity. *Ab Imperio* 2003(2): 257–266.

Baunov, A. 2014. Rossii ne do smekha. *Otechestvennye Zapiski* 2014(6). www.strana-oz.ru/2014/6/rossii-ne-do-smeha (accessed May 20, 2016).

BBC Russian Service. 2015. Opros: rossiiane odobriaiut poezdki dobrovol'tsev v Donbass. *BBC Russian Service*, March 20. www.bbc.com/russian/russia/2015/03/150320_russia_polls_volunteers (accessed May 20, 2016).

Bindman, Eleanor. 2015. The state, civil society and social rights in contemporary Russia. *East European Politics* 31 (3), 342–360.

Cheskin, Ammon, and Luke March. 2015. State–society relations in contemporary Russia: new forms of political and social contention. *East European Politics* 31 (3): 261–273.

Clover, Charles. 2016. *Black Wind, White Snow: The Rise of Russia's New Nationalism*. New Haven, CT: Yale University Press.

Colton, Timothy J. 1999. Understanding Iurii Luzhkov. *Problems of Post-Communism* 46 (5): 14–26.

Donadio, R. 2016. Svetlana Alexievich, Nobel laureate of Russian misery, has an English-language milestone. *New York Times*, May 20. www.nytimes.com/2016/05/21/books/svetlana-alexievich-a-nobel-laureate-of-russian-misery-has-her-english-debut.html (accessed May 20, 2016).

Finkel, Evgeny, and Yitzhak M. Brudny. 2012. No more colour! Authoritarian regimes and colour revolutions in Eurasia. *Democratization* 19 (1): 1–14.

Frye, Timothy, Ora John Reuter and David Szakonyi. 2014. Political Machines at Work: Voter Mobilization and Electoral Subversion in the Workplace. *World Politics* 66 (2): 195–228.

Goode, J. P. 2012. Nationalism in quiet times. *Problems of Post-Communism* 59 (3): 6–16.

Gordy, Eric D. 1999. *The Culture of Power in Serbia: Nationalism and the Destruction of Alternatives*. University Park, PA: Penn State University Press.

Greene, Samuel A., and Graeme B. Robertson. 2014. Explaining Putin's popularity: rallying round the Russian flag. *WashingtonPost.com*, September 9. www.washingtonpost.com/news/monkey-cage/wp/2014/09/09/explaining-putins-popularity-rallying-round-the-russian-flag/ (accessed May 20, 2016).

Greene, Samuel A., and Graeme B. Robertson. 2019. *Putin v the People: The Perilous Politics of a Divided Russia*. London: Yale University Press.

Gudkov, L. 2015. Russian public opinion on the aftermath of the Ukraine crisis. *Russian Politics and Law* 53 (4): 32–44.

Hale, Henry E. 2018. How Crimea pays: media, rallying 'round the flag, and authoritarian support. *Comparative Politics* 50 (3): 369–391.

Hemment, Julie. 2015. *Youth Politics In Putin's Russia*. Bloomington: Indiana University Press.

Higgins, A., and S. Erlanger. 2014. Gunmen seize government buildings in Crimea. *New York Times*, 27 February.

Howard, Philip N. 2006. *New Media Campaigns and the Managed Citizen*. Cambridge: Cambridge University Press.

ICG. 2016. Russia and the separatists in eastern Ukraine. IN *Europe and Central Asia Briefing No. 79*. Brussels: International Crisis Group. www.crisisgroup.org/en/regions/europe/ukraine/b079-russia-and-the-separatists-in-eastern-ukraine.aspx (accessed May 20, 2016).

Ingram, Alan. 1999. "A Nation Split into Fragments": The Congress of Russian Communities and Russian Nationalist Ideology. *Europe-Asia Studies* 51 (4): 687–704.

Kashin, O. 2014. Vezhlivye liudi s pushkami. *openDemocracy Russia*, April 16. www.opendemocracy.net/od-russia/%D0%BE%D0%BB%D0%B5%D0%B3-%D0%BA%D0%B0%D1%88%D0%B8%D0%BD/vezhliviye-lyudi-s-pushkami (accessed May 20, 2016).

Kerr, David. 1995. The new Eurasianism: the rise of geopolitics in Russia's foreign policy. *Europe-Asia Studies* 47 (6): 977–988.

Kostiuchenko, E. 2014. Armiia i dobrovol'tsy. *Novaya Gazeta*, September 3. www.novayagazeta.ru/society/65096.html (accessed May 20, 2016).

Kuzio, Taras. 1997. Borders, symbolism and nation-state building: Ukraine and Russia. *Geopolitics and International Boundaries* 2 (2): 36–56.

Laruelle, M. 2004. The two faces of contemporary Eurasianism: an imperial version of Russian nationalism. *Nationalities Papers* 32 (1): 115–136.

Laruelle, Marlène. 2004. The two faces of contemporary Eurasianism: an imperial version of Russian nationalism. *Nationalities Papers* 32 (1): 115–136.

Laruelle, Marlène. 2014. Alexei Navalny and challenges in reconciling "nationalism" and "liberalism." *Post-Soviet Affairs* 30 (4): 276–297.

Linz, Juan J. 2000. *Totalitarian and Authoritarian Regimes*. Boulder, CO: Lynn Rienner.

Magaloni, Beatriz. 2006. *Voting for Autocracy: Hegemonic Party Survival and Its Demise in Mexico*. Cambridge: Cambridge University Press.

Matveeva, Anna. 2018. *Through Times of Trouble: Conflict in Southeastern Ukraine Explained from Within*. London: Lexington Books.

McCarthy, John D., and Mayer N. Zald. 1977. Resource mobilization and social movements: a partial theory. *American Journal of Sociology* 82 (6): 1212–1241.

McNutt, J. G., and K. M. Boland. 2007. Astroturf, technology and the future of community mobilization: implications for nonprofit theory. *Journal of Sociology and Social Welfare* 34 (3): 165–179.

Medvedev, S. (2014) Russkii resentiment. *Otechestvennye Zapiski* 2014(6). www.strana-oz.ru/2014/6/russkiy-resentiment (accessed May 20, 2016.

Oliphant, R. 2014. Ukraine crisis: "polite people" leading the silent invasion of Crimea. *The Daily Telegraph*, March 2. www.telegraph.co.uk/news/worldnews/europe/ukraine/10670547/Ukraine-crisis-Polite-people-leading-the-silent-invasion-of-the-Crimea.html (accessed May 20, 2016).

Owen, Catherine. 2015. "Consentful contention" in a corporate state: human rights activists and public monitoring commissions in Russia. *East European Politics* 31 (3): 274–293.

Petlianova, N. 2014. Lev Shlosberg prosit glavnogo voennogo prokurora rassledovat' gibel' desantnikov 76-oi pskovskoi divizii VDV. *Novaya Gazeta*, September 17. www.novayagazeta.ru/news/1687093.html (accessed May 20, 2016).

Petrov, Nikolay, Maria Lipman and Henry E. Hale. 2013. Three dilemmas of hybrid regime governance: Russia from Putin to Putin. *Post-Soviet Affairs* 30 (1): 1–26.

Putin, V. 2014. *Address by President of the Russian Federation, 18 March*. Moscow: Presidential Administration. http://en.kremlin.ru/events/president/news/20603 (accessed May 20, 2016).

Robertson, Graeme B. 2007. Strikes and labor organization in hybrid regimes. *American Political Science Review* 101 (4): 781–798.

Robertson, Graeme B. 2009. Managing society: protest, civil society and regime in Putin's Russia. *Slavic Review* 68 (3): 528–547.

Robertson, Graeme B. 2011. *The Politics of Protest in Hybrid Regimes: Managing Dissent in Post-Communist Russia*. Cambridge: Cambridge University Press.

Romanov, A. 2016. UniSocial4. A cloud-powered high-performance system for data collection from social networks. https://github.com/NewMediaCenterMoscow/UniSocial4.

Sorkin, K. 2014. Obshchii iazyk nenavisti. *Otechestvennye Zapiski* 6. www.strana-oz.ru/2014/6/obshchiy-yazyk-nenavisti (accessed May 20, 2016).

Stokes, Susan C., Thad Dunning, Marcelo Nazareno and Valeria Brusco. 2013. *Brokers, Voters, and Clientelism: The Puzzle of Distributive Politics*. Cambridge: Cambridge University Press.

Strelkov, I. 2014. Interview zhurnalista Aleksandra Chalenko s I.I. Strelkovym. *VKontakte post*, December 1. http://vk.com/strelkov_info?w=wall-57424472_32149 (accessed May 20, 2016).

Tarasenko, Anna. 2015. Russian welfare reform and social NGOs: strategies for claim-making and service provision in the case of Saint Petersburg. *East European Politics* 31 (3): 294–313.

TASS. 2015. Donbas Volunteer Union set up in Russia. *TASS*, August 27. http://tass.ru/en/russia/816955 (accessed May 20, 2016).

Tsygankov, Andrei P. 1998. Hard-line Eurasianism and Russia's contending geopolitical perspectives. *East European Quarterly* 32 (3): 315–334.

Umland, Andreas. 2002. Contextualizing the decline of post-Soviet Russian parties of the extreme right wing. *Demokratizatsiya* 10 (3): 362–391.

Verkhovsky, Alexander. 2000. Ultra-nationalists in Russia at the onset of Putin's rule. *Nationalities Papers* 28 (4): 707–722.

Walker, Edward. 2014. *Grassroots for Hire: Public Affairs Consultants in American Democracy*. Cambridge: Cambridge University Press.

Weiss, Jessica Chen. 2013. Authoritarian signaling, mass audiences, and nationalist protest in China. *International Organization* 67 (1): 1–35.

Weiss, Jessica Chen. 2014. *Powerful Patriots: Nationalist Protest in China's Foreign Relations*. Oxford: Oxford University Press.

9

Mirroring Opposition Threats

The Logic of State Mobilization in Bolivarian Venezuela

Sam Handlin

9.1 INTRODUCTION

Hugo Chávez and his Bolivarian Movement came to power in 1999 promising to refound the Venezuelan state and restructure the polity in ways that would build "popular power" through the promotion of grassroots participation, organization, and mobilization. Once in office, the Bolivarian forces launched a series of initiatives to sponsor organization and mobilization among supporters, which ranged widely in their functions and strategic purpose. State-mobilized organizations can be seen as operating in three different arenas of politics: the local governance arena; the electoral arena; and the protest arena. From an ideological standpoint, the Bolivarian Movement was oriented toward sponsoring organizations that could operate in the first of these arenas, helping realize Chávez's vision of constructing a "protagonistic democracy" by establishing vehicles for citizen participation in local governance. In the terminology of this volume, these activities are best seen as a form of "infrastructural mobilization," working to solidify political support and achieve the government's longer-term aims. As the polarizing Bolivarian government met with opposition, however, its initiatives in social mobilization often became geared toward sponsoring organizations suited to operating in the electoral and protest arenas. These activities are best seen as forms of "reactive" and "proactive" mobilization, ways to defend against threats posed by an increasingly powerful opposition.

I propose a mirroring theory for explaining the evolution of state-mobilized groups in Venezuela and their respective emphases, which reduces to two claims. First, the degree to which the government has engaged in infrastructural mobilization, with state-mobilized groups geared toward the local governance arena, vis-à-vis proactive or reactive mobilization, with those groups geared toward the protest or electoral arenas, has been inversely related to the seriousness of the threat posed by the opposition. Second, when engaged in the latter forms of mobilization, the government has focused on sponsoring organizations best suited to operate in whichever of these two arenas – that of protests or elections – has corresponded to the focus of opposition strategies during particular time periods. This mirroring theory, which has some resemblance to the notion of "mirror-image design" advanced in Chapter 8, helps us think systematically about the motives behind mobilizational initiatives and how incumbents decide between multiple strategic option, one of the key issues highlighted in this volume's introduction. While governments may draw on an extensive repertoire of mobilizational strategies to "rule by other means," the imperative of dealing with open opposition threats may tends to trump other motivations when making these choices.

The chapter proceeds as follows. Section 9.2 highlights two contextual variables – the competitiveness of autocratic regimes and strength of states – that serve as scope conditions, shaping the strategic environment and giving state-mobilized movements (SMMs) a distinctive character in Venezuela when compared to other autocracies examined in this volume. The bulk of the chapter – Sections 9.3 through 9.7 – then presents the mirroring theory. To do so, I break the Bolivarian era into four periods distinguished by variation in the degree and nature of opposition threats and examine how mobilizational initiatives changed in response to this shifting landscape.

9.2 CONTEXTUAL CONDITIONS SHAPING STRATEGY CHOICE

Bolivarian Venezuela possessed two important contextual conditions – a highly competitive autocratic regime and a very weak state – that differentiate the case from many others examined in this volume and which greatly influenced the logic and nature of SMMs. This section first offers some background information on Venezuela before the rise to power of the Bolivarian Movement. I then explicitly discuss these two contextual conditions and how they shaped SMMs in Bolivarian Venezuela.

9.2.1 Background

Venezuela possessed one of Latin America's longest-standing democracies prior to the Bolivarian era. This democratic regime was established in 1958 after a broad opposition movement successfully overthrew the dictatorship of Marcos Pérez Jiménez. As democracy collapsed across South America in the 1960s and 1970s, Venezuela's "Punto Fijo" democracy (so named after the location at which its founding pact was agreed upon) proved remarkably resilient and stable. During the 1970s and early 1980s, scholars frequently invoked the idea of "Venezuelan exceptionalism," referring to an island of democratic rule and relative political stability amid a sea of military regimes

Mirroring Opposition Threats: Bolivarian Venezuela

or, as in neighboring Colombia, seemingly intractable civil conflicts (Ellner and Tinker Salas, 2005).

Punto Fijo democracy was also beset by several severe pathologies, which eventually fostered great citizen alienation and discontent. Perhaps most consequentially, Venezuelan democracy was erected on a very weak state in which corruption and patrimonialism were widespread. While the oil economy boomed in the 1970s, such issues were easy to sweep under the rug. When oil prices crashed and the country experienced other economic challenges in the 1980s, these long-standing problems with corruption increased in salience. The last decades of the twentieth century therefore saw Venezuela mired in a deep "state crisis," a situation in which the state proved highly ineffective in the delivery of basic goods and highly venal in its treatment of citizens, leading to widespread discontent with basic state institutions (Handlin, 2017).

The Bolivarian Movement led by Hugo Chávez emerged in this context, promising to refound the Venezuelan state and create a "protagonistic democracy" that would open up new avenues for popular participation. These ideas were already developed in many of the programmatic documents that Chávez and other conspirators drew up to present to the public before launching a coup against the Venezuelan government in 1992. While the coup failed, Chávez and other leaders of the MBR-200 elicited great sympathy from a highly anti-systemic public fed up with the country's political class. Therefore, Chávez and the MBR-200 were able to garner a pardon and contest the 1998 elections, running on a program centered on the convocation of a constituent assembly to rewrite the constitution, refound the Venezuelan state, and implement a more participatory form of government that would address the deficits of representation and social citizenship in the Punto Fijo system.

9.2.2 A Highly Competitive Autocracy

After winning power, Chávez and the Bolivarian forces utilized the constituent process not only to write a new constitution but also to remove opponents from the state and neuter institutions of horizontal accountability (Coppedge, 2002; Corrales and Penfold, 2011; Handlin, 2017). Domination over the state subsequently allowed the Bolivarian forces to tilt the playing field against opponents, such that by 2004 the political regime was best considered competitive authoritarian (Levitsky and Way, 2002).

Competitive authoritarianism in Venezuela involved a relatively contested and liberal autocracy, even when compared to other hybrid regimes. Throughout the Bolivarian period, the opposition has been given fairly wide latitude to mobilize and protest in the streets. Only after the start of a large protest cycle in 2014 did serious repression begin, and that repression was not extensive enough to dissuade activity in the protest arena altogether. The electoral arena in Venezuela has also been unusually competitive (see Table 9.1). From 1999 through 2003, no election was held to which the opposition

TABLE 9.1 *Major elections and referenda during the Fifth Republic, 1999–2017*

Year	Election	Margin
1999	Constituent Assembly	+44 (Semi-boycotted)
2000	Presidential	+22 (Semi-boycotted)
2001	None	
2002	None	
2003	None	
2004	Recall referendum	+16
2005	Legislative	Boycotted
2006	Presidential	+26
2007	Constitutional referendum	−1
2008	Gubernatorial	+12
2009	Constitutional referendum	+10
2010	Legislative	+1
2011	None	
2012	Presidential, Gubernatorial	+11
2013	Presidential	+2
2014	None	
2015	Legislative	−15
2016	None (cancelled)	
2017	Gubernatorial	+9

wholeheartedly committed. From 2004 onward, however, highly contested elections or referendum were held nearly every year, due to renewed opposition commitment to electoral strategies, the nonconcurrent electoral calendar, and the plebiscitarian nature of the Bolivarian Revolution, which sometimes led to major referenda being held in years without regularly scheduled elections.

The highly competitive nature of the authoritarian regime in Venezuela strongly shaped the government's approach to SMMs, incentivizing reliance on social mobilization as a tool for countering opposition in the protest arena and for building a set of grassroots organizations that could coordinate with party structures for campaigning and electioneering. The Bolivarian government entered office greatly invested in using social mobilization for other purposes, especially activities in the local governance arena that most closely mirror the concept of "infrastructural development" advanced in the introduction of this volume. Faced with high levels of opposition threat in both the protest and electoral arenas given the regime context, however, the government was pressed into activities that more neatly fit into the categories of "reactive" and "pro-active" mobilization. The case points to a more general proposition about autocracies: the more competitive the regime, the more likely that governments will focus on reactive and proactive strategies rather than other forms of social mobilization less directly geared toward dealing with open opposition.

9.2.3 State Weakness

After rising to prominence and power through critiques of the Venezuelan state crisis and the political status quo, the Bolivarian Movement inherited this weak state in office (Handlin, 2017). State weakness shaped the nature of SMMs in Bolivarian Venezuela in several ways. For one, the weak state further fueled reliance on state-mobilized groups in general. At the head of a state that had proven highly corrupt and frequently incapable of delivering services and providing public goods, Chávez's options for using established state structures to mobilize support were limited. It is no surprise, for example, that his first major initiative in social policy – Plan Bolívar 2000 – was implemented mainly through the military, the one wing of the state apparatus in which he placed confidence. As we will see, the subsequent reliance on SMMs and the formation of para-statal entities like the Communal Councils to mobilize support and achieve local governance objectives reflected a similar logic. While the Bolivarian Movement had an ideological commitment to such notions, necessity – in this case, a weak state apparatus – was also the mother of invention.

The Venezuelan experience also demonstrates that state weakness is likely to place substantial limitations on the ability of governments to control state-mobilized groups. Principle-agent problems are inherent to situations in which states mobilize parts of society to do their bidding and accomplish particular goals. Those societal groups, once formed and mobilized, may operate according to their own incentives and goals, which may not fully align with those actors within the state who supported and pushed their mobilization. Following analyses of principle-agent dynamics from many other settings, we might conclude that the ability of states to monitor the activities of state-mobilized groups and to credibly sanction them for bad behavior will be critical to limiting principle-agent problems that might arise. Weak states are likely to have less capacity for both monitoring and sanctioning. Entities tasked with liaising with state-mobilized groups – whether relevant bureaucratic agencies or, in some cases, security services – are likely to have less potent tools for covert surveillance, less capacity for organizing and maintaining records related to the activities of state-mobilized groups, and less ability to decisively act to punish state-mobilized groups that pursue nonsanctioned activities.

As we will see, a recurrent dynamic during the Fifth Republic, observable even in its earliest years and particularly notable more recently, has involved state-mobilized groups affiliated with the Bolivarian Movement engaging in activities that compromise or complicate the broader goals of the government. In particular, certain state-mobilized groups (a subset of Bolivarian Circles in the early years, a subset of colectivos, or community-based support groups, more recently) have often engaged in violence and crime. The Venezuelan government has supported at least some of this violence, using state-mobilized groups as vehicles for sowing fear among the opposition. But the activities of these groups have also seemed beyond the control of the government at times. And the government's association with them has tended to be viewed very negatively by the Venezuelan public, leading to losses of mass support. To a less spectacular degree, the principle-agent problem can also be seen as relevant to the government's attempt to use certain state-mobilized groups as vehicles for electoral mobilization. One of the constant challenges the government has faced has involved creating groups that would work cooperatively with Bolivarian parties.

9.3 MIRRORING THREATS: EXPLAINING VARIATION IN STATE MOBILIZATION OVER TIME

The chapter now turns to an explanation of change over time within the Venezuelan case. The focus is not so much to test the propositions established in the previous section regarding state and regime context but to analyze how and why – with this context largely taken as a given – the Venezuelan government's approach to mobilization shifted so much during the Bolivarian era.

State-mobilized organizations serve many functions and often operate in multiple arenas of politics in authoritarian contexts. The logic animating state decisions to create or cultivate these organizations (and to create or cultivate particular types of organizations in particular situations) can involve calculations that take into account political action occurring across multiple arenas. One part of this calculation may involve activities in the protest arena, the engagement of state-mobilized organizations in contention and countermobilization to support the government or, more darkly, in violence against opposition protesters. But the calculation may also involve the activities of state-mobilized organizations in the electoral arena, such as getting out the vote on behalf of pro-regime parties and politicians or action in the realm of local governance. To best understand the shifting landscape of state-mobilized organizations over time in Venezuela (and elsewhere), we have to appreciate this broader strategic landscape composed of multiple arenas.

In considering the Venezuelan case, it is heuristically useful to think of these three arenas of action – the protest arena, the electoral arena, and the local governance arena – and to locate the major Bolivarian initiatives in state-mobilized organizations with respect to their respective emphases. Figure 9.1 displays this notion graphically. It should be emphasized that this is a heuristic

Mirroring Opposition Threats: Bolivarian Venezuela

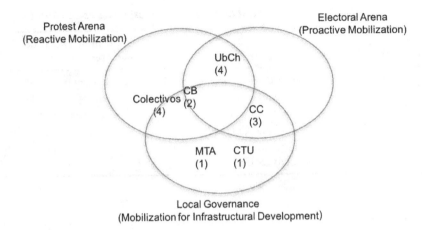

FIGURE 9.1 Arenas of operation and dominant types of mobilization

and that the locations in this space are not precisely fixed: For example, Communal Councils (CCs) have engaged in activity in the protest arena, but it has not been an emphasis for that group of organizations. Therefore, they are located in the figure only at the intersection of the electoral and local governance arenas. The numbers in parentheses refer to the phases of the Fifth Republic in which each organization was created or, in the case of the colectivos, increased in prominence.

We can also match these three arenas of politics with nominal values from the typology of mobilization strategies developed in the volume's introduction. The local governance arena is marked by mobilization for infrastructural development, attempts to use organize society to accomplish development projects that local state officials are incapable or unwilling to undertake. The protest arena is most likely to be characterized by defensive or reactive mobilization, as government mobilizes supporters to engage in counterprotest against contentious forces in society. Finally, proactive mobilization seems likely to be the dominant form in the electoral arena: state incumbents build up grassroots organizing capacity in advance of elections, seeking to establish an organizational advantage that will allow them to withstand anticipated opposition challenges.

Figure 9.1, when supplemented by the additional information provided in Table 9.2, also helps us better consider the logic of temporal change among state-mobilized organizations in Venezuela. We can see two broad trends. First, the emphasis of SMMs on local governance has risen and fallen with the threat level of the opposition. In the first few years of the Chávez era, with the opposition in total disarray, initiatives almost exclusively focused on stimulating citizen participation and organization in local governance, a longtime ideological emphasis of the Bolivarian Movement. This focus

TABLE 9.2 *Opposition threats and state mobilization responses across four phases*

Phase	Rough Dates	Key Organizations	Opposition Threat Level and Arena
1	1999–2000	Urban Land Committees (CTU), Water Tables (MTA)	Very low, none
2	2001–2003	Bolivarian Circles (BC)	High, protest arena
3	2004–2012	Communal Councils (CC)	Moderate, electoral arena
4	2013–	Colectivos, Battle Units Hugo Chávez (UBCh)	High, both arenas.

dropped off somewhat as the opposition threat swelled in 2001–2003, was accentuated again as the opposition threat level diminished in 2004–2012, and then dropped off again in the current period, when the opposition threat has been at its highest.

Second, to the extent that state-mobilized organizations have been geared toward countering opposition threats, their relative emphasis on the protest or electoral arena has mirrored the nature of the gravest threat. When the opposition was contesting power in the streets during the 2001–2003 period, the government launched the Bolivarian Circle program to meet that challenge. Once the opposition returned to the electoral arena from 2004 to 2012, the government launched the Communal Council program. And with the opposition presenting grave threats both in the streets and at the ballot box from 2013 onward, the government has emphasized groups like the colectivos and UbCh that are explicitly politicized and together can operate in both spheres. Less well conveyed, but discussed further in Section 9.7, is that these groups are not just active in the protest arena but have shifted increasingly toward repression rather than simple counterprotest.

9.4 VERY LITTLE OPPOSITION THREATS, 1999–2000

The years immediately following Chávez's 1998 election were marked by a rapid sequence of controversial institutional reforms and a reeling opposition that presented very little threat to the new government. The arrival to power of Chávez in early 1999 was followed by a referendum on writing a new constitution, elections to select a constituent assembly to author the document (which were rigged to favor the Bolivarian Movement), another referendum to approve the document, and then "mega-elections" in July 2000 for all elected positions mandates by the new magna carta. With the population largely supportive of the constitutional reform process, a bitterly divided opposition provided little threat to Chávez and the Bolivarian Movement during this stage in either the protest or electoral arenas.

9.4.1 Water Tables and Urban Land Committees

With the Chávez administration focused on institutional reform and remaking the state, initiatives to mobilize society were modest and had great trouble getting off the ground. Nevertheless, the government did at least attempt to push forward two such programs to sponsor local-level organization and mobilization among supporters. As predicted by the theory, in the absence of a meaningful opposition threat these initiatives focused overwhelmingly on local governance or, in the terminology of this volume, infrastructural mobilization, in keeping with the ideological commitments of the new government.

As the Bolivarian Movement came to power, lack of access to potable water and improved sanitation presented a serious and all-too-common problem, especially in rural communities. The most concerted action of the government to support social organization and mobilization as a means of fighting poverty was the extension of a program to sponsor the formation of Mesas Técnicas de Agua (MTA), community-based associations that would work with government agencies to improve water and sanitation infrastructure in underserved neighborhoods. During Chávez's first months in office, the government organized a series of workshops and meetings to discuss the national expansion of the program (Arconada Rodríguez, 2005). Attempts to translate plans into policy action proved difficult, given that they required larger-scale changes to the regulation of water provision in the country. While it took several further years for MTA to proliferate, the key point for present purposes is that they were born in a context of low threat and designed exclusively for infrastructural mobilization in the local governance arena.[1]

A similar program also emerged during this period in the area of housing. One of the more ambitious initiatives to emerge in the first year of the Chávez administration was El Programa de Habilitación Física de Barrios, a comprehensive policy agenda developed by El Consejo Nacional de la Vivienda (CONAVI), a national entity established a decade previously to address the systemic housing problems in the country. In laying out a new approach for dealing with housing problems, CONAVI declared that "to incorporate and support the organizations of residential communities" should be a central aspect of the process of addressing housing problems (Giménez, Rivas, and Rodríguez, 2007). This plan would eventually lead to a program to support and sponsor thousands of Comités de Tierra Urbana (CTU), neighborhood organizations in poor areas devoted to dealing with housing issues such as land titling and infrastructure. As with the MTA, implementation of these plans was slowed and complicated by the political

---

[1] According to official documents from HIDROVEN (n.d.), the number of MTA rose from 100 in 2001 to 960 in 2003.

context. But, like the MTA, the program again showed the government's focus on infrastructural mobilization when not facing serious opposition threats.

9.5 STRONG OPPOSITION THREATS IN THE PROTEST ARENA, 2001–2003

By 2001 opposition forces had regrouped enough to pose a real challenge to the Chávez government. This year inaugurated an extremely polarizing period in which the opposition attempted to oust Chávez through a variety of nonelectoral means and during which the ability to mobilize supporters into the streets and control the public sphere was critical for both sides in the conflict. Reactive forms of mobilization in the protest arena became the dominant strategy of the government.

Opposition protest mobilizations occurred frequently throughout 2001 but increased notably at the end of the year, after the Chávez administration controversially used an enabling law to implement a sweeping package of new economic policies by decree. As opposition protests became more regular and swelled in size, they were increasingly met by loyalist counterprotests. Each side was putting tens of thousands, sometimes hundreds of thousands, of people onto the streets of Caracas on an almost weekly basis. This increasingly tense atmosphere reached a peak in April 2002 when the opposition launched a complex coup attempt, which began with a massive march on Miraflores Palace that was met by a large loyalist mobilization, a clash that left several people dead, violence used as a pretext for a military takeover. While the opposition plotters succeeded in removing Chávez from Miraflores and taking him to a remote island military base, the coup broke down after disagreements emerged among the key players and after loyalist forces mobilized thousands of Venezuelans into the streets in protest.

Even after the failure of the April 2002 coup, opposition protest activity and attempts to oust Chávez remained ongoing. The opposition continued to mobilize into the streets on a semi-regular basis throughout the rest of the year and then launched a massive general strike, including a shutdown of the oil industry, spanning December 2002–February 2003. It was not until the disastrous failure of this strike, which had dire economic consequences and greatly discredited the opposition in the minds of the Venezuelan public, that the opposition moved away from contentious strategies and began to focus on the electoral arena. They did so through activating a clause in the Bolivarian constitution allowing for referenda to be convened to recall elected officials. Ultimately, after considerably delays, a referendum to recall Chávez failed in August 2004. This sequence of events augured the dawning of a new phase in Venezuelan politics, taken up in Section 9.6, marked by a substantial decrease in protest on both sides and contestation largely occurring at the ballot box.

9.5.1 The Bolivarian Circles

While Chávez and the MVR had long made the sponsorship of social organization a central part of their program, initiatives in this regard were relatively small in scale in the initial years of the Bolivarian era. As protest activity by the opposition picked up, the government launched a much more ambitious effort to sponsor organization and collective action among loyalists, calling for the formation of Bolivarian Circles by supporters around the country (Arenas and Gómez Calcaño, 2005). Chávez had first mentioned the possibility of forming the Circles in mid-2000, but the initiative really picked up steam in late 2001, with the president conducting a massive rally that December to swear-in members, publicize the initiative, and galvanize support. Estimates of the total number of Circles have varied widely, but there is little doubt that this was a very large – if relatively short-lived – initiative.[2] The program was relatively informal, particularly compared to later initiatives. It established a set of coordinating structures and a formal registry of Circles, enabling some degree of contacting and joint action. But these structures were poorly institutionalized, many Circles appear to have been formed and then quickly gone defunct, and the program was supported with very few resources (Hawkins and Hansen, 2006).

The Circles played roles in local governance but also were clearly oriented toward activity in the protest arena, organizations capable of mobilizing supporters and other community members into the streets on short notice in defense of the Bolivarian Revolution. Scholars have commonly seen the Circles as playing particularly important roles in the countermobilizations that became increasingly frequent, particularly in Caracas, during the extremely tense months of late 2001 and early 2002 (García-Guadilla, 2004). At times, the Circles also engaged in contentious activity for other strategic purposes, beyond simply providing a counterbalance to opposition protests. For example, in one episode, Circles led a major protest alleging unfair treatment of the government in *El Nacional*, one of Venezuela's leading newspapers, which succeeded in shutting down the newspaper for a day (Inter-Press Service, 2002). Nevertheless, countermobilization was clearly the dominant purpose of Circle activity in the protest arena.

The Bolivarian Circles became best known for the roles they played in the events of the 2002 coup. The days leading up to the coup had been filled with tension, with both sides suspecting that a breaking point was nearing. In this context, Chávez and close advisers discussed plans for having armed Circles surround Miraflores palace in case of an opposition attempt to besiege the house of government (Nelson, 2009). When the opposition did begin its

---

[2] Coordinators of the Bolivarian Circle program at times claimed as many as 200,000, numbers that seem unrealistic. In contrast, Hawkins and Hansen (2006) estimate that the true number is more likely between 9,500 and 11,000 active Circles at the height of the program.

massive march on Miraflores, the Circles were central actors in rallying the pro-government countermobilization. More ominously, members of Circles were responsible for at least some of the deadly violence when the two marches clashed, with footage capturing a known Circle leader firing a gun at the opposition from an overpass. After the coup occurred, and Chávez was taken by force out of Miraflores, Circles are also widely credited with helping lead the massive popular protest that surrounded Miraflores and demanded the return of the president (Roberts, 2006). After the coup, the Circles continued to be important actors during the remainder of this period of intense polarization. During the extremely tense 10-week general strike of late 2002 and early 2003, the Circles were also active in community provisioning and leading counterprotests denouncing the general strike.

When the opposition renounced attempts to remove Chávez by extra-constitutional means and shifted its strategic focus toward the electoral arena, however, several drawbacks and strategic limitations of the Circle program became particularly pronounced. First, the Circle program revealed a dynamic that would recur repeatedly in later years. The Bolivarian government relied heavily on state-mobilized groups as allies and actors in the political struggle but had difficulty controlling the actions of these groups, with adverse consequences for its larger campaign to win public opinion. Due to the activities of some groups during the 2002–2003 struggle, the Circles acquired a reputation as violent and repressive. The opposition certainly influenced this negative portrayal, taking every opportunity to denounce them as thugs and which probably unfairly exaggerated the centrality of violence and intimidation (versus more benign community work) to their activities. Nevertheless, surveys showed that a substantial majority of Venezuelans disapproved of the Circles. They were one of the least popular political actors in all of Venezuela – on either the pro-government or pro-opposition side – during the 2002–2004 period.

The limited ability of the government to control, monitor, and direct the activities of the Circles also manifested itself in their limited use in the electoral arena. The Circles participated heavily in the campaign to defeat the recall referendum in 2004 (Hawkins and Hansen, 2006). As poorly financed and largely informal groups that operated with a substantial degree of independence, and which were often very skeptical of the MVR, the Circles were not well designed to be mobilizers of electoral support. In sum, the Circle program revealed some problems that would not go away – a basic limitation in the ability of the government to monitor and control such groups – but also possessed some specific drawbacks related to the informal and uninstitutionalized way the program had developed. In this latter respect, they were a poor fit for the next phase of the Fifth Republic, when contestation returned to the electoral arena.

9.6 MODERATE OPPOSITION THREATS IN THE ELECTORAL ARENA, 2004–2012

The aftermath of the recall referendum saw Venezuela move into a new phase in which the opposition gave up trying to oust Chávez through nonconstitutional channels and committed to the electoral arena. This strategic reorientation did not occur immediately and did not receive universal support. The opposition ended up strategically boycotting the 2005 legislative elections at the last minute. While leaders cited concerns regarding fraud as their rationale, the fact that polls predicted a massive defeat – partly a product of a lack of opposition unity and continued sectors bent on electoral abstention – probably also played into their calculus. From the presidential elections of 2006 onward, however, the opposition launched a committed effort in every subsequent major election and referendum in the country and did so increasingly unified as the Democratic Unity Roundtable (MUD) front. These elections were not just fully contested but also, as Table 9.1 earlier in the chapter indicated, very frequent. From 2005 through 2012, a major election or referendum occurred every year except 2011.

Opposition activity in the protest arena did not cease completely during this period. The opposition still took to the streets during campaign season and to protest particularly egregious actions by the government. The most notable protest cycle occurred in 2007, when a wave of student-led protests occurred in response to the government's closing of RCTV, an unabashedly pro-opposition broadcaster (Brading, 2012). Some of the same student groups that led these protests then continued to mobilize actively in late 2007 in opposition to the government's referendum of that year on planned changes to the constitution. In the big picture, however, this period marked a sea change in activity within the protest arena. Contentious action by the opposition was less frequent and no longer posed an existential threat to the Chávez government – rather than hundreds of thousands of protesters, thousands or perhaps 10,000 might take to the streets of Caracas. And rather than street mobilizations being led by an opposition bent on removing the government through any means possible (such as coups or massive strikes), this protest activity occurred in a context in which the opposition had renounced such strategies and was grimly determined to contest power at the ballot box.

During late 2004, coming off the victory in the recall referendum, a high-level meeting of Bolivarian officials took place in which Chávez and a close coterie of advisers proposed what was termed a "New Strategic Map" for navigating a new era in which they had emerged triumphant, would have much more leeway to implement their policy agenda, and expected the opposition to keep trying to take power through elections and not the streets. This document laid out a great variety of policy and strategy proposals, most of which are irrelevant for present concerns. Two particularly pertinent features were a call to rethink and reinvigorate Bolivarian political parties – an idea that eventually led to the dismantlement of the MVR and the creation of a new party, the PSUV, with a much stronger emphasis on grassroots organization – and an emphasis on reinvigorating commitments and programs to enhance citizen participation and organization in local governance.

9.6.1 The Communal Councils

In early 2006, the government launched the Communal Council program, an initiative of unprecedented scope and ambition geared toward building popular power through state-sponsored community organizations (García-Guadilla, 2007; Machado, 2008). Unlike the Bolivarian Circle initiative, the Communal Council program was implemented through the legislature, with the passing of the Ley de Consejos Comunales, which established a very detailed set of procedures by which small communities of about 200 households (fewer in rural areas) could join together and form a state-sanctioned neighborhood organization that would assume a variety of local governance functions. Requirements in this process included the conducting of a local census, advertising the planned formation of the Council, holding votes for a variety of council offices and leadership positions, and filing substantial paperwork with government officials. The program was supported and pushed forward by multiple entities of the Venezuelan government. At the national level, the agency Fundacomunal was repurposed and tasked with helping implement the Communal Council program, holding workshops and events to publicize the program, meeting with communities to help them navigate the process, handling the formal registration, and also disbursing a great deal of funding. But many municipal and state governments also became involved with the administration and support of the program in various ways. By early 2008, over 18,000 Councils had been formally registered with the government. Later estimates would place that number over 30,000.

While overtly cast as organizations tasked with local governance functions, the Communal Councils also became de facto grassroots organizations of the PSUV, heavily involved in electoral mobilization (Handlin, 2013, 2016). PSUV leaders referred to the Councils openly as the "base units" of the new party. The Councils played important roles in the process of building the party, particularly in signing up party members and helping recruit people into party activism. Perhaps most notably, the Councils also engaged in various forms of electoral mobilization in the elections and campaigns held from 2006 onward, holding joint events with PSUV politicians in communities, helping mobilize people to campaign rallies, serving as channels for the distribution of patronage, and urging voters to the polls. To the extent that the Communal Councils operated outside the local governance arena, then, their primary function was clearly to support the Bolivarian Movement and PSUV in the electoral arena during a time in which the opposition made contestation at the ballot box the focus of its efforts.

Mirroring Opposition Threats: Bolivarian Venezuela 231

In contrast, the Communal Councils played only relatively minor roles in the protest arena. They often engaged in discrete forms of local claim-making, which in some instances might escalate into small-scale contentious activity (e.g. organizing a group of people to march on city hall in a provincial city and demand better water and sanitation services). But the Communal Councils were not major actors in organizing larger-scale counterprotests or otherwise managing the protest arena. For one, the opposition did not make contentious activity in the protest arena a central thrust of its own strategy during this time, so the need to use state-sponsored groups like the Communal Councils as vehicles for regularly mobilizing regime supporters into the streets was far less acute than in the 2001–2004 period.

Moreover, to the extent that the opposition did engage in major protest activity during the 2005–2012 period, the student movement tended to be the protagonist. Just as the Putin government in Russia learned from the color revolutions and sponsored the pro-Kremlin student group Nashi to counter student opposition, the Chávez government reacted to the upsurge in student activism and mobilization by creating its own pro-government student groups. These Chavista student organizations engaged in regularized activities on campuses. But they were also engaged in selective counterprotests to show the country that part of the younger generation was aligned with the Bolivarian Project. The specific form of opposition protest activity during this period therefore called for a more specific form of SMMs for which the Communal Councils, in which older community leaders and activists tended to be most involved, were a poor demographic fit.

9.7 VERY SERIOUS OPPOSITION THREATS IN BOTH ARENAS, 2013–2017

Two shocks massively altered the political environment in Venezuela after 2012, with great implications for the strategies and threat level of the opposition and, in consequence, for the government's approach to state mobilization of loyalist groups. First, Chávez died in early 2013 after a long battle with cancer, the details of which had been mainly kept hidden from the public. The death of personalistic leaders is famously difficult for autocratic regimes, often setting off messy succession conflicts. Chávez ameliorated this problem to some degree by naming Maduro as a designated successor, but fissures within the Bolivarian coalition still became much more pronounced, especially divides between a radical leftist sector (which Maduro headed) and a more cynical, nonideological sector with backgrounds in the military and security forces (exemplified by Cabello). Just as importantly, Chávez had great charisma and had developed very personalized forms of linkage with many followers. It was never likely that another politician, particularly one as inept as Maduro, would be able to replicate this appeal.

The strength of Chavismo after Chávez was soon put to the test, since the Venezuelan constitution mandated that a new election be held, Chávez having died before being able to begin his new presidential term. Whereas Chávez had won the 2012 presidential election by about 11 percentage points against Henrique Capriles, Maduro won an election six months later against the same opponent by only 2 percentage points. Chavismo did not fall apart without Chávez, but the nine-point swing was significant. Just as importantly, the razor-thin victory did nothing to quell uncertainties regarding whether Maduro would be able to hold together the Bolivarian coalition at the elite and mass levels, particularly in times of difficulty. The death of Chávez, the close margin of the 2013 election, and allegations of fraud in that election emboldened a more hard-line wing of the opposition to launch an extended cycle of protests in early 2014. While the protests subsided over time, they would return on a grand scale in 2016, substantially in response to the government's blocking opposition attempts to trigger a referendum to recall Maduro from office. These cycles of protest, which involved massive mobilizations and semipermanent roadblocks, represented the biggest threat to the Bolivarian government in the protest arena since the 2001–2003 period.

The government's troubles were greatly accentuated by a subsequent economic collapse, stemming from both long-term macroeconomic and fiscal mismanagement and a steep fall in global oil prices that began in the middle of 2014. Despite the opposition's reinvigorated contentious activity, the Maduro government maintained decent approval ratings up through mid-2014 and looked to have successfully stalemated the new wave of protest. The collapse of global oil prices plunged Venezuela into a massive recession, also marked by growing scarcities of basic goods, which turned public opinion sharply against the government and drove the opposition to a historic rout in the 2015 legislative elections. In the following year, the economy further collapsed in tragic ways, leading to hyperinflation, widespread hunger, and unprecedented deprivation. Meanwhile, political tensions ratcheted up, as the Maduro government effectively acted as if the legislature possessed no power while using its hold over the Supreme Court to thwart opposition attempts to trigger a constitutional provision to hold a referendum on recalling the president. In sum, the government came under very high levels of threat – truly unprecedented levels – in both the protest and electoral arenas during this period.

9.7.1 Colectivos and UBCh

The government's response in terms of state mobilization during this period was to reinvigorate or create new groups composed of extreme loyalists that had little to do with local governance and were explicitly geared toward action in the protest and electoral arenas. After the formation of the PSUV, the government had begun to experiment with the creation of formal local party organizations to augment the more informally affiliated, albeit very numerous and well-resourced, Communal Councils. In 2009, assemblies were held across the country to begin the process of forming "Socialist Patrols," local groups of activists that would be individually matched to every voting center in the country and responsible for electoral mobilization within that territory. While active in certain elections, however, these Socialist Patrols had never been fully institutionalized within the party, and many had become defunct.

After the death of Chávez in early 2013, and with a new presidential election now scheduled, the PSUV launched a major initiative to restructure and reinvigorate its formal local party organization through the creation of the UBCh, which would become the new base organizational unit of the party. The push to create UBCh was clearly motivated by the death of Chávez and the realization among leaders of the Bolivarian Movement that the opposition threat in the electoral arena would be heightened. But the UBCh were not just another temporary iteration of local party organization like the Socialist Patrols. Rather, they were intended to be a "permanent element of propaganda and mobilization" that would "strengthen and expand the vanguard" of the Bolivarian Revolution every day" and which should assume some ill-defined responsibilities in local governance in their communities. In effect, the UBCh were designed to be highly politicized organizations that would be agents of electoral mobilization but also capable of acting the protest arena and establishing permanent positions within communities. This put them into potential conflict with Communal Councils operating in the same neighborhoods. In the Bolivarian mediascape, substantial debate surrounded the question of what the relationship between the Councils and UBCh should be and whether the UBCh were undermining the "popular power" exercised by the Councils.

The second consequential form of state mobilization during this period was the activation, or reactivation, of a more informal set of organizations, many of which were rooted in the Bolivarian Circle initiative, known colloquially as colectivos. These colectivos are informal, highly revolutionary neighborhood-based organizations that view themselves as defenders of the Bolivarian Revolution, although they may maintain critical postures toward the government. Generalizing further about the colectivos is difficult. As with the Bolivarian Circles, the activities of a set of high-profile colectivos may not be representative of the activities of the broader population of colectivos. Many colectivos do not engage in violence and are simply groups of militant revolutionary leftists who view themselves as defenders of their communities and the vanguard of the Bolivarian Revolution. Nevertheless, a subset of armed colectivos came to play a salient and controversial role in Venezuelan politics in the 2013–2017 period.

Both the UBCh and colectivos were actively involved in standard forms of countermobilization, organizing demonstrations and pouring into the streets in response to opposition protest cycles and as ways to rally support for a beleaguered government. For example, the Maduro government used the UbCh and colectivos as key grassroots mobilizational actors for massive national-scale events in late 2016 labeled the "Anti-Coup March" and the "Venezuela, Indestructible Heart Campaign," which both sought to cast opposition attempts to remove Maduro as undemocratic, to blame the opposition for launching a financial war that was destroying the Venezuelan economy, and to rally the government's dwindling support more generally. Similar types of countermobilizational events were also held in previous years during this period of elevated opposition threats.

The armed colectivos, and some portion of the UBCh, were centrally involved in the Venezuelan government's heightened attempts to control and manage the protest arena through repression and intimidation. When massive protests first broke out in February 2014, PSUV leader Francisco Ameliach tweeted, "UBCh prepare yourselves for an immediate counter-attack. Diosdado will give the order." The following months were marked by numerous notorious instances in which armed colectivos and UBCh violently clashed with protesters. When the opposition announced plans for a massive mobilization to protest the government's blocking of an attempted recall referendum in 2016, Vice President Aristóbulo Istúriz responded by saying that the government would fill the streets of Caracas with colectivos and their "iron horses," a reference to the motorcycles that armed colectivos have often used when making a show of force on the streets (Infobae, 2016). An extensive report from Human Rights Watch (2014) documents high degrees of collaboration between armed Bolivarian civilian groups – colectivos and UBCHs – and government security forces. This collaborative activity took different forms. In some instances, security forces policing a protest suddenly disappeared, and colectivos or UBCh descended soon after to beat up protesters. In other instances, armed civilian groups and security forces operated side-by-side in forcefully detaining, and even opening fire upon, protesters.

Empowering a subset of colectivos and UBCh in this way had doubled-edged consequences for the Maduro government. The armed civilian groups allowed the government to exert a higher degree of repression on opposition protesters, therefore helping stalemate the initial wave of protests in 2014, while minimizing the degree to which security forces were directly implicated in the violence. While serious investigations of the violence would still conclude that the government was responsible for substantial repression, either directly or because they empowered the armed civilian groups, this more nuanced perspective is not necessarily dominant among Venezuelans or international audiences. In this sense, the use of state-mobilized groups to repressively manage the protest arena can be seen within a larger pattern in which autocratic regimes like Venezuela and Russia often engage in disinformation campaigns or other deliberate attempts to "muddy the water" in ways that allow them to get away with certain types of behavior without facing the full consequences in terms of domestic or international opinion.

On the other hand, the colectivos and – to a lesser degree – UBCh proved difficult to control, much like the Bolivarian Circles of a decade earlier, creating various unintended consequences and forms of blowback. While it is hard to know whether any given instance of colectivo repression is sanctioned or not, it seems likely that the government tried to curtail their repressive activities yet was not able to fully stop the violence, hurting them in the court of public opinion. Part of the issue seems to be the limited ability, or willingness, of the Venezuelan security services to fully control these groups, with which they otherwise may act in concert at times.

Some colectivos also likely function as criminal organizations involved in the drug trade and racketeering, activities that may bring them into cooperation, conflict, or both with parts of the Venezuelan security forces. The murkiness of these connections was put on display in a sequence of events in October 2014. First, Robert Serra, a young rising star within the PSUV known to be heavily linked to colectivos – he had also been a central figure in organizing youth counterprotests in the 2007 protest cycle – was found mysteriously murdered in his Caracas home. Several days afterward, an armed standoff occurred in Caracas between security forces and a major colectivo, which left five colectivo leaders dead, including one very closely linked to Serra. In response, this colectivo went public with demands that Interior Minister Miguel Rodríguez Torres, long associated with close relationships with armed Bolivarian Circles and Colectivos, resign for his role in the murders, and not long afterward the minister was shuffled to a new post. While the true relationship between all these events remains unknown, they underscore the murky territory created when the government empowers and mobilizes armed civilian groups, which may not only play roles in the protest arena but which may clash with state forces or become pawns in power struggles between competing government factions.

The ability of Bolivarian governmental forces to control at least some of the colectivos further deteriorated in 2016 (Stratfor, 2016). As the economic collapse took on truly dire dimensions, marked by widespread shortages and hunger, some colectivos increased their criminal activity while growing increasingly disenchanted with the Maduro government, which they increasingly viewed as corrupt (Casey, 2016). Many colectivos exerted de facto control over neighborhoods in major cities, sometimes in cooperation with security forces but often in open defiance of them. While some residents may see the local colectivo as a source of aid and provisioning, others may view them as exploitative criminals empowered by the Bolivarian government. At the very least, this fracturing of control over state-mobilized groups in Venezuela further complicated and undermined the Maduro government's already tenuous ability to exert social and political control over the country.

In sum, the recent period has been one in which unprecedented threats in both the protest and electoral arenas led the Bolivarian government to emphasize the mobilization of a new set of highly loyal and politicized organizations, much more explicitly geared toward political action rather than local governance and, most ominously, much more willing to engage in repression and violence as a means to counteract opposition activity in the protest arena. While the colectivos and UBCh proved useful in some ways, helping the government stave off the opposition for the moment, they also created other troubles. State weakness in Venezuela meant that government bureaucrats and security services had great difficulty controlling state-mobilized groups once these entities had been called into life through the Bolivarian Revolution. The dramatic and tragic economic collapse of the country greatly exacerbated this dynamic, leading to an increasing fracturing of authority and control.

9.8 CONCLUSION

This chapter examined the evolution and logic of state mobilization in Bolivarian Venezuela from 1999 to 2017. Two contextual conditions help explain important aspects of the case and differentiate it from others examined in this volume. The extremely competitive nature of the Venezuelan regime created great incentives for the government to use state-mobilized groups mainly for the purposes of proactive and reactive mobilization, as a means to counter opposition threats in the protest and electoral arenas. The weak Venezuelan state, in turn, has meant that the government has faced great difficulties in controlling state-mobilized groups, as bureaucracies and security services did not have substantial capacity to monitor their activities and credibly punish those groups for non-sanctioned behavior.

The bulk of the chapter then focused on explaining the logic underlying change over time in state mobilization, developing and testing a mirroring theory that centered on two propositions. First, the government's emphasis on infrastructural mobilization, most keeping with its ideological commitments, waxed and waned with the degree of opposition threat. The imperative of dealing with threats to power, through proactive and reactive mobilization, has clearly taken precedence over the use of infrastructural mobilization to achieve longer-term programmatic goals. Second, when mobilizing society to deal with opposition threats, the government has focused on sponsoring movements and organizations suited to operating in whichever arena of politics, that of protests or elections, the opposition was most threatening at the time. The need to respond to a shifting threat landscape helps explain why the Bolivarian Movement has sponsored the formation of so many different kinds of organizations and movements during its nearly twenty years in power.

This should be a useful framework for understand the logic of SMMs in other authoritarian cases. As the scope conditions make clear, authoritarian regime type delimits relevant arenas of politics and whether or not incumbents are liable to face open challenges in the protest and/or electoral arenas. State elites in closed autocracies face a very different strategic landscape than in competitive authoritarian regimes, and the logic of their mobilizational choices will differ accordingly. The mirroring theory seems like it might produce the greatest traction, however, when applied within other competitive autocracies. Other chapters of this volume note that autocratic incumbents engage in reactive mobilization of protest-oriented movements to deal with opposition threats in that arena (Chapters 2 and 7). Others find that electoral authoritarian governments that anticipate genuine threats at the ballot box also often seek to mobilize society to help in electioneering (Chapter 10). A versatile and shifting repertoire of mobilizational strategies, which can be tailored to the needs and threats of the day, may be particularly helpful in ruling by other means.

REFERENCES

Arconada Rodríguez, Santiago. 2005. Seis Años Después: Mesas Técnicas y Consejos Comunitarios de Aguas. *Revista Venezolana de Economía y Ciencias* 11: 3.

Arenas, Nelly, and Luis Gómez Calcaño. 2005. Los Circulos Bolivarianos: El Mito de la Unidad del Pueblo. *América Latina Hoy* 39: 167–193.

Brading, Ryan. 2012. The anti-Bolivarian student movement: new social actors challenge the advancement of Venezuela's Bolivarian bocialism. *Asian Journal of Latin American Studies* 25 (3): 23–46.

Casey, Nicholas. 2016. In a brutal year in Venezuela, even crime fighters are killers. *The New York Times*, December 30.

Coppedge, Michael. 2002. "Venezuela: Popular Sovereignty Versus Liberal Democracy." Kellogg Institute Working Paper #294, University of Notre Dame.

Corrales, Javier, and Michael Penfold. 2011. *Dragon in the Tropics: Hugo Chávez and the Political Economy of Revolution in Venezuela*. Washington, DC: Brookings Institution Press.

Ellner, Steve, and Miguel Tinker Salas. 2005. The Venezuelan exceptionalism thesis: separating myth from reality. *Latin American Perspectives* 32 (2): 5–19.

García-Guadilla, María Pilar. 2004. Civil society: institutionalization, fragmentation, autonomy. In Steve Ellner and Daniel Hellinger (eds.), *Venezuelan Politics in the Chávez Era: Class, Polarization, and Conflict*. Boulder, CO: Lynne Rienner, pp. 179–196.

García-Guadilla, María Pilar. 2007. El Poder Popular y la Democracia Participativa en Venezuela: los Consejos Comunales. Paper prepared for the congress of the Latin American Studies Association. Montreal.

Giménez, Claudia, Mariela Rivas, and Juan Carlos Rodríguez. 2007. Estado y Participación Ciudadana en las Políticas de Intervención Urbanística del Barrio en Venezuela: Del Puntofijismo a la Revolución Bolivariana. In *Seminario Internacional. Procesos Urbanos Informales*. Bogotá: Procesos Urbanos Informales.

Handlin, Samuel. 2013. Social protection and the politicization of class cleavages during Latin America's left turn. *Comparative Political Studies* 46 (12): 1582–1609.

Handlin, Samuel. 2016. Mass organization and the durability of competitive authoritarian regimes. *Comparative Political Studies* 49 (9): 1238–1269.

Handlin, Samuel. 2017. *State Crisis in Fragile Democracies: Polarization and Political Regimes in South America*. Cambridge: Cambridge University Press.

Hawkins, Kirk, and David Hansen. 2006. Dependent Civil Society: The Circulos Bolivarianos in Venezuela. *Latin American Research Review* 41 (1): 102–132.

HIDROVEN. n.d. "Gerencia de Desarrollo Comunitario: Mesas Técnicas de Agua, Proceso Evolutivo." Official document.

Human Rights Watch. 2014. *Punished for Protesting: Rights Violations in Venezuela's Streets, Detention Centers, and Justice System*. Washington, DC: Human Rights Watch.

Infobae. 2016. El vicepresidente de Venezuela amenaza de la oposición con llenar las avenidas de Caracas con colectivos armados. October 27.

Inter-Press Service. 2002. Venezuela: Tensión en los Medios de Prensa. January 8.

Levitsky, Steven, and Lucan Way. 2002. The rise of competitive authoritarianism. *Journal of Democracy* 13 (2): 51–65.

Machado, Jesús. 2008. *Estudio de los Consejos Comunales in Venezuela*: Caracas: Fundación Centro Gumilla.

Nelson, Brian. 2009. *The Silence and the Scorpion: The Coup Against Chávez and the Making of Modern Venezuela*. New York: Nation Books.

Roberts, Kenneth. 2006. Populist Mobilization, Socio-Political Conflict, and Grass-Roots Organization in Latin America. *Comparative Politics* 38 (2): 127–148.

Stratfor. 2016. In Venezuela, armed groups find opportunity in calamity. March 1.

10

Mobilizing against Change

Veteran Organizations as a Pivotal Political Actor

Danijela Dolenec and Daniela Širinić

10.1 INTRODUCTION

On 18 November 2016, around 100,000 people marched from the Vukovar city centre to the cemetery, commemorating Vukovar Remembrance Day, the twenty-fifth anniversary of the day when Vukovar fell into the hands of Serbian occupying forces in 1991. The event was organized by local veteran organizations and attended by the prime minister and his cabinet, the president, army chiefs of staff, numerous MPs, generals, and other notables from the political elite. Following the September election that year, both the parliamentary majority and the presidency were in the hands of the right-wing party Hrvatska Demokratska Zajednica (HDZ), and the entire party leadership was in attendance. Participants came to Vukovar from all parts of Croatia, including some from neighbouring Bosnia and Herzegovina, many of them draped in Croatian flags, others carrying military insignia from the Homeland War. After laying the wreaths at the city cemetery to commemorate soldiers and civilians who died in Vukovar during the war, the Catholic archbishop held mass.

Though this was a mass gathering, we justifiably hesitate to call it a 'protest'. The organizers were not making claims against the government. To the contrary, the prime minister, the president of Croatia and top government representatives were heading the march, while the powerful leadership of the Catholic Church was shaping key messages during the event. Indeed, this event bears striking resemblance to the one described in the introduction, organized in Warsaw by the Law and Justice (PiS) party in April 2016 to commemorate the Smolensk plane crash. In both cases the ruling party coordinated and actively

---

Research funded by the Swiss National Science Foundation, IZ11Z0_166540 – PROMYS as part of the project 'DISOBEDIENT DEMOCRACY: A Comparative Analyses of Contentious Politics in the European Semi-periphery'.

supported the mass mobilization, defying the standard scenario from contentious politics literature according to which protests represent weapons of the weak. Both in Warsaw and in Vukovar, what we saw was *pro-active mobilization*, where the state mobilizes social actors to enhance its own legitimacy and pre-empt potential challenges by the opposition. Such collective actions instigated by the state to advance its interests seem to be best captured by the concept of state-mobilized movements (SMMs).

In the case of Croatia, further insights about this dynamic can be drawn by comparing the described event from 2016 with the same Remembrance Day ceremony from three years earlier. On 18 November 2013, around 70,000[1] people marched from the Vukovar city centre to the cemetery. The event was organized by veteran organizations, responsible for directing participants through the designated route and ensuring everyone's safety. Like in 2016, the event was attended by the prime minister and his ministers, the president of Croatia, army chiefs of staff, many retired generals, MPs, heads of political parties, and other notable guests. The key distinction was in the fact that both the parliamentary majority and the presidency were at that time held by a coalition of Social Democrats and Liberals. At one point during the march, veterans blocked the way for government representatives, not allowing them to proceed along the designated route towards the cemetery. National TV stations were broadcasting perplexed and worried faces of the heads of state as they stood in the middle of a crowded street. In the next moment, they started moving backwards, giving up on completing the route to the city cemetery. The veteran organizations successfully prevented top government officials from taking part in the closing ceremony.

What was happening there? Why did the veteran organizations block government representatives from marching to the cemetery? Was this a protest, a war commemoration, or both? These two contentious episodes are intended to introduce the main protagonists in our analysis of the dynamic between veteran organizations as the main agent of protest politics and the right-wing political party HDZ, which dominates Croatia's politics since the country's independence in 1990. Between winning the first multi-party election in 1990 and the current government in 2019, HDZ has headed the state for more than twenty years. In addition to heading the government after seven out of nine rounds of parliamentary elections so far, in many counties and municipalities HDZ has enjoyed uninterrupted rule throughout the past three decades. It seems fair therefore to treat it as a hegemonic political actor which, though operating in a multi-party environment, is in many ways closely entwined with state institutions since their inception in the 1990s. As a political party that grew during the 1990–5 Homeland War, HDZ has learned how to rely on mass mobilization as 'a tactic of the state to exercise

---

[1] According to regional TV station Slavonska Televizija, broadcast on 18 November 2013, available at www.youtube.com/watch?v=plDk9XqaHGQ (accessed 14 February 2020).

Veterans as a Pivotal Political Actor

power and promote its own objectives' (see Ekiert and Perry in the Introduction). Through a series of decisions and events that we describe in this chapter, HDZ has managed to, firstly, successfully claim war victory and completion of the state-building project as the party's doing; and secondly, tie a large veteran population into a clientelist relationship with the party. As a result, when HDZ is in power – which has been almost always – veteran organizations proactively mobilize in order to strengthen HDZ legitimacy and weaken oppositional claims to power. In contrast, during the two terms when HDZ was in opposition, veteran mobilization became contentious, aiming to destabilize the incumbent government and rally the vote for HDZ.

In this chapter we first describe the broad social mobilization for the war that created the veteran population and the dominant role of HDZ in the politics of the 1990s. We also outline the institutional architecture of veterans' rights that was implemented under HDZ governments in the 1990s, creating a client–patron relationship between this political party and the veteran population. In the second part of the chapter we focus on the period after 2000, analysing this interaction both in the arena of political institutions and in the protest arena. Recent analyses suggest that veterans represent HDZ's voting constituency, while veteran organizations' recourse to citizens' petitions for referenda reveal both close ties to HDZ and at the same time some serious friction. Veteran organizations are those that ultimately possess the capacity for mass mobilization, which means that the power relationship between them and the party is not entirely asymmetric. Since 2000 HDZ was in opposition twice – 2000–3 and 2011–15 – so we contrast periods when HDZ was in power with those when they were in opposition in order to establish whether levels of contention by veteran groups support the logic of a party-mobilized movement. Using protest event data, we show that in periods when HDZ was not in power the level of contentious mobilization of veterans was substantially higher; we suggest that the aim of this mobilization was to reinstate HDZ into government.

10.2 A SOLDIERS' STATE

The case of Croatia fundamentally departs from the general storyline of the third wave of democratization in Eastern Europe as a top-down, elite-driven 'transition' to multiparty electoral democracy and capitalism (Merkel, 2011; Dolenec, 2016). This is a country which underwent democratization through war (Dolenec, 2013), so the new state was born out of large-scale nationalist mobilization.

Still within the Socialist Federal Republic of Yugoslavia (SFRY), in May 1990 the first multiparty election was held in Croatia, in which HDZ won 42 per cent of the vote and 58 per cent of seats. Soon after that, the Yugoslav National Army confiscated all weapons from the Croatian Territorial Defence, setting in motion a series of belligerent steps that led to war. Not being able to rely on existing defence institutions, the new Croatian state founded the Croatian National Guard (CNG), initially as a crossover between police and army (Marijan, 2008), which was in 1991 transformed into the Armed Forces of the Republic of Croatia (AFRC). The armed insurrection of Serb-populated areas of Croatia escalated into full-blown war, and in 1991 a quarter of Croatia's territory was occupied by insurgent forces (Šterc and Pokos, 1993; Živić, 2005). Full numbers for participation in the AFRC are difficult to ascertain. According to Marijan (2008), at the end of 1991 the AFRC had 200,000 people under arms. Other sources estimate that around 300,000 people were under arms during 1991–2.[2] According to Smerić (2009), mass participation in the armed forces of the Republic of Croatia during the Homeland War therefore represents one of the fundamental formative institutions of contemporary Croatian state, impacting the entire institutional configuration of Croatian society.

The Official Register of Veterans, published only in 2012, estimates the number of veterans[3] in Croatia at 503,112. If this number is correct, veterans make up about 12 per cent of the population of Croatia,[4] and so it seems safe to say that in the 1990s this society underwent dramatic social upheaval and mobilization. It is also worth mentioning that Croatian society draws on a legacy of mass mobilization from during and after World War II. According to Unkovski Korica (2017), in the spring of 1945 the People's Liberation Movement (Narodno-Oslobodilački Pokret, NOP) in Croatia numbered 800,000 people. Similarly, at the end of 1947 the Popular Front had 955,450 members (Spehnjak, 1987). Rothschild (1993) describes the Yugoslav regime in the 1940s and 1950s as possessing a 'deep reservoir of authentic popularity, prestige, and legitimacy that Tito, his Partisan movement and his Communist party amassed during the war' (p. 105).

This experience with party-led mass mobilization from Yugoslav times might help in part account for HDZ's large party membership, as well as its growing experience with and reliance on mass mobilization as a way of exercising power while in government. Čular and Nikić Čakar (2017) categorize HDZ in the 1990s as a charismatic movement party. As numerous analyses have shown (see e.g. Kasapović, 1996; Zakošek, 2002; Čular, 2005; Dolenec, 2013), HDZ has decisively shaped politics in Croatia. Since 1990, HDZ has been in power for 20 years; out of nine elections, the party was in opposition only twice (Čular and Nikić Čakar, 2018). At the same time, despite being in government most of the time since Croatia's independence, in the early 1990s HDZ was 'the leader of

---

[2] Prolexis Online Encyclopedia, Miroslav Krleža Institute of Lexicography, http://proleksis.lzmk.hr/18243/

[3] We use the term 'veteran' since this is the standard term for this population in academic literature, but in Croatia this population self-identifies with the name 'defenders'. This term was encoded in relevant legislation during the 1990s and is now the most frequently used name for this social group, both by themselves and the general public.

[4] Croatian Bureau of Statistics quotes 4,284.889 inhabitants in 2011.

a broad nationalist movement seeking independence and democratization of Croatia' (Čular and Nikić Čakar, 2018, p. 2). Even though it institutionalized into a strong organization with a large membership, the initial circumstances of its development suggest a resemblance to Kitschelt's (2006) movement parties. The party's rapid growth and Franjo Tuđman's charismatic leadership pushed HDZ towards relying on movement-type linkages with citizens while sidelining formal institutional procedures (Čular and Nikić Čakar, 2018). In parallel, the party grew a strong membership base and a loyal electorate, both of which helped maintain its political dominance. In 1995, the party had 400,000 members, and the number continued to grow until 2001, reaching 432,000 members (Čular, 2010). In contrast, its main competitor party on the left, the Social Democratic Party (SDP), never reached above 30,000 members. In summary, throughout the 1990s more than half a million people in Croatia were party members, an overwhelming majority of which were HDZ supporters (Čular, 2010).

The Yugoslav war legacy also meant that Croatia had experience with welfare programmes for veterans before the Homeland War. Partisans who fought in the Second World War in Croatia were awarded the status of veterans during SFRY, and many received state-insured pensions.[5] The rights of Homeland War veterans were legislated from 1994 onwards, under successive HDZ governments. Significant changes to the legislation were made in 1996, 2001, and 2004 (Begić, Sanader, and Žunec, 2007). By 2004, the law awarded thirty-seven different material entitlements to this population, most importantly pensions, disability compensation, health services, housing, child allowance, unemployment benefits, financial help in securing employment, tax cuts, scholarships, guaranteed university entry, and others (Begić, Sanader, and Žunec, 2007). According to the last available report[6] published by the Croatian government in 2013, the total annual material compensation to veterans amounted to 5 per cent of the state budget and around 1.8 per cent of Croatia's GDP.[7] Veteran pensions represent the largest share of material compensations. Of the total number of veterans, in 2016, 72,001 were recipients of state pensions, 80 per cent of which receive disability pensions (Croatian Pension Fund 3/2016). Veteran pensions are around three times higher than standard pensions and higher than the average net salary (Bađun, 2009). In comparison, in Israel, a welfare state with comprehensive provisions for veterans, fully disabled veterans receive benefits at the level of 66 per cent of the average wage (Gal and Bar, 2000). A comparative study of eleven countries,

---

[5] In 2009, there were 64,000 participants in the Second World War, both partisans and NDH soldiers (Bađun, 2009).
[6] Reports regarding the implementation costs of veteran-related legislation were discontinued by HDZ coalition governments.
[7] Historical data on GDP taken from the website of the Central Bank of Croatia, available at www.hnb.hr.

including the United States, Israel, and Germany, found Croatia at the very top regarding the extent and quality of privileges accorded to veterans (Ferenčak, Kardov, and Rodik, 2003; see also Žunec, 2006; Dobrotić, 2008).

The Act from 2004 was further amended in 2005; twice in 2007; twice in 2009; in 2010, 2011, and 2012; three times in 2013, and once in 2014; an entirely new Act with significant increases in rights and material entitlements was introduced in 2017. In other words, after the HDZ government put in place welfare state entitlements for veterans in the mid-1990s, all subsequent governments were compelled to deal with these state programmes for veterans. Data from the Croatian Policy Agendas Project (Širinić, 2018; Širinić et al., 2016)[8] shows that, after the initial focus on building the armed forces, from mid-1992 to 2015 there is remarkable stability in the share of government attention on the policy issue of veterans and their dependents. The key question is whether veteran benefits get extended or reduced under HDZ and SDP governments respectively. Under the first SDP-led government 2001–2003, state pensions, disability support, and other benefits for veterans were reduced and discontinued (Begić, Sanader, and Žunec, 2007). Conversely, the largest increases in the number of disability pension entitlements for veterans occurred in 1999, 2007, and most recently in 2017, election years when HDZ was in power (Stubbs and Zrinščak, 2011). As an illustration, the number of disabled veterans registered in the pension system grew three times between 2003 and 2010, years of the first and second Sanader government, with the largest increase in election year 2007, with 5,500 new insurances issued for veterans with disability (Bađun, 2011). After returning to power, HDZ adopted a new Act on Veterans in 2017, substantially increasing various material benefits for this population, reducing thresholds for accessing state pensions, and opening access to state pensions to soldiers who fought in Bosnia and Herzegovina.[9]

In the following section we portray the evolution of veteran organizations into pivotal political actors, delving further into the complexity of their interaction with HDZ. Though HDZ mobilizes veterans both to protect the status quo and to win back elections, this case also shows that veteran contention possesses strong blackmail potential and is ever only partially under the party's control.

---

[8] Longitudinal data from the Croatian Policy Agendas Project, covering the period from 1990 to the end of 2015 (Širinić et al., 2016). The government agenda dataset coded agendas of all cabinet weekly meetings from 1990 to 2015, amounting to over 40,000 agenda items (Širinić, 2018). All items were coded following the methodology of the Comparative Agendas Project (Bevan, 2015), where each unit of analysis is coded into 21 major policy topics and 214 subtopics.

[9] 'Novi zakon: branitelji će lakše u mirovinu, imat će i veće penzije', Jutarnji list, 4 August 2017, www.jutarnji.hr/vijesti/hrvatska/novi-zakon-branitelji-lakse-u-mirovinu-imat-ce-i-vece-penzije-uvodi-se-i-naknada-za-nezaposlene-te-ubrzava-njihovo-stambeno-zbrinjavanje/6435139/ (accessed 14 February 2020).

10.3 VETERAN ORGANIZATIONS AS PIVOTAL POLITICAL ACTORS

HDZ governments in the early 1990s instituted welfare programmes for the veteran population, but arguably much of the welfare package would not have happened without veterans organizing to put pressure on the state. In the spring of 1992 the first veteran non-governmental organization (NGO) was founded, and in 1993 it held a federative assembly of over fifteen chapters. The assembly meeting was attended by the then-president of Croatia, Franjo Tuđman, while General Martin Špegelj, the first chief of staff of the Croatian Armed Forces, was elected president of the association. The Association of Patriotic War Volunteers and Veterans of the Republic of Croatia (UDVDR), as the federation is called, today numbers 21 member organizations at county level, over 200 chapters on the local level, and around 80 social clubs. Its website boasts a membership of 220,000, 'representing the population of around 350,000 Croatian veterans, who together with their families come close to one million citizens of Croatia'.[10] The Association of Disabled Veterans of the Homeland War (HVIDR-a) is similarly federated across Croatia, with member organizations on county level.[11] According to Mihalec, Pavlin, and Relja (2012), HVIDR-a has a membership of 35,000, with 20 regional and 105 local chapters. Its president served as HDZ's MP and he headed the parliamentary Board for Veterans. During 2010, veteran NGOs participated in thirteen advisory and consultative bodies of the government, spanning issues from employment policies to regional development (Mihalec, Pavlin, and Relja, 2012). Finally, the Association of Volunteer Veterans, the third-largest federation of veteran NGOs, has member organizations in eight of the twenty-one counties, with chapters and clubs like UDVDR.[12] In addition to large veteran federations, in 2016, no less than 795 NGOs in Croatia registered veteran issues as their primary objective.[13]

Though the generosity of the welfare package for veterans creates the impression of a highly privileged population, compensatory government programmes have in fact created a passive, state-dependent population (Dobrotić, 2008). Given that during the war these were generally young people, most often with only secondary education qualifications, with little or no job experience prior to going to war, the compensatory approach has contributed to their social isolation (Dobrotić, 2008). In the 1990s, veterans were overrepresented in lower socioeconomic groups such as the unemployed, welfare recipients, and the poor (Žunec, 2006). Studies showed that only 37 per cent had returned to their jobs from before the war (Grizelj and

---

[10] Quoted from the website of the organization, accesible in Croatian at www.udvdr.hr/povjesnica-2/.
[11] The website of HVIDR-a is much less informative about its size and composition: see www.hvidra.hr/.
[12] See www.uhbddr.hr/pdf/ustrojbeni%20oblici%20udruge.pdf.
[13] Information from Ministry of Administration, Official Registry of NGOs.

Vukušić, 1996; Žunec, 2006). According to a survey by veteran associations, around 50 per cent of former soldiers were unemployed, a third of them claimed they were unsatisfied with their socioeconomic position, and 50 per cent thought they were disadvantaged compared to the population that did not fight in the war (Žunec, 2006).

The contradictory social position of being perceived as privileged but at the same time feeling marginalized contributed to the emergence of a politically explosive social group. Though over time both the symbolic and material politics tied veterans to HDZ, this relationship was neither straightforward nor harmonious. Such a large population, officially encompassing over half a million people, unavoidably entails social, economic, and cultural heterogeneity. In addition, significant differences exist between those 70,000 who receive handsome pensions and the rest who do not, as well as between those who cultivate close links to HDZ party leadership, who work in government agencies or serve as MPs, and again the large majority which does not have access to these social and economic privileges. At the same time, the leadership of veteran organizations has repeatedly proven their ability to mobilize veterans in the hundreds of thousands. Having all this in mind, mass mobilization of veterans in Croatia perhaps carries similarities to what Beissinger (see Chapter 6 in this volume) terms 'composite' mobilization of various strands of motivations and incentives pulled together.

The UDVDR was the first veteran organization to exert political pressure on the government, starting in 1993, when it adopted its first Declaration on Veterans in the Homeland War, and 1994, when it adopted the Resolution on Rights of Croatian Veterans of the Homeland War. Both documents were advocacy initiatives for regulating social rights of veterans and their families. In October 1996 UDVRD organized a high-profile event in the Zagreb Concert Hall, in the presence of high-ranking government officials, at which they presented their '15 Fundamental Demands', together with a petition signed by 90,000 veterans to support the introduction of these demands into the Act on Rights of Croatian Veterans.[14] Though the initial reaction of President Tuđman to these demands was unfriendly, two months later the government legislated a new Act on the Rights of Croatian Veterans from the Homeland War and their Families (NN 108/96, 23.XII.1996). Following that, in 1997 the government set up a separate Ministry for Croatian Veterans of the Homeland War, fulfilling another request by veteran organizations.

Overall, between 1993 and 1996 – partly of its own volition and party in response to pressures from veteran organizations – HDZ governments created a comprehensive institutional architecture of rights and entitlements for veterans and their families. This in turn created a strong bond between HDZ and the veteran population (Kasapović, 1996), described as a powerful client-

---

[14] Information based on the report on UDVRD website, www.udvdr.hr/kategorija/aktivnosti-od-1992-1999/.

Veterans as a Pivotal Political Actor

patron axis charged with both symbolic meaning and material benefits (Čular, 2000). In other words, during the 1990s in their struggle for state recognition and state benefits, veterans evolved from unorganized cohort to client group, they became a prominent social identity and through their strong network of federative organizations they became a powerful pressure group. We know from welfare state literature that once social protection mechanisms are instituted, interest groups organize to defend them (Gal and Bar, 2000; Brooks and Manza, 2007; Maddaloni, 2014), creating an ongoing dynamic of negotiation and confrontation with the state. If the veteran group is large enough, like was the case in the late-nineteenth-century United States, and in Croatia in the 1990s, veteran organizations can become pivotal political players, forging alliances with political parties and influencing election outcomes.

In the United States, the veteran organization Grand Army of the Republic (GAR) was organizationally and ideologically central to late-nineteenth-century politics, influencing the soldiers' vote to affect outcomes of presidential and congressional races (Skocpol, 1995; Ainsworth, 1995). The case of Croatia, we argue, exhibits some important parallels to this dynamic. At the same time, the relationship between HDZ and the veteran population is not a straightforward case of mobilization by the state. The evolution of veterans as an interest group with large mobilization capacity is not the result of HDZ deliberate design but rather of the party using state resources and institutions during the 1990s in seeking to proactively manage this interest group and securing a loyal constituency base. When wielding state control, HDZ uses veteran mobilization in an *order-producing* process (Slater and Smith, 2016), with the dual purpose of both dissuading the opposition and persuading veteran leadership that it is in their best interest to continue to work together (Robertson, 2009). The overall effect is similar to what Beissinger (Chapter 6 in this volume) describes in the case of counterrevolutionary mobilization in Ukraine, of demonstrating the continuing coherence of the regime's institutional control.

By locking in comprehensive welfare programmes for veterans, funding the work of veteran NGOs and enabling veteran representation in many state and party[15] bodies, HDZ managed to co-opt not only veteran organizations but a significant part of the veteran population as well. However, the fact that it is the veteran organizations that ultimately possess capacity for mass mobilization unavoidably contains the potential of backfiring. For this reason, as Ekiert and Perry argue in the introduction to this volume, mass mobilization – even when undertaken with clear state support – unavoidably carries a degree of ambivalence and anxiety for the state.

---

[15] In 2014 HDZ formed an advisory body called the Community of Veterans ('Gojko Šušak') to reinforce the position of veterans within the party. The Community is also open for veterans who are not registered members of the party.

In the following two sections of the paper, partly mirroring the structure of Handlin's analysis of Venezuela (see Chapter 9 in this volume), we explore how this relationship plays out in the arenas of political institutions and of protest.

10.3.1 HDZ and Veterans: The Arena of Political Institutions

In this section we analyse the representation of veteran interests in Parliament, veteran voter preferences in recent elections, and the use that veteran organizations have made of citizen petitions for referenda since 2000.

Parliamentary questions by MPs are used both as an opposition pressure tool and as a way to promote government policies (Vliegenthart and Walgrave, 2011). In our analysis, MP questions pertaining to veteran issues may be revealing of whether one political party stands out in terms of representing veteran interests. Figure 10.1 shows the share of questions of government and opposition MPs, summarized by the SDP and HDZ government terms between 2000 and 2015.[16]

Figure 10.1 shows that, during SDP-led governments, 71.05 per cent of parliamentary questions related to veteran issues were posed by HDZ MPs and their coalitional partners. More interestingly though, even during terms when HDZ held parliamentary majorities and led governments, again their MPs

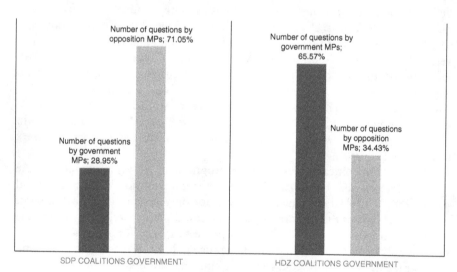

FIGURE 10.1 Share of MP questions on veteran-related issues from 2000 to 2015
Source: Croatian Policy Agendas Dataset (Širinić et al., 2016)

---

[16] CAP dataset (Širinić et al., 2016) includes all MP questions for parliamentary terms between 2000 and 2015. Out of 3,111 MP questions, 99 were devoted to veteran issues.

posed most of questions related to veteran issues (65.57%). In other words, compared to all other parties, HDZ invests by far the greatest energy in representing veteran interests in the parliamentary arena.

Regarding the veteran vote, a long academic silence on this topic in Croatia has been broken recently by a few studies, including ours. In the absence of individual data on veteran vote, Glaurdić and Vuković (2016) analysed voting outcomes at municipal level to investigate whether veterans represent HDZ's voter base. They used the indicator 'war disabled per 1,000 inhabitants' as a proxy for the effects of war violence on individual municipalities, looking at the extent to which this indicator is related to HDZ vote share on municipal level. Since this indicator spatially closely mirrors war impact, being highest in areas of direct combat, it seems like a reasonably reliable proxy for the impact of war on local communities, as well as for a higher density of veteran population. Analysing voting outcomes on municipal level for five rounds of parliamentary elections between 2000 and 2015, Glaurdić and Vuković (2016) found that this indicator had a consistently positive, statistically significant relationship with the vote for HDZ and a negative relationship with the vote for SDP-led coalitions.

We introduce another way of indirectly relating veteran voting behaviour with voting for HDZ, by correlating the density of veteran NGOs[17] with HDZ vote share on the county level, for the 2013 local election.

Figure 10.2 suggests a relatively strong relationship between the density of veteran NGOs and vote share for HDZ (r=0.64), further corroborating the claim that HDZ captures a significant part of the veteran vote.

Along the same lines, Bagić and Kardov's (2018) survey of veteran political orientations finds that veterans more often describe their political orientation as right-wing: 37 per cent of veterans do so, in comparison to 27 per cent of the general electorate. Furthermore, 14 per cent of veterans self-identify as far-right, compared to around 6 per cent of non-veteran voters. While 21 per cent of voters did not declare their ideological self-positioning, only 13 per cent of veterans failed to, which suggests that this social group is more politicized than the average voter. And indeed, veterans seem to vote somewhat more often than the general voter – 69.9 per cent as opposed to 66.2 per cent, though in this study this does not translate into a statistically significant difference.

Regarding veteran vote choice, Bagić and Kardov (2018) sorted results into preferences for right-wing, centre, and left-wing political parties. They grouped HDZ together with five other small right-wing parties, so these findings do not establish a direct correspondence between the veteran vote and HDZ. However, given that most of the other parties in the group barely manage to cross the electoral threshold for parliamentary representation, and that they often form

---

[17] Density is calculated as the number of veteran NGOs (in 2016), divided by the number of inhabitants in each of the twenty-one counties.

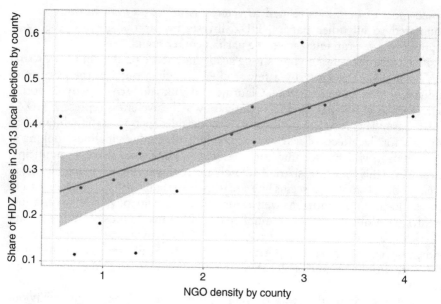

FIGURE 10.2 Density of veteran NGOs and HDZ vote share in 2013 local election

coalitions with HDZ, it seems plausible to assume a high correspondence between voting right-wing and voting for HDZ. Bagić and Kardov's (2018) main finding is that 51 per cent of veterans voted for right-wing parties in the 2011 election, compared to 38.7 per cent of general voters. The survey also asked about vote choice in the 2015 presidential election, as well as the intended vote in the then-upcoming 2015 parliamentary election. Logistic regression models for each of these three elections returned statistically significant results, with veteran status increasing the likelihood of a right-wing vote by 1.5 times. Also, results for each of the three elections are very similar, suggesting stability in the vote choice. This finding is in line with Čular and Nikić Čakar (2018), who show that HDZ has the most stable electorate among political parties in Croatia. Measuring stability of the party vote at the individual level between 1990 and 2016, they find that on average 75 per cent of HDZ voters voted for HDZ in the previous election as well (Čular and Nikić Čakar, 2018).

Another dimension of veteran – HDZ political alignment became apparent after 2000, when HDZ went into opposition for the first time. The Social Democratic government immediately initiated the process of EU integration, which brought on pressure from the EU towards improving Croatia's cooperation with the Hague Tribunal and the prosecution of war crimes (Dolenec, 2013). At the same time, several reforms to welfare programmes for veterans, as well as a downsizing of the army and police, were initiated. Unsurprisingly, the veteran population feared that their material interests, social standing, and – for some – personal freedom were under threat, and this population mobilized to an unprecedented level.

Amendments to the constitution implemented by the SDP-led government in 2001 introduced, among other institutional reforms, the option of citizens' initiatives for referenda. Though the conditions were very prohibitive, requiring that the initiative collect signatures from 10 per cent of voters in Croatia within fifteen days,[18] for large veteran organizations with member organizations across Croatia it opened an avenue of political mobilization. A few months after the Constitutional amendments were approved by Parliament, veteran organizations submitted a citizens' initiative to Parliament with the aim of preventing Croatia's cooperation with the Hague Tribunal (Smerdel, 2010). Their immediate grievance was the fact that in February 2001 warrants for the arrest of suspects in a wartime murder were issued, including for General Mirko Norac (Dolenec, 2013). In an impressive show of mobilizational capacity, veteran organizations collected over 400,000 signatures in two weeks, reaching the legal threshold for holding a referendum. The referendum did not take place, however. The loophole that the SDP government used was the fact that the Referendum Act had not been amended in line with the new constitutional framework. Nevertheless, though the government managed to diffuse this particular threat, 2001 and 2002 would prove to be highly contentious, as we show in Section 10.3.2.

The second citizens' initiative for referendum by veteran organizations was launched in 2007, with the same objective of preventing Croatia's cooperation with the Hague Tribunal. However, there was a crucial difference in the political opportunity structure: HDZ was now in government. Under the leadership of Ivo Sanader, HDZ maintained the course of European integration as the fundamental policy objective event at the cost of serious friction with parts of its constituency (Dolenec, 2013). In June 2004 the EU proposed to open accession negotiations with Croatia on the condition that it 'maintain full cooperation with the ICTY' (Council of the European Union, 2004). Capturing and extraditing General Ante Gotovina became the crucial bone of contention between the Croatian government and the ICTY, with Sanader playing a game of nerves in an effort to both stay in power and acquiesce to European demands (Dolenec, 2013). Croatia's candidacy status hung in the balance until the very last moment in 2005, when Gotovina was finally arrested and brought before the ICTY to stand trial. How costly this move was for HDZ is reflected in the party membership: in the period between 2001 and 2005 the party's membership fell from 432,000 to 220,000. Though this was a trying period for HDZ, it also showed that veteran organizations

---

[18] By comparison, in Switzerland the required percentage of signatures is less than 2 per cent of registered voters, while the period for the collection of signatures is eighteen months (Kriesi, 2011). Closer to home, in Slovenia around 2 per cent of voters' signatures must be collected in thirty-five days (Erceg, 2011).

were not as strong without HDZ support. The 2007 initiative for referendum was not able to collect the required number of signatures, though a respectable number of 296,000 (Dolenec, 2014) testifies to the serious rift that the party's stance towards the Hague Tribunal caused in its voter base.

After the 2007 initiative against cooperation with the Hague Tribunal, veteran organizations retreated from mass mobilizations, only to return after the SDP government came into office in December 2011. With HDZ in opposition, veterans' organizations again started disrupting public events organized on important state holidays, especially those related to the Homeland War. The prime minister and president were booed and in other ways disrespected during public appearances, in particular during the annual celebration of Victory Day in Knin and on Vukovar Remembrance Day, when demonstrations and other types of disruptive activities were organized against the government. As described in the introduction, in November 2013 the commemoration of Vukovar Remembrance Day came close to violence, in a culmination of a month-long crisis in which veterans were tearing down placards in Cyrillic letters from public buildings in Vukovar. After months of clashes with police, arrests and public demonstrations, veteran associations started their referendum initiative under the slogan 'In defence of Croatian Vukovar'. The initiative proposed to exempt Vukovar from the implementation of Cyrillic alphabet placards in public locations. This time the initiative collected 632,165 signatures, which was more than enough for initiating a referendum (Dolenec, 2014). Again, the referendum did not take place, this time due to the ruling of the Constitutional Court, which argued that the formulation of the question on the referendum ballot was unconstitutional.

Analysed together, the three campaigns for referenda by veteran organizations show that they possess impressive mobilization capacity and resources necessary to collect hundreds of thousands of signatures in a span of fifteen days. At the same time, it also highlights that veteran organizations were successful in crossing this high threshold only when supported by HDZ. In the next section we look specifically into the dynamic between veteran organizations and HDZ in the protest arena.

10.3.2 HDZ and Veterans: The Protest Arena

The 2000 election that brought a Social Democrat–led coalition to power was counted as a democratic turning point by relevant international and domestic assessments (Schimmelfennig, 2005; Čular, 2005). The SPD-led government initiated constitutional reform to strengthen parliamentarism and reduce the powers of the president (Kasapović, 2008), secured WTO membership, signed the CEFTA, joined NATO's Partnership for Peace, signed the SAA, and secured candidacy for the EU (Dolenec, 2013). The process of EU integration created strong pressures on the government to cooperate with the Hague Tribunal, including extraditing Homeland War generals. It was in this context that the

Veterans as a Pivotal Political Actor

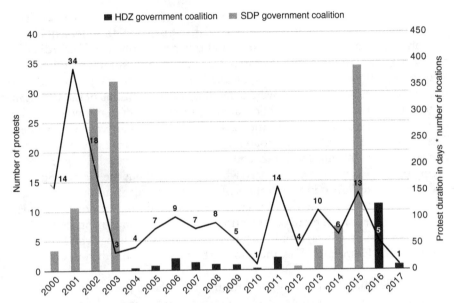

FIGURE 10.3 Veteran protests between 2000 and 2017
Source: Dolenec et al. (2019)

veteran population moved full force into the protest arena, hoping to destabilize the government and bring HDZ back into power.

Figure 10.3 shows veteran protests in Croatia between 2000 and 2017.[19] The left axis shows the number of protests in a given year, while the right axis shows their duration, calculated as number of protest days multiplied by the number of locations where protests were held. Years when HDZ is in power are marked in black, while years when SDP is in power are marked in grey.

Taking the number of protests and protest duration together shows a clear picture of strong episodes of contention by veteran groups during the two periods of SDP-led governments. Looking at the number of protests, the year 2001 is most contentious of the whole period, while years 2002 and 2014 stand out as most contentious on the indicator of protest duration. Both these periods when HDZ was in opposition represent crucial contentious episodes which we describe in the following sections.

The first contentious episode starts in February 2001, when warrants for the arrest of several veterans suspected of involvement in a wartime murder were issued, including General Mirko Norac, who failed to appear before a judge. In response to the issuing of the warrant, veteran groups blocked the main north–

---

[19] PEA data collected by the research project 'DISOBEDIENT DEMOCRACY: A Comparative Analyses of Contentious Politics in the European Semi-periphery', funded by the Swiss National Science Foundation, IZ11Z0_166540 – PROMYS.

south highway route in the Sinj, a city close to General Norac's home town. The road blockade protest made it to newspaper front pages, with statements from veteran organizations as well as HDZ and other party officials. According to media reports,[20] veteran organizations threatened that Norac's arrest would lead to the whole of Croatia being blocked. They accused the government of treason and affirmed that they were defending the foundations of the Croatian state. HDZ leadership made public statements to the effect that it was time for more radical steps, mass mobilizations, and blocking of main transport routes. The following day protests and road blockades took place in at least six towns across Croatia. In Sinj, the HDZ county president addressed the protesters, saying that it was not General Norac who was on trial but the Homeland War and Croatia itself. Also in Sinj, leaders of the veteran organizations announced a big demonstration in Split, stating, 'Either they fall, or we do!'[21] In Pula, another member of a veteran organization made a public statement, saying that 'in case the prime minister and his government did not change their position regarding the Homeland War, there might be massive disobedience, even civil war'.[22]

On 11 February, veteran organizations held a large protest in the city of Split. The organizers estimated the number at 200,000, while the media and the police put the number at between 100,000 and 150,000 protesters.[23] The same day supporting demonstrations of between 3,000 and 10,000 people were held in five other cities in Eastern Croatia.[24] The slogan of the protest was 'We are all Mirko Norac'. Many retired generals were in attendance, as well as HDZ president Ivo Sanader (who addressed the audience), many other HDZ notables, and party leaderships of other right-wing parties. Veteran organizations issued a declaration demanding amnesty for all Croatian generals and calling for early parliamentary and presidential elections.[25] During the protest, both the president and prime minister were insulted and accused of treason, and the language used towards the SDP government was insulting and inflammatory. Harnessing veteran revolt, at that moment HDZ had hoped to topple the SDP-led coalition government (Babić, 2003).

Veteran organizations announced another protest in front of the Parliament in Zagreb on February 15, but in the few days between the Split and Zagreb protests it became clear that veteran organizations were not united about the next move. The protest in Zagreb was considerably smaller, estimated at around 13,000 people, and none of the HDZ politicians addressed the

---

[20] 'Branitelji u Sinju pozvali Hrvate da odaberu stranu', Večernji list, 9 February 2001.
[21] 'Poruka stožera u Sinju: Ovih dana padamo ili mi, ili oni', Jutarnji list, 10 February 2001.
[22] Ibid.
[23] 'U ovoj zemlji i odlučujemo', Jutarnji list, 12 February 2001; 'Na skupu u Splitu više od 150,000 ljudi', Večernji list, 12 February 2001.
[24] 'Mirko ne predaj se! Nemaš kome', Večernji list, 12 February 2001.
[25] 'U ovoj zemlji i odlučujemo', Jutarnji list, 12 February 2001.

crowd.[26] It seems that HDZ, though initially riding the wave of this mass mobilization, decided to hit the brakes. Responding to a journalist asking him whether the situation was a potential threat to the legal order in Croatia, a top HDZ official said that it was 'necessary to do everything to stop an uncontrollable avalanche of events' and that it was irresponsible of his party to have used the protests to demand early elections.[27] Though the slogans used by the protesters in Zagreb used inflammatory rhetoric and displayed far-right Ustasha insignia, overall the moment of serious instability for the government had passed.[28] When Mirko Norac appeared before the court on February 22, claiming that he was not aware that a warrant for his arrest had been issued,[29] veteran organizations initiated new protests. Overall, during 2001 there were thirty-four and during 2002 eighteen veteran protests recorded by national newspapers. The most protracted of them was a 600-day sit-in on St Mark's Square in Zagreb, the seat of the parliament and government. Discharged police officers who were Homeland veterans camped on the square with the intention of annulling the government's decision. This government measure was part of a large reform effort aimed at downsizing and reforming the armed forces and the police. Between 2001 and 2004 the number employed in the armed forces was cut by around 40 per cent.[30]

The second contentious episode started after the SDP government returned to office in 2011. This time veteran grievances were directed against the implementation of Serbian-minority language rights pertaining to the use of Cyrillic alphabet in public spaces in Vukovar. In March 2013, veteran organizations campaigned in the local election against the incumbent Social Democratic mayor, supporting the HDZ candidate in exchange for his endorsement of their demand to exempt the city of Vukovar from the introduction of Cyrillic signs on public buildings. When the government went on to pursue the implementation of the said policy, this was met with acts of civil disobedience, including repeated tearing down of Cyrillic placards and several arrests. As described in the introduction, the stand-off between veteran organizations and the SDP-led government culminated during Remembrance Day, when the march through the streets of Vukovar with the prime minister, the president, and other government officials was blocked, leading the situation to the brink of violence.

A year later, in October 2014, veteran organizations occupied the public square in front of the Ministry of Veterans in 66 Savska Street, demanding the

---

[26] 'Viđene i desnice u zraku uz pozdrav Za dom spremni', Večernji list, 16 February 2001.
[27] 'HDZ je sam kriv što ga vlast optužuje za ekstremizam', Večernji ist, 14 February 2001.
[28] In the summer of 2002, the second-largest party in the SDP-led coalition, HSLS, suffered serious fractioning leading to government reconstruction, but the parliamentary majority was maintained (Kasapović, 2005).
[29] 'Norac u pritvoru i negira optužbe', Večernji list, 23 February 2001.
[30] Data from website of the Armed Forces of the Republic of Croatia, available at www.osrh.hr/#rub211.

resignation of the minister and his key aids. Through this action they initiated a sit-in that lasted 555 days, ending after HDZ returned to power. The placard that the veteran organizations displayed at their tent read '1991: they both fell, 2015: they will both fall'. The phrase 'they both fell' is common knowledge in Croatia, referring to the excited exclamation of a soldier recorded on tape after the successful knocking down of two YNA aircraft flying over Zadar in 1991. 'They will both fall' in 2015 alluded to the presidential and parliamentary elections, for posts at that time held by Social Democrats. The start of the veteran protest was aligned with the electoral campaign for presidential elections, which the incumbent Social Democratic president Ivo Josipović lost to HDZ candidate Kolinda Grabar Kitarović. The first place she visited on election night, and again upon assuming office, was the veterans' tent on 66 Savska Street. Though the 2015 election was close,[31] HDZ won the November 2015 parliamentary election too. An HDZ party member who had been an active participant in the veteran protest on 66 Savska Street became the new minister of veterans.[32]

In the summer before this election, with the SDP-led government in power, the annual celebration of Victory Day that always took place in Knin was exceptionally moved to Zagreb. The previous year in Knin, the SDP prime minister and the president, together with their entourage, received a hostile reception, and they were booed during their speeches.[33] Echoing the Vukovar Remembrance Day experience, there was uncertainty as to how the heads of state would join the march of the Armed Forces and veteran organizations. In the end, the government officials refrained from joining the march.

In stark contrast, with HDZ back in power, on 5 August 2016 Victory Day was again celebrated in Knin, with the prime minister, the president of Croatia, generals of the Armed Forces, top HDZ officials, and numerous veteran organizations in attendance. News sources estimated that around 100,000 people[34] attended the event, while HDZ politicians gave fiery speeches exulting the war victory, celebrating veteran sacrifice and denigrating the Social Democrats. In other words, similarly to the Law and Justice party (PiS) in Poland, HDZ actively supports and coordinates mass mobilization around key commemorative events of the Homeland War, through which they repeatedly renew their symbolic ties to veterans as fathers of the state. These mass gatherings with high symbolic resonance resemble Scott's (1990)

---

[31] HDZ won 33.4 per cent of the vote, in comparison with the coalition led by the Social Democrats which won 33.2 per cent of the vote.
[32] See www.vecernji.hr/hrvatska/tomo-medved-je-novi-ministar-branitelja-1070056.
[33] 'Milanovića i Josipovića izviždali, premijer uzvratio: Dođite na Markov trg!', Večernji list, 5 August 2014, www.vecernji.hr/vijesti/drzavni-vrh-na-proslavi-190bljetnice-oluje-u-kninu-954116 (accessed 30 October 2017).
[34] 'Poruka onima koji su Hrvatsku nazvali slučajnom: Država je stvorena voljom naroda', Večernji list, 5 August 2016, https://www.vecernji.hr/vijesti/u-kninu-se-slavi-21-obljetnica-akcije-oluja-1104271 (accessed 30 October 2017).

ritualized protest which serves to reinforce the party's domination and demonstrate the continued coherence of the regime (Beissinger, Chapter 6 in this volume).

HDZ went on to win the early parliamentary election a month later, on 8 September 2016. Consolidating their victory though pre-emptive mobilization, and once again demonstrating how mobilization can be used as a deliberate state tactic, they organized the mass gathering for Vukovar Remembrance Day on November 18, described at the opening of this chapter.

10.4 CONCLUDING REMARKS

This chapter explores the complex three-way dynamic between veteran organizations, the evolution of state support for veterans and veteran organizations, and the right-wing political party HDZ which has dominated Croatia's politics since the country's independence in 1990. Despite heading state institutions during the entire decade in the 1990s, HDZ at the same time led a broad nationalist movement and, in that process, learned how to rely on mass mobilization as 'a tactic of the state to exercise power and promote its own objectives' (Ekiert and Perry in the introduction). The party's rapid growth pushed HDZ towards relying on movement-type linkages with citizens and sidelining formal institutional procedures, while also growing a strong membership of several hundred thousand. In parallel, a comprehensive state institutional architecture of veterans' rights was implemented under HDZ governments, creating a three-way client–patron relationship between the state, HDZ, and the veteran population, producing an interesting variety of a state-mobilized movement instigated to enhance the state's legitimacy.

Our analysis showed how the combined reliance on comprehensive state resources as well as symbolic mass gatherings has helped align the veteran vote and maintain the loyalty of veteran organizations to HDZ. This case also shows that the mobilization capacity of veteran organizations is ever only partially under outside control. This was best illustrated by the 2007 petition for referenda which the veteran organizations organized in defiance of the state's decision to maintain full cooperation with the Hague Tribunal. Veteran organizations are fundamentally dependent on the state for financing of their activities, but it is they that ultimately possess mobilization capacity, so this power relationship is not entirely asymmetric. However, since HDZ has been in government most of the time, and since it operates an admirable party machine, the party is able to wield state infrastructure and substantial funding in support of veteran organizations and hence rely on them for mass mobilization. This has created a powerful political dynamic in Croatia whereby veteran organizations are motivated to stop reforms to state institutions designed during the 1990s. In other words, betraying the standard image of social movements as challengers to the state, our case shows veteran organizations proactively mobilizing in order to maintain the status quo. As a result, handsomely financed and supported to help the state 'rule by other means', veteran organizations have played a pivotal role in the outcomes of elections in Croatia.

REFERENCES

Ainsworth, S. 1995. Electoral strength and the emergence of group influence in the late 1800s: the Grand Army of the Republic. *American Politics Quarterly* 23 (3): 319–338.
Babić, J. 2003. Hrvatska napokon smogla snage da osudi svoje ratne zločince. Nacional, 26 March. www.nacional.hr/clanak/10546/hrvatska-napokon-smogla-snage-da-osudi-svoje-ratnezlocince.
Bađun, M. 2009. Korisnici mirovina koji su pravo na mirovinu ostvarili pod povoljnijim uvjetima. *Newsletter of the Institute for Public Finance* 44: 1–8.
Bađun, M. 2011. Why are there so many disability pensions beneficiaries in Croatia? *Newsletter of the Institute for Public Finance* 56: 1–9.
Bagić, D., and K. Kardov. 2018. Politička participacija i stranačke preferencije ratnih veterana u Hrvatskoj. *Politička misao : časopis za politologiju* 55 (3): 82–103.
Begić, N., M. Sanader, and O. Žunec. 2007. Ratni veterani u Starom Rimu i u današnjoj Hrvatskoj. *Polemos: časopis za interdisciplinarna istraživanja rata i mira* 10 (20): 11–30.
Bevan, Shaun 2015. General Comparative Agendas Project Coding Guidelines. http://sbevan.com/cap-master-codebook.html.
Brooks, K., and J. Manza. 2007. *Why Welfare States Persist: The Importance of Public Opinion in Democracies.* Chicago, IL: University of Chicago Press.
Council of the European Union. 2004. *Presidency Conclusions – European Council.* Brussels: Council of the European Union.
Croatian Pension Fund. 2016. Statistical Information Report, Year 14, No. 3, October 2016 [in Croatian].
Čular, G. 2000. Political development in Croatia. *Politička misao* 37 (5): 30–46.
Čular, G. 2005. Politčke stranke i potpora demokraciji. In G. Čular (ed.), *Izbori i konsolidacija demokracije u Hrvatskoj.* Zagreb: Fakultet političkih znanosti, pp. 123–179.
Čular, G. 2010. Treba li suvremenim strankama članstvo? *Političke analize* 1 (3): 20–24.
Čular, G., and D. Nikić Čakar. 2017. Organizational structures of political parties in Croatia. In K. Sobolewska-Myślik, B. Kosowska-Gąstoł and P. Borowiec (eds.), *Organizational Structures of Political Parties in Central and Eastern European Countries.* Crakow: Jagiellonian University Press, pp. 109–131.
Dobrotić, I. 2008. Sustav skrbi za branitelje iz Domovinskog rata. *Revija za socijalnu politiku* 15 (1): 57–83.
Dolenec, D. 2013. *Democratic Institutions and Authoritarian rule in Southeast Europe.* Colchester: ECPR Press.
Dolenec, D. 2014. Zašto SDP-ova vlada nije socijaldemokratska? *Političke analize* 5 (20): 33–38.
Dolenec, D. 2016. Democratization in the Balkans: the limits of elite-driven reform. *Taiwan Journal of Democracy* 12 (1): 125–144.
Dolenec, D., A. Balković, K. Kralj, and D. Širinić. 2019. Croatia Protest Event Analysis Dataset, Version 1.0.

Erceg, M. 2011. Referendumska demokracija u Sloveniji. *Političke perspektive* 2 (6): 59–61.
Ferenčak, N., K. Kardov, and P. Rodik. 2003. Booklet on war veterans entitlements and welfare systems. Unpublished authors' manuscript.
Gal, J., and M. Bar. 2000. The needed and the needy: the policy legacies of benefits for disabled war veterans in Israel. *Journal of Social Policy* 29 (04): 577–598.
Gerber, D. A. 2003. Disabled veterans, the state, and the experience of disability in Western societies, 1914–1950. *Journal of Social History* 36 (4): 899–916.
Glaurdić, J., and V. Vuković. 2016. Voting after war: legacy of conflict and the economy as determinants of electoral support in Croatia. *Electoral Studies* 42: 135–145.
Grizelj, D., and H. Vukušić. 1996. Zakon ne smije praviti razlike među braniteljima. *Glas Slavonije*, 25 September. (Interview with Herman Vukušić.)
Kasapović, M. 1996. *Demokratska tranzicija i političke stranke: razvoj političkih stranaka i stranačkih sustava u Istočnoj Europi*. Zagreb: Fakultet političkih znanosti.
Kasapović, M. 2008. Semi-presidentialism in Croatia. In R. Elgie and S. Moestrup (eds.), *Semi-Presidentialism in Central and Eastern Europe*. Manchester: Manchester University Press, pp. 219–238.
Kasapović, M. 2005. Koalicijske vlade u Hrvatskoj: prva iskustva u komparativnoj perspektivi. In G. Čular (ed.), *Izbori i konsolidacija demokracije u Hrvatskoj*. Zagreb: Biblioteka Politička misao, pp. 181–212.
Kitschelt, H. 2006. Movement parties. In R. S. Katz, and W. Crotty (eds.), *Handbook of Party Politics*. London: Sage, pp. 278–290.
Kriesi, H. 2005. *Direct Democratic Choice: The Swiss Experience*. Plymouth: Lexington Books.
Maddaloni, D. (2014). *The Warfare-Welfare Nexus. An Ecological-Evolutionary Conceptual Framework for the Analysis of the Rise and Decline of National Public Welfare Systems* (No. 132). CELPE-Centre of Labour Economics and Economic Policy, University of Salerno, Italy.
Marijan, D. 2008. Sudionici i osnovne značajke rata u Hrvatskoj 1990–1991. *Časopis za suvremenu povijest* 40 (1): 47–63.
Merkel, W. 2011. *Transformacija političkih sustava: uvod u teoriju i empirijsko istraživanje transformacije*. Zagreb: Fakultet političkih znanosti.
Mihalec, I., P. Pavlin, and M. Relja. 2012. Utjecaj društvenih skupina na kreiranje javnih politika u Hrvatskoj. Unpublished student paper.
Robertson, G. B. 2009. Managing society: protest, civil society, and regime in Putin's Russia. *Slavic Review* 68 (3): 528–547.
Rothschild, J. 1993. *Return to Diversity: A Political History of East Central Europe Since World War Two*. New York: Oxford University Press.
Schimmelfennig, F. 2005. Strategic calculation and international socialization: membership incentives, party constellations, and sustained compliance in Central and Eastern Europe. *International Organization* 59 (4): 827–860.
Scott, J. C. 1990. *Domination and the Arts of Resistance: Hidden Transcripts*. New Haven, CT: Yale University Press.
Slater, D., and N. R. Smith. 2016. The power of counterrevolution: elitist origins of political order in postcolonial Asia and Africa. *American Journal of Sociology* 121 (5): 1472–1516.
Skocpol, T. 1995. *Protecting Soldiers and Mothers: The Political Origins of Social Policy in United States*. Cambridge, MA: Harvard University Press.

Smerić, T. 2009. Uz temu: Hrvatska vojska – hrvatsko društvo. *Društvena istraživanja: časopis za opća društvena pitanja* 18 (3(101)): 337–337.
Smerdel, B. 2010. Direct decision-making and its constitutional limits. *Hrvatska pravna revija* 10 (11): 1–9.
Spehnjak, K. 1987. Organiziranost i oblici djelovanja Narodnog fronta Hrvatske 1945–1953. godine. *Povijesni prilozi* 6 (6): 1–57.
Stubbs, P., and S. Zrinščak. 2011. Rethinking clientelism, governance and citizenship in social welfare: the case of Croatia. ESPANet Annual Conference.
Širinić, D., D. N. Čakar, A. Petek, J. Šipić, V. Raos, and A. Kekez. 2016. *Croatian Policy Agendas Project – Datasets* (v.1.0). Zagreb: Center for Empirical Research in Political Sceince, Faculty of Political Science of the University of Zagreb.
Širinić, D. 2018. Political Attention of Croatian Governments 1990–2015. In Z. Petak and K. Kotarski (eds.), *Policy-Making at the European Periphery: The Case of Croatia*. London: Palgrave Macmillan, pp. 65–82.
Šterc, S., and N. Pokos. 1993. Demografski uzroci i posljedice rata protiv Hrvatske. *Društvena istraživanja* 2 (2–3 (4–5)): 305–333.
Unkovski Korica, V. 2017. *The Economic Struggle for Power in Tito's Yugoslavia: From World War Two to Non-Alignment*. London: I. B. Tauris.
Vlada Republike Hrvatske (2014). *Izvješće o provedbi Zakona o pravima hrvatskih branitelja iz Domovinskog rata i članova njihovih obitelji za 2013. godinu*. Zagreb: Vlada Republike Hrvatske.
Vliegenthart, R., and S. Walgrave. (2011). Content matters: the dynamic of parliamentary questioning in Belgium and Denmark. *Comparative Political Studies* 44 (8): 1031–1059.
Zakošek, N. 2002. *Politički sustav Hrvatske*. Zagreb: Fakultet političkih znanosti.
Živić, D. 2005. Demografski ratni gubici kao determinanta razvoja stanovništva Istočne Hrvatske u razdoblju 1991–2001. *Migracijske i etničke teme* 1–2: 123–142.
Žunec, O. 2006. Apsolutna žrtva i relativna kompenzacija: proturječja društvenog položaja veterana i državne skrbi za ratne veterane i invalide. *POLEMOS: časopis za interdisciplinarna istraživanja rata i mira* 9 (18): 11–42.

11

The Dynamics of State-Mobilized Movements
Insights from Egypt

Ashley Anderson and Melani Cammett

11.1 INTRODUCTION

On February 2, 2011, pro-regime loyalists swept into Tahrir Square in central Cairo to attack protesters calling for the ouster of President Hosni Mubarak, who had governed Egypt for nearly three decades. In the attacks, government-hired thugs rode horses and camels through the protest camp, attacking demonstrators with whips and other weapons and leaving several dead and wounded. The attack, which came to be as the "Battle of the Camel," is a violent example of regime-orchestrated contentious action (Kandil, 2012, p. 227; Ketchley, 2017, p. 67). State-mobilized movements (SMMs), however, can take more peaceful forms, such as demonstrations and rallies organized to express support for incumbent authoritarian rulers. Indeed, the Egyptian uprising witnessed multiple episodes of nonviolent, SMMs in which citizens took to the streets to convey their support of the incumbent regime, whether orchestrated by elites from the Mubarak government or from one of his successors in the tumultuous years following his departure.

Egypt is hardly the only Middle Eastern regime to have deployed or promoted SMMs. During the Arab uprisings, citizens in Bahrain, Jordan, and Saudi Arabia all took to the streets to express support for their incumbent rulers against a growing tide of anti-regime opposition (Al-Jazeera, February 21, 2011; Shah, 2011). In the face of direct challenges to their rule from below, such pro-state action helped to substantiate the legitimacy of authoritarian elites, counterbalancing oppositional narratives and redirecting citizen prerogatives from revolution to mere reform (Ryan, 2011; Al-Rasheed, 2011). Beyond the Middle East, pro-government demonstrations have been used to buttress authoritarian regimes in Russia, China, and Venezuela, as well as in several other countries ruled by hybrid and authoritarian regimes.

Yet despite the prevalent use of SMMs as a tool for social control and regime survival, the dynamics of this phenomenon remain largely unexplored in the current literature on social movements. In the Middle East in particular, scholars have typically eschewed a full examination of SMMs in favor of analyses which center on ordinary citizens and disenfranchised actors as the primary agents of contentious action. Departing from this tradition, in this chapter we explore the dynamics of SMMs, which we define as collective action to support or defend an established political order and its associated body of elites against actual or perceived challenges from below. Using original data on protest mobilization in Egypt from 2011 to 2013, we seek to answer the following question: "Under what conditions do Egyptian regime elements and their societal allies organize contentious actions in support of the state?" To anticipate our findings, we trace the use of SMMs during this period, noting that they tended to follow rather than precede opposition mobilization, arose in response to larger-scale protests, and occurred after anti-regime protests involving organized civil society actors rather than more spontaneous and disparate opposition groups. More generally, we argue that SMMs should be incorporated more fully into the growing literature on the dynamics of authoritarianism in Egypt and elsewhere in the Middle East. While most existing literature emphasizes the use of coercion and cooptation in maintaining social control, SMMs constitute another possible means of buttressing authoritarian regimes.

Of the possible cases within the Middle East, Egypt presents an ideal context in which to investigate the dynamics of SMMs for at least three reasons. First, Egypt experienced multiple episodes of SMMs in the time span we cover between 2011 and 2013, permitting us to trace the evolution of this phenomenon across distinct time periods. Second, given that this period coincided with an especially contentious moment in Egyptian history during which the country witnessed numerous waves of anti-state mobilizing, the Egyptian case affords us the unique opportunity to explore the interplay between pro- and anti-regime mobilization. Third, between early 2011 and mid-July 2013, Egypt experienced multiple regime changes, enabling us to examine the phenomenon of SMMs under various political conditions; however, as we discuss in Section 11.3, there is more evidence for this phenomenon during the Mubarak period than under SCAF rule. Indeed, although we cannot claim that Egypt is representative of the Middle East and North Africa given the wide array of authoritarian regime types and political economies in the region, the diversity of regime types witnessed in Egypt during the period makes it roughly comparable to many other neighboring countries and hybrid regimes around the world.

The remainder of the chapter is organized as follows. Section 11.2 provides a more detailed discussion of SMMs, adding conceptual precision to the term and distinguishing it from other, more well-known forms of social control. In Section 11.3, we provide essential background on SMMs in Egypt, outlining

Insights from Egypt

three main episodes of SMMs that occurred during the period of study. In Section 11.4, we then build on this discussion and the relevant literature on countermovements and social control to develop a series of hypotheses about the conditions under which regime elements and their societal allies are likely to organize pro-state contentious actions. In Section 11.5, we describe the data and methods used in the chapter, followed by a discussion in Section 11.6 of the empirical analyses and the ways in which they complement existing studies of contentious mobilization in Egypt. Finally, Section 11.7 concludes by summarizing the main findings and delineating important areas for further research on SMMs within and beyond Egypt.

11.2 STATE-MOBILIZED MOVEMENTS AS A TOOL OF AUTHORITARIAN SOCIAL CONTROL

A robust body of research on pre-2011 Egypt analyzes the various forms of carrots and sticks – or concessions and repression – that the Mubarak regime and its predecessors employed to maintain social control (Blaydes, 2010; Brown, 1990; Brownlee, 2007; Kassem, 2004; Lust, 2005; Masoud, 2014; Stacher, 2012). Similarly, the broader literature on authoritarianism highlights these and other strategies utilized by dictators to defuse popular protest and defend against political challenges, including repression, concessions, toleration, and neglect (Bishara, 2015; Cai, 2008; Conrad, 2011; Earl, 2003; Franklin, 2008; Gamson, 1990; Levitsky and Way, 2006; Tilly, 1978). As highlighted in the introductory chapter, however, a distinct set of tools entailing mass mobilization in favor of the regime has received less attention, despite its growing prominence in various global regions. While a rich literature on elections under authoritarian rule (Blaydes, 2010; Gandhi, 2010; Gandhi and Lust Okar, 2009; Greene, 2007; Lust-Okar, 2005; Magaloni, 2006) has examined the motivations for holding elections and their effects on political behavior in nondemocratic settings, fewer scholars have focused on how regimes deploy or benefit from more banal forms of political participation to cement their rule (Robertson, 2007; Wedeen, 2002). Alongside coercion and cooptation, some hybrid and authoritarian regimes foster or directly organize activities that are ostensibly aimed at promoting regime legitimacy or at least employ the trappings of institutional and civic legitimacy as part of regime strategies of maintaining control. As the contributions to this volume convincingly show, such SMMs have been integral to the survival of authoritarian and democratic regimes alike, allowing them bolster their popular legitimacy and fend off challenges from political opponents (see Chapters 2, 7, and 12 in this volume).

In this chapter, we define SMMs as collective action aimed at supporting or defending an established political order and its constituent body of elites against actual or perceived challenges from below. Several aspects of this definition warrant further specification. First, and most important for our analysis, we acknowledge that the question of which actors actually organize pro-state demonstrations is difficult to determine. In theory, pro-state contention may operate autonomously of the state, although this is less likely in authoritarian regimes that maintain strict social control. Highlighting this caveat is especially important given the opacity around the role of state agents in many incidents of SMMs in Egypt and the virtual impossibility of empirically verifying the role of regime officials in the organization of contentious actions. Thus, SMMs may emerge as apparent grassroots mobilization organized by civilians or societal actors, or it may take the form of ersatz social movements orchestrated directly by state forces to rally support for the regime in moments of crisis.

Second, our definition of SMMs allows for variation in the tactical forms taken by pro-state demonstrations, both subnationally and cross-nationally. Much like contentious action more generally, SMMs can be expressed through a variety of different strategies including marches, occupations, protests, and political rallies.

Finally, SMMs can vary in terms of which elements of the state serve as the agents of mobilization. As in this volume's introduction, we do not treat the state as a unitary actor but rather recognize that it comprises distinct components such as the coercive apparatus and its associated organizations, political institutions, and different groups or factions of political elites. As a result, SMMs may express support for the state as a whole or may advocate for specific elements of the state while remaining indifferent or antagonistic toward others. In case of Egypt, for example, the Interior Ministry and police force were the key protagonists behind particular violent episodes of SMMs during the 2011 uprisings, while the army was either uninvolved or perceived to oppose such actions (Kandil, 2012, p. 227).[1] Furthermore, to the extent that the identity of the state is contested by different members of society – as is often the case during civil wars or revolutionary episodes – it may also be possible to speak of competing or even conflicting episodes of SMMs, with some actions defending one component of the state apparatus and others mobilizing in favor of another. In this case, SMMs are akin to what the introductiory chapter refers to as "interstate conflict," in which SMMs are used to signal competition among contenders for power within the state.

However, the concept of SMMs employed here is important not only for what it includes but also for what it excludes. As an analytical tool and conceptual approach, SMMs differ from extant categories of regime responses to societal threats in several ways. First, SMMs are distinct from strategies of

---

[1] This reflects a larger shift under the Sadat regime, during which the military was relegated to the barracks after the 1979 Camp David Accords and became more involved in economic activities. Sadat's successor, Hosni Mubarak, increasingly favored globally oriented capitalists with distinct economic interests from those of the military and constructed a "police state" that relied heavily on the Interior Ministry and domestic security forces to safeguard his rule (Kandil, 2012, pp. 181–201).

social control that have received more extensive scholarly attention like repression and cooptation in terms of its form and strategies of mobilizing. For example, although sharing some commonalities with low-intensity coercion in the use of covert tactics to undermine opposition, SMMs entail a more complex strategy which simultaneously allows anti-regime protests to occur and seeks to neutralize their effectiveness through concomitant mobilization. Moreover, while coercion and channeling typically necessitate the restriction of civil liberties and rights to assembly, SMMs leverage these rights to organize campaigns in favor of the state. Second, SMMs are distinct from toleration in that they entail an active response to contentious mobilization. Rather than acceptance or conscious disregard of protests, state actors either proactively or retroactively counter the opposition by mobilizing support for the regime vis-à-vis its adversaries. Finally, SMMs can differ from counterrevolutionary mobilization in its timing and character. While counterrevolutionary actions, by definition, emerge in response to the presence of a revolutionary movement, SMMs can occur before such mobilization has materialized, serving more as a prophylactic against the emergence of organized or anticipated opposition than a reaction to existing threats. Thus, the timing and sequencing of SMMs vis-à-vis other forms of mobilization may vary, raising important theoretical and empirical questions about the conditions under which pro-state action is proactive or reactive.

11.3 STATE-MOBILIZED MOVEMENT IN EGYPT (2011–2013)

In this chapter, we explore the dynamics of SMMs in the case of Egypt from the beginning of 2011, when the Arab Spring uprisings first erupted, until July 2013, when a military coup upended the rule of Mohamed Morsi, Egypt's first democratically elected president. We seek to address the first two questions posed in this volume's introductory chapter: notably, why state agents (or their societal allies) mobilize non-state collective actors and the conditions under which they deploy this strategy. Before expanding on these questions, however, it is useful to provide general background on the Egyptian case and review the evolution of SMMs in this context.

11.3.1 Pre-uprising Politics in Egypt

Before the ouster of President Hosni Mubarak, who ruled from 1981 to 2011, the Egyptian political regime was characterized by a highly centralized system with authority concentrated in the executive. The president worked closely with the dominant party, the National Democratic Party (NDP), which commanded the vast majority of seats in parliament. While both presidential and parliamentary elections were held regularly during Mubarak's tenure, the Ministry of Interior routinely intervened to block opposition candidates. In addition, the state imposed restrictions on the freedom of association, and the security apparatus regularly monitored and harassed opposition groups and sometimes even directly blocked voters from casting ballots during elections.

At the same time, Egypt's competitive authoritarian system permitted a modicum of political freedom, allowing for the development of an increasingly robust and active opposition. As early as 1981, the Mubarak regime liberalized the political system to include a handful of legal opposition parties (e.g. New Wafd Party, al-Tagammu, al-Nassery) and allowed room for maneuver to a variety of others debarred from receiving formal recognition (e.g. the Muslim Brotherhood[2]). Although throughout much of the 1980s and 1990s these groups remained confined to a largely representative, nonconfrontational political role, by the mid-2000s this outgrowth of opposition spawned a new era of activism in Egypt, marked by rapid growth in contentious activity and the rise of several new anti-regime social movements. From 2000 to 2008 alone Egypt witnessed three major episodes of contentious mobilization – the movement against the war on Iraq (2003), the rise of the Kifaya prodemocracy movement (2004–2006), and Mahalla labor protests (2008) – which brought together millions of Egyptian citizens from diverse sociopolitical backgrounds, at times in a direct challenge to the political hegemony of the Mubarak regime (El-Mahdi, 2014). While these movements were ultimately dismantled through a combination of repression, cooptation, and limited prostate mobilization, their actions dramatically shifted the landscape of contention in Egyptian society in a more militant direction and laid the foundation for the wave of anti-regime demonstrations witnessed in 2011 (El-Mahdi, 2014).

11.3.2 Protests during the Egyptian Uprisings

Indeed, between 2011 and 2013, the period of focus in this chapter, Egypt witnessed especially high levels of contentious politics, with extensive bouts of opposition protests and periodic episodes of pro-state activities.[3] On January 25, 2011, ten days after the departure of President Zine El Abedine Ben Ali from Tunisia, thousands of protesters gathered in Cairo's central Tahrir Square in a "Day of Rage" against poverty and repression in Egypt. The massive demonstration was timed to coincide with National Police Day in order to highlight mounting police brutality. Afterward, a large group of citizens remained in Tahrir Square and, one week later, held a large scale demonstration dubbed the "March of Millions" in which protesters explicitly

---

[2] In the 1980s the Muslim Brotherhood began fielding candidates for parliament as independents on the slate of the Wafd Party. In the 2005 elections, the organization won 20 percent of parliamentary seats while running independent candidates, a number which vastly exceeded the number of seats won by legal opposition parties, prompting a state crackdown on the group and a 2007 constitutional amendment banning parties with a religious base.

[3] For a complete history and analysis of the Egyptian uprisings, see Ketchley (2017).

Insights from Egypt

called for Mubarak's resignation. Henceforth, Tahrir Square became the epicenter of anti-regime protest, playing host to daily demonstrations of thousands of Egyptian citizens in the weeks leading to Mubarak's departure.

Yet, even during the height of the Egyptian uprising, contentious activity was never the sole provenance of opposition forces. Alongside anti-regime protests, a number of pro-state sympathizers staged their own demonstrations to lobby in favor of the Mubarak regime. In the first reported episode of pro-state action, NDP parliamentarians and local authorities in Damietta staged a sit-in on January 28, 2011, praising the Mubarak government and calling for an end to the demonstrations in Tahrir Square (al-Masry al-Youm, January 29, 2011; Ketchley, 2016). Moreover, although the army officially announced it would not use force against protesters, a decision that marked a critical turning point in the uprisings, other pro-state elements cracked down on anti-government demonstrations. For example, in the aforementioned "Battle of the Camel," which took place on February 2, 2011, hired thugs on horse- and camelback charged through anti-regime protests, throwing rocks at demonstrators and attacking people with whips and assorted weapons. In the days that followed (February 3–5), pro-Mubarak forces borrowed from the contentious tactics used by anti-regime protesters to stage a series of marches and sit-ins intended to counterbalance the growing opposition. In addition to appropriating several strategically important locations as protest sites, pro-government demonstrators launched a number of counterrevolutionary slogans that directly challenged the legitimacy of anti-government protests in Tahrir, including "He who loves Egypt, doesn't destroy Egypt" and "Yes to Mubarak, to protect stability" (Agence France Presse, February 2, 2011). Although ultimately these demonstrations were unable to cause the tide of anti-regime opposition to ebb, they successfully amassed thousands of citizens to express support for the state apparatus, providing a pretext for the continual harassment and repression of government opponents even after the fall of the Mubarak regime.

11.3.3 Shifting Political Regimes and Competing Cycles of Protest

11.3.3.1 *State-Mobilized Movement under the SCAF*

Indeed, following Mubarak's departure, Egypt continued to experience significant episodes of contention characterized by competing waves of pro- and anti-government demonstrations.[4] As early as April 2011, citizens once again returned to Tahrir Square to call for the resignation of Mubarak's successor, Field Marshall Hussein Tantawi, and demand that the ruling Supreme Council of the Armed Forces (SCAF) hand over power to

---

[4] We discuss the coding rules for "pro-" and "anti-"state protests in Section 11.5 on "Data and Methods."

a transitional civilian government. While these initial demonstrations were often met with repressive violence, by late November state authorities once again turned to street mobilization to counter the growing anti-government threat. In the midst of a month-long protest wave calling for a host of political reforms and the end to military rule, SCAF sympathizers launched a massive demonstration in Cairo's Abasseya Square to stimulate popular support for the military regime. Despite being overshadowed by anti-SCAF demonstrations in Cairo and elsewhere, the Abasseya Square protest marked the largest pro-state demonstration to date, bringing together an estimated 10,000 citizens in support of the SCAF regime (Agence France Presse, November 25, 2011).

Once again, state-sponsored demonstrations strategically mimicked the mobilization tactics popularized by anti-regime protesters in an effort to undermine the effectiveness of the opposition movement. Like the Tahrir Square protests, the pro-SCAF demonstrations were scheduled to be held on a Friday, a day which had become known as a focal point of contention during the January 25 Revolution (Ketchley and Barrie, 2019). Moreover, in television and print media, organizers billed the Abasseya protest as a "million-man march" (milyuniyya), a term routinely used by opposition forces to encourage widespread participation in protest events and reinforce the legitimacy of their demands. Finally, like the Tahrir Square protesters, the organizers of the pro-SCAF demonstrations utilized a diverse array of tactics to express their demands. In addition to the main demonstration in Abasseya Square, government supporters held complimentary protests in Alexandria and Cairo and circulated a petition demanding that the SCAF government remain in power indefinitely (al-Masry al-Youm, November 26, 2011).

Yet, beyond merely mimicking opposition protests, pro-state forces also actively contested these demonstrations, generating competing cycles of contention that lasted throughout the rest of the year. For example, pro-SCAF protests were routinely held near anti-regime marches and sit-ins, providing cover for SCAF supporters, many of whom were off-duty officers and soldiers, to repress opposition demonstrations (Armbrust, 2013). Further, slogans from anti-regime demonstrations were frequently retooled by pro-SCAF militants in efforts to delegitimize the ongoing protests in Tahrir Square. A commonly invoked refrain during the January 25 demonstrations – "The army and the people are one hand" – for example, was repurposed by SCAF protesters to emphasize the harmony between Egyptian citizens, the security apparatus, and the military government ("The people, the police, and the army are one hand"). At the same time, other protest slogans openly questioned the validity of the Tahrir Square demonstrations ("Oh Field Marshal, Egypt isn't in Tahrir Square") and denounced the protests as the work of foreign dissidents (Agence France Presse, November 25, 2011; al-Masry al-Youm, November 26, 2011).

Thus, as in the era that preceded it, SMMs during the SCAF period operated according to a simple logic: faced with mounting pressure from below to relinquish power, pro-state forces mobilized popular support in order to

Insights from Egypt

protect the interests of regime elites. While it is impossible to gauge the extent to which these demonstrations were truly the work of government authorities themselves, it is clear that regime elites utilized pro-state protests to serve their own ends, eventually using them to mount a successful counterrevolutionary campaign against the subsequent Morsi regime.

11.3.3.2 State-Mobilized Movement under Morsi

If state-sponsored protests during the Mubarak and SCAF periods can be more-or-less described as top-down demonstrations intended to counter democratic pressures from below, pro-state mobilization under the Morsi regime presents a much more complex picture. On the one hand, the beginning of the Morsi presidency marked a quantitative shift in the frequency of SMMs – in comparison to the SCAF period, which witnessed an average of 0.7 pro-state demonstrations per month, the Morsi period witnessed 87 such protests over the course of a year, from June 2012 to July 2013. Additionally, from a qualitative standpoint, SMMs under Morsi appear to be the result of an effort not to counteract revolutionary pressures from below but rather to resist a counterrevolutionary movement orchestrated by former regime elites.

Indeed, one of the largest waves of SMMs during the Morsi regime emerged in response to the rise of the Tamarrod (Rebellion) movement, a pro-military campaign seeking the restoration of SCAF rule in Egypt. Organized in April 2013, the Tamarrod campaign joined revolutionaries from the January 25 movement, Mubarak-era elites, and security forces in a broad front against the Morsi presidency, which had become increasingly divisive in the wake of a series of controversial constitutional reforms and contentious government appointments. Claiming that Morsi ruled in a dictatorial and exclusionary way, forcibly imposing an Islamist agenda on Egypt and abusing his power, members of Tamarrod called upon Morsi to hold early presidential elections and threatened to initiate a civil disobedience campaign if he did not step down by July 2, 2013. In the months leading up to this date, Tamarrod activists launched an extensive, and often violent, series of demonstrations against the Brotherhood-dominated government and the Morsi presidency, culminating in his eventual ouster via military coup on July 3, 2013.

As in previous periods, pro-regime forces responded to such mobilization with their own protest movement, Tagarrod (Impartiality), to reinforce the legitimacy of the Brotherhood-dominated government and support the continuation of Morsi's rule. However, unlike previous instances of SMMs, pro-Morsi mobilization differed in two key ways. First, as already noted, SMMs under Morsi was much more *extensive* than they were in previous periods. In addition to comprising a greater number of protests, SMMs during the Morsi period were also distributed over a larger proportion of the Egyptian territory, with concurrent pro-state demonstrations being held in Cairo, Alexandria, Dakhalia, Mansoura, Suez, and Qalubiya (Aswat al-Masriya, July 1, 2011;

Xinhua General News Agency, July 2, 2011). In many cases, these demonstrations were organized as ad hoc mobilizations, intended to protect local government institutions and Brotherhood offices from attacks by opposition protesters. In this sense, SMMs during the Morsi period can also be characterized as more defensive or reactionary than in previous periods.

Second, in contrast to previous episodes of SMMs, pro-Morsi demonstrations exhibited a lesser degree of regime organization. Particularly when juxtaposed to pro-Mubarak and Tamarrod protests – whose close linkages with government officials and security forces have been well documented (Kandil, 2012; Ketchley, 2017; Mohsen, 2011) – pro-Morsi demonstrations appear to have been grounded in a stronger base of genuine, grassroots support, undoubtedly owing to the Brotherhood's rootedness in Egyptian society and their dense formal and informal networks of support. Indeed, many of the organizers of and participants in protest events originated from the pro-Islamist camp – members of the Muslim Brotherhood, Salafists, and those who voted for Morsi in the presidential election. Moreover, although focal protests at Rabaa' al-Adawiyah Mosque[5] exhibited some degree of coordination by Brotherhood elites, much of their assistance was material (i.e. providing buses to transport people to protest sites) and dissipated quickly following the success of the coup movement (Ketchley, 2017). Thus the Morsi period marked a qualitative shift in dynamics of SMMs in post-Mubarak Egypt – rather than a top-down mobilization orchestrated by authoritarian elites to protect their own interests, SMMs during the Morsi presidency emerged more as a bottom-up movement designed to express support for a popularly elected, although embattled, leader and therefore may be more appropriately labeled "pro-state mobilization" rather than SMMs per se. While such grassroots support was ultimately unable to overwhelm the volume of anti-regime contention, it created the foundations for a robust anti-coup movement that endured well into the early months of the Al-Sisi military regime and continues to exist in some form to this day.

11.4 THE POLITICS OF STATE-MOBILIZED MOVEMENT

11.4.1 Motivations

Given the numerous protest control strategies available at their disposal, and the risk that SMMs may backfire (see the introductory chapter), the question

---

[5] In a direct response to the success of the Tammarod movement, in July 2013 Rabaa Al-Adawiya Mosque and the adjacent Rabaa Square became a sit-in protest area for supporters of then ex-president Mohammed Morsi following his removal from power. Although protests at Rabaa Al-Adawiya served as a focal point for the pro-Morsi movement, they were ultimately unsuccessful, and the mosque was ultimately destroyed in a violent massacre between the police and Islamist forces on August 14, 2013 (Ketchley, 2017).

Insights from Egypt

remains – why did Egyptian regime elites resort to SMMs as a means to quell opposition threats? In the absence of interviews with government officials, we can only speculate about the motivations for SMMs; however, a growing literature on the dynamics of authoritarian rule suggest a host of reasons why regime elites might resort to such demonstrative forms of social control rather than other tactics. Indeed, as the introductory chapter to this volume notes, incumbents and their societal allies may engage in SMMs for a variety of reasons, targeting both domestic and international audiences. On the domestic front, SMMs can play an important role in shoring up support among elites, which in some respects echoes the concept of *factional intra-state conflict* described in this volume (see introductory chapter). Like electoral victories, SMMs may deter elite defection by demonstrating that opposition to the regime is futile and may therefore help to co-opt potential elite opposition. Similarly, SMMs can create or reinforce "divided structures of contestation" that fragment potential opposition forces and promote further investment in the regime by at least some elites (Gandhi and Lust-Okar, 2009, p. 405). As Robertson (2010, pp. 168–169) notes in his study of protest in hybrid regimes, government-orchestrated contention performs an important signaling role to elites as they contemplate whether to stick with or defect from the regime: "At any given moment, key elite players, whether from the security apparatus, business, or politics, can choose to ally themselves with the incumbent leadership, or they can decide they are better off throwing their lot in with the opposition and challenging for power."

Conversely, SMMs can be a useful strategy for elites to convey their commitment to the regime. For example, Blaydes (2010) argues that elections in Mubarak's Egypt enabled elites to communicate their potential influence and power within their communities to the regime and to reaffirm their loyalty. Likewise, organizing pro-state rallies may enable aspiring elites or existing regime allies to demonstrate their usefulness to the regime, thereby facilitating or perpetuating their access to power, economic opportunities, or other resources.

Pro-state contentious action can also be aimed at broader domestic audiences beyond elites as the strategy of *defensive or reactive mobilization* implies (see introductory chapter). As the literature on elections in authoritarian and hybrid regimes suggests, SMMs can serve as a signal that leaders enjoy popular support and even quasi-democratic legitimacy (Schedler, 2006). This function may be especially salient during economic crises, when authoritarian rulers may be most vulnerable (Gandhi and Lust-Okar, 2009, p. 415; Greene, 2007; Magaloni, 2006). Moreover, a desire to boost perceptions of regime legitimacy for international audiences may also factor into regime calculations to organize or encourage SMMs. International pressure for political liberalization may compel authoritarian rulers to adopt the trappings of democratic rule such as elections or increased civil freedoms. In this regard, pro-state collective action acts as a fig-leaf measure promoting the fiction of increased liberalization in an authoritarian context.

Yet legitimacy may not factor into regime calculations at all, especially when there is little pretense of widespread popular consent for the regime. Instead, SMMs may be deployed as a strategy of *spoiler or pro-active mobilization* (see introductory chapter). Rulers might launch or sanction pro-state contentious actions in order to exhaust the civic energies of citizens or to signal their power in a deterrent fashion. As Robertson (2010, pp. 168–169) emphasizes, deterring civil unrest is a primary concern in authoritarian regimes because, "maintaining the incumbent advantage … depends to a significant extent on maintaining an air of invincibility or permanence." Thus, elites may undertake SMMs perpetuate an image of regime strength, effectively neutralizing opposition before it has a chance to materialize in a protest cascade (Kuran, 1991; Lohmann, 1994). On the other side, citizens may be compelled to take part in pro-state rallies or demonstrations as part of a patronage bargain. In her discussion of authoritarian social control in Syria, Wedeen (2002, pp. 33–49) argues that pro-regime symbols "clutter public space," making it impossible or at least harder for "alternative symbols, discussions, and language" to be introduced. For Wedeen, the organization of "spectacles" serves multiple useful purposes for the regime, even if people know they are fraudulent, by inducing compliance as citizens become accomplices in the spectacle, setting boundaries for acceptable and unacceptable action, upholding norms and ideas about state domination, isolating would-be regime opponents from each other, and crowding out other forms of contention in the public sphere. By forcing people to articulate sentiments that are patently absurd and to behave as if they support the regime, the state can project its power (Wedeen, 2002). Even in more open authoritarian systems than Syria, where there is little pretense of voluntary consent for the political system, SMMs may serve similar purposes.

11.4.2 Dynamics

A second key question about SMMs raised in this volume centers on the conditions under which authoritarian regimes are likely to resort to this strategy. Do authoritarian rulers and their allies organize pro-state events proactively, as a means of deterring opposition activism (i.e. *spoiler or proactive mobilization*), or reactively, in response to anti-regime protests, sit-ins or other expressions of mass discontent (i.e. *defensive or reactive mobilization*)? If SMMs occur in a reactive sequence, what scale and scope of opposition protests compel incumbent rulers to employ SMM tactics? Do short or isolated protests incite state responses, or do authoritarian regimes reserve SMMs for protracted and widespread opposition mobilization? Finally, are some opposition demands more likely to invite SMMs than others, such as calls for the ouster of the ruler or other demands that call for radical changes to the status quo? Although most existing research on social mobilization addresses such

Insights from Egypt

questions only peripherally, in the discussion that follows we focus on these questions directly, drawing on the vast literature on countermobilization to derive hypotheses about the conditions under which SMMs are likely to occur.

Although specific research on the dynamics of SMMs is scarce, research on the dynamics of movement development and decline yields some relevant insights, particularly in its emphasis on the interplay between opposing social movements. In his discussion of "tactical interaction" between opposition and countermovements, for example, McAdam (1983, p. 736) argues that movements constantly engage in tactical innovation, devising new ways to protest, express opposition, and advance their claims, in efforts to "offset the moves of the other ... in a chess-like fashion." Similarly, Meyer and Staggenborg highlight the dynamic interactions between movements and countermovements, pointing to several factors that may increase the likelihood of SMMs: "[F]irst, the movement shows signs of success; second, the interests of some population are threatened by movement goals; and third, political allies are available to aid oppositional mobilization" (Meyer and Staggenborg, 1996, p. 1635). Extrapolating from these insights, SMMs are more likely to emerge as a reactive response to the success of opposition movements – when opposition activism is gaining traction, or when a movement threatens interests of the regime or its allies, societal actors should be more willing to organize pro-state demonstrations. These observations give rise to our first hypothesis:

H_{1a}: *Authoritarian rulers organize protests reactively, in response to anti-regime protests and perceptions of threats to the regime, rather than proactively.*

On the other hand, authoritarian rulers face compelling incentives to organize protests proactively rather than reactively. Indeed, research on various forms of SMMs in hybrid and authoritarian regimes yields conflicting insights on the dynamics of SMMs. In an account of the formation of Nashi, a political youth movement that is closely linked to the Kremlin, Atwal, and Bacon (2012) suggest that the movement emerged in a reactive fashion – but not necessarily to opposition mobilized or mobilization at home. In particular, the 2004 Orange Revolution in Ukraine inspired pro-Kremlin forces to mobilize even as opposition movements in Russia became emboldened (see also Chapter 7 in this volume). At the same time, other scholars note that incumbents do not always wait for challenges to their authority but can be proactive in attempting to deter dissent (Davenport and Inman, 2012, pp. 625–626). Regime elites may aim to cut off potential opposition before it has the opportunity to gain traction (Francisco, 2005; Robertson, 2010) or to crowd out opposition activity before it has time to develop (Wedeen, 2002). Additionally, because pro-state protests also signal regime power, they may be used to deter opposition activity from developing in the first place. Even if SMMs do not fool or convince citizens of the regime's legitimacy, they may at least convince fence-sitters that the regime remains powerful and that resistance is futile (Kuran, 1991; Lohmann, 1994). This logic conceivably applies to a greater degree to hybrid regimes, where some measure of dissent is tolerated, and to stricter authoritarian regimes, where opponents have less room to operate. For the former, incumbents may deploy SMMs as a way of bolstering perceptions of the legitimacy of their rule. For the latter, the regime may be more likely to use all available tools – including protests and "spectacles" – in order to exert control over all aspects of political and civic life and to "fill up" the space for expression with pro-regime activities. These points generate an opposing hypothesis: H_{1b}: *Authoritarian rulers organize protests proactively rather than in response to opposition mobilization.*

In addition to yielding insights about the timing of SMMs, extant research on social movements also offers preliminary suggestions about what types of opposition protests are likely to generate a regime response. As Zald and Useem (1982) and Meyer and Staggenborg (1996) note, opposition success incentivizes regimes to launch countermobilization efforts – when protests are more protracted or large-scale, regimes and their societal allies may perceive them as more significant threats and thus may be more compelled to act. From the regime's perspective, short-lived opposition mobilization may not require a response, which entails the outlay of scarce resources, whereas more enduring opposition activities calls for direct action. Similarly, larger anti-state protests, measured either in terms of event counts or participation, may be more threatening to the regime and, hence, more worthy of a response in the form of pro-state demonstrations. Beyond calculations based on the costs and benefits of deploying material resources, repression is often insufficient to suppress widespread unrest (Davenport, 2005). Under these circumstances, regime elites and their allies will employ strategies that emphasize their legitimacy and attempt to boost consent – or at least foster the appearance of consent. These considerations give rise to an additional hypothesis: H_2: *More protracted periods of anti-state contention or larger-scale opposition protests are more likely to elicit SMMs.*

11.5 DATA AND METHODS

To test these hypotheses, we draw upon an original dataset of protest mobilization in Egypt spanning from January 1, 2011 to July 3, 2013, the date of the military coup. Following definitional criteria outlined in Horn and Tilly (1988), we classify protests as "occasions on which at least ten or more persons assembled in a publicly accessible place and either by word or deed made claims that would, if realized, affect the interests of some person or group outside their own number." As such, our data excludes events that might otherwise be categorized under the rubric of protest actions: (1) so-called "micro-demonstrations" in which lone or small groups of individuals engage in protest behavior; (2) protest actions in which no specific claim (either a grievance or expression of support) can be identified; and (3) events occurring in private locations or total institutions – mental institutions, prisons, and jails – existing outside of the public sphere. Nonetheless, our data set encompasses a wide variety of protest actions including demonstrations, marches, strikes, sit-ins, blockades, and violent riots. Moreover, given our deliberately expansive definition of protest, this data set is among the first to contain systematic information on both contentious and pro-state collective action, allowing for an analysis of the relationship between opposition protests and SMMs.

Data on protest events were collected from Lexis-Nexis, a database of electronic news drawn from the archives of over 10,000 press agencies and newspapers. In selecting Lexis-Nexis as a primary data source, we draw upon a rich tradition in the field of social movement research, while simultaneously working to address known problems associated with deriving data from news media. For example, by choosing a database that aggregates multiple news sources, we combat common biases of underreporting and unreliability that plague events data derived from single newspapers (Franzosi, 1987; Maney and Oliver, 2001; Earl, 2003). Moreover, because our sources include both international and local news media, we reduce the risk of "selection bias" and thus are able to capture smaller, more quotidian protest events that are typically ignored by foreign news sources (McCarthy, McPhail, and Smith, 1996; Nam, 2006). Finally, unlike most studies using newspapers to classify protest events, we examine daily editions of selected newspapers rather than sampled issues or indices in order to identify the full range of protest actions reported during our period of interest. Ultimately, this method yielded a final collection of 1,805 protest events, which were then content-coded by supervised research assistants on the basis of their tactics, actors, targets, demands, and location.

Using this rich data source, we empirically assess our hypotheses using an event-history approach, following recent developments in protest research (Olzak, 1989; Koopmans and Statham, 1999; Jung, 2010). As Olzak (1989) argues, this modeling strategy better conceptualizes the cyclical and temporally dependent nature of protests, particularly in instances where protests exhibit phasic dynamics or are subject to contagion effects. Unlike event-count models which arbitrarily aggregate individual events within fixed time periods, event-history analyses take the issue of time seriously by examining both the changing frequency of protest occurrence and the time spans that occur between individual events. As a result, protests can be analyzed at a higher level of disaggregation such as the protest-event or protest-day, which reduces the likelihood of biased parameter estimates or causal inferences caused by improper aggregation techniques (Shellman, 2004). Further, an event-history approach allows for the inclusion of time-dependent covariates in statistical models, thereby enabling researchers to capture the time-varying effects that specific explanatory factors have on the outcome of interest. In this way, this approach combines the advantages of time-sensitive analysis with the utility of stochastic models, allowing scholars to analyze protest events as outcomes of processes that unfold over time rather than singular phenomena.

11.5.1 Dependent Variable

In keeping with the event-history approach, we operationalize our dependent variable as the occurrence of a pro-state protest, using the definitional criteria for SMMs outlined in the beginning of the chapter. Given that our unit of analysis is the country-day, this variable indicates whether a pro-state protest occurred on a given day, irrespective of whether the protest was the sole event to occur on that day or whether it was one of a series of pro-state protest events. As such, the data comprises 63 pro-state event-days, within which 109 pro-state demonstrations occurred, out of a total of 913 days. Figure 11.1 depicts the frequency of these events from January 1, 2011 to July 3, 2013.

From this data, two distinct features of SMMs are readily apparent. First, in contrast to other forms of contention, SMMs are a relatively rare occurrence. As demonstrated in Figure 11.1, the trajectory of SMMs is dominated by substantial periods of inactivity punctuated by relatively short spells of intensive mobilization. Indeed, the average inter-event duration between pro-state demonstrations is 14.72 days, while the maximum is 113 days. Moreover, over one-third of SMM event-days occur consecutively, indicating the possible presence of contagion effects or interdependence in the organization of SMMs.

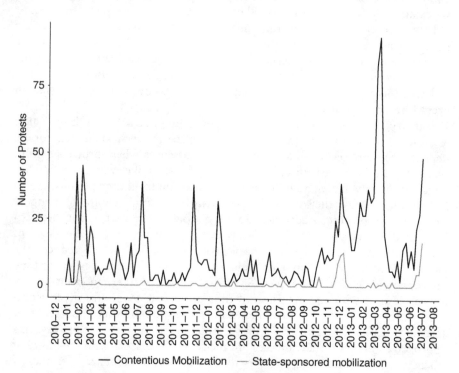

FIGURE 11.1 State-sponsored and contentious mobilization in Egypt, 2011–2013

Insights from Egypt

Apart from indicating the sporadic nature of pro-state protests, the data also hint at likely correlations between spells of SMMs and the occurrence of central events in the Egyptian political landscape (Figure 11.1).

Indeed, as noted in Section 11.2 in our discussion of SMM in the Egyptian case, spikes in pro-state activity were commonly organized in response to waves of anti-state contention. The rise in pro-state demonstrations witnessed in February 2011, for example, directly coincided with foundational moments in the anti-Mubarak rebellion such as the "March of Millions" and the "Friday of Departure." Similarly, the waves of SMMs witnessed in December 2012 and June 2013 corresponded with crisis periods during the Morsi presidency brought on by opposition to the expansion of his presidential powers and the onset of the Tamarrod rebellion, respectively. Thus, rather than a general trend in SMMs, the data display infrequent bursts of activity that appear connected to individual regime officials or events. This highlights the need to take regime identity seriously when analyzing SMMs and, further, provides preliminary evidence of a reactive pattern of pro-state action and contentious mobilization.

11.5.2 Independent Variables

11.5.2.1 Protest Timing

To test our hypothesis regarding the timing of SMMs, we include a lagged measure of contentious mobilization indicating whether an opposition protest occurred in the day or days prior to the onset of SMMs. If regime officials are organizing protests proactively, we should expect protest at t-1[6] to have no significant relationship with pro-state action, whereas a reactive pattern of mobilization should lead us to expect a positive and significant relationship between the incidence of SMMs and oppositional protests.

11.5.2.2 Protest Intensity

In order to capture the effects that protest intensity has on the likelihood of SMMs, we include three variables that measure the frequency, duration, and magnitude of protest activity, respectively. First, to measure the frequency of contention we construct a lagged variable that records the total number of opposition protests that occurred at time t-1. Given that our event catalogue records each protest held by a distinct group of actors in a specific location as an individual observation, this variable provides a sense of the volume of opposition prior to the occurrence of pro-state action as well as a rough proxy of the geographic distribution of contentious mobilization. As noted in

---

[6] In addition to a one-day lag, we also ran robustness checks with independent variables lagged by two and three days. These results largely confirmed those of the original estimation, although it is worth noting that, on average, most pro-state demonstrations occurred immediately after anti-state contention.

the theoretical discussion in Section 11.1, we expect that pro-state protests of the reactive variant are more likely to occur when the volume of opposition protests witnessed previously is high, and we anticipate that SMMs are less likely when the volume of prior contention is low.

Second, to model the effects of protest duration on the incidence of SMMs, we include a variable that records the number of consecutive days on which opposition protests have occurred. In simple terms, this variable measures the longevity of a protest cycle – during more protracted periods of conflict, the number of successive protest-days will be high, whereas more ephemeral cycles of contention will have fewer consecutive protest-days. Consistent with H_2, we expect this measure to be positively correlated with the incidence of SMMs.

Third, to account for the magnitude of contentious mobilization, we include a lagged measure that records the total number of protest participants reported by news media for the previous day's protests. In our data set, specific numbers of demonstrators were reported by press reports in nearly half of all recorded events. For the remaining 50 percent, coders were instructed to estimate the total number of protesters based on verbal cues present in the articles and to place them in distinct ranges given pre-established coding rules (e.g. "small," "few," or "handfuls" were all estimated to be in the 1–100 range).[7] Based on these figures, estimates of daily protest participation were calculated by summing the participation figures for each protest occurring on a specific day, with nonspecific values coded as the midpoint of their given range. This aggregation strategy yielded a minimum daily protest participation figure of 10 and a maximum of 930,350 individuals. To account for potential uncertainty in our estimates, these figures were then recoded into categorical measures representing the approximate magnitude of protest events (i.e. "hundreds," "thousands," "tens of thousands," etc.). In line with the theoretical discussion outlined in H_2, we expect larger numbers of protest participants to increase the risk of SMMs.

11.5.3 Control Variables

In addition to the variables specified, we control for several additional factors that have previously been identified as important predictors of SMMs. Following Zald and Useem (1982), Griffin, Wallace, and Rubin (1986), and Soule and Olzak (2004), we include a variable that indicates whether social movement organizations (SMOs) were present during opposition protests. This binary variable is coded as "1" if a political party or recognized civil society organization is listed as one of the principal actors in a given demonstration and zero otherwise. Because formal associations tend to have more committed activist networks (Zald and Useem, 1982; McAdam, 1982) and possess the resources necessary to

---

[7] More detailed information on coding procedures is available in Appendix A.

launch an effective challenge to the state (Zald and McCarthy, 1987), demonstrations organized by SMOs should be of concern to regime officials wishing to maintain their hold on power. Thus, we expect protests with a heavy SMO-presence to be more likely to elicit pro-state action, due to the increased threat that formally organized social movements pose to extant rulers.

Additionally, drawing on a distinction made by Gamson (1975) and later taken up by Gartner and Regan (1996) and Regan and Henderson (2002), we control for severity of protester demands by including a binary variable that indicates whether protests at time $t\text{-}1$ expressed radical goals. We define radical goals as protest claims advocating for the dissolution of a governing institution or calling for the dismissal and/or prosecution of high-ranking officials at the regional or national level. As Gartner and Regan note, demands to dramatically alter the status quo through regime change or civil war should engender a more robust state response because elites are more likely to view such demands as threatening to their key interests (Gartner and Regan, 1996). In such a circumstance, offering concessions to the opposition is infeasible, requiring a more robust form of state response, whether it be through countermobilization or through repression (Goldstone and Tilly, 2001). Thus, we expect that authorities will be more likely to respond to dissent with pro-state protests when challengers wish to displace current political leaders and/or the political-economic system.

For similar reasons, we also include a control variable denoting the use of violent tactics during opposition protests. As the literature on protest policing has shown, authorities are more likely to respond to protests that utilize violent tactics, due to the inherent threat that such actions pose to the state's monopoly over the exercise of force (Earl, Soule, and McCarthy, 2003; Soule and Davenport, 2009; Earl and Soule, 2006). Consequently, we control for the use of violent tactics by constructing a binary indicator that records whether opposition protests at time $t\text{-}1$ involved the use of violence against persons or property. Consistent with the literature, we expect the use of violent tactics to increase the likelihood that SMMs occur at time t.

Finally, to account for the potential effects that regime identity may have on the incidence of SMMs, we include a control variable that identifies the head of state at the time under observation. The multiple executives that held power during our period of study correspond to distinct regime types. Under Mubarak, Egypt was classified as a single-party hegemonic authoritarian system. During the period of SCAF rule, Egypt was ruled by a military regime. Finally, under Morsi, the country can be formally classified as a multiparty democracy, although in practice it exhibited numerous traits of a competitive authoritarian regime.

11.5.3.1 *Estimation Technique*

We analyze the occurrence of SMMs using a Cox proportional hazards model. As a semi-parametric model, this approach allows us to estimate the probability that a pro-state demonstration occurs at time *t*, without assuming a specific distribution for the baseline hazard function. Thus, our model follows the form

$$h(t \mid X) = h_0(t)\exp(X\beta)$$

where $h_0(t)$ refers to the baseline hazard that will be unspecified because of no distributional assumption, t denotes the inter-event time span, X represents the matrix of all covariates, and β references the estimated coefficients. Put simply, then, our model specification tests whether opposition protest timing, intensity, and demands affect the hazard rate of pro-state protest occurrence, conditional upon the control variables mentioned in Section 11.5.3.

11.6 ANALYSIS

Table 11.1 presents the results of the analysis. Coefficient values are reported as hazard ratios, with values greater than one indicating an increase in the hazard rate and thus a greater likelihood of SMM occurrence, and values below one indicating the opposite. Robust standard errors are reported in parentheses.

The principal finding emerging from these results is that the existence of protest activity is positively correlated with the onset of SMMs. Specifically, the incidence of opposition protest at time *t-1* increases the hazard rate of SMMs at time *t* by nearly 250 percent, an effect that is significant at the 95 percent confidence level. This suggests that, consistent with H_{1a}, Egyptian authorities use pro-state demonstrations not as a prophylaxis against future conflict but rather as a response to existing unrest that poses a threat to their rule. This finding largely accords with the analysis of SMMs presented in the qualitative case study in Section 11.4 – faced with growing anti-government opposition, Egyptian elites and their allies countermobilized in an attempt to generate popular support for extant regime interests. It is important to note, however, that – in line with observations made by Francisco (2005) and Robertson (2010) – such forces appear particularly sensitive to the threat of opposition and mobilize pro-state demonstrations almost immediately after a wave of contentious activity begins. Indeed, a sensitivity analysis (results not shown) demonstrates that increasing the lag on our measure of protest by one to three days has no discernible effect on the likelihood of SMMs, emphasizing the rapidity of pro-state response.

Turning to our secondary hypotheses, we find mixed support for the notion that more intense periods of opposition elicit pro-state activity. Contrary to our expectations, experiencing a higher number of opposition protests on a given day has a slightly negative effect on the

TABLE 11.1 *Cox proportional hazards model for SMMs, 2011–2013*

	Incidence of SMMs	
	(Model 1)	(Model 2)
Incidence of opposition protest	3.501	3.285
	(0.502)**	(0.515)**
Number of opposition demonstrations	0.955	0.969
	(0.030)	(0.030)
Consecutive protest days	0.996	1.017
	(0.003)*	(0.011)
Consecutive protest days – squared		1.000
		(0.001)**
Total participants:		
1,000–9,999	0.654	0.453
	(0.329)	(0.408)
10,000–99,999	0.855	0.671
	(0.357)	(0.421)
100,000–499,999	0.706	0.549
	(1.011)	(1.031)
500,000+	4.362	3.202
	(0.546)***	(0.547)**
Radical demands	1.234	1.287
	(0.366)	(0.376)
SMO presence	2.469	2.133
	(0.340)***	(0.347)**
Use of violent tactics	0.798	0.845
	(0.408)	(0.404)
SCAF regime	0.228	0.210
	(0.567)***	(0.574)***
Morsi regime	1.166	1.010
	(0.506)	(0.517)
Observations	913	913
R^2	0.041	0.045

Note: *p<0.1; **p<0.05; ***p<0.01

incidence of SMMs, although this effect is not significant at conventional confidence levels. More surprisingly, the occurrence of SMMs appears less likely during periods of protracted conflict, as indicated by the coefficient on our duration measure. While this result appears somewhat counterintuitive, it is likely that it indicates a potential nonlinear relationship between conflict duration and regime response. Indeed, in the Egyptian case, some of the most protracted periods of conflict were also the most banal – a six-month wave of contention from October 2012 to April 2013, for example, persisted mainly due to the existence of protracted labor conflicts unlikely to elicit an immediate pro-state response. If longer-standing conflicts are indicative of lack of interest by elites or are associated with more measured responses, we might expect protest duration to have a curvilinear relationship with SMMs. In other words, the risk of SMMs should increase as the duration of opposition activity increases up to a certain threshold; but it should decrease thereafter due to the government's desensitization to conflict or decision to pursue resolution by other means. As Model 2 shows, adding a quadratic term to our analysis demonstrates preliminary support for this interpretation: while protest duration is positively associated with pro-state action, its square is negatively correlated with SMMs, indicating a concave relationship between the length of a protest cycle and the likelihood of SMMs.

Further, our hypotheses regarding the magnitude of opposition activity receive only partial support. While exceptionally large demonstrations significantly increase the risk of SMMs, this effect does not hold for moderately sized protests. As the coefficient estimates from Table 11.1 indicate, protests with 500,000 or more demonstrators are nearly four times more likely to trigger an immediate pro-state response than those with fewer than 1,000 participants, an effect which is significant at the 99 percent confidence level. While this threshold appears relatively high, it is reasonable in the context of the Egyptian case, given the frequent use of "million man marches" as a form of contention during the January 25 and Tamarrod uprisings. Nevertheless, this finding generally confirms the notion that SMMs are most likely to occur in cases where opposition is extreme, convincing incumbent authoritarian rulers and their allies that less-costly options such as repression or conciliation are infeasible.

Regarding our set of controls, we find mixed support for the effects of organizational presence, opposition demands, and violence on pro-state mobilization. In contrast to Gamson (1990) and others, we find no support for a significant positive relationship between the severity of protest demands and the organization of pro-state demonstrations. While expressing radical demands increases the risk of pro-state protest occurrence by 23 percent, this effect is not significant at conventional levels. In fact, what appears more influential in generating SMMs are the presence of social movement organizations (SMOs) at opposition events. The hazard ratio for SMO presence indicates a 146 percent increase in the hazard of SMMs when formal associations participate in opposition demonstrations – an effect which is highly statistically significant. Figure 11.2 depicts the same results graphically, showing the duration of spells between pro-state protests when SMOs are present and absent from opposition demonstrations.

As Figure 11.2 shows, pro-state action is more immediate and more likely following protest events with significant SMO presence, a logical finding given

Insights from Egypt

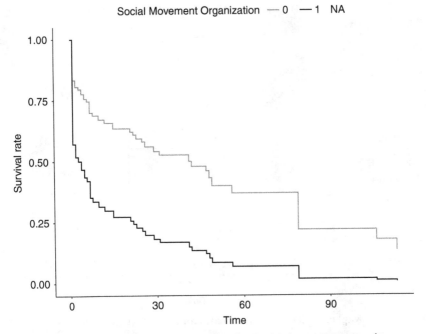

FIGURE 11.2 Kaplan-Meier survival estimates for SMMs by organizational presence

that mobilization by these groups is likely to pose a more formidable challenge to regime stability.

Finally, while theoretical expectations regarding the connection between violence and SMMs are unsubstantiated in our analysis, it is important to note that we find significant support for a relationship between regime identity and SMMs. In comparison to the Mubarak and Morsi regimes, SMMs were a much more rare occurrence under SCAF rule. As Table 11.1 shows, the hazard rate of SMM was reduced by nearly 88 percent under the military regime, indicating a significant departure from the Mubarak-era pattern of pro-state action (Figure 11.3).

This finding suggests that SMM is more likely to occur under hegemonic party systems or hybrid regimes, where rulers may be especially sensitive to public displays of unrest (Magaloni, 2006; Gandhi, 2010) or face greater constraints on the use of overt repression to subdue opposition (Davenport, 2007). Viewed in this way, this trend can be seen as potential evidence of a repression-mobilization trade-off, whereby rulers substitute actions aimed at eliciting support or displacing opposition through peaceful means for outright physical coercion.

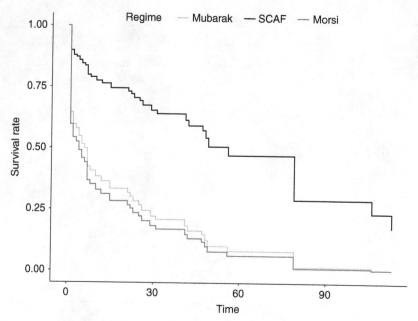

FIGURE 11.3 Kaplan-Meier survival estimates for SMM by regime identity

11.7 CONCLUSION

Authoritarian leaders in the face of crisis can select from multiple defense strategies beyond the traditional use of "carrots and sticks." In this chapter, we explore one such strategy – SMMs – and illustrate its application in the case of Egypt during and after the Arab uprisings. As our theoretical and empirical discussions underscore, SMMs constitute a distinct category of social control employed by hybrid and authoritarian regimes that has largely been overlooked in the literatures on social movements and on authoritarian politics. Conceptually, we propose a general definition of SMMs and outline a set of tentative hypotheses to explain the conditions under which different rulers and their allies might resort to this strategy to fend off or guard against popular unrest. Testing these hypotheses using an original data set of protest mobilization under multiple regimes in Egypt, we find that SMMs were largely a reactive response to perceived societal threats. Our findings suggest that regimes employ this tactic in order to counteract episodes of contention that involve significant crowds or attract the engagement of established social movements. Moreover, our analysis of Egypt suggests that hegemonic party systems and hybrid regimes may be more likely to employ SMMs as a countermobilization tactic, pointing to potential divergence in preferred strategies of social control across regime types. Absent cross-national data

Insights from Egypt

across distinct regime types, however, we cannot adjudicate this claim more definitively.

Our empirical analyses are based on the Egyptian case; however, our findings have implications for discussions of regime responses to contentious action and autocratic survival more generally. First, in broadening the typology of protest control tactics to include SMMs, this chapter joins the other contributions to this volume in highlighting the need to move beyond repression and concessions when analyzing strategies of autocratic survival. While scholars have taken steps in this direction by introducing new categories of regime response such as toleration and neglect (Bishara, 2014; Cai, 2008; Franklin, 2009), a focus on the more active ways in which regimes can challenge protests without resorting to violence or compromise forces us to treat SMMs as more than just a residual category entailing the mere absence of repression and concessions. Indeed, more systematic treatments of the distinct motivations for using SMMs would likely illuminate the ways in which the goals of SMMs overlap with or, in some cases, contradict those of better-theorized strategies such as the repression of and concessions to regime opponents. As our analyses demonstrate, the rationales for employing repression and SMMs are not necessarily similar: while violence and radical demands have been shown to increase the likelihood of repressive activity against opposition elements (Earl, Soule, and McCarthy, 2003; Soule and Davenport, 2009; Earl and Soule, 2006), these factors had little effect on the incidence of SMMs in the case of Egypt.

Second, the recognition of SMMs as a distinct category of regime response invites further exploration of the ways in which various modes of authoritarian survival strategies interact. To be sure, as the social movements literature implies, regimes facing opposition threats do not adhere strictly to a single mode of response but rather strategically combine and modify tactics for maintaining social control to adapt to the changing nature of contentious mobilization. Our research provides a useful point of departure for analyzing when and why SMMs serve as a substitute or complement for other types of responses to societal threats. In this sense, our work prompts a reconsideration of the well-theorized "repression-concessions dilemma" to include the possibility of SMMs.[8]

At the same time, our chapter raises a host of new questions about SMMs, suggesting fruitful avenues for future research. One such avenue would be to refine the concept of SMM itself – although our analysis takes tentative steps in this direction, a fuller exploration of SMMs could reveal new insights about the actors, motivations, and dynamics that underlie this unique regime response.

---

[8] Analyzing the interaction between repression and SMM is a critical, albeit difficult, next step for future research. Although data on the state's use of repressive force was collected to undertake such an analysis in this project, unfortunately the sparsity of such data and the inherently biased nature of media reporting on repression (Ortiz et al., 2005), we elected not to include measures of repression in our analyses as explanatory variables nor controls.

For example, future work could delve more deeply into the core actors at the heart of SMMs. Under what conditions do regime officials themselves organize pro-regime demonstrations, rallies, or other forms of collective action? Alternatively, when do regime elites turn to their societal allies to do this work on their behalf, and when do their elite supports opt to organize pro-state demonstrations on their own? More generally, is pro-state mobilization always synonymous with SMMs, or can it have purely societal roots?

Another line of inquiry could explore the motivations for and varieties of SMMs in different types of authoritarian regimes. As the contributions to the volume usefully illustrate, regimes adopt varied rationales for the use of pro-state demonstrations – while in some cases such mobilization is used to reactively defend the regime against political challengers (see Chapters 2 and 12 in this volume for prominent examples) in others it is used to proactively stimulate support for the state's developmental agenda (Looney and Rithmire, 2017). Similarly, a growing body of research identifies marked differences in the use of repression and countermovements among totalitarian, hybrid, and democratic regimes (Davenport, 2007). It is thus worth asking whether we can identify distinct patterns of SMMs within different regimes, and whether various regimes consider trade-offs when selecting SMMs over other response methods such as repression or concession.

Finally, future research should devote greater attention to the likely consequences of SMMs for contentious action. While our analysis supports a reactive view of SMMs, it is still worth exploring in a broader set of cases whether SMMs are ultimately aimed at quelling or preempting the opposition. Further, research should consider how protesters perceive and respond to pro-state demonstrations and how this action may affect their own organizational capacities and choices. Thus, in line with the ongoing research program on the repression–mobilization nexus (Davenport, 2005), an important line of inquiry would examine the conditions under which SMMs have their intended effects on would-be opposition.

Undoubtedly, any future work on SMMs would be a necessary and welcome addition to the current literature on social movements. As rulers in hybrid and authoritarian regimes become more sophisticated in their strategies of social control, scholars must adapt their approaches to the study of social mobilization and politics in nondemocracies.

REFERENCES

Al-Rasheed, Madawi. 2011. Sectarianism as counter-revolution: Saudi responses to the Arab Spring. *Studies in Ethnicity and Nationalism* 11 (3): 513–526, doi:10.1111/j.1754-9469.2011.01129.x.
Armbrust, Walter. 2013. The trickster in Egypt's January 25th revolution. *Comparative Studies in Society and History* 55 (04): 834–864, doi:10.1017/S0010417513000431.

Atwal, Maya, and Edwin Bacon. 2012. The youth movement Nashi: contentious politics, civil society, and party politics. *East European Politics* 28 (3): 256–266, doi:10.1080/21599165.2012.691424.

Bishara, Dina. 2015. The politics of ignoring: protest dynamics in late Mubarak Egypt. *Perspectives on Politics* 13 (04): 958–975, doi:10.1017/s153759271500225x.

Blaydes, Lisa. 2010. *Elections and Distributive Politics in Mubarak's Egypt* [electronic Resource]. New York: Cambridge University Press.

Blaydes, Lisa. 2014. *Elections and Distributive Politics in Mubarak's Egypt*. Cambridge: Cambridge University Press.

Brown, Nathan J. 1990. *Peasant Politics in Modern Egypt: the Struggle against the State*. New Haven, CT: Yale University Press.

Brownlee, Jason. 2007. *Authoritarianism in an Age of Democratization*. Cambridge: Cambridge University Press.

Cai, Yongshun. 2008. Power structure and regime resilience: contentious politics in China. *British Journal of Political Science* 38 (03): 411–432, doi:10.1017/s0007123408000215.

Conrad, Courtenay R. 2011. Constrained concessions: beneficent dictatorial responses to the domestic political opposition. *International Studies Quarterly* 55 (4): 1167–1187, doi:10.1111/j.1468-2478.2011.00683.x.

Davenport, Christian. 2005. Understanding covert repressive action: the case of the U.S. government against the Republic of New Africa. *Journal of Conflict Resolution* 49 (1): 120–140, doi:10.1177/0022002704271285.

Davenport, Christian. 2007. State repression and political order. *Annual Review of Political Science* 10 (1): 1–23, doi:10.1146/annurev.polisci.10.101405.143216.

Davenport, Christian, and Molly Inman. 2012. The state of state repression research since the 1990s. *Terrorism and Political Violence* 24 (4): 619–634, doi:10.1080/09546553.2012.700619.

Earl, Jennifer. 2003. Tanks, tear gas, and taxes: toward a theory of movement repression. *Sociological Theory* 21 (1): 44–68, doi:10.1111/1467-9558.00175.

Earl, Jennifer, and Sarah Soule. 2006. Seeing blue: a police-centered explanation of protest policing. *Mobilization: An International Quarterly* 11 (2): 145–164.

Earl, Jennifer, Sarah Soule, and John McCarthy. 2003. Protest under fire? Explaining the policing of protest. *American Sociological Review* 68 (4): 581–606, doi:10.2307/1519740.

El-Mahdi, Rabab. 2014. Egypt: A Decade of Ruptures. In Ellen Lust and Lina Khatib, (eds.), *Taking to the Streets*. Baltimore, MD: Johns Hopkins University Press, pp. 52–76.

Francisco, Ronaldo. 2005. The dictator's dilemma. In Christian Davenport (ed.), *Repression and Mobilization*. Minneapolis: University of Minnesota Press, pp. 58–82.

Franklin, James C. 2008. Contentious challenges and government responses in Latin America. *Political Research Quarterly* 62 (4): 700–714, doi:10.1177/1065912908322405.

Franzosi, Roberto. 1987. The press as a source of socio-historical data: issues in the methodology of data collection from newspapers. *Historical Methods: A Journal of Quantitative and Interdisciplinary History* 20 (1): pp. 5–16, doi:10.1080/01615440.1987.10594173.

Gamson, William. 1975. *The Strategy of Social Protest*. Homewood, IL: Dorsey.

Gamson, William A. 1990. *The Strategy of Social Protest*. Belmont, CA: Wadsworth.

Gandhi, Jennifer, and Ellen Lust-Okar. 2009. Elections under authoritarianism. *Annual Review of Political Science* 12 (1): 403–422, doi:10.1146/annurev.polisci.11.060106.095434.

Gandhi, Jennifer. 2010. *Political institutions under dictatorship.* Cambridge: Cambridge University Press.

Gartner, Scott Sigmund, and Patrick M. Regan. 1996. Threat and repression: the non-linear relationship between government and opposition violence. *Journal of Peace Research* 33 (3): 273–287, doi:10.1177/0022343396033003003.

Goldstone, Jack, and Charles A. Tilly. 2001. Threat (and opportunity): popular action and state response in the dynamics of contentious action. In Ronald Aminzade et al. (eds.), *Silence and Voice in the Study of Contentious Politics.* Cambridge: Cambridge University Press.

Greene, Kenneth F. 2007. *Why Dominant Parties Lose: Mexico's Democratization in Comparative Perspective.* Cambridge: Cambridge University Press.

Griffin, Larry J., Michael E. Wallace, and Beth A. Rubin. 1986. Capitalist resistance to the organization of labor before the New Deal: Why? How? Success? *American Sociological Review* 51 (2): 147–157, doi:10/2307/2095513

Horn, Nancy, and Charles Tilly. 1988. *Contentious Gatherings in Britain, 1758–1834.* Ann Arbor, MI: Inter-University Consortium for Political and Social Research.

Jung, Jai. 2010. Disentangling protest cycles: an event-history analysis of new social movements in Western Europe. *Mobilization: An International Quarterly* 15 (1): 25–44.

Kandil, Hazem. 2012. *Soldiers, Spies, and Statesmen: Egypt's Road to Revolt.* London: Verso.

Kassem, Maye. 2004. *Egyptian Politics: The Dynamics of Authoritarian Rule.* Boulder, CO: Lynne Rienner.

Ketchley, Neil. 2016. Elite-led protest and authoritarian state capture in Egypt. *POMEPS Studies* 20: 34–36.

Ketchley, Neil, and Christopher Barrie. 2019. *Fridays of revolution: focal days and mass protest in Egypt and Tunisia.* Political Research Quarterly.

Koopmans, Ruud, and Paul Statham. 1999. Political claims analysis: integrating protest event and political discourse approaches. *Mobilization: An International Quarterly* 4 (2): 203–221.

Kuran, Timur. 1991. Now out of never: the element of surprise in the East European revolution of 1989. *World Politics* 44 (01): 7–48, doi:10.2307/2010422.

Lohmann, Susanne. 1994. The dynamics of informational cascades: the Monday Demonstrations in Leipzig, East Germany, 1989–91. *World Politics* 47 (01): 42–101, doi:10.2307/2950679.

Looney, Kristen, and Meg Rithmire. 2017. China gambles on modernizing through urbanization. *Current History* 116 (791): 203–209.

Lust-Okar, Ellen. 2005. *Structuring Conflict in the Arab World: Incumbents, Opponents, and Institutions.* Cambridge: Cambridge University Press.

Magaloni, Beatriz. 2006. *Voting for Autocracy: Hegemonic Party Survival and Its Demise in Mexico.* Cambridge: Cambridge University Press.

Maney, Gregory M., and Pamela E. Oliver. 2001. Finding collective events: sources, searches, and timing. *Sociological Methods & Research* 30 (2): 131–169, doi:10.1177/0049124101030002001.

Masoud, Tarek. 2014. *Counting Islam: Religion, Class, and Elections in Egypt.* Cambridge: Cambridge University Press.

McAdam, Doug. 1982. *Political Process and the Development of Black Insurgency: 1930–1970.* Chicago, IL: University of Chicago Press.

McAdam, Doug. 1983. Tactical innovation and the pace of insurgency. *American Sociological Review* 48 (6): 735–754, doi:10.2307/2095322.

McCarthy, John D., Clark McPhail, and Jackie Smith. 1996. Images of protest: dimensions of selection bias in media coverage of Washington demonstrations, 1982 and 1991. *American Sociological Review* 61 (3): 478–499, doi:10.2307/2096360.

Meyer, David S., and Suzanne Staggenborg. 1996. Movements, countermovements, and the structure of political opportunity. *American Journal of Sociology* 101 (6): 1628–1660, doi:10.1086/230869.

Mohsen, Ali Abdel. 2011. Thug life: pro-Mubarak bullies break their silence. *The Egypt Independent*, March 18.

Nam, Taehyun. 2006. What you use matters: coding protest data. *PS: Political Science & Politics* 39 (02): 281–287, doi:10.1017/s104909650606046x.

Olzak, S. 1989. Analysis of events in the study of collective action. *Annual Review of Sociology* 15: 119–186.

Olzak, S. 2005. Analysis of events in the study of collective action. *Annual Review of Sociology* 10 (3): 397–419.

Ortiz, David G., Daniel Myers, Eugene Walls, and Maria-Elena Diaz. 2005. Where do we stand with newspaper data? *Mobilization: An International Journal* 68 (4): 397–419, doi:10.2307/1519740.

Regan, Patrick M., and Errol A. Henderson. 2002. Democracy, threats and political repression in developing countries: are democracies internally less violent? *Third World Quarterly* 23 (1): 119–136, doi:10.1080/01436590220108207.

Robertson, Graeme B. 2010. *The Politics of Protest in Hybrid Regimes: Managing Dissent in Post-Communist Russia.* Cambridge: Cambridge University Press.

Robertson, Graeme B. 2007. Strikes and labor organization in hybrid regimes. *American Political Science Review* 101 (04): 781–798, doi:10.1017/s0003055407070475.

Ryan, Curtis R. 2011. Identity politics, reform, and protest in Jordan. *Studies in Ethnicity and Nationalism* 11 (3): 564–578, doi:10.1111/j.1754-9469.2011.01135.x.

Schedler, Andreas. 2006. *Electoral Authoritarianism: The Dynamics of Unfree Competition.* Boulder, CO: Lynne Rienner.

Shah, Angela. 2011. Why the Arab Spring never came to the U.A.E. Time, July 18.

Shellman, Stephen M. 2004. Time series intervals and statistical inference: the effects of temporal aggregation on event data analysis. *Political Analysis* 12 (01): 97–104, doi:10.1093/pan/mpg017.

Stacher, Joshua. 2012. *Adaptable Autocrats: Regime Power in Egypt and Syria.* Stanford, CA: Stanford University Press.

Soule, Sarah, and Susan Olzak. 2004. When do movements matter? The politics of contingency and the Equal Rights Amendment. *American Sociological Review* 69 (4): 473–497, doi:10.1177/000312240406900401.

Soule, Sarah, and Christian Davenport. 2009. Velvet glove, iron fist, or even hand? Protest policing in the United States, 1960–1990. *Mobilization: An International Quarterly* 14 (1): 1–22.

Tilly, Charles. 1998. *From Mobilization to Revolution.* New York: McGraw-Hill.

Way, Lucan A., and Steven Levitsky. 2006. The dynamics of autocratic coercion after the Cold War. *Communist and Post-Communist Studies* 39 (3): 387–410, doi:10.1016/j.postcomstud.2006.07.001.

Wedeen, Lisa. 2002. *Ambiguities of Domination: Politics, Rhetoric, and Symbols in Contemporary Syria*. Chicago, IL: University of Chicago Press.

Zald, Meyer, and John McCarthy. 1987. Social movement industries: competition and conflict among SMOs. In M. Zald and J. McCarthy (eds.), *Social Movements in an Organizational Society: Collected Essays*. New Brunswick, NJ: Transaction Books, pp. 161–182.

Zald, Mayer, and Bert Useem. 1982. Movement and countermovement: loosely coupled conflict. *Annual Meetings of the American Sociological Association*.

12

State-Mobilized Campaign and the Prodemocracy Movement in Hong Kong, 2013–2015

Eliza W. Y. Lee

12.1 INTRODUCTION

The events surrounding the prodemocracy movement in Hong Kong from 2013 to 2015 represent the latest chapter in a long and torturous struggle for democracy that can be dated back to the early 1980s when Britain and China held their negotiations over the city's future (So, 1998). The Occupy Central Movement (OCM), initiated by three prodemocracy activists, exhorted supporters to block major roads and exercise civil disobedience in the struggle for full democracy. It soon provoked the Chinese Communist Party-state ("party-state") to initiate a campaign to counter OCM. Executed mainly through their unofficial agents and sponsored organizations in Hong Kong, its scale of operation was almost unprecedented, at least since the social riot in 1967 (which was largely the spillover of the Cultural Revolution).

This chapter will analyze the characteristics and role of state-mobilized movements (SMMs) in countering a prodemocracy movement. The specific movement in question mostly operated through state-sponsored social organizations in Hong Kong and went through several stages: from 2013 to June 2014, it successfully countered the mobilization of OCM through launching a countermovement (anti-OCM). From June to August 2014, the party-state stepped up its attack on OCM and revealed its hard line in controlling Hong Kong's democratization, thus intensifying state–society confrontation. The announcement of an extremely restrictive democratic reform plan by the National People's Congress on August 31 followed by the Hong Kong government's use of excessive police force against protesters finally triggered a large-scale popular rebellion, termed the Umbrella Movement by the media, with tens of thousands of protesters occupying major roads in various places of the city. At this stage, state-sponsored social organizations were deployed to demobilize the Umbrella Movement, largely through gang violence, street-level clashes, and legal procedures. From late 2014 to 2015, state-sponsored organizations were involved in remobilizing social support for the stringent political reform plan imposed by the party-state as well as regaining political control over society, or re-equilibration, after the partial breakdown of order in the Umbrella Movement. The idea of re-equilibration is based on Ekiert (1996), who uses the concept to analyze the aftermath of political crisis in East Central Europe and underscore the significance of post-crisis development in state–society relations. The case study will show that the state-mobilized campaign was reactive (or defensive) in some stages and proactive in other stages. Altogether, they epitomize a mode of operation of the party-state in the liberal enclave of Hong Kong. Our conclusion will reflect on the limitation of this form of indirect rule under the "One Country, Two Systems" arrangement.

12.2 THE PRODEMOCRACY MOVEMENT IN HONG KONG AND ITS CONSTRAINTS

The study of this particular case has to be put in the context of the prodemocracy movement since the 1980s. The Sino-British negotiations for the return of Hong Kong to Chinese rule in the early 1980s represented the beginning of a long democratic transition that remains unfinished. Hong Kong has been undergoing partial democratization at a slow pace starting from the introduction of popularly elected seats in the legislature in 1991. The process was mostly arrested after 2004 as the percentage of popularly elected seats reached 50 percent, with the chief executive remaining a nonelected figure. During this period, the prodemocracy movement has gone through phases of mobilization and demobilization. It has witnessed the international emergence of third and fourth waves prodemocracy movements, each of which have inspired activists to try out different strategies for challenging the party-state – the single major external force that has been blocking the progress in democratization. Successive waves of mobilization saw increasing radicalization in the repertoires of contention adopted by movement activists, as well as the proliferation of new leaders, new internal conflict and fragmentation due to disagreement over strategies, ideological differences, and generational change.

The protracted democratic transition was also complicated by broader political and socioeconomic development that gave rise to changes in collective identities and values of citizens. The decolonization process in the 1980s heightened the rights and democratic consciousness of the general population and, with the handover of sovereignty, led to the search for a new political identity. From 1984 to 2014, GDP per capita in Hong Kong increased by almost threefold from USD13,190 to USD35,596. The percentage of the population with post-secondary educational attainment increased from 9.2 percent in 1986 to 30.8 percent in 2015, with a significant gap between the younger and older generation: 46.9 percent among the 20–29-year-old group had post-secondary educational attainment, as opposed to 13.7 percent among the 50–59-year-old group.[1] It was also during this period that civil society and new social movements flourished. Civil society in Hong Kong went through an important period of maturity in the decade after the handover in 1997 (Chan and Chan, 2007). In particular, new social movements in relation to the environment, heritage conservation, and urban planning strongly question the government's developmentalist approach in policymaking inherited from the colonial era, testifying to the emergence of a postmaterial society in search of a postcolonial identity, particularly among the younger generation (Law, 2018; Ma, 2011; Sing, 2010).

The combined effect of these factors on the prodemocracy movement is complex. On the one hand, they offered Hong Kong some of the most favorable textbook conditions for democratization (and thus the most challenging conditions for authoritarian rule to persist). Further supporting democratization are: hyper-free flow of information in a cosmopolitan city and thus an extremely well-informed citizenry; the low political salience of ethnic, linguistic, religious, or urban–rural divides; and relatively low political cost of public activism compared with other authoritarian states thanks to its common law system that affords constitutional protection of civil liberties.

On the other hand, these same factors might also have paradoxically hindered the prodemocracy movement. Rapid socioeconomic development has brought about generational and class differences in values (Wong and Wan, 2009). While among the population there are substantial grievances and dissatisfaction with the current regime, the prodemocracy movement has not been driven by an urgent need to remove a brutal dictator or corrupt government. Categorized as a high-income place by the World Bank, currently ranked seventh in the world in the Human Development Index by the United Nations, the postindustrial city has a well-developed public administrative system and rule-based governance structure, all of which constitute favorable conditions for a high-performing authoritarian state to maintain stability and endure (Przeworski and Limongi, 1997). There are major differences in people's interpretation of the colonial experience, the relationship between Hong Kong and China, the legitimacy of the party-state, etc. Studies on voting behavior in the 1990s have already discovered "the China factor," meaning attitude toward and feelings about China, as the major political cleavage among voters (Leung, 1993, 1996). All these mean that the prodemocracy movement is bound to suffer serious frame disputes. These conditions – internal fragmentation of the democratic movement and social division within the broader Hong Kong society – have offered the party-state

---

[1] For details, see Census and Statistics Department, HKSAR Government, "Education and Training Characteristics," www.censtatd.gov.hk/hkstat/sub/gender/education_and_training/index.jsp.

much room for maneuver, to either divide or contain the prodemocracy movement.

12.3 STATE-SPONSORED ORGANIZATIONS AGAINST THE AUTONOMOUS CIVIL SOCIETY

Social organizations sponsored by the party-state have a long history of existence in Hong Kong. Way back in the early colonial period, the Chinese Communist Party (CCP) had penetrated Hong Kong society through its united front strategy, guided by the objectives of propagating communist revolutionary doctrine and winning nationalist sympathizers (Loh, 2010; Kiang, 2011). During the political transition in the 1980s, capitalists were among the major groups to be co-opted. Upon the handover of sovereignty, the party-state had lined up a range of social and political organizations, including political parties, business associations, labor unions, clan associations, women's organizations, community-based and neighborhood-based organizations, recreational clubs, arts and culture organizations, schools, etc. Also growing in number in recent years are professional groups, alumni associations, think tanks, and student organizations. Aside from formal organizations, new issue-based social groups and alliances led by new faces have proliferated. While some long-time party loyalists are still the core members of united front organizations, the expansion and differentiation of united front groups have brought in new recruits who tend to be opportunists that willingly provide their service for material rewards. In short, united front networks have evolved into patron–client networks, with the "Liaison Office" (the Central Government's de facto local agency in charge of overseeing Hong Kong),[2] assuming the role of the patron with the power and resource to reward and discipline followers (Lee, 2019).

The clientelization of the united front operation contributes to its "composite" character similar to the counterrevolutionary mobilization described by Beissinger in Chapter 6 of this volume: its members are a mixture of underground CCP members, party-state loyalists, nationalists, political clients, and sheer opportunists. Together they act as agents for the party-state to manage Hong Kong society. The party-state, restricted by the arrangement of "one country, two systems," which precludes its direct dictatorship over Hong Kong and makes outright repression a costly option, has resorted to indirect rule to exercise political control, executed through the tactical configuration of extralegal personnel and institutions to control the local state of Hong Kong and penetrate its local society. The composite character of state-sponsored organizations is also beneficial for manufactured

---

[2] The full name is the Liaison Office of the Central People's Government in the Hong Kong Special Administrative Region. Its predecessor during the colonial era was the New China News Agency, which was widely recognized as the de facto party machinery in Hong Kong. See Loh (2010).

ambiguity, the concept developed by Krusewska and Ekiert in Chapter 2 of this volume, in the sense that the role of the party-state was rendered invisible without state personnel being seen to be involved.

As mentioned, the postcolonial era witnessed the growing maturity of civil society. The watershed was a mass rally on July 1, 2003, in which as many as half a million people protested against a local legislation on national security (which is required under Article 23 of the Basic Law) that was widely felt to threaten civil liberties. The event continued to mobilize civil society afterward, triggering wave upon wave of social protests. Beijing's decision to arrest democratization in Hong Kong further prolonged political conflict and deepened the legitimacy crisis of the HKSAR government (Lee et al., 2013).

The party-state responded by tightening its grip on Hong Kong through the Liaison Office, which stepped up its behind-the-scenes intervention in all areas of Hong Kong affairs, from taking an interest in the Hong Kong government's public policymaking, coordinating pro-Beijing political parties in fielding candidates for elections, deploying manpower for electoral campaigns, and funding social organizations. United front organizations were expanded in size and number, including mass associations and their subsidiary organizations, estimated to include hundreds of thousands of members in total (Wong, 2015, pp. 97–129). Hometown associations (*tongxianghui*) were revived and proliferated. New forms of populist organizations emerged, led by figures who portrayed themselves as unaffiliated concerned citizens.

Many of these state-sponsored organizations have actively participated in contentious activities in the form of signature campaigns, rallies in support of unpopular government policies, patriotic marches, protests, and counterprotests. Organizational leaders were often "foot soldiers" in making counterclaims to dilute the voice of civil society. Vocal representatives competed for media attention and airtime to shape public perceptions. Smear campaigns were carried out to attack opponents and intimidate potential opposition. Street-level clashes among the contending groups frustrated the moderate majority and alienated them from politics. In sum, a party-state–cultivated social sphere has variously played both reactive and proactive roles in counterbalancing the autonomous civil society.

12.4 OCCUPY CENTRAL MOVEMENT AND COUNTERMOBILIZATION THROUGH ANTI-OCM

Over the past three decades, Beijing has used tactics of delay in response to demand from the Hong Kong society for democracy.[3] The prodemocracy forces, which first arose in the 1980s, have been faced with multiple incidents of defeat and dismay.

---

[3] In this paper, the term Beijing refers to the Central Government of the People's Republic of China (PRC).

Despite Beijing's promise in 2006 for universal suffrage of the chief executive in 2017, there was widespread skepticism as to whether it would be a free election, as Beijing can manipulate the process and outcome through crafting the details of the electoral system. Particularly, Article 45 of the Basic Law (the mini-constitution of the Hong Kong Special Administrative Region, or HKSAR) stipulates that "[t]he ultimate aim is the selection of the Chief Executive by universal suffrage upon nomination by a broadly representative nominating committee in accordance with democratic procedures." It has long been the prodemocracy camp's worry that Beijing would try to manipulate the composition and operational rules of the Nominating Committee with the purpose of controlling the choice of candidates and even the outcome of the election. Beijing has also set down procedures for amending the relevant provisions, and in practice it has complete control over when to initiate the process and what constitutional reform plans to submit to the local legislature for voting.

The Occupy Central Movement (OCM) started with a commentary written by Benny Tai, a law professor at the University of Hong Kong, published in *Hong Kong Economic Journal* (a local newspaper) on January 16, 2013, in which he expressed pessimism that Beijing would honor its promise to let Hong Kong choose its own Chief Executive by free elections in 2017. Given that past strategies of contention, such as mass rallies, sit-ins, protests, and so on, had proven rather ineffective, he argued that Hong Kong people needed to step up their pressure on Beijing by arming themselves with "more deadly weapons." The article proposed a plan of nonviolent civil disobedience, with over 10,000 people gathering in Central (the central business district and financial center in Hong Kong), occupying the major roads and paralyzing the heart of the city's economy. His idea caught the media's immediate attention and soon went viral among prodemocracy activists. In March 2013, an organization named Occupy Central with Love and Peace (OCLP) was officially formed with Benny Tai, Kin-man Chan (a sociology professor teaching at the Chinese University of Hong Kong), and Reverend Yiu-ming Chu as the leading figures, signifying the formal inauguration of OCM. This soon instigated the party-state to launch a countermovement (anti-OCM) in order to mobilize the population to oppose to OCM.

In the social movement literature, the emergence and development of a movement are often explained by three variables: namely, political opportunities, mobilizing structures, and framing (McAdam et al., 1996). An examination of OCM and anti-OCM through the lenses of these three variables is useful for understanding the dynamics between them and the outcomes of the contention.

12.4.1 Political Opportunities

The OCM activists (or at least some of them) were acting not on the perception that there was an opening up of political opportunities. Quite the contrary,

The Prodemocracy Movement in Hong Kong, 2013–2015

since around 2008, Beijing had increased its repression against dissenting voices in the mainland, thus reversing a decade of loosening up political control. The leadership in China, paranoid about the destabilizing potential of increasing social unrest, resorted to heavy-handed measures "to nip any sign of unrest in the bud," a phrase popularly used by officials in defense of their stability maintenance (*weiwen*) policy. This negative atmosphere had set the stage for Beijing's approach toward the increasingly contentious civil society in Hong Kong and its demand for more democracy, and Xi Jinping's ascendance to power officially signified China's switch from soft authoritarianism to hard authoritarianism (Shambaugh, 2016).

These signs – that Beijing was unwilling to offer a more liberal political reform – made prodemocracy activists pessimistic about the future but also more determined to attempt a radical approach to pressure Beijing. There was a strong sense of threat and urgency over the cost of inaction, that Beijing would resort to a delaying tactics and reveal an offer at the last minute, thus making it too late for societal mobilization and negotiation.

Not surprisingly, Beijing was both threatened and outraged by OCM. It was seen as threatening particularly for its potential to evolve into a strong movement that united democratic forces across a wide spectrum, hence seriously limiting Beijing's room for maneuver. Among officials the dominant view was that giving in to such pressure would only encourage more provocative behavior in the future. In that regard, OCM strengthened the hardliners' voice within Beijing's policymaking circle.

The latest radicalization of the activists was thus met with a turn to repression on the part of the authoritarian state. The state–society dynamics were such that actions on both sides triggered a strong sense of threat and outrage against the other. Beijing perceived an urgent need for countermobilization in order to dissuade the general public from participating in OCM. Consistent with its tactics of SMMs in the past few years, it encouraged the proliferation of new social groups through offering resources and material rewards. For the agencies in charge of Hong Kong affairs such as the Liaison Office, it represented a chance for an increase in budget and influence. Establishment elites (or those who aspired to be become one) saw this as an opportunity to gain recognition and/or material reward.

12.4.2 Mobilizing Structures

The leaders of OCLP (the lead organization of OCM) had strong personal ties with many prodemocracy activists that facilitated the organization of collective action through overlapping membership and social ties. It was also able to count on a few prodemocracy media, including a couple of newspapers, online news, and social media, to propagate its ideas. OCLP leadership tried to build a platform engaging the prodemocracy political parties, civil society organizations, and the public in order to generate consensus among them. The idea was that if they could produce a consensus plan for the 2017 Chief Executive election, it would allow the prodemocracy camp to speak with one voice. Deliberative forums were held, followed by an unofficial referendum that would allow the public to choose their most preferred political reform plan. The latter was conducted through an electronic voting system developed by the Public Opinion Programme of the University of Hong Kong that would enable all permanent residents aged eighteen or older to vote via their mobile phones. Through these processes OCLP hoped to generate a unified reform proposal that enjoyed public mandate (particularly that of the moderate middle class), thus pressuring Beijing to get to the bargaining table and not to impose an electoral plan unilaterally. This ambitious idea, however, did not quite materialize. Throughout, there were conflicts between the moderates and the radicals. The radicals were more eager to push for a model that met their image of an ideal democratic system. The deliberation forums ended up attracting mostly members of radical groups rather than the average citizens.

In sum, the movement lacked organizational capacity to reach out to communities. The problem was exacerbated by a narrow social base of support, internal fragmentation, and the precarious balance it needed to maintain among public opinion, the different factions within the movement camp, and the party-state.

In contrast to the relatively weak mobilizing structure of OCM, the anti-OCM camp showcased the mobilizational strength of the party-state in Hong Kong. Delineating its formal organization can be difficult, however. While observers agree that the party-state was behind the countermobilization, we simply do not have enough concrete information to ascertain the precise role of the party-state or to unravel many of its operations, which remain a black box to researchers. Besides the Liaison Office which is tasked with managing and coordinating state-sponsored organizations, reports have also named the United Front Work Department of the CCP and the National Security Bureau as very active in infiltrating the society of Hong Kong, and both have very likely played key roles in organizing contentious activities.[4]

New social organizations were formed to carry out the anti-OCM initiative. Among them, the Silent Majority of Hong Kong set up in August 2013 soon became the de facto lead organization of anti-OCM. (It was reorganized as the Alliance for Peace and Democracy in July 2014.) Initiated by a former journalist Yung Chow along with some academics and businesspeople, it was not a highly structured organization but rather gave the countermovement the appearance of being part of civil society.

Anti-OCM relied on the mobilizing capacity of party-state agencies and the extensive organizational networks they had built over the years. State-sponsored organizations are often linked to extensive patron–client networks

---

[4] See *Insider Magazine*, Issue 31, July 22, 2014 (in Chinese).

The Prodemocracy Movement in Hong Kong, 2013–2015

or umbrella organizations representing many subsidiary organizations. Political parties are supported by local branches and neighborhood-based organizations. Investigatory reports have revealed the operation of a "responsibility" system whereby cell leaders were responsible for getting a certain number of people to turn up, often using monetary and other material rewards as incentives (Chan, 2014; Liu, 2014).

Beyond mobilization through state-sponsored organizational networks, anti-OCM was able to gain some support from the general public. Aside from the new organizations led by "new faces" that conferred an image of independence, the involvement of professionals (e.g. senior academics) also offered the movement some "credibility" to the public. One strategy of gaining support was through imitating the repertoires of contention commonly adopted by civil society in contentious activities, such as mass signature campaigns and rallies. There was also rather sophisticated use of social media, including Facebook and Youtube, to publicize their ideas.

12.4.3 Framing

Frame analysis is useful for analyzing the dynamics of the two camps. Snow and Benford (1988) argue that the construction of collective action frames involves "diagnostic framing" (stating what the problem is), "prognostic framing" (stating what tactics or solutions should be adopted), and "motivational framing" (stating the rationale for action).

For the OCM camp, diagnostic framing asserted that the prodemocracy movement has repeatedly utilized various forms of contention such as protests, sit-ins, mass rallies, mass gatherings, etc, to no avail. Beijing was likely to offer the Hong Kong people "fake universal suffrage" for 2017 by manipulating the composition of the Nominating Committee and the method of returning candidates. Prognostic framing called for a more disruptive form of contention to put pressure on Beijing. Motivational framing called upon the public to support the operation of occupying Central and to reject any arrangement short of genuine universal suffrage that met international standards.

OCM defined occupying Central as an act of civil disobedience, a rather unfamiliar concept for many Hong Kong people then. The idea of blocking the major roads of the business center represented a new repertoire of contention. OCM's typical supporters were young (below forty) and well-educated (with tertiary-level education). While the approach had considerable idealistic appeal among this demographic, it was a rather uphill battle for OCM leaders to obtain more general social support. The average citizen was worried about social disruption, deterred by the possible consequences of illegal behavior, and skeptical of its effectiveness in pressuring Beijing.

Benford and Snow (2000) regard experiential commensurability, meaning how the framing resonates with everyday experiences of the targets of mobilization, as one of the major factors affecting the salience of a collective action frame. The major problem with OCM's framing was in persuading the public to accept civil disobedience, a rather new and radical idea for the average population. Bridging, which is "the linkage of two or more ideologically congruent but structurally unconnected frames regarding a particular issue or problem" (Snow and Benford, 2000, p. 624), was attempted as a frame alignment process. OCM activists proclaimed that during the occupation they would surrender to police arrest as a way to morally indict Beijing for refusing to give Hong Kong democracy. They cited Mahatma Gandhi and Martin Luther King as their role models. Gandhi's idea of nonviolent resistance, in particular, was much proffered to the public. Through linking this mode of resistance with the principles of peace and nonviolence (which were well-recognized and resonated with the public), they attempted to bridge OCM with the city's more traditional modes of contention.

The skepticism of the general public provided space for the anti-OCM camp to promote their counterframe. While party-state agencies might have done a lot of the mobilization work behind the scene, most of the explicit counterframing was constructed by leaders of anti-OCM, particularly the Silent Majority of Hong Kong. Their focus was on countering the prognostic framing of OCM, arguing that Occupy Central was a violation of the right of innocent people, a destruction of the rule of law, and a disaster for the economy. They also questioned whether Beijing would bow to the pressure of the movement. They countered OCM's motivational framing by calling upon Hong Kong people to oppose occupying Central in order to defend democracy and the rule of law.

Exploiting the low resonance of OCM's collective action frame among the general public, anti-OCM forces adopted a strategy of frame amplification through skillfully appropriated terms such as democracy, civil rights, and the rule of law to justify their opposition, framing OCM as the enemy of these values. At the same time, they appealed to the fear of the public by painting a bleak picture of the consequence of OCM: economic loss, social chaos, lack of harmony, arrests of youths attracted to Occupy Central, all of which would destroy Hong Kong – the home that many people held dear. Through integrating the democratic discourse and the stability discourse, the framing by anti-OCM leaders captured the worry, fear, and pragmatism of a definite sector of the population. The Chinese name for the Alliance for Peace and Democracy (保普選反佔中大聯盟) means "The Protect-Universal Suffrage and Anti-Occupy Central Alliance,"[5] which portrayed the anti-OCM camp as the true defender of democratic values, dismissing the OCM camp's claim that universal suffrage under the framework prescribed by Beijing was fake democracy.

---

[5] This literal translation from the Chinese name appears in https://en.wikipedia.org/wiki/Alliance_for_Peace_and_Democracy_(Hong_Kong).

The failure of OCM to attract popular support could be seen in the tracking polls done by the Public Opinion Programme mentioned earlier. From April 2013 to May 2014, the percentage of respondents agreeing with the movement promoted by OCLP stayed at 24 to 25 percent most of the time, while those that disagreed increased from 51 to 56 percent (Public Opinion Programme, 2014). Arguably, anti-OCM has successfully countermobilized public opinion against OCM.

12.5 HYPERMOBILIZATION AND HEIGHTENED TENSION BETWEEN THE STATE AND SOCIETY

In the eighteen months after the idea of Occupy Central was made public, OCM was not able to gain strong support among the general public. OCLP's attempt to engage the moderate middle class in deliberative forums in order to afford them a voice in formulating the constitutional reform plan was largely a failure. Radical groups pushed for Occupy Central to be launched sooner rather than later. Student activist groups, namely, the Federation of Students (an organization that represented all university students) and Scholarism (a secondary-school students organization), were insistent that the nominating procedure for the election of the Chief Executive must include civic nomination, a demand that was seen by Beijing officials as a blatant violation of Basic Law Article 45 (which requires the candidates to be nominated by a Nominating Committee). OCM was thus confronted with internal frame disputes and low salience among the population.

At the same time, anti-OCM was gaining momentum. From June through September 2014, anti-OCM entered a state of hypermobilization. Various pro-Beijing organizations advertised their opposition against Occupy Central in newspapers. There were instances of intense street confrontations between opposing groups that turned violent at times. Silent Majority sent letters to all the school boards alerting them there were teachers encouraging students to participate in Occupy Central. In July, the Alliance for Peace and Democracy held a mass signature campaign and claimed that over a million signatures were collected. This was followed by a rally in August, which it claimed to have attracted 190,000 participants. What is more, the state-sponsored network was operating in a mode of "total mobilization," penetrating organizations such as business enterprises, mainland Chinese student organizations, etc. Critics regarded this as an adaptation of the *biaotai* (making explicit one's attitude) practice inherent in the party-state culture.

These activities of the anti-OCM camp, which largely operated behind the facade of civil society, were complemented by more overt state action. Party-state-sponsored newspapers and the mainland media (such as the *Global Times*) made strong-worded commentaries. The People's Liberation Army in Hong Kong staged multiple drills that mimicked operations in the crowded downtown of the city. The Secretary for Security and directors of various disciplinary forces visited Beijing and were received and praised by high-level officials. The Secretary for Education urged schools and parents not to let students participate in Occupy Central, and warned teachers that they could be arrested and would lose their teaching licences if convicted.

In June 2014, on the eve of the civic referendum organized by OCLP, the State Council of the PRC announced the *One Country, Two Systems White Paper*, in which it stated that all the major institutions in the HKSAR, including the executive, the legislature, and the judiciary, must be led by "patriots" and that the Central Government had "comprehensive jurisdiction" over Hong Kong. The tough-worded statements added fuel to an already very tense atmosphere. It was widely taken as a clear signal that Beijing intended to impose an extremely restricted arrangement for the 2017 election and reduce Hong Kong's autonomy.

In July, the influential online newspaper *The House News* that was sympathetic to OCM suddenly ceased operating after its founder Tony Tsoi was discovered missing for a weekend in mainland China. Allegedly under duress, Tsoi reappeared in public announcing and apologizing for his decision to close the newspaper.

These repressive measures actually backfired and helped boost OCM's dwindling public support. Days before the unofficial civic referendum was due to be held on June 22, POP's electronic voting system encountered large-scale cyber attacks (Olson, 2014). The sabotage was widely suspected to have originated from mainland China. Public outrage with the repressive atmosphere boosted the turnout to almost 800,000 people, a figure much higher than expected.

12.6 STATE REPRESSION AND POPULAR UPRISING

On August 31, the Standing Committee of the National People's Congress (NPCSC) announced its resolution regarding the 2017 election, in which it stated that majority support of the Nominating Committee would be required for a person to run for Chief Executive. This was tantamount to giving Beijing full power to control the process of nominating chief executive candidates. The prodemocracy political parties and activists regarded the resolution as completely objectionable and a clear indication that Beijing had no intent to offer Hong Kong real democracy. Beijing's decision further alienated the prodemocracy activists, both radicals and moderates. The tracking polls of the Public Opinion Programme (2014a) showed an increase in popular support of OCM (from 24 percent to 27 percent) and decline in those that were against it (from 56 percent to 54 percent) after the NPCSC announcement. Another opinion poll conducted by Centre for Communication and Opinion Survey (2014) of The Chinese University of

Hong Kong in mid-September showed a strong support of OCM among young people (46.7 percent for the 15–24 age group; 39.8 percent for the 25–39 age group). These were signs that the resolution of the NPCSC had radicalized the population, with more people inclining to express their grievance through drastic actions.

OCLP announced that they would soon carry out Occupy Central. Nevertheless, the organizers were still not hopeful that there would be a high turnout of participants. The grand plan of OCLP was to choose October 1, the National Day, to carry out their operation, with the expectation that only a few thousand people would be occupying the street. The choice of National Day was tactical: aside from its symbolic meaning, it was a public holiday and the actual disruption was reckoned to be minimal.

By then, some activists, particularly students, felt that OCLP's operation was too moderate. The Federation of Students announced that it would launch class boycott in all universities. Social mobilization spread to secondary schools, as students set up their own concern groups, organized class boycotts, and joined the mass gathering of the university students. To deter the activism of young students, the Alliance for Peace and Democracy set up a "Save the Children hotline" for informants to report any case of organized class boycott activities in secondary schools (with the implication that this could subject such students to disciplinary action by the school authorities).

On September 26, as students and protesters assembled at the front gate of the government headquarters, some students suddenly climbed into the fenced-off area outside the government building (a move they labelled as "reclaiming the civic square," as that area was once open space where many public protests had taken place). A few student leaders were arrested, and pepper spray and physical force were used to dispel unarmed students. Enraged citizens came to show their sympathy and support for the students, culminating in thousands of protesters, including the leaders of OCLP. On September 28 after midnight, OCLP announced that it would commence Occupy Central on the spot. This came as a surprise, as it departed from the original plan of launching a small-scale occupation in another location in Central on October 1. A large number of police blocked all roads and footbridges to prevent people from joining the protesters in front of government headquarters, and pepper spray was used to dispel the crowd. The police escalated their operation with the use of multiple tear gas grenades, inciting tens of thousands of protesters to take to the street and leading to the eventual occupation of major roads in Central and other areas of the city. The outbreak of the Umbrella Movement, as it was subsequently called, represented a dramatic turn of events that was beyond the original expectations of both camps.

12.7 BREAKING THE STALEMATE AND DEMOBILIZING THE UMBRELLA MOVEMENT

Another twist that led to the widespread occupation of roads was, that hours after the midnight of September 29, having fired eighty-seven teargas grenades, the riot police abruptly halted their operation and retreated. There were widespread media reports that in the midst of the clash the authorities in Beijing had prohibited the Hong Kong government from escalating the confrontation. Options such as the use of lethal weapons or the deployment of PLA troops in Hong Kong were ruled out by the highest authorities, which instead ordered a strategy of "no compromise" and "no bloodshed" to be adopted (Bradsher and Buckley, 2014). In the first week of the Umbrella Movement, as many as hundreds of thousands of citizens turned up at the "occupied sites" offering their support for the student leaders and the occupiers. Thousands of secondary school students participated in class boycotts; there were small-scale strikes initiated by some workers and shop owners in reaction to the government's crackdown.

Within the Hong Kong government, Chief Executive C. Y. Leung and the police commissioner were seen as the hardliners who preferred heavy-handed measures to deal with the protesters. From the moderate camp, Chief Secretary for Administration Carrie Lam agreed to hold a meeting with the student leaders. Her effort was nearly sabotaged by an instance of gang violence against protesters, which student leaders alleged to be government orchestrated (to be elaborated below). After weeks of negotiation and mediation involving unnamed third parties behind the scene, both sides appeared on a live-televised meeting, which Lam hoped would offer a goodwill gesture and a dignified climb-down for all parties. Instead, the student leaders rejected any symbolic concession and demanded that the NPCSC resolution be withdrawn. The meeting failed to break the deadlock, and the student leaders announced that they would continue with the occupation.

Lam had little room for maneuver in actuality, as the authorities in Beijing were in command of the political situation. Under the party-state's strategy of no negotiation and no repression, state-sponsored social organizations and agents were called upon to help demobilize the Umbrella Movement. Both Beijing and Hong Kong officials also reckoned that public support and tolerance would dissipate and the movement would burn itself out. Multiple organizations, some of them newly set up, intervened in the Umbrella Movement and confronted their activists. The most prominent was the involvement of gangsters in beating up protesters at various occupied sites. Investigations revealed that the gangs received handsome payment for the jobs (Cheng and Yuen, 2017). A "blue-ribbon campaign" was organized to counter the "yellow ribbon," the public symbol in support of the students and the Umbrella Movement. The blue-ribbon campaigners claimed to represent the public opinion in support of police's use of force to restore law and order. Organizations with evocative names such as "The Alliance in Support of Our Police Force," "Justice League," and "Loyalists Association" similarly advocated social support for police officers. Ironically, their members, often wearing blue ribbons, frequently caused violence, verbal abuse, and sexual assault at occupied sites. Other organizations, carrying names such as "Cherish Group," protested at universities and occupied sites against the academic and student leaders, often resorting to profanities to escalate confrontation with the opposing camp. Groups of protesters that appeared to be from mainland China were seen bused in to protest in places such as the headquarter of *Apple Daily*, a notable prodemocracy newspaper. The Alliance for Peace and Democracy was at the forefront in mobilizing public opinion against the illegal blocking of roads. Among its activities were rallies, meeting government officials, and a large-scale signature campaign in which they claimed to have collected over 1.8 million signatures.

Lawyers, merchants, coach companies, and taxi associations collaborated and successfully obtained injunctions from the court to clear roadblocks. While these plaintiffs looked like ordinary citizens that were harmed by the blocking of roads, reports revealed that they were politically affiliated with pro-Beijing political parties (Apple Daily, 2014). Finally, on December 11, the occupation was cleared and protesters were arrested.

In sum, state-sponsored social organizations and agents played a crucial role in the demobilization of the Umbrella Movement through acts of intimidation and violence, provoking confrontation and social division and through which the state was spared the need to escalate the use of force or negotiate with the protesters. Their impact can be further studied through two sets of poll figures. The tracking polls done by the Centre for Communication and Public Opinion Survey (2014) from September to December 2014, in which residents fifteen years old and above were randomly sampled and interviewed, show that the level of public support peaked in October after the riot police's use of teargas grenades; otherwise, the percentage of public support actually remained quite steady from early September (after NPCSC's announcement) to December right before the final clearance of the occupation. This shows that the operation of state-sponsored social organizations during this period had no particular impact on the level of public support toward the Umbrella Movement and that the support did not dissipate with time (see Table 12.1).

At the same time, when the same survey asked respondents in November and December whether the protesters should retreat, 67.4 percent and 76.3 percent respectively answered very much so/quite so respectively. This shows that while

TABLE 12.1 *Public support of the Occupy Movement*

	September 9–17, 2014 (N=1006)	October 8–15, 2014 (N=802)	November 5–11, 2014 (N=1030)	December 8–12, 2014 (N=1011)
Supportive/very supportive (%)	31.1	37.8	33.9	33.9
Unsupportive/very unsupportive (%)	46.3	35.5	43.5	42.3

Source: Centre for Communication and Opinion Survey (2014)

TABLE 12.2 *Survey on whether the Occupy Movement should continue or stop*

	Percentage (%)
Continue	24
Stop, use other ways to fight for universal suffrage	36
Stop, because the goals have been attained	8
Stop, because occupying is wrong	26

N=1005
Source: Public Opinion Programme (2014b)

the public's moral support for the Umbrella Movement remained steady, with time more people felt that the occupation should end. A survey conducted by the Public Opinion Programme (2014) in early November 2014 offers more insight. When asked whether the Occupy movement should stop, 36 percent said it should and people should use other ways to fight for universal suffrage; 8 percent said it should because the goals have been attained (see Table 12.2).

Taken together, one can infer that with time, more people were in favor of retreat for pragmatic reason: that continuing with the occupation would not help achieve the intended goal of fighting for democracy. In this regard, state-sponsored organizations played an important role in decreasing the public's support over the movement through increasing the cost of contention.

Another consequence of this demobilization process was the deepening of social division. The blue ribbon campaign successfully divided citizens into "yellow ribboners" (the pro–Umbrella Movement camp) and "blue ribboners" (the anti-Umbrella Movement camp). Arguments and tensions extended to family members, social circles, and social media where acquaintances "unfriended" each other due to their different political views. More importantly, being "blue" or "yellow" constructed the political identity of citizens based on ideological division and constituted the new political cleavage in the post–Umbrella Movement period.

12.8 THE AFTERMATH: RE-LEGITIMATION AND RE-EQUILIBRATION

With the clearance of the occupied sites, public governance appeared to return to normalcy. The HKSAR government still had to go through the remaining "steps" of political reform – i.e. to present a political reform proposal modelled after the resolution of the NPCSC and introduce a bill to the Legislative Council for approval with two-thirds majority support. According to the Basic Law, the final step of approving or rejecting political reform rests with the legislature of the HKSAR. The prodemocracy camp, which controlled just over one-third of the seats in the legislature, held the veto power over the reform (as the amendment to the relevant provisions requires a two-third majority).[6] For the party-state, the successful veto by the prodemocracy camp would be a blow to its authority and would render democratization a lingering issue of contention between the party-state and the Hong Kong society.[7] For the local state of Hong Kong, after such intense state–society confrontation, it badly needed re-legitimation through convincing the majority that the political reform proposal met the promise of democracy while blaming the prodemocracy camp for sabotaging the reform. The Alliance for Peace and Democracy, together with other organizations, continued to be strongly relied upon in campaigning for social support. After months of public campaign by both the Alliance and the Hong Kong government, public opinion remained divided. According to the tracking poll jointly conducted by three universities, 46.7 percent supported and 37.6 percent opposed the reform proposal in late April of 2015. By mid-June, the result was 47.0 percent in favor and 38.0 percent against the proposal.[8] The divided public opinion strongly supported the prodemocracy parties to veto the political reform in June 2015.

There were also state attempts at re-equilibration (Ekiert, 1996), i.e. restoration of political domination and stability after the partial breakdown of social order and loss of political control. This included punishing the culprits and deterring further acts of transgression. While over 1,000 people were reported to have been arrested due to unlawful activities, and quite a few leading activists prosecuted and sentenced to jail, under the "one country, two

---

[6] For details, see Basic Law, Annex II, www.basiclaw.gov.hk/en/basiclawtext/annex_2.html.
[7] A different speculation was that the party-state did not expect the prodemocracy parties to approve the political reform and that vetoing the proposal would actually allow it to further delay the process of democratization. While this might be the thought of some Beijing officials, there is no concrete evidence to show that the party-state actually preferred the reform proposal to be vetoed.
[8] For details, see "Joint University Rolling Survey on 2017 Chief Executive Election Proposal," www.hkupop.hku.hk/english/features/jointUrollingSurvey/.

systems" setting, arbitrary arrest and imprisonment were still not readily available as means for sanctioning dissidents.

Instead, state-sponsored organizations were deployed for a witch-hunt campaign. In late November, 2014, *Wen Wei Po*, a local party-state–sponsored newspaper, started a smear campaign against Professor Johannes Chan, former dean of the Faculty of Law, The University of Hong Kong, for his poor leadership as dean and for corroborating with Benny Tai (one of the leaders of OCM), even though Chan actually had no involvement in OCM or the Umbrella Movement. At that time, Chan was being recommended by the Search Committee to the University Council as the candidate for the next vice president of the University. Party-state–sponsored newspapers, street banners, protest signs, and social media campaigns launched fierce personal assaults against Chan's character, qualification, and competence. Members of the University Council were reported to have been under intense political pressure to stop Chan from being appointed. In the end, the Council went against procedural propriety to veto the recommendation of the Search Committee on Chan's appointment. Even that did not stop the president of the university from being castigated for failing to discipline his staff. Various protest groups continued to visit universities, demanding that the "black hands" be rounded up and punished.

Even though supporters and participants of OCM and the Umbrella Movement came from numerous universities, The University of Hong Kong, particularly its Faculty of Law, was singled out as the major target of attack. Styles of personal assault reminiscent of political struggles in communist regimes were used. The persecution was intended for its chilling effect, warning academics to distance themselves from political activism, and putting political pressure on universities to discipline their staff's political behavior. The political struggle against university personnel was apparently also an attempt of the party-state to penetrate the institutional infrastructure of universities that have hitherto afforded strong protection for academic freedom and independence but which in the eyes of the party-state have allowed universities to become bases of political subversion. Chan was also probably a scapegoat for party-state officials who had to be answerable to party authorities for the eruption of the Umbrella Movement.

12.9 CONCLUSION AND OVERALL ANALYSIS

In recent years, state-mobilized contentions have become a pertinent part of indirect rule by the party-state over Hong Kong. The major objective is to counterbalance the voice and impact of a contentious civil society that has demonstrated strong mobilizational potential. To compete with the local Hong Kong civil society for public support over major political and policy issues, one typical strategy is to deploy state-sponsored agents and organizations to exploit, construct, and augment social division. Unlike the

The Prodemocracy Movement in Hong Kong, 2013–2015

cases of Communist China and Poland discussed in this volume (see Chapters 2, 3, and 13), where workers were recognized as the legitimate revolutionary agent and class conflict (such as workers against students) could be readily deployed for the purpose of instant mobilization, social division – and hence political cleavage – had to be situationally constructed in the case of Hong Kong.

In many ways, the case of anti-OCM represents the pinnacle of the party-state's mobilization in Hong Kong. Anti-OCM's initial success in countering OCM was partly attributed to the inherent weakness of the latter, which was conceived in a situation of unfavorable political opportunities, weak mobilizing structure, and the lack of resonance from the mainstream population toward the movement's collective frame. On the contrary, anti-OCM was backed by the resources and mobilizing structures supported by the extensive state–sponsored network. Most importantly, its framing strategy intelligently appropriated the language and ideas that were well-understood and accepted by the mainstream population. Differed from some of the state–sponsored mobilization in the past, anti-OCM forwent the nationalistic frame, which tended not to be well-received by the mainstream local population. Instead, the counterframe deployed languages such as "rights," "rule of law," "democracy," "economic cost" to directly compete with civil society organizations to win social support. The necessary condition for such countermobilization to be successful was the presence of real social division (over the action of pressuring Beijing for democracy through occupying Central and civil disobedience). Anti-OCM built on and fortified this social division.

The subsequent hypermobilization led to public backlash. Reviewing its operation, one can query whether actions such as the cyber-attack were unwise and unnecessary, particularly in a situation where OCM was actually failing to attract public support. Also, state-sponsored organizations and agents tended to overmobilize (i.e. mobilize more than was necessary for achieving the goal) out of their competition for recognition and reward. These problems illustrate the limits of state-sponsored mobilization in a situation of indirect rule, where the mobilization work is "outsourced" and remote from the party-state's enforcement apparatus (unlike the cases of Poland and Communist China described in this volume; see Chapters 2 and 3). Other provocative actions might be necessary from the point of view of the party-state. For instance, the announcement of the *One Country, Two Systems White Paper* was probably intended to signal its policy turn toward stronger political control over Hong Kong. Mobilizing all their social organizations and establishment elites to participate in activities like signature campaigns could be seen as essential for disciplining elites and maintaining the cohesion of its united front. Thus, at this stage, the mobilization had gone beyond a reactive mode to being proactively used for signaling policy change and elite management. More importantly, while the hyper-mobilization had definitely intensified the atmosphere of confrontation between the state and society, the Umbrella Movement probably would not have occurred had the NPCSC not announced its extremely restrictive political reform decision and had the police not taken repressive measures against student protesters.

The subsequent stalemate between the state and the protesters can be understood as the outcome of bargaining failure between a strong civil society and a strong authoritarian state, between which there is no institutionalized or even effective informal channel of communication. The party-state's strategy of "no compromise, no bloodshed" was implemented through the deployment of state-sponsored organizations and agents to provoke confrontation, harassment, and physical assaults against the protesters, effectively demobilizing the movement through increasing the cost of participation and exploiting and augmenting social division. The success of this strategy was also much aided by the internal problem of the Occupy Movement itself. The Umbrella Movement was the second episode of the Occupy Movement, with an almost spontaneous change in leaders and repertoires of contention from OCM. While OCM was led by the three leaders of OCLP, the outpouring of public support was incited by their sympathy toward the student leaders, who then became the legitimate leaders of the Umbrella Movement. Deviating from the original plan of OCM, the repertoire of contention has changed from a small-scale occupation of roads for a short period of time to a large-scale defiance of political authority demanding the withdrawal of the decision of NPCSC. Accompanying this change in leaders and repertoire was the change in mobilizing structure into a form of "connective action" (Lance and Segerberg, 2012): the participants in the Umbrella Movement have quickly developed into self-organizing micro-communities, literally turning the occupied sites into anarchist communes, embracing the ideals of bottom-up participatory democracy. The political situation made it difficult for the student leaders to back down without significant concession from the government, still less to secure majority support from the unexpected massive number of protesters on any retreat plan.

After the occupation ended, the party-state continued to utilize state-sponsored organizations and agents to help regain political legitimacy and control over society following such major social upheaval in defiance of state authority. At this stage, state-sponsored mobilization also turned proactive. The social division constructed during the Umbrella Movement, dividing people into yellow- and blue-ribbon camps, endured as a source of political cleavage and provided the social basis for state-sponsored organizations to carry out their mission in re-legitimation and re-equilibration. Paradoxically, this rigidified political cleavage might have caused the state's failure in affecting public support in the battle for public opinion over the political reform proposal. Some analyses regard that, in such situations, battle for public opinion does not usually change the position of either side and that campaigns from both sides will often counterbalance and thus cancel out each other (Lee, 2015). The political struggle against university personnel provoked strong reaction among the academics and students who felt threatened by such political infringement, testifying to the limit of SMMs in achieving re-equilibration when there was a strong civil society. Indeed, in the later phase of re-equilibration (after 2016) the state did step in to assert its power directly, especially with the emergence of advocates for self-determination and separatism. Candidates were barred from running political offices through administrative procedures (Radio Free Asia, 2018); *Financial Times* journalist Victor Mallet was denied a work visa after hosting a talk given by the leader of a separatist political party (Reuters, 2018), and this party was latter banned on the grounds that it posed a threat to national security and public safety (South China Morning Post, 2018).

In conclusion, from the party-state's perspective, the mobilization of state-sponsored organizations and agents for contentious activities has at least the following advantages: new forms of organizations can be formed and new agents can be recruited when needed. As well, they can be deployed to construct new frames and thus new social division that are necessary for counterbalancing the civil society. This mode of operation is necessary for the party-state to counter an autonomous civil society where instruments for high intensity repression cannot be readily deployed. On the other hand, the operation carries limitation, as over-mobilization may occur as a result of internal competition among agents and failure of the state to control agents' behavior, thus leading to backlash from civil society. As well, such attempt to demobilize civil society and re-equilibrate state–society relations may lead to the remobilization of civil society activism and thus result in highly uncertain outcome in state–society dynamics. Where state-mobilized contention is ineffective, the state is compelled to impose its repressive power directly.

REFERENCES

Andrews, K. T. 2002. Movement-countermovement dynamics and the emergence of new institutions: the case of "white flight" schools in Mississippi. *Social Forces* 80: 911–936.

Apple Daily. (2014). Disclosing the background of the taxi association that applied for court injunction. October 31. https://hk.news.appledaily.com/local/daily/article/20141031/1891887.

Benford, R. D., and D. A. Snow. 2000. Framing processes and social movements: an overview and assessment. *Annual Review of Sociology* 26: 611–639.

Bennett, W. L., and A. Segerberg. 2012. The logic of connective action: digital media and the personalization of contentious politics. *Information, Communication and Society* 15: 739–768.

Bradsher, K., and C. Buckley. 2014. Beijing is directing Hong Kong strategy, government insiders say. *New York Times*, October 17. www.nytimes.com/2014/10/18/world/asia/china-is-directing-response-to-hong-kong-protests.html.

Cheng, E. W., and S. Yuen. 2017. Neither repression nor concession? A regime's attribution against massive protests. *Political Studies* 65 (3): 611–630.

Centre for Communication and Opinion Survey, The Chinese University of Hong Kong. 2014. Public opinion and political development in Hong Kong survey results. September 21. www.com.cuhk.edu.hk/ccpos/research/TaskForce_PressRelease_English_140920c.pdf.

Chan, E., and J. Chan. 2007. The first ten years of the HKSAR: civil society comes of age. *Asian Pacific Journal of Public Administration* 29: 77–98.

Derichs, C. (ed.). 2014. *Women's Movements and Countermovements: The Quest for Gender Equality in Southeast Asia and the Middle East* Cambridge: Cambridge Scholars Publishing.

Ekiert, G. (1996). *The State against Society: Political Crises and Their Aftermath in East Central Europe.* Princeton, NJ: Princeton University Press.

Kiang, K. S. (2011). *The Chinese Communist Party in Hong Kong Volume 1.* Hong Kong: Cosmos Books. (In Chinese.)

Law, W. S. (2018). Decolonisation deferred: Hong Kong identity in historical perspective. In Lam W. and L. Cooper, *Citizenship, Identity and Social Movements in the New Hong Kong: Localism after the Umbrella Movement.* New York: Routledge, pp. 13–33.

Lee, E. W. Y. (2019. United Front, clientelism, and indirect rule: Theorizing the role of the "Liaison Office" in Hong Kong. *Journal of Contemporary China*, published online, 19 December.

Lee, E. W. Y., J. C. W. Chan, E. Y. M. Chan, P. T. Y. Cheung, W. F. Lam, and W. M. Lam. 2013. *Public Policymaking in Hong Kong: Civic Engagement and State–Society Relations in a Semi-Democracy.* London: Routledge.

Lee, F. 2015. Did the battle for public opinion affect public opinion in the political reform? *Ming Pao Daily News,* June 25, A38 (in Chinese).

Leung, S. W. 1993. The "China factor" in the 1991 Legislative Council election: the June 4th incident and anti-Communist China syndrome. In S. K. Lau and K. S. Louie (eds.), *Hong Kong Tried Democracy: The 1991 Elections in Hong Kong.* Hong Kong: The Chinese University Press, pp. 187–235.

Leung, S. W. 1996. The "China factor" and voters' choice in the 1995 Legislative Council Election. In *The 1995 Legislative Council Elections in Hong Kong.* Hong Kong: Hong Kong Institute of Asia-Pacific Studies, The Chinese University of Hong Kong, pp. 201–244.

Liu, J. (2014). Were some Hong Kong marchers paid? BBC News, August 19. www.bbc.com/news/blogs-china-blog-28832294.

Loh, C. 2010. *Underground Front: The Chinese Communist Party in Hong Kong.* Hong Kong: University of Hong Kong Press.

Ma, N. (2011). Value changes and legitimacy crisis in post-industrial Hong Kong. *Asian Survey* 51: 683–712.

McAdam, D., J. D. McCarthy, and M. N. Zald (eds.). 1996. *Comparative Perspectives on Social Movements: Political Opportunities, Mobilizing Structures, and Cultural Framings.* Cambridge: Cambridge University Press.

McAdam, D., S. Tarrow, and C. Tilly. 2001. *Dynamics of Contention.* New York: Cambridge University Press.

Meyer, D. S. and S. Staggenborg. 1996. Movements, countermovements, and the structure of political opportunity. *American Journal of Sociology* 101 (6): 1628–1660.

Olson, P. 2014. The largest cyber attack in history has been hitting Hong Kong sites. *Forbes*, November 20. www.forbes.com/sites/parmyolson/2014/11/20/the-largest-cyber-attack-in-history-has-been-hitting-hong-kong-sites/#3342ae103fc4.

Przeworski, A., and F. Limongi. (1997). Modernization: Theories and facts. *World Politics* 49: 155–183.

Public Opinion Programme, The University of Hong Kong. 2014a. Survey on CE election and Occupy Central campaign (Sixth round). September 10. www.hkupop.hku.hk/english/report/mpCEnOCCw6/index.html.

Public Opinion Programme, The University of Hong Kong. 2014b. Survey on CE election and Occupy Central campaign (Seventh round). November 10. www.hkupop.hku.hk/english/report/mpCEnOCCw7/index.html.

Radio Free Asia. (2018). Hong Kong bans another election candidate over "implied support" for independence. December 3. www.rfa.org/english/news/china/candidate-12032018113911.html.

Reuters. (2018). Hong Kong press freedom in question as FT journalist denied visa. October 5. www.reuters.com/article/us-hongkong-politics-visa/hong-kong-press-freedom-in-question-as-ft-journalist-denied-visa-idUSKCN1MF0XH.

Shambaugh, D. 2016. *China's Future*. Cambridge: Polity Press.

Sing, M. (2010). Explaining mass support for democracy in Hong Kong. *Democratization* 17: 175–205.

Snow, D. A., and R. D. Benford. 1988. Ideology, frame resonance, and participant mobilization. *International Social Movement Research* 1: 197–218.

So, A. 1998. *Hong Kong's Embattled Democracy: A Societal Analysis*. Baltimore, MD: Johns Hopkins University Press.

South China Morning Post. (2014). As it happened: police estimate more than 110,000 marchers attended anti-occupy Central rally. August 19. www.scmp.com/news/hong-kong/article/1575403/live-anti-occupy-central-march-due-kick-amid-controversy.

South China Morning Post. (2018). Ban on Hong Kong National Party over "armed revolution" call met with both cheers and fear. September 24. www.scmp.com/news/hong-kong/politics/article/2165439/hong-kong-issues-unprecedented-ban-separatist-party.

Tarrow, S. 1998. *Power in Movement: Social Movements and Contentious Politics*. Cambridge: Harvard University Press.

Tsang, S. (ed.). 1995. *A Documentary History of Hong Kong: Government and Politics*. Hong Kong: Hong Kong University Press.

Wong, S. H. W. 2015. *Electoral Politics in Post-1997 Hong Kong: Protest, Patronage, and the Media*. Singapore: Springer Science+Business Media.

13

The Resurrection of Lei Feng
Rebuilding the Chinese Party-State's Infrastructure of Volunteer Mobilization

David A. Palmer and Rundong Ning

13.1 INTRODUCTION

Following the Sichuan earthquake of 12 May 2008, hundreds of thousands of volunteers spontaneously joined the relief effort – a loosely organized grassroots movement that caught both the Chinese government and international observers by surprise. A few months later, at the Beijing Olympic games, over 100,000 well-organized volunteers efficiently catered to the needs of visitors. With these two events, volunteerism became visible as a mass phenomenon in China. From then on, the state gave volunteering an increased level of support and legitimacy, in order to promote and channel volunteering as a form of social service. The Communist Party Youth League and the Ministry of Civil Affairs, with their networks reaching down to student cells in schools and residents' committees in the neighbourhoods, developed increasingly comprehensive and systematic programmes to recruit and deploy volunteers to care for the elderly, help out at major sporting and diplomatic events, give tutoring support for migrant children, engage in environmental cleanups, or travel as volunteer teachers to remote rural and ethnic minority regions. In 2012, the Politburo's Leading Group on Spiritual Civilization Building, following guidance from the 6th Plenum of the 17th Central Committee of the CCP, officially linked this mobilization with the 'permanent implementation' of the campaign to learn from the revolutionary hero Lei Feng, which was ramped up to a level unseen since the years immediately following the crackdown on the Tiananmen student movement in 1989. Volunteer mobilization has thus become a vehicle for the revival, reconstruction, and expansion of technologies of neo-

---

This article is an output of the project 'Volunteerism in China: Moral discourse and social spaces' funded by the General Research Fund of the Hong Kong University Grants Council as well as the Contemporary China Strategic Research Theme of the University of Hong Kong. We gratefully acknowledge the generous support of these two grants for the research and writing of this project.

socialist governmentality (Palmer and Winiger, 2019) through an organizational and propaganda infrastructure dating from the revolutionary era.

These infrastructures have long been considered by many Chinese (as well as foreign observers) as anachronistic relics of a bygone era of mass political campaigns, increasingly irrelevant to people's lives as individualistic consumers in the market economy who are highly cynical about appeals to 'Serve the People' (Ning and Palmer, 2020). Thus the puzzle posed by this phenomenon: could forms of voluntaristic mobilization derived from Maoist mass politics gain any traction in a depoliticized population with little inclination to invest itself in party-led activities? How and why has this infrastructure been redeployed, and what have been the consequences? This chapter traces the evolution of state-sponsored volunteer practices, discourses, and organizational forms from the Mao era until today. We pay special attention to the shifting representations of the revolutionary hero and model volunteer Lei Feng, as well as the incorporation of Western-derived conceptions of volunteering and volunteer management into the institutions of the party-state and its revolutionary rhetoric on altruistic service. We conclude that state-led volunteering in contemporary China paradoxically redeploys discursive and organizational legacies of revolutionary mobilization to attain the opposite goal of demobilization or depoliticization, channelling popular altruism and energies into forms of social service that reinforce market-driven governance and party-led nation-building. In comparison with the cases presented in this volume, this mobilization can be called 'pre-emptive' in that it aims to create a 'state-mobilized civil society' that absorbs the altruistic energies of the youth and middle class, filling the space that might otherwise be taken by independent organizations and networks that could, eventually, turn into oppositional social movements (see Perry, 2014; Xu, 2017). To use the typology presented in the introductory chapter to this volume, state-sponsored volunteering channels popular energies into an 'infrastructural mobilization' in order to assist the party-state in its project of society-building by means other than routine bureaucratic policy implementation and regulation. In contrast to many of the cases discussed in this volume, such as Hemment's study of the Nashi movement in Russia (Chapter 7) – in which the state lacks its own direct means of mobilization and tries to indirectly and covertly form and fund popular groups to carry out its agenda, sometimes with unforeseen consequences – here the role of the party-state is fully open and transparent. Rather than dissimulating itself behind purportedly independent popular movements, the Chinese Communist Party (CCP), in our case, attempts to openly and directly re-establish its organic connection to the grassroots, both symbolically and organizationally.

Volunteering in China, indeed, presents the coexistence of two realities of popular spontaneity and high levels of state mobilization. At one level, it can be seen as a poorly organized phenomenon, a movement in which individuals perform acts of service in a rather unstructured way. Many volunteers operate at an even more 'grassroots' level than NGOs and civil society movements, since their actions are usually temporary, their connections are often loose networks that are rarely organized formally, and, since the same individual often gets involved in several groups simultaneously or consecutively, their volunteer trajectories might not be encapsulated within a single organization or institutional formation.

At another level, however, volunteering is highly organized and institutionalized. Notably, the Ministry of Civil Affairs and the Communist Party Youth League – and, more recently, the Office of Spiritual Civilization – have been playing a significant role in mobilizing volunteers. Official discourse and policy reflect a strong will to organize and to institutionalize volunteers, to convert the party-state's network of mass mobilization and surveillance of youth and neighbourhood residents, notably through the Youth League and neighbourhood committees, into the institutional framework of volunteering. The deployment of the institutional network aims to channel this engagement, in ways that show both continuities and ruptures with revolutionary-era campaigns, in order to contribute to Chinese nation-building and reinforce the presence of the party-state at the grassroots.

As part of a broader research project on volunteering in contemporary China, this chapter specifically focuses on state-organized process of volunteer mobilization, rather than other, more autonomous organizations and forms of volunteer social engagement. It is based primarily on official discourses, documents, and press reports and reflects primarily the top-down perspective of the state. The discourses and experiences of volunteers themselves, based on interviews and ethnographic participant observation among educational volunteers organized in a wide range of programmes and organizations, both within and outside the party-state, are the subject of a series of forthcoming articles.[1]

In her work on volunteering in the United States, sociologist Nina Eliasoph has highlighted the contrast between volunteering, which tends to be apolitical, and more politicized forms of activism (Eliasoph, 2011; 2013). Volunteering has been actively promoted since the 1990s in the West and elsewhere as part of a neo-liberal restructuring of governance with the goal of drawing on the goodwill of grassroots volunteer efforts, in which individual and community 'self-help' are seen as the solution to social problems, rather than state interventions. While volunteers often consciously avoid discussing and acting on the political dimensions of the problems that they are trying to alleviate through their altruistic efforts, volunteering can lead to a deeper awareness of the structural political roots of social issues and draw volunteers into more activist and politicized forms of social action. Thus, while volunteering and contentious political activism are distinct categories, the boundaries between them can be fluid and ambiguous.

This is precisely the risk that has led the party to proactively take the lead in structuring the wave of volunteering. The genealogy and development of volunteerism in China are closely tied to the evolution and transformations of state-led mobilization from the revolutionary era until today. In the 1990s, the

---

[1] See, for example, Ning and Palmer (2020; n.d.).

promotion of modern forms of volunteering represented an attempt to move away from the politicized flavour of revolutionary forms of mass mobilization widely perceived as ritualistic and ineffective and thus was aligned with a global trend towards depoliticized volunteering and social engagement in the context of rising neo-liberalism. But 'neo-liberalism' is a problematic concept in China, given that the apparent retreat of the state in the first two decades of 'reforms and opening up' in the 1980s and 1990s, was a tactical move serving the longer-term aim of consolidating the rule of the party-state (see Palmer and Winiger 2019; Breslin, 2006; Nonini, 2008; Zhao, 2008; Tomba, 2014, pp. 18–19). By the early twenty-first century, indeed, and increasingly in the past few years, this 'neo-socialist' programme has been promoted by a party-state that is once again expanding its reach and increasingly drawing on and adapting the symbols, discourses, and techniques of control and mobilization of the revolutionary era (Pieke, 2009, pp. 9–10). In the case of volunteering, the goal is to activate and channel non-political forms of altruism and social service, while preventing such engagement from slipping into contentious forms of activism. What we witness, then, is a ramping up of the revolutionary legacy of the propaganda and infrastructure of political mobilization, in order to attain the goal of a *depoliticizing* and *non-contentious* mobilization.

When we speak of a *depoliticizing* mobilization, we contrast contemporary voluntarism to the Communist Party's heritage of revolutionary mobilization, which explicitly aimed to politicize the masses as full participants in the struggles of which the party was the vanguard. Indeed, the Communist Party under Mao developed a broad, deep, and multifaceted culture of voluntarism, in which the stirrings of popular protest at the root of revolutionary action were incorporated into the party's institutional mode of operation. The top-down, rational-bureaucratic diktat of a Leninist party is complemented by the free and enthusiastic rising-up of the masses to fight the enemy, to engage in class struggle, to build the New China, to feed the nation, to develop industry, to advance modernization, and so on. In its revolutionary history, the party gained experience in mobilizing striking coal miners against their capitalist bosses in the 1920s (Perry, 2012), peasants against landlords from the Jiangxi Soviet in the 1930s until the land reform movement of the 1950s (see, for example, Averill, 2006; Lin, 2009), intellectuals in the movement to go 'up the mountains and down to the countryside' 上山下乡 that took place in several waves from the Yan'an period in the 1930s until the Cultural Revolution in the 1970s (Bonnin, 2013), and military recruits against the American Imperialists in the Korean War (Junshi kexueyuan junshi lishi yanjiubu, 2000). These troops were called the 'Volunteer Army' *zhiyuan jun* 志愿军, in what appears to be the first usage in the Peoples' Republic of China of the term that is now used to express the concept of the 'volunteer'. The Red Guard movement can be seen as the climax of politicized Mao-inspired voluntarism in the early years of the Cultural Revolution, in 1966–7. This movement led to the formation of highly politicized youth and popular groups that eventually turned against each other, leading the country to the verge of a civil war.[2] The ultimate outcome was a cynical demobilization of the masses and, among the reformist party leadership under Deng Xiaoping, a visceral horror for any type of mass protest that, it was feared, could degenerate into another wave of fanaticism and chaos reminiscent of the Red Guards. This was one of the main fears that justified, for Deng, the ruthless suppression of the Tiananmen student movement of 1989 (Vogel, 2011). The challenge for the party in the post-revolutionary era, then, was how to mobilize the masses without politicizing them with potentially uncontrollable consequences.

13.2 OFFICIAL DISCOURSES ON VOLUNTEERING

The short book *Volunteers in Action*, published as part of the 'Stories of National Conditions' series (国情故事), provides an excellent window into how volunteering is recounted within party-state narratives of nation-building (see Zhang, 2009). The book begins with a chapter on '2008: Year One 元年 for volunteering in China', with portraits of volunteers conducting disaster relief at the site of the Sichuan earthquake and helping at the Beijing Olympic games. In the state narrative of the post-quake volunteers, the Chinese nation comes into expression through mutual help and compassion. The diversity of backgrounds – students, businesspeople, workers, peasants, freelancers, laid-off workers – all spontaneously arise to rescue their fellow Chinese. Young people of the post-Mao generation, previously seen as selfish individualists lacking a social conscience, reveal their altruism and their courage. Taxi drivers turn off their meters; droves of volunteers climb over landslides and mountains, risking their lives, reaching out to stranded victims, carrying food and supplies, offering first aid, sanitation, and psychological counselling. Crowds of volunteers flow into Chengdu from all over China, lining up to offer their services at the Red Cross, the Youth League, and improvised coordination offices of a network of local and national NGOs. Altogether, the number of volunteers was estimated by the China Social Work Commission to amount to 100,000 persons who came to Sichuan from other parts of China, while 1 million volunteers assisted within Sichuan, and 10 million persons across China participated in publicity, fundraising, and contributing and transporting materials. According to the China Youth Volunteer Association, 4.91 million persons volunteered nationally (Zhang, 2009, p. 6).

The stories of volunteers emphasize the mutual care of Chinese people from different classes, regions and ethnic groups. For example, one group of thirteen peasants from a village near Tangshan, Hebei, as soon as they heard news of the quake, embarked on buses and moto-taxis to Beijing, Zhengzhou, Xi'an, Chengdu and Beichuan to rescue victims isolated behind the mountains. Another group of ten peasants from Shandong loaded thirty-eight cases of

---

[2] On the Red Guards, see Andreas (2007); Walder (2009).

bottled water and fifty cases of instant noodles onto a tractor and set off for Sichuan, driving across China for four days and three nights until they joined the ranks of the on-site volunteers. Meanwhile, a millionnaire entrepreneur from Jiangsu donated 8 million yuan and organized for 60 bulldozers and 120 technicians to be sent from Jiangsu and Anhui to Dujiangyan, bringing along 2,300 tents, 23,000 radios, 1,000 TV sets, and 8,000 schoolbags, saving 128 lives. A seventy-three-year-old hospital director and his wife drove down from Yizhou in Hebei, carrying 300 types of drugs and 60 items of medical equipment. A twenty-three-year-old Tibetan from Aba descended to Deyang; organized other volunteers to carry the wounded, examine the victims, set up the tents, lay down the cots; and, with his own hands, carried stretchers holding the critically injured up and down the stairs of a hospital whose elevators had broken down. In these stories, rich and poor, peasants and millionaires, young and old, northerners and southerners, Han and Tibetans all come together in solidarity, saving lives, tending wounds, rescuing the body of the nation in a redemptive moment, a time when the Chinese could, in the midst of disaster, celebrate their moral goodness.

In her account of the Beijing Olympics, Zhang Chunxia emphasizes the patriotic enthusiasm of the youth, displaying Chinese goodwill and friendship to the world. Over 1 million applied to be volunteers when only 100,000 were required; of the applications, 70 per cent were from the post-Mao youth generation of only children (Zhang, 2009, p. 23). They were dispatched to the sports venues and to 'volunteer stations' throughout the city to carry out support work for the athletic events and to offer tourist information, translation, and first aid services. Praise for the Chinese volunteers by members of the IOC, and positive coverage by the overseas media, figures prominently. The participation of schoolchildren, the elderly, the handicapped, and scholars is highlighted, as are beautiful women: fashion models were trained for the flag-raising ceremonies, while a comely young woman was caught on camera, bringing water and comfort to a handsome blond foreign boy who had fainted on a sidewalk in the summer heat – she symbolizes the humanistic spirit of the Olympics and displays the inner spiritual beauty behind the beautiful appearance of the volunteer.[3]

Zhang Chunxia stresses that, in 2008, volunteering acquired a level of public recognition that had never existed before. Since the events of 2008, she says, society has shown a greatly increased level of openness to and respect for volunteering, and more common people are now joining the ranks of volunteers. She states that, after over a decade of the development of volunteering in China, the trend is for greater regulation, organization, and institutionalization of volunteering, in order to give it more 'rational' guidance and norms. But volunteering still lags behind the developed world: where about 40 per cent of Westerners take part in volunteer activities, the number of urban

---

[3] Zhang, 2009, pp. 38–9. On volunteers at the Beijing Olympics, see Chong (2011).

Chinese volunteers only amounts to 3 per cent of the urban population (Zhang, 2009, pp. 110–11). Thus, how could China gain ever-increasing numbers of volunteers, without causing social chaos? How could volunteering be better guided, regulated, organized, and institutionalized?

Tan Jianguang, a scholar in the Youth League's university system, writes that, with globalization, the rise of NGOs, and the emergence of global civil society, volunteerism as a form of social service spread beyond the West to other parts of the world. Tan notes that volunteerism in this context is closely tied to NGOs rather than to the government or business sectors, since volunteerism are the main workforce of NGOs and volunteerism cannot be forced on people by governmental fiat, nor can it be promoted by economic incentives. At the same time, he stresses that international NGOs often have political objectives and hope to promote 'Western-style democracy' in China. But most international NGOs, he stresses, have no political objectives and are motivated by humanism and charity. While being alert to the potential political motives of foreign NGOs, China cannot stem a global tide; it should absorb their positive elements and develop a 'volunteer service with Chinese characteristics', spread the advantages of socialist spiritual civilization, and change the current unilateral radiation of volunteer service outward from Europe and America to a diversified trend of development (Tan, 2005, pp. 4–5).

Tan Jianguang's account reflects the ambiguities of China's official approach to volunteering at the turn of the century. Western models of volunteering clearly presented an attractive solution to palliating for the shortcomings of the state in a market economy. Encouraging people to do good deeds was certainly something that should be encouraged – but how could it be done without undermining the political control of the party? How could volunteering be developed without becoming a 'fifth column' of Western democratization?

13.3 RETURNING TO LEI FENG

Party and state organs discussed these questions over the next few years and considered the experience of the previous three decades, in which, as described in Section 13.6, the party-state had already built a large infrastructure for recruiting, managing, and deploying volunteers. This infrastructure had adapted and built on mobilization techniques and methods inherited from the revolutionary era – notably, the campaigns for 'Learning from Lei Feng', an altruistic soldier who had been turned into a revolutionary saint in the 1960s (see Figure 13.1), as described in Section 13.4. The crystallization of this emerging official discourse on 'volunteer service with Chinese characteristics' can be dated to 2012, when the Politburo's Leading Group on Spiritual Civilization Building issued a document entitled 'Notification about Promoting the Lei Feng Spirit and Energetically Launching Voluntary Service Activities' (Zhongyang Wenming Ban, 2012). The document stressed that voluntary service was closely related with and very important for promoting

FIGURE 13.1 The iconic image of Lei Feng

the 'Lei Feng spirit', which was now to be promoted at an increasingly higher pitch.

At about the same time, the News Channel of China Central Television launched a series of reports named 'I Learn from Lei Feng, I volunteer' (*Xue Lei Feng, wo zhiyuan*). This program showcases people who kindheartedly help others, such as jumping into a river to save someone who was drowning. In addition to such 'ad hoc' actions of doing good deeds which are in line with the classic interpretation of the 'Lei Feng spirit', this series also highlights various kinds of more organized, systematic, and lasting actions and programs; more importantly, these reports make explicit use of the rubric 'volunteer'. For example, the episode broadcast on 7 April 2012 was about college student volunteers acting as guides and helpers in a hospital.[4] They all wore blue waistcoats, showing their volunteer identity, and were recruited directly by the hospital. In the same year when the program was aired, the same or slightly modified slogans of 'I learn from Lei Feng, I volunteer' served as the name of numerous governmental activities. Clearly, in this wave of promotion of the 'Lei Feng spirit', volunteering has taken a central place. This campaign marked the intensification of a campaign to re-integrate discourses and propaganda on the revolutionary tradition of serving the masses with the discourses and practices of 'volunteering', which had, from the 1990s until then, been evolving in an ambiguous space between state-sponsored mobilization and informal actions at the grassroots.

13.4 LEARNING FROM LEI FENG IN THE REVOLUTIONARY ERA

The 'Learning from Lei Feng' slogans and activities hark directly back to the Maoist era, when, starting in the early 1960s, promoting selfless sacrifice was elevated to a national campaign, at the centre of which stands a heroic yet mysterious soldier who died at the age of twenty-two. In this section, we focus on the historical shifts in the official discourse on helping others by 'Learning from Lei Feng' (LLF).

---

[4] The video is available at https://goo.gl/NwbMMJ (accessed 29 September 2017).

Prominent as he is, Lei Feng has not been studied extensively. Most of the existing literature in Chinese aims at interpreting the figure of Lei Feng in different ways as an instrument of governance.[5] Sociological research has focused on the ways in which the official and popular discourse of Lei Feng has changed with the social context.[6] These studies suggest that Lei Feng propaganda has become de-politicized since the 1980s and now places more emphasis on such personal virtues as diligence and helping others. However, they failed to notice how the Lei Feng movement was hybridized with the new social trend of volunteerism and has thus smoothly acquired a new life. Here we will briefly introduce the rise of LLF and its marriage with volunteer service.

Lei Feng (雷锋), originally named Lei Zhengxing (雷正兴), was born on 18 December 1940. He was orphaned at the age of seven. He began his career in his township government in 1956, at the age of sixteen. In 1960, when he was twenty, he was enlisted in the People's Liberation Army (PLA) and joined the CCP. During his service, he won numerous honorary titles and awards, including 'Chairman Mao's good soldier'. He reportedly died on 15 August 1962, hit on the head by a wooden column that had been accidentally struck down in a collision by a military truck. Most of the propaganda about him was launched after his death.

Lei Feng had already been the subject of one major article in the *People's Daily* (*Renmin Ribao*) before his death (RMRB, 1961, p. 4), in which he was described as a warm-hearted and diligent soldier who had endured a miserable childhood to become a hard-working and enthusiastic young 'builder of socialism'. The article relates that Lei Feng once insisted on donating 200 yuan to a people's commune. When the leader of the commune finally accepted his donation and asked his name, he simply replied, 'I used to be an orphan, now I'm a soldier of the PLA.' The article finished with two other short stories about him. One told about how he had accompanied an elderly woman who had lost her way back to her home; the other told of him stopping to help the workers at a construction site while on his way to the hospital. Lei Feng's remarks and the two stories were constantly cited in subsequent LLF campaigns, until they became among the most widely known citations from the press in the revolutionary era.

While these acts of altruism are what Lei Feng is most remembered for today, the article also contained other stories about him that cast him firmly into the revolutionary narratives of his time. For instance, he was the leader of a children's group in 1950. During a struggle session against a landlord of his village, who had slashed the hands of Lei with a knife when he had tried to stop the landlord's dog from eating his meager meal, an 'intense hatred surged into the heart of this ten-year-old boy; he jumped onto the stage, stretched out his wounded hand, grabbed the neck of that landlord whose [exploitation] had

---

[5] See, for example Chen (2010); Hua (1990). For a more detailed literature review, see Liu (2013).
[6] Examples include Lu (2013); Chen (2008).

caused the death of his mother; and condemned his crimes. With his own eyes, he watched as the People's Government, in accordance with the law, shot dead that evil landlord, taking revenge for him and for countless class brothers.'

Soon after his death, his deeds were publicized extensively in Liaoning province, where the army troop in which he served was stationed (RMRB, 1963a, p. 1). Then, on 21 January 1963, around five months after his death, the Ministry of Defense approved naming Lei Feng's squad after him (RMRB, 1963b, p. 2). During the naming ceremony, General Du Ping (杜平), the head of the Department of Politics of Shenyang division of the PLA, called on all the youth in the squad to launch a movement to learn from Lei Feng. At the same time, an exhibition hall about Lei Feng's life was inaugurated, which featured memorial inscriptions written by Luo Ruiqing (罗瑞卿), the chief of staff of the PLA, and Song Renqiong (宋任穷), the secretary-general of the Northeastern Bureau of the Central Committee of the CCP.

Despite the fact that Lei Feng was still a regional hero at this time, these inscriptions showed recognition of Lei Feng from the highest leadership in China. In February, the movement became nationwide in scope. On 7 February a front page article of the *People's Daily* detailed how influential the publicity activities aboutABei Feng had been in Liaoning province. An enriched version of the article published in 1961 and an editorial extolling him also appeared on the second page. Excerpts from his diary and a set of photos of him were published on page five. In the following two months, the *Peoples' Daily* published articles every week calling on the masses to learn from Lei Feng. One of the most frequently cited phrases from Lei Feng's diary was his resolution to become 'a screw that never rusts' for the revolution. This phase of the campaign culminated on 5 March, when the *People's Daily* reported that Mao Zedong, Zhou Enlai, and other party and state leaders had written inscriptions to promote 'Learning from Lei Feng' on the front line. From then on, 5 March was designated as Lei Feng Memorial Day, and various activities would be held across the country on this date every year.

The content, implications, and discourses of LLF today, however, are quite different from fifty years ago. Lei Feng was all too perfect. Then what exactly did the party want the masses to learn from him? The answers have varied dramatically with the times.[7]

Initially, LLF was a highly politically charged campaign. In the 1963 announcement of the campaign in the PLA, the soldiers were exhorted to learn the following four points from Lei Feng: (1) to be firm in one's class position, loyal to the party, to Chairman Mao, and to the revolutionary spirit of liberating humanity; (2) to put the interest of the party first, to base oneself on the needs of the revolution, to resolutely become a 'screw that never rusts' and wholeheartedly serve the people; (3) to uphold the noble communist virtues of

---

[7] For a more detailed description and analysis of this change, please see Chen (2008) and Liu (2013).

simplicity, hard work, self-abnegation and altruism; (4) to study the works of Chairman Mao with effort and enthusiastically accept the party's indoctrination, to be strict to oneself and adopt a spirit of learning and self-improvement (RMRB, 1963c, p. 1). The focus was almost entirely on loyalty and service to the party and the people; warm-hearted help to others that would, much later, become the focus of LLF campaigns was still marginal in the LLF movement.

During the Cultural Revolution, the political significance of Lei Feng was most salient, and he was used as a token in political struggles (see Liu, 2013). This was most clearly shown by the fact that Lei Feng was invoked to justify two events instigated by opposing factions: the attack on former PRC president and senior party leader Liu Shaoqi in 1966; and the sacking of the 'Gang of Four' in 1976. During the Cultural Revolution, Lei Feng was presented not as a helping hand but as a diligent builder of socialism who always followed the party line without question; the evocation of direct service to others was downplayed.

13.5 DEPOLITICIZING LEI FENG, 1978–1981

After 1978 and the launch of the Opening-up policy, the LLF campaign was gradually depoliticized and turned into the promotion of moral deeds at a personal level. Admittedly, most of the LLF discourse at that time was still highly political, but new interpretation of LLF was emerging. A new slogan was attached to the campaign: 'Establish a new atmosphere, do good deeds' (*Shu xinfeng, zuo haoshi*, 树新风, 做好事) (RMRB, 1978, p. 1). This was originally the title of an activity for youth, proposed by the Ministry of Education and other state agencies, during the winter break and Spring Festival of 1978. The activity was aimed at pushing the Lei Feng campaign to a 'new climax', in order to further eliminate the 'poisonous influence of the Gang of Four' and restore the lustre of the revolutionary tradition. The proposal contained three detailed components which were in stark contrast to the initial focus of the campaign in 1963: (1) during the spring festival holiday, each person, according to their personal circumstances, was encouraged to do one meaningful deed for his people's commune, factory, school, work unit, or the masses; (2) during the holiday, to visit and comfort relatives of revolutionary martyrs, PLA soldiers, teachers, and comrades who were still working during the festival; (3) Red Guard organizations in schools and in party units,[8] and teams of sent-down youth in the countryside, could organize reading meetings, singing gatherings, scientific experiments, or meet exemplars and heroes. The overtly ideological and political elements of the campaign, if not completely eliminated, became less obvious; modest acts of direct care to others were emphasized instead of revolutionary grandstanding. In fact, the third component of the plan seemed to

---

[8] This is a literal translation of the original news report in the *RMRB*. The Red Guards had been largely demobilized as early as 1968, and the wording here might be referring to the remnants of Red Guard groups.

The Resurrection of Lei Feng

liberate the 'red guard' groups and the sent-down youth from purely political activities.

Indeed, the reports about LLF following the appearance of the new slogan were largely about outstanding, diligent, or warm-hearted people; they no longer mentioned whether they enthusiastically read Mao's works or if they actively criticized class enemies. This signalled the gradual depoliticization of the LLF campaign: the regime had decided to abandon class struggle, to move away from the turmoil and conflicts of the Cultural Revolution, and to release the people's energies into the market economy.

Revolutionary ideology and mass political mobilization fit uncomfortably with the new orientation. At the same time, the increasingly self-interested and individualistic pursuit of private gain in the market economy were seen as having a corrosive effect on public morality and on the collectivist ethos. The party thus outlined a complement to the construction of 'material civilization' in a campaign to construct 'spiritual civilization', an ambiguous category that encompassed both ideological work and increasing the population's level of education, culture, manners, and civility (Palmer and Winiger, 2019). Under the category of spiritual civilization, the moral resources of the revolution would, during the next two decades, be converted into the depoliticized public virtues of a market economy and consumer culture – and this would include the transformation of Lei Feng from a loyal 'nail' of the party into a model of unreflexive help to others.

Since the 1980s, the LLF campaign increasingly emphasized acts of community service. On 4 March 1980, one day before the Lei Feng Memorial Day of that year, some 30,000 middle and primary school students in Beijing went out to clean streets, help the elderly, and publicize traffic rules – activities that would be called 'voluntary service' today. The *People's Daily* reported the event and cited a remark from a passerby: 'the Lei Feng spirit has come back to the youth' (RMRB, 1980, p. 4), an expression that would reappear in the *People's Daily* in the same period next year (RMRB, 1981a, p. 4). It was not until this point that the LLF campaign became less emphatic on being loyal to the party and highlighted more, if not solely, the moral qualities related with doing good deeds.[9]

Another step was made in the 1980s as well. Before this time, the LLF campaign referred more often to individual acts. In the 1960s, there were hardly any reports about people forming groups to help others; rather, they highlighted exemplary individuals. 'LLF groups' began to appear in news reports from the mid-1970s on and were extensively publicized in the 1980s. The first 'LLF group' was reported in 1973. This group belonged to the Guangzhou People's Trolley Bus Company and consisted of twenty-two members who were primarily bus attendants. In the report they narrated how the deeds of Lei Feng inspired them to be more kind and helpful to bus

---

[9] The public speeches given by political and military leaders continued to attach various virtues to Lei Feng, such as studying hard and being faithful to Marxism, but most reports of 'Lei Feng cases' in this period were now about helping others.

passengers, to give them detailed directions, to return lost wallets, and so on (RMRB, 1973, p. 3). And yet the report did not describe any systematic group work done by them, so coordinated volunteering was unlikely the primary mode of their service. Moreover, 'LLF groups' were rarely mentioned in the *People's Daily* before 1980. That year, however, an article reported that PLA troops in Xiamen organized 'LLF groups' to help with providing service to tourists. These groups also regularly helped to repair damaged buildings and to maintain parks. After this report came out, the phrase 'LLF groups' showed up repeatedly in the *People's Daily*. Groups with other titles emerged as well. A 'Youth Service Corps' (YSC, *qingniang fuwu dui* 青年服务队), for example, was first reported in 1981 (RMRB, 1981b, p. 3). According to this article, the first YSC arose from branches of the Youth League in a bicycle factory in Shanghai. The members of this YSC first helped fellow workers in the factory with daily chores such as repairing bikes, haircutting, washing clothes, and so on. Soon other factories organized their YSCs as well, and they offered their service outside the factories. They helped in hospitals, schools, army barracks, and ports. In an article published three months later, it was reported that more than 6,000 Youth Service Corps had emerged in Shanghai. These groups marked a new phase of LLF, in which helping acts were carried out in groups, and this practice was recognized and vigorously publicized. This transition rendered the organizational structure of traditional LLF more powerful to mobilize and manage people to offer help, and it would facilitate the shift towards the volunteer movement in 1990s.[10]

13.6 THE CATEGORY OF 'LABOUR BY OBLIGATION' (YIWU LAODONG)

Corresponding to this trend, the term 'yiwu laodong', once closely associated with LLF but separated from it during the Cultural Revolution, was resurrected in the 1980s. This phrase has an ambiguous meaning. Literally, it means 'obligatory labor'. If the labor is obligatory, one has no choice but do it. However, the usage in the Chinese context by no means implied compulsion. Nearly all the reports related to *yiwu laodong* suggest that, despite the obligatory implication in the name, the work was done ad hoc and out of willingness. Thus *yiwu* or 'obligatory' in this term does not mean a burden or a lack of choice. Rather, such labor was an 'obligation' in the sense that material or financial reward to the laborers was neither necessary nor desirable. The word implies that, out of a deep sense of obligation to serve the party, the state, and the people, one voluntarily offers help. Compared to the earlier discourse on 'doing good deeds', 'labor' in this phrase also carried a subtle change. While helping an elderly person cross the street or offering someone a seat in a bus

---

[10] On the LLF campaigns of the early 1990s, see Li and Geng (1993). On the ironic appropriations of Lei Feng in Chinese pop culture, see Jeffries and Su (2016).

The Resurrection of Lei Feng

could well count as good deeds, they are hardly 'labor' in the formal sense of the term. Labor implies systematic work and usually takes place in organized groups. Specifically, *yiwu laodong* includes such activities as working for construction projects, planting trees, and reaping for farmers. Therefore *yiwu laodong* was a very sophisticated expression connoting patriotism, willingness, complexity of the work, and teamwork at the same time. It almost captured the entire essence of what would be called 'volunteerism' today.

It should be noted that *yiwu laodong* came into public use much earlier than 'learning from Lei Feng'. Reports about *yiwu laodong* can be found in the *People's Daily* going back to 1947. The term was also associated with the earliest reports on LLF: on 16 March 1963, when LLF was still in its first high tide, the term was first used in conjunction with LLF in the *People's Daily*. The original sentence went 'ten members of the Chinese Communist Youth League and young people spontaneously organized a *yiwu laodong* group and helped clean the workshops'.

However, for most of the time before the 1980s, especially during the Cultural Revolution, *yiwu laodong* referred to volunteerism in other countries in the Soviet Bloc. Starting from the 1980s, the term was used less for describing foreign activities and more for domestic ones. Indeed, *yiwu laodong* heralded the emergence of volunteerism in public discourse in the 1980s. The stress on intentional service is the first step of LLF on the road to incorporating volunteerism.

13.6.1 Emergence of the Category of the 'Volunteer' in the 1990s

Although the 1980s had seen the emergence of a conception of organized unpaid service activity that prefigured the modern notion of volunteering, the Lei Feng and *yiwu laodong* campaigns still had the form and coloration of mass political campaigns and propaganda that were increasingly seen as meaningless formalism, with exhortations to 'serve the people' seen as being completely out of sync with people's enthusiastic rush to make money by any means. Most Chinese today remember *yiwu laodong* as activities such as that attended by one of us in 1993 in Chengdu, where, on LLF day, teachers and students of a school were instructed to uproot plants from one part of the schoolyard and replant them in another location, in what seemed to be a futile exercise mostly enjoyed by students as an opportunity to get out of the classroom on a springtime Saturday morning.[11]

In the late 1980s, however, residents of Shenzhen and Guangdong imported more individualistic discourses and practices of volunteering from Hong Kong.[12] In those territories, volunteering is called 'yigong' 義工 – which also translates literally as 'work by obligation' but, in the Hong Kong context, is the term used to convey the Western category of 'volunteering', often carried

---

[11] The work and school week was still six days long at that time.
[12] United Nations Volunteers, 1999. This unpublished report contains a detailed description of volunteerism in China in the late 1980s and early 1990s.

out by religious groups and charities. Exchanges with Hong Kong thus played a major role in facilitating the semantic and conceptual shift from the revolutionary obligation to sacrifice for the collective, to less politicized and more individualistic conceptions of volunteering. In one source, which focuses on Guangdong, the 'first' volunteer service in China is identified as a group of Lei Feng enthusiasts who, in 1987, tired of the 'political movement' flavour of Lei Feng activities and, after reading books about volunteer service overseas and consulting with Hong Kong volunteer groups, decided to set up a telephone hotline, the 'hand-in-hand youth hotline service' ('手拉手'青春热线电话服务) to provide psychological counselling to people in need, with the support of the Guangdong branch of the Youth League. In 1990, the first independent volunteer association, the Shenzhen Volunteer Social Service Federation, registered with the Shenzhen Civil Affairs Bureau.[13] This association's founders included lawyers who were familiar with foreign experiences of NGOs and who were in touch with Hong Kong volunteer associations.[14] The association was, in its early years, lodged in the Municipal offices of the Youth League and primarily offered a hotline service. When the Municipal Party leader first met the group in 1994, he expressed strong support for the organization, which led to funds and office space being allocated, staff being hired, and the expansion of services into several new areas, including a volunteer teachers' corps (义工讲师团), a volunteer artist troupe, and so on (Ding and Jiang, 2001).

In the early 1990s, several municipalities in Guangdong experimented with new ways to celebrate Lei Feng Memorial Day on 5 March. In Jiangmen, groups from Hong Kong and Macau and overseas Chinese groups were invited to share the traditional culture and customs of overseas Chinese, under the theme of 'caring for our overseas relatives', and also to provide examples and models of volunteer service, leading to the establishment of the first rural youth volunteer service centre, in the Xinhui district of Jiangmen. Similarly, Zhuhai invited volunteer groups from Hong Kong and Macau to establish pilot projects. Shantou used the visits of overseas Chinese to promote philanthropy and volunteer service.[15]

Meanwhile, in north China, the term of *zhiyuan* started to acquire the connotations associated with the modern concept of 'volunteering' and would become the preferred term in official discourse to designate the practice. The first 'volunteer organization' in China is traced in the official literature as having been formed in March 1989 by thirteen members of the residents' committee of a lane in Tianjin (天津市和平区新兴街朝阳里), who organized a group of forty to fifty volunteers, the 'serve the people volunteer group' (为民服务志愿者小组) to help with lone and widowed elderly, the handicapped, and people with special needs in the neighbourhood. The earliest activities were helping the

---

[13] The name in Chinese was 深圳市青少年义务社会工作者联合会. It changed in 1995 to 深圳市义务工作者联合会 and again in 2005 to 深圳市义工联合会.
[14] Tan (2005), pp. 10–11.   [15] Tan (2005), p. 52.

elderly to buy and deliver vegetables and coal (Zhang Chunxia, 2009, p. 61; Tan Jianguang, 2005, p. 10).[16]

In 1990, the Asian Games were held in Beijing. Of all the 17,000 staff of the organizing committee, most were actually volunteers. However, the official report used the phrase '*zhiyuan renyuan*' (志愿人员, voluntary personnel) instead of 'volunteers' (*zhiyuanzhe* 志愿者) (RMRB, 1990, p. 4). The first *People's Daily* article dedicated to 'volunteers' per se (*zhiyuanzhe*) appeared in 1992. The report described volunteers who were active in helping residents in need in many neighborhoods in Hangzhou (RMRB, 1992, p. 4). Citing an old member of the residents' committee, the journalist wrote 'Here, "Learning from Lei Feng" is no longer a seasonal song but a daily show!'

Indeed, this quote served as an overture for a national campaign starring millions of volunteers across the nation in the following decades. The emergence of youth volunteers is traced in the official literature to 19 December 1993, when, in preparation for the spring festival peak season, 20,000 youth, holding flags with the words 'youth volunteer' 青年志願者, provided help to travellers in 33 trains and 120 stations along the Beijing–Guangzhou line (RMRB, 1993, p. 4). Subsequently, 40,000 secondary school and university students were deployed on all major lines and stations during the Spring Festival rush. Shortly thereafter, on Lei Feng memorial day of 1994, which inaugurated the two-day weekend in China, over 10 million youth volunteers were mobilized to conduct labour in homes, farms, and factories (Zhang, 2009, p. 64).

13.6.2 Institutionalizing volunteerism

Volunteering was not only a category deployed in official discourses and large-scale event mobilisation; increasingly systematic efforts began to organize volunteers on a permanent basis. The establishment of the Tianjin volunteer group (described in Section 13.6.1) in 1989 was followed by the successive establishment of neighbourhood volunteer organizations throughout China until, in 2005, the Commission on Community Volunteers of the China Association of Social Work was formally established. According to figures compiled by the Ministry of Civil Affairs, by December 2007 over 270,000 volunteer organizations had been established, triple the number from the year before. The number of community volunteers was estimated at 20 million, including over 5.67 million 'registered volunteers'. In December 2007, a system of registration and management of volunteers began to be implemented nationally (Zhang, 2009, p. 58; Ding and Jiang, 2001, p. 126; see also Tan and Zhou, 2008, pp. 18–23). The growth in numbers, organizations, and activities

---

[16] By the early 2000s, this 'volunteer's association' (志愿者协会) worked to help residents find jobs and provided them with health training. Every year the association conducted a survey of the residents' needs; and at the entrance to each building, a list of resident volunteers and contact information was posted.

was an expression of the growing interest among China's middle classes for engaging in some form of helping activity – an interest that the party-state was learning to structure and to channel through the deployment of its official volunteering infrastructures. The volunteer movement, however, was far from limited to state-sponsored initiatives; it was also manifested through the upsurge in grassroots networks and NGOs (Hsu, 2017). Thus, while the 2008 Sichuan Earthquake and Beijing Olympics gave the phenomenon of both grassroots and state-organized volunteering an unprecedented public visibility and legitimacy, it reflected a trend that had been building up for the past two decades.

As Elizabeth Perry has noted, 'Chinese university students are at present devoting more energy to community service than to political mobilization. Hostile as the top leadership is towards the whole idea of civil society, the Communist Party-state's survival has actually been prolonged by its emergence' (Perry, 2014, p. 217). This has been largely thanks to the regime's efforts to take the initiative to organise and control community service opportunities. At present, in spite of the large number of volunteer organizations with little or no background in the party or the government, state-driven volunteering programs are still among the most influential and most popular ones in China. The Chinese Communist Youth League appeared before, the Ministry of Civil Affairs (*minzhengbu* 民政部), and the CPC Central Committee's Central Commission for Guiding the Construction of Spiritual Civilization (official English name: Central Commission for Guiding Cultural and Ethical Progress) (*Zhongyang jingshen wenming jianshe zhidao weiyuanhui* 中央精神文明建设指导委员会 or 中央文明委) are the main state agencies promoting volunteerism. The first, an affiliate of the CCP, aims to govern, organize, and train the youth of China as future party members and cadres. The second is a branch of Chinese government focusing on the management of social work, social welfare, and social organizations. The third is a ministry-level organ of the Central Committee of the CCP, which, since its establishment in 1997, has been tasked with civilizing missions such as enhancing the civility of towns and cities, embellishing the rural and ethnic character of villages, promoting 'civilized families', 'civilized work units', and 'civilized campuses', improving the civilized behavior of tourists, enhancing trust between people, and encouraging volunteering (Zhongguo Wenming Wang, 2016).

There is also often a parallel infrastructure of agencies and programs at the provincial, municipal, county (*xian* 县), and even more local levels of government. Local governments may have their own versions that follow the general ideas of the centrally promoted programs. Therefore, there is an effervescence of volunteer programs with different names, aims, and types of people under the same banner of a central program.

Volunteers are a major component in the organization of major events and sports meets. This practice began with the Beijing Womens' Summit in 1995, for which the Youth League recruited thousands of volunteers from schools, universities, and work units in Beijing; this was the first time this approach was used to welcome foreign visitors and give a smiling image of China. Other major events include the Kunming World Horticulture Exhibition of 1999, the *Fortune* forum in Shanghai in 2001, the Beijing Olympics of 2008, and the Shanghai Expo of 2010 (Zhang, 2009, pp. 75–6; Ding and Jiang, 2001, pp. 149–54). Overseas volunteer service began in 2002, with volunteers of the Youth League being sent to Laos. By 2009, 300 volunteers had been sent to Myanmar, Ethiopia, Guyana, and other developing countries, for periods of six months to one year, to serve in the areas of Chinese-language education, health, computer training, etc. (Zhang, 2009, p. 78). A widely known Chinese international agency, the Confucius Institute (CI), which aims at promoting Chinese language and culture in other countries, also recruits a large number of volunteers each year from China to teach Chinese in its overseas branches. The CI recruits its volunteers independently from the state institutions already mentioned. Instead, it relies heavily on the educational agencies at provincial and lower levels for recruitment. Universities also play an indispensable role in this process, for fresh graduates are the most important source of new volunteers for the CI, and it is the universities that directly arrange the selection and recruitment of new volunteers. Intriguingly, in the statements addressed to prospective volunteers, the CI does not mention Lei Feng. Instead, it is the personal growth and transformation of volunteers themselves, triggered by the experience of volunteering, that are foregrounded.[17] This absence of Lei Feng discourse reflects the flexibility of the state organizations in recruiting new volunteers, which adds to its effectiveness in absorbing and channelling the force of fervent youth through volunteer programs.

Among the various state institutions with volunteer programs being among their routine tasks, the Youth League is arguably the most visible and among the most influential ones. It takes the responsibility to organize youth volunteers, especially in schools and universities. On 5 December 1994, the Youth League established the China Youth Volunteer Association – laying the foundation for an institutionalized system of youth volunteering which, by 2009, included thirty-five provincial Associations; local associations in two-thirds of China's municipalities, districts and counties; 2,000 institutions of higher education; and 190,000 'volunteer service stations' (Zhang, 2009, p. 65). In Guangdong, for example, the Provincial Youth Volunteer Association was established in 1995; by 2005, there were 180 local Youth Volunteer Associations, 5,500 'youth volunteer service stations' (青年志愿服务站), and 64,708 'Youth Volunteer Teams' (青年志愿服务队) (Tan, 2005, p. 3). In this system, the provincial association is responsible for establishing the legal status of volunteers and providing broad guidance, while municipal-level associations and 'service stations' at the county level or below have a coordinating role, to link volunteers with service recipients, gradually establishing a broad-based service network (Tan and Zhou, 2008, pp. 31–8). There are local variations

---

[17] For more discussion on volunteers in the CI, please see Ning (2019).

in the system: the provincial association and the municipal associations of Guangzhou, Foshan, Zhuhai, Shantou, and other areas have followed the national model with 'Youth Volunteer Associations', with an emphasis on combining large-scale campaigns with specific service activities, while Shenzhen, taking inspiration from Hong Kong, spearheaded another model, of the 'Volunteer Federation' (义务工作者联合会), which tries to coordinate government and non-governmental initiatives. There has been some competition between the two models (Tan, 2005, p. 53). The Central Committee of the Youth League sent representatives several times to try to persuade Shenzhen to adopt the national nomenclature, but Shenzhen persisted in retaining its name; other cities such as Panyu, Nanhai, Shunde, and Lianzhou even adopted the 'Yigonglian' name, in order to match the language used in Hong Kong (Tan and Zhou, 2008, p. 58).

The organization of youth volunteers was quickly followed by regulation. In August 1999, the Guangdong People's Congress passed the first set of 'regulations for youth volunteer service' (青年志愿服务条例), an example which was followed at the provincial and municipal levels by Shandong, Nanjing, Fujian, Henan, and so on (Zhang, 2009, p. 65). The Guangdong regulations guarantee the right of citizens to participate in volunteer activities, ensuring that they enjoy normal rights during volunteer service and can sue for compensation in cases of abuse; that volunteers' resources cannot be misappropriated or volunteers forced to do unreasonable work; that volunteers deserve social recognition; and that volunteers are prohibited from engaging in illegal activities or harming the interests of the recipients of their services (Tan, 2005, p. 11). In 2000, the Youth League announced that Lei Feng Memorial Day would be designated as the 'Chinese Youth Volunteer Service Day' (中国青年志愿者服务日). The following year, a system of youth volunteer registration was put into place by the Youth League Central Committee, in which youth aged fourteen years or older could acquire the status of a volunteer, provided that they did at least forty-eight hours of volunteer service per year. Thus, by 2007, 25.1 million youth were registered as volunteers (Zhang, 2009, p. 67).

Youth volunteer work is organized into a series of areas: poverty alleviation in rural areas; urban community building; environmental protection; large events; emergency rescue and disaster relief; and public interest (shehui gongyi 社会公益). Organizational models include 'one-to-one' 一助一 assistance (started in 1995), in which a long-term relationship is established between a volunteer individual or volunteer group with an individual or area, to provide service at regular intervals and places. The targets of this type of service include isolated and widowed elders, the handicapped, retirees, laid-off workers, and students with special difficulties. They also include relationships with old-age homes, welfare homes, orphanages, health rehabilitation centres, etc. The youth provide company, medical care, culture and entertainment, repairs of electrical appliances, Internet training, legal advice, etc. (Ding and Jiang, 2001, pp. 114–15; Zhang, 2009, p. 71).

According to Tan Jianguang, in the early stages of the development of volunteer organizations the role of the Youth League in mobilizing resources was crucial. Most groups evolved from 'a model of management by league cadres, assisted by league members, and the participation of youth, to a model of support by league cadres, management by volunteer activists [gugan 骨干], and participation in service by league members and youth'. Early efforts continued LLF activies of helping poor families, the handicapped, and lonely and widowed elders with daily chores and moral support as well as propaganda for public morality (obeying traffic regulations, hygiene, etc.). Later, the Guangdong Youth League promoted youth volunteerism in new areas such as environmental action and technological literacy. The Youth League also acts as a bridge between the party and government and youth volunteers, consulting with the party and government to launch volunteer projects which dovetail with government policies, such as support for poor rural areas (Tan, 2005, pp. 21–2).

13.7 THE GO WEST PROGRAMME

One of the most high-profile programmes sponsored by the Youth League involves sending university graduates as volunteer teachers to rural regions of western China. Initially, small-scale experiments began in 1996; these were consolidated in 2003 under the name of the 'Go West Plan' (*xibu jihua* 西部计划). In June of that year, the Youth League, the Ministry of Education, the Ministry of Finance, and the Ministry of Personnel co-issued a document which announced the commencement of the program, which makes use of the category of volunteerism to mobilize fresh college graduates to serve in western China in the fields of education, medical care, and agricultural technology. The official document was issued to relevant governmental branches on 8 June, and little more than two months later, in late August, the groups of college students set out for their volunteer service. At an internal meeting about the Go West plan in 2003, Zhao Yong, then the standing secretary of the Secretariat of the Youth League, remarked: 'This year we have fought a sudden fight; [we] finished a series of tasks including recruitment and dispatch within a very short time' (Tuanzhongyang qingnian zhiyuanzhe gongzuobu, 2006, p. 72).

While the reason for this hasty action is unclear, the urgency of this program may be related to the special situation of college graduates in 2003. In 1999, under the influence of the new policy of 'expanding enrollment' (扩招), the number of students admitted into college increased by 44 per cent compared to the previous year, whereas the annual rate of increase had averaged at 3.3 per cent in the period from 1993 to 1998.[18] This dramatic change in the scale of admission resulted in a huge wave of inexperienced new job-seekers in 2003. To make things worse, in 2003 China's major cities were severely stricken by SARS, an acute and

---

[18] Calculated from the data in the website of the National Bureau of Statistics of China, http://goo.gl/v8VKgS (accessed 24 February 2015).

frequently fatal infectious disease. Both factors led to uncertain prospects in the job market for college graduates in that year. The Go West program, born in such unusual circumstances, might well be understood as a way to channel the surplus of college-level labour from the cities to the countryside and thus temper the urgent issue of youth employment. In fact, a 2003 governmental notification about the employment of college students issued by the State Council listed as the first point the encouragement of college students to work 'at the grassroots' (基层) and in areas in hard conditions. Moreover, this notification explicitly expressed the governmental support of the Go West program and the career advantages the volunteers would enjoy after they finished their service (Guowuyuan Bangongting, 2003). The document about the implementation of the Go West program cited this notification and claimed that the aims of the program included 'widening the channel of employment and entrepreneurship of college students' (Gongqingtuan Zhongyang, Jiaoyubu, Caizhengbu, Renshibu, 2003). Apart from the pressing problem of employment, training of new talents with work experience at the 'grassroots' was another basic aim of the Go West Plan. Therefore, Go West is a program as much for helping volunteers as it is for helping the western areas. Although promoting the development of western China is still a key component of the guiding aims, the channelling and training of volunteers carry equal, if not more, importance.

Another program, the 'triple rustication' (*san xiaxiang* 三下乡), launched in 1997 and jointly sponsored by the Central Propaganda Department, the Ministry of Education, and the Youth League Central Committee, involves sending hundreds of thousands of students at professional schools (大中專专) down to the countryside during their summer holidays to conduct literacy, cultural, technological, and health work and to 'promote applied agricultural technology and health, and civilized lifestyles' (Zhang, 2009, p. 72; Ding and Jiang, 2001, pp. 116–19).

The 'Go West' and 'Triple Rustication' programmes both evoke the movement to send urban youth to the countryside during the Cultural Revolution, from 1966 to 1976. The latter programme employs the same term of *xiaxiang* – 'going down to the villages', denoting an explicit and unambiguous link with the Mao-era campaign, while the slogan of the Go West programme employs a slogan that is almost identical to one associated with the Cultural Revolution. Figures 13.2 and 13.3 illustrate both the continuities and the changes in the presentation of these campaigns to send educated urban youth to 'serve the people' in the countryside. Figure 13.2 is a poster for sent-down youth in the Cultural Revolution, showing zealous young revolutionaries, holding Mao's *Little Red Book*, departing on the train from Shanghai en route to their remote inland destination. On the red banner, educated youth are told of the necessity to be re-educated by the poor, lower and middle peasants. The vertical slogan on the right of the poster states, 'Go to the countryside, Go to the frontier areas, Go wherever the fatherland needs you most!'

FIGURE 13.2 Propaganda poster for sent-down youth in the Cultural Revolution

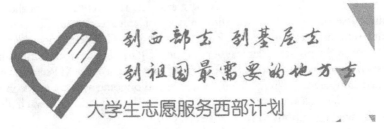

FIGURE 13.3 Banner for the Go West Programme's website

An almost identical slogan can be found on the banner for the Go West programme's website in 2015 (see Figure 13.3): 'Go to the West, Go to the grassroots, Go wherever the fatherland needs you most!' But this time, the cheering youth portrayed beside the slogan are not heading off to be re-educated by the peasants but to bring education to the peasants as volunteer teachers. And the militant aesthetics of the revolutionary poster are replaced by alluring images of grasslands and snow-capped mountains, as well as China's official logo for volunteering, showing a dove-shaped helping hand inside a heart, conveying a message of peace and love.

13.8 CONCLUSION

This chapter has provided an overview of the official discourse and institutionalization of volunteering in China from the Mao era until the present. It reveals a process of conversion of the party's network of mass mobilization of youth and neighbourhood residents, notably through the Communist Party Youth League and neighbourhood committees, into the institutional framework of volunteering. With their growing affluence and sophistication, urban residents have a greater desire to contribute and participate in society through engagement as volunteers. The deployment of the institutional network aims to channel this engagement, in ways that show both continuities and ruptures with the campaigns of the revolutionary era. The aim is to contribute to Chinese nation-building and to prevent the emergence of Western-style civil society by co-opting the altruistic impulses of the people into party-led programmes.

In tracing the changes in the party's techniques of implementing its policies since the Maoist era, Elizabeth Perry describes a shift from 'mass campaigns' to 'managed campaigns'. For her, mass campaigns are more ideologically intensive and exclusive, stressing revolutionary moral virtues such as struggle against class enemies and sacrifice for the masses, and more frequently use coercive means in their implementation. While managed campaigns retain some of the characteristics of mass campaigns, they are more pragmatic and more inclusive of interpretive and practical diversity at the grassroots. In this sense, the case of volunteerism described in this chapter illustrates the shift from a mass campaign to a managed campaign and the continuing importance of campaigns in the political life of contemporary China (Perry, 2011). However, the two forms of campaign are not easily separated once and for all. As this case shows, the government is never willing to entirely divorce itself from the legacy of the Maoist era. The recurrent surges of the image and discourse of Lei Feng in the short history of volunteerism in China and the uncanny reminiscence between the Rustication and the Go West Program are both vivid proof of the proactive endeavours of the CCP to 'recycle' its traditions in the Maoist era in innovative and accommodative ways (Siu, 1990). As Perry has put it, managed campaigns originate from 'an active and ongoing attempt to reconfigure elements of China's revolutionary tradition in order to address new challenges under changed conditions' (Perry, 2011, p. 51).

The Resurrection of Lei Feng

TABLE 13.1 *Frequency of key terms in the* People's Daily

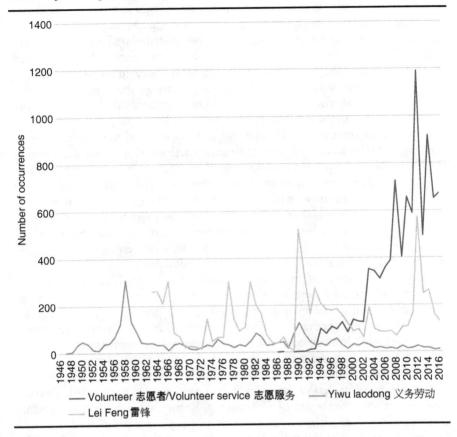

Table 13.1 compares the currency of three key phrases – 'volunteer', '*yiwu laodong*', and 'Lei Feng' – in official discourse in the history of the People's Republic of China, by counting the number of occurrences of the terms in the *People's Daily*. Peaks on the graph correspond to political campaigns. *Yiwu laodong* was most frequently used during the Great Leap Forward in 1958 and reached a second peak, together with Lei Feng, in 1990, in the year following the crackdown on the Tiananmen student movement, when the 6th Plenum of the 13th CCP Central Committee called for a renewal of the LLF campaign. The first peak for the term 'volunteer' was in 2008, associated with the Olympics and the Sichuan earthquake, while the second peak, for both 'volunteer' and Lei Feng, was in 2012, corresponding to the campaign by the Office of Spiritual Civilization to promote the Lei Feng spirit through volunteer service.

If the concept of 'managed campaign' captures the changes in the means of the CCP's campaigns, it raises questions about changes in the ends, or rather about the formulation of the ends, of such campaigns. Mass campaigns in the Maoist era are usually characterized by their being formulated in terms of 'anti-' (such as the 'three anti- and five anti-', 三反五反, to name only a few). Managed campaigns, in contrast, are marked by a notable decrease in the use of 'anti-' in their names (the anti-corruption campaign being the most noticeable exception); instead, contemporary campaigns are formulated in much more affirmative and constructive terms.

How can we theorize this change and identify some of the nuances among campaigns that look very similar in their constructive and affirmative discourse? We would like to venture the following: if the 'Constructing a new socialist countryside' campaign, an example analyzed by Perry, can be seen as an 'inventive mobilization' in which the state is trying to engender something that goes against a social trend (in this case, the migration of the Chinese peasantry to the cities, leading to the dilapidation of the countryside), then, using the comparative framework of this volume, contemporary state-sponsored discourses and institutions of volunteering in China can be considered as a form of 'preventive mobilisation', which aims to actively organize and structure the existing and even vigorous impulse for social service and engagement in order to prevent and pre-empt mobilization by other actors or for other causes. This complicates Juan Linz's characterisation of forms of mobilization and political regimes in his comparative study of totalitarian and authoritarian regimes (Linz, 2000): Chinese state-sponsored volunteering does not reflect a totalitarian state's efforts to mobilize citizens into pro-regime *political action*; nor can it be characterized as an authoritarian state's efforts to actively *demobilize* citizens. Rather, what we find is an effort to actively *mobilize* citizens but towards pro-regime *depoliticized action*.[19] Perhaps it can be considered a form of 'quasi-mobilization' as defined by Hankiss 1988 in his study of post-socialist Hungary, in which the elite simultaneously fosters and curbs self-mobilization among the population (Hankiss, 1988).

Institutionally and ideologically, contemporary Chinese volunteerism can trace its genealogy to the protest movements at the root of the Chinese revolution, which the CCP learned to organize, to nurture, and to channel to its purposes, both before and after Liberation, in campaigns ranging from labour strikes and peasant struggles to the intellectuals' rustication movement, the volunteer army to the Korean War, Red Guard activism, and 'Learning from Lei Feng'. In this rich repertoire of forms of party- and state-led popular mobilization, it was the figure of Lei Feng that lent itself most readily to being recast from a paragon of class struggle into an

---

[19] For more detailed discussion on the relations between the state and grassroots actors providing social services, please see Hsu (2017), especially chapter 5.

embodiment of humble acts of kindness and virtue, allowing for the reappropriation of revolutionary symbolism and discourses for the party's new strategies and technologies of rule in an individualized market economy. In this way, a tinge of the collectivism of the socialist era continues to be felt in the institutions of state-led volunteering. As Yan Hairong has argued, 'the emerging hegemony of capitalism in China must deal with living socialist legacies, claims, and structures of feeling that surround the current relations of production and sociality' (Yan, 2008, p. 13). Similarly, the emerging volunteerism cannot be fully separated from LLF, and volunteers' experience and practice are influenced by this socialist legacy.

At the same time, the new configuration does not fully resolve the ambiguous tensions between the collectivist discourses on Lei Feng and the more individualistic notions of volunteer service in a market economy. Tan Jianguang notes that while the LLF movement's emphasis on 'doing good deeds and helping others' (做好事, 帮助他人) is similar to the 'volunteer service' emphasis on 'serving society, serving others' (服务社会, 服务他人), they differ in that the Lei Feng movement was 'political, movement-oriented and collective' (政治性, 运动性, 集体性), while volunteer service is 'personalized, routinized and individualized' (人性化, 日常化, 个体化) (Tan, 2005, p. 6). There was a conscious transition from the 'selfless sacrifice' of revolutionary era to the 'volunteer service' and 'non-profit service' of the reform era. Organizers reflected that the Cultural Revolution had overly politicized serving others, and the 'movement' style of the LLF campaigns of the 1980s involved sporadic actions that lacked continuity. A leading youth volunteer from Guangzhou noted in an essay that many people speak of Lei Feng and of volunteers as if they were the same thing, but he stressed that while 'Lei Feng was a volunteer [yigong], volunteers need not be Lei Fengs, volunteers need not have such noble thoughts and spiritual awareness as Lei Feng'. 'A volunteer is only an ordinary person who does ordinary things. But Lei Feng was the product of a specific age, who was fabricated as a model to imitate. He has a high level of enlightenment [觉悟]; he has an attitude of sacrifice for the people; his heart is committed to the common good; he has unswerving perseverance. But a volunteer does not necessarily have these qualities and is not required to have them. The main thing that volunteers and Lei Feng have in common is all have a heart that takes joy in helping others.' This author criticized media reports on volunteers that exaggerate the sacrifices of volunteers, depicting them like heroic Lei Fengs, creating the negative effect of causing people to misunderstand the notion of volunteering and even to resist it (Wutuobang, 2006).

Such comments reflect the tensions between the revolutionary ethic of selfless sacrifice and the more individualized ethic of most contemporary volunteers who do not recognize themselves in Lei Feng, deny any pretension to heroism, and, for the most part, seek self-discovery and self-expression through their volunteering (Bannister, 2013). Thus, while the party-state is able to re-deploy discourses, practices, and institutions dating from the revolutionary era, the volunteers who are mobilized pursue their own dreams, emotions, and desires (Ning and Palmer 2020; n.d.).

REFERENCES

Andreas, J. 2007. The structure of charismatic mobilization: a case study of rebellion during the Chinese Cultural Revolution. *American Sociological Review* 72: 434–58.

Averill, S. C. 2006. *Revolution in the Highlands: China's Jinggangshan Base Area.* New York: Rowman & Littlefield Publishers.

Bannister, Tom. 2013. Heirs of Lei Feng or Re-organised Independence? A Study of Individualization in Chinese Civil Society Volunteers. PhD diss., University of Sheffield.

Bonnin, M. 2013. *The Lost Generation: The Rustication of China's Educated Youth (1968–1980).* Hong Kong: Chinese University Press.

Breslin, S. 2006. Serving the market or serving the party: neo-liberalism in China. In R. Robison (ed.), *The Neo-liberal Revolution: Forging the Market State.* New York: Palgrave Macmillan, pp. 114–34.

Chen, X. (陈曦). 2010. Lun Lei Feng fengxian jingshen (论雷锋奉献精神) (On the Lei Feng spirit of devotion). Unpublished PhD thesis, Zhonggong zhongyang dangxiao (中共中央党校) (Party School of the Central Committee of the CCP).

Chen, Y. (陈阳). 2008. Qingnian dianxing renwu de jiangou yu shanbian: Renmin Ribao suzao de Lei Feng xingxiang (青年典型人物的建构与嬗变：人民日报塑造的雷锋形象) (The construction and evolution of model youth: a study on Lei Feng's image construction in *People's Daily*). *Guoji Xinwenjie* (国际新闻界) (Journal of International Communication) 3: 18–22.

Chong, G. P. L. 2011. Volunteers as the 'new' model citizens: Governing citizens through soft power. *China Information* 25: 33–59.

Ding, Y. (丁元竹) and X. Jiang (江汛清). 2001. *Zhiyuan huodong yanjiu: leixing, pingjia yu guanli* (志愿活动研究：类型，评价与管理) (Research on volunteer activities: types, evaluation and management). Tianjin: Tianjin Renmin Chubanshe, pp. 146–9.

Eliasoph, N. 2011. *Making Volunteers: Civic Life after Welfare's End.* Princeton, NJ: Princeton University Press.

Eliasoph, N. 2013. *The Politics of Volunteering.* Cambridge: Polity Press.

Gongqingtuan Zhongyang, Jiaoyubu, Caizhengbu Renshibu (共青团中央，教育部，财政部人事部) (The Central Committee of the Youth League, Ministry of Education, and Department of Personnel of the Ministry of Finance). 2003. Guanyu shishi daxuesheng zhiyuan fuwu xibu jihua de tongzhi (关于实施大学生志愿服务西部计划的通知) (Notification on implementing the Program of Volunteer Service in the Western Area for College Students. No. 26).

Guowuyuan Bangongting (国务院办公厅) (The Office of the State Council). 2003. Guowuyuan Bangongting guanyu zuohao 2003 nian putong gaodeng xuexiao biyesheng jiuye gongzuo de tongzhi (国务院办公厅关于做好2003年普通高等学校毕业生就业工作的通知) (Notification about effectively working on the employment of graduates of regular universities and colleges in 2003 by the Office of the State Council. No. 49).

Hankiss, E. 1988. The second society: is there an alternative social model emerging in contemporary Hungary? *Social Research: An International Quarterly* 55: 13–42.

Hsu, C. L. 2017. *Social Entrepreneurship and Citizenship in China: The Rise of NGOs in the PRC*. London: Routledge.

Hua, Q. (华琪). 1990. *Lun Lei Feng jingshen* (论雷锋精神) (On the Lei Feng Spirit), Beijing: Jiefangjun Chubanshe.

Jeffreys, E., and X. Su 2016. Governing through Lei Feng: A Mao-era role model in Reform-era China. In D. Bray and E. Jeffreys (eds.), *New Mentalities of Government in China*. London: Routledge, pp. 30–55.

Junshi kexueyuan junshi lishi yanjiubu (军事科学院军事历史研究部) (Military History Department of the Academy of Military Sciences). 2000. *Kangmeiyuanchao zhanzheng shi* (抗美援朝战争史) (The History of the War of Supporting Korea against America). Beijing: Junshi Kexue Chubanshe.

Li, K., and Y. Geng 1993. On the upsurges in the emulate Lei Feng movement and some sober reflections. *Chinese Education & Society* 26: 23–47.

Lin, Y. (林蘊暉). 2009. *Xiang shehuizhuyi guodu: Zhongguo jingji yu shehui de zhuanxing (1953–1955)* (向社會主義過渡: 中國經濟與社會的轉型 (1953–1955)) (Moving toward Socialism: The transformation of China's economy and society (1953–1955)). Hong Kong: Chinese University Press.

Linz, J. J. 2000. *Totalitarian and Authoritarian Regimes*. Boulder, CO: Lynne Rienner Publishers.

Liu, J. (刘佳). 2013. Xue Lei Feng: Yige guojia yundong shijiao de yanjiu (学雷锋: 一个国家运动视角的研究) (Learning from Lei Feng: a study from the perspective of national movement). Unpublished master's thesis, Lanzhou University.

Lu, Y. (逯延津). 2013. Lei Feng: ni cong nali lai (雷锋: 你从哪里来) (Lei Feng: where are you from?). Unpublished master's thesis, Shandong University.

Ning, R (宁润东). 2019. Hao geti, huai shehui: Zai fei huaren dui Feizhou renzhi de liangmianxing (好个体, 坏社会? 在非华人对非洲认知的两面性坏——以孔子学院志愿者为例) (Good indiviiduals, bad society? The paradoxical perception toward Africa of Chinese in Africa–A case study of Confucius Institute volunteers) Annual Review of African Studies in China 7: 182–196.

Ning, R., and D. A. Palmer. n.d. Intimate utopias: volunteering, tiny publics, and micro-civil spheres in China. Article manuscript in preparation.

Ning, R., and D. A. Palmer. 2020. Ethics of the heart: moral breakdown and the aporia of Chinese volunteers. *Current Anthropology*. In press.

Nonini, D. M. 2008. Is China becoming neoliberal? *Critique of Anthropology* 28: 145–76.

Palmer, D. A., and F. Winiger. 2019. Neo-socialist governmentality: managing freedom in the People's Republic of China. Economy and Society 48

Perry, E. 2011. From mass campaigns to managed campaigns: 'constructing a new socialist countryside'. In S. Heilmann and E. Perry (eds.), *Mao's invisible hand: the political foundations of adaptive governance in China*. Cambridge, MA: Harvard University Asia Center, pp. 30–61.

Perry, E. 2012. *Anyuan: Mining China's Revolutionary Tradition*. Berkeley: University of California Press.

Perry, E. 2014. Citizen contention and campus calm: the paradox of Chinese civil society. *Current History* 113: 211–17.

Pieke, Frank, N. 2009. *The Good Communist: Elite Training and State Building in Today's China*. Cambridge: Cambridge University Press, pp. 9–10.

RMRB (人民日报) (*People's Daily*). 1961. Kuhaizi chengzhang wei youxiu renmin zhanshi (苦孩子成长为优秀人民战士) (A poor child grows into an outstanding peoples' soldier). 5 May: 4.

RMRB (人民日报) (*People's Daily*). 1963a. Aizeng fenming lichang jianding haobu liji zhuanmen liren: Xiang Lei Feng nayang zhongyu geming shiye (爱憎分明立场坚定 毫不利己专门利人：像雷锋那样忠于革命事业) (Clearly distinguish between love and hatred; show no self-interest, and focus on benefiting others: be loyal to the revolutionary cause like Lei Feng). 7 February: 1.

RMRB (人民日报) (*People's Daily*). 1963b. Guofangbu pizhun shouyu Shenyang budui gongchengbing moubu siban guangrong chenghao 'Lei Feng Ban' (国防部批准授予沈阳部队工程兵某部四班光荣称号'雷锋班') (The Ministry of Defense approved to award the Squad 4 of a certain division of the engineer army of Shenyang Troop the glorious title 'Lei Feng Squad'). 25 January: 2.

RMRB (人民日报) (*People's Daily*). 1963c. Jiefangjun zongzhengzhibu he tuanzhongyang fenbie fachu tongzhi: Guangfan kaizhan 'xuexi Lei Feng' de jiaoyu huodong (解放军总政治部和团中央分别发出通知：广泛开展'学习雷锋'的教育活动) (The General Political Department of the People's Liberation Army and the Central Committee of the Youth League respectively issued the following notification: widely carry out the educational activity 'Learning from Lei Feng'). 16 February: 1.

RMRB (人民日报) (*People's Daily*). 1973. Renmin de qinwuyuan: ji Guangzhoushi Renmin Dianche Gongsi 'Xue Lei Feng xiaozu' de shiji (人民的勤务员：记广州市人民电车公司'学雷锋小组'的事迹) (A note on the deeds of the 'Learning from Lei Feng Group' in the Guangzhou People's Trolleybus Company). 3 March: 3.

RMRB (人民日报) (*People's Daily*). 1978. Ba 'Xiang Lei Feng tongzhi xuexi' de yundong tuixiang xin gaochao (把'向雷锋同志学习'的运动推向新高潮：春节和寒假开展'树新风、做好事'活动) (Push the campaign of 'Learning from Comrade Lei Feng' to a new climax: carry out 'establishing a new atmosphere, doing good deeds' in the Spring Festival and the winter break). 27 January: 1.

RMRB (人民日报) (*People's Daily*). 1980. Gongqingtuan Beijing shiwei zuzhi kaizhan 'Xue Lei Feng huodongri' huodong: shoudu sanwan zhongxiao xuesheng shangjie gao weisheng (共青团北京市委组织开展'学雷锋活动日'活动：首都三万中小学生上街搞卫生) (The Beijing Municipal Committee of the Youth League organizes 'Learning from Lei Feng Day': thirty thousand middle school and primary school students go to the streets to do cleaning in the capital). 5 March: 4.

RMRB (人民日报) (*People's Daily*). 1981a. Dao chezhan, matou, dajiexiaoxiang wei qunzhong zuohaoshi: Nanjing qingshaonian juxing xue Lei Feng huodong zhou (到车站、码头、大街小巷为群众做好事：南京青少年举行学雷锋活动周) (Do good deeds for the masses at train and bus stations, ports, and streets: the youth in Nanjing hold Learning from Lei Feng Week). 3 March: 4.

RMRB (人民日报) (*People's Daily*). 1981b. Tamen zijue de wei qunzhong zuohaoshi: ji Shanghai qinggong xitong qingnian fuwudui (他们自觉地为群众做好事：记上海轻工系统青年服务队) (They spontaneously do good deeds for the masses: a note on the youth service team of Shanghai's light industry system). 27 February: 3.

RMRB (人民日报) (*People's Daily*). 1990. Yayunhui gexiang choubei gongzuo jiuxu (亚运会各项筹备工作就绪) (All preparatory work for the Asian Games is ready). 16 August: 4.

RMRB (人民日报) (*People's Daily*). 1992. Hangzhou 'zhiyuanzhe huodong' pengbo xingqi (杭州'志愿者活动'蓬勃兴起) (Vigorous rise of 'volunteer activities' in Hangzhou). 6 June: 4.

RMRB (人民日报) (*People's Daily*). 1993. Rexin xian shehui zhenqing nuan renxin: Qingnian zhiyuanzhe huodong lakai weimu (热心献社会 真情暖人心: 青年志愿者活动拉开帷幕) (Devote a warm heart to society, warm others' hearts through true affection: the youth volunteer activity opens up). 20 December: 4.

Siu, H. F. 1990. Recycling tradition: culture, history, and political economy in the chrysanthemum festivals of south China. *Comparative Studies in Society and History* 32: 765–94.

Tan J. (谭建光). 2005. Zhongguo Guangdongsheng Zhiyuanfuwu Fazhan Baogao (中国广东省志愿服务发展报告) (Report on the Development of Volunteer Service in Guangdong Province, China). Guangzhou: Guangdong Renmin Chubanshe.

Tan, J. (谭建光) and H. Zhou (周宏峰) (eds.). 2008. *Shehui zhiyuan fuwu tixi: Zhongguo zhiyuan fuwu de 'Guangdong jingyan'* (社会志愿服务体系: 中国志愿服务的'广东经验') (The system of social volunteer service: the 'Guangdong experience' of volunteer service in China). Beijing: Zhongguo Shehui Chubanshe.

Tomba, L. 2014. *The Government Next Door: Neighborhood Politics in Urban China*, Ithaca, NY: Cornell University Press.

Tuanzhongyang qingnian zhiyuanzhe gongzuobu (团中央青年志愿者工作部) (Youth Volunteers Work Office of the Central Committee of the Youth League). 2006. *Xibu jihua wanli caifeng zhiyuan xingdong cankao ziliao* (西部计划万里采风志愿行动参考资料) (Reference Materials on the Volunteer Action of the Go West Program).

United Nations Volunteers. 1999. *Zhiyuan jingshen zai Zhongguo* (志愿精神在中国) (The spirit of volunteerism in China).

Vogel, E. F. 2011. *Deng Xiaoping and the Transformation of China*. Cambridge, MA: The Belknap Press of Harvard University Press.

Walder, A. 2009. *Fractured Rebellion: The Beijing Red Guard Movement*. Cambridge, MA: Harvard University Press.

Wutuobang. 2006. Jintian women zenme zuo yigong (今天我们怎么样做义工) (How do we do volunteer work today). In J. Tan (谭建光), S. Li. (李淼) and L. Zhu (朱莉玲) (eds.), *Yu zhiyuanzhe tongxing: Zhongguo Guangdong zhiyuan fuwu diaocha jishi* (与志愿者同行: 中国广东志愿服务调查纪实) (Hand-in-hand with volunteers: an investigation of volunteer service in Guangdong, China). Guangzhou: Guangdong Renmin Chubanshe, pp. 151–5.

Xu, Bin. 2017. *The Politics of Compassion: The Sichuan Earthquake and Civic Engagement in China*. Stanford, CA: Stanford University Press.

Yan, H. 2008. *New Masters, New Servants: Migration, Development, and Women Workers in China*. Durham, NC: Duke University Press.

Zhang, C. (张春霞). 2009. *Zhiyuanzhe zai xingdong* (志愿者在行动) (English title given as *Volunteer campaigns in China*). Beijing: Xin Shijie Chubanshe.

Zhao, Y. 2008. Neoliberal strategies, socialist legacies: communication and state transformation in China. In P. Chakravartty and Y. Zhao (eds.), *Global Communications: Toward a Transcultural Political Economy*. Lanham, MD: Rowman & Littlefield, pp. 23–50.

Zhongguo Wenming Wang (中国文明网). 2016. Zhongyang wenming ban queding jinnian 10 xiang zhongdian gongzuo (中央文明办确定今年10项重点工作) (The Office of Spiritual Civilization Building of the Central Committee determined ten key projects for this year). 15 January. www.wenming.cn/specials/zxdj/2016wmbzrh/yw_wmbzrh/201601/t20160115_3089937.shtml (accessed 26 December 2016).

Zhongyang Wenming Ban (中央文明办). 2012. Guanyu hongyang Lei Feng jingshen dali kaizhan zhiyuanfuwu huodong de tongzhi (关于弘扬雷锋精神 大力开展志愿服务活动的通知) (Notification on promoting the spirit of Lei Feng and energetically carrying out volunteer service. No. 2).

Index

Abasseya Square, 267–268
Accelerated Rural Development Program (ARDP), 92
Act on Rights of Croatian Veterans, 246
Act on the Rights of Croatian Veterans from the Homeland War, 246
administrative grassroots engagement, 102
AFRC. *See* Armed Forces of the Republic of Croatia
African Americans, 111–112, 122, 124–125, 128, 135
   neighborhoods restricted to, 115
   tenant farmers, 124
   voting rights of, 113
   vulnerability of, 123–124, 125
agency, 4, 5–6, 18, 20, 196–197
agricultural development, 90–91
agricultural economy, 99
agricultural laborers, 58, 117
agricultural production, 86–87, 89
agricultural society, 86–87
All-China Federation of Trade Unions, 75, 76
Alliance for Peace and Democracy, 300–302, 303, 305, 307
The Alliance in Support of Our Police Force, 304–305
Ameliach, Francisco, 234
American Revolution, 143–144
Americans for the Preservation of the White Race (APWR), 119–120, 121–122, 123, 127, 131–132, 134
Aminzade, Ronald, 2
Anders, Odell, 121
anti-communism, 41
Anti-Coup March, 233–234

antifascist direct action, 181
anti-gay legislation, 198
anti-intelligentsia frame, 43–45
anti-leafleting ordinance, 132–133
Anti-Maidan drive, 203, 212
anti-minority prejudices, 41
anti-OCM, 295–296, 298
   leaders of, 300
   momentum of, 301–302
   party-state and, 298
   social division and, 309
anti-Semitism, 27–28, 39–41, 53
   campaigns of, 51
   Moczar, and, 46
   MSW and, 50–51
   nationalism and, 41–42
anti-Zionism, 34, 38, 40–41, 45, 46, 47–48, 50–51
Apple Daily (newspaper), 305
APWR. *See* Americans for the Preservation of the White Race
Arab Spring, 189, 284–285
Arab–Israeli War, 40
ARDP. *See* Accelerated Rural Development Program
Armed Forces of the Republic of Croatia (AFRC), 241–242
Association of Disabled Veterans of the Homeland War (HVIDR-a), 245
Association of Patriotic War Volunteers, 245
Association of Volunteer Veterans, 245
astroturfing, 10–11, 112, 195
   Nashi and, 167–168, 178–179
   negative connotations of, 195
   propaganda and, 193

Atwal, Maya, 273
authoritarian contexts, 6, 11, 284–285
authoritarian regimes, 4–5, 8, 13–14, 236–237
　highly institutionalized, 15
　legitimacy of, 263
　political mobilization in, 196
　populist, 8, 10
　recalibration of governance under, 168
　representative institutions and, 10–11
　savvy, 7
　SMMs and, 15
　strategies of social control, 286
　strong, 310
authoritarian rule, 7, 261, 273, 274
　dynamics of, 270–271
　postmodern form of, 189
　pro-state demonstrations and, 272–273
authoritarianism, 10, 111, 194, 219–222, 262, 296–297
Autonomous Association of Workers, 75

backwardness, 87, 95
Bacon, Edwin, 273
Bagić, Dragan, 249–250
Bahrain, 147–148, 261
Bailey, Philip, 132
Baltic republics, 148
Barnett, Ross, 119
Battle of Moscow, 166
Battle of the Camel, 147, 149, 261, 267
Battle Units Hugo Chávez (UBCh), 224, 232–236
Bayesian Information Criterion (BIC), 159
Beijing, 58–59, 60, 65, 70–73, 196, 295–296, 318–319
　Basic Law Article 45 and, 301
　counter-deployment in, 70
　OCM and, 297
　People's Liberation Army and, 72–73, 81
　pressure on, 299
　proletariat and, 67–68
　Shanghai and, 74–77
　student protest and, 70
　Workers' Propaganda Teams in, 81
Beijing Daily (newspaper), 72, 76, 78–79
Beijing Garrison Command, 62
Beijing Olympics, 314, 318, 319–320, 329–330, 337
Beijing Women's Summit, 330
Ben Ali, Zine El Abedine, 266–267
Benford, Robert D., 299
Bennett, Gordon, 88, 90

BIC. *See* Bayesian Information Criterion
Black Hundred, 146
Blaydes, Lisa, 271
Blue Bucket Brigade, 182–183
Bolivarian Circle program, 224, 227–228, 233, 235
Bolivarian Movement, 217, 219, 236
　divided opposition to, 224
　groups affiliated with, 221–222
　local governance and, 223–224
　rise to power of, 218, 225
Bolivarian Project, 231
Bolivarian Revolution, 219–220, 227, 233
Bolivarian Venezuela, 9–10, 13, 218, 221–222, 236
Bolotnaya protests, 212
bombing campaigns, 132, 135
Bosnia and Herzegovina, 239, 244
Bowers, Sam, 120–121
Brenton, Tony, 170
Brodzki, Stanisław, 38
Brown v. Board, 117, 118, 127
Brumfield, Robert, 132
Bryant, C. C., 130
Building a New Socialist Countryside, 104
Bujak, Zbigniew, 49
Burt, Gordon, 131, 132

Cairo, Egypt, 267–268
Camp David Accords, 264
campaign coordination committees, 93–94, 97, 98
Capital Iron and Steel Corporation, 75
capitalism, 156, 241
Capriles, Henrique, 232
Carter, Hodding, 129–130
Catholic Caucus, 34
Catholic Church hierarchy, 51
CCA. *See* Citizens' Councils of America
CCP. *See* Chinese Communist Party
CCs. *See* Communal Councils
Ceausescu, Nicolae, 19
CEFTA. *See* Central European Free Trade Agreement
Cell, Charles, 88
Central Commission for Guiding the Construction of Spiritual Civilization, 330
Central Cultural Revolution Group, 66
Central European Free Trade Agreement (CEFTA), 252–253
Chan, Johannes, 308

Index

charismatic mobilization, 57–58, 63–66, 70, 77–80, 81–82
Chávez, Hugo, 217, 219, 226
  attempts to oust, 229
  death of, 231, 233
  failure of the April 2002 coup against, 226, 227–228
  first few years of, 223–224
  MTA and, 225
  New Strategic Map and, 229–230
  social organization and, 227
  winning power, 219–222, 224
Chiang Ching-kuo, 93, 95–96, 102
Chiang Kai-shek, 93, 95
Chief Executive election, 2017, 297–298
China, 7, 11, 261, 293–294, 318. *See also* Hong Kong
  Basic Law Article, 45, 301
  blogging factories from, 14
  Confucian idea of Mandate of Heaven, 11–12
  contemporary, 9–10
  Mainland, 302
  mass associations and, 12–13
  national interests of, 196
  nation-building and, 336
  neoliberalism and, 316–317
  political life in, 336
  revolutionary successors in, 59
  SMMs and, 18, 20
  Tiananmen Uprising, 15–16
  urban bias, shift away from, 104–105
  volunteerism and, 315–316
China Youth Volunteer Association, 318
Chinese Communist Party (CCP), 19, 58, 82, 314, 315, 337
  Deng and, 77–78
  guerrilla warfare and, 89
  Hong Kong and, 294
  land reform, 86
  social organizations of, 294
Chinese Communist Youth League, 330
Chinese Nationalist Party. *See* Kuomintang regime
Chinese revolution, 19
Chinese Youth Volunteer Service Day, 332
The Chosun Ilbo (newspaper), 103–104
CI. *See* Confucius Institute
Citizens' Councils, 114, 119–120, 123, 127, 134, 135–136
Citizens' Councils of America (CCA), 118–119, 122

civil disobedience, 299
civil liberties, 293, 295
civil rights
  activists, 117
  challenges, 135
  era, 115
  organizers, 125
  programs, 134–135
  reform, 112–113, 135
  struggle, 124
Civil Rights Commission, U.S., 113, 117
Civil Rights Movement, 9, 17, 111–112, 118
civil society, 180, 181–182, 295, 311, 320, 330
  in Hong Kong, 292–293
  Kremlin and, 198
  nationalism and, 199
  participation in, 152–153
  repression of, 18
  SMMs and, 294–295
  social media and, 14
  state–society cooperation and, 7
  strong, 310
  voice of, 295
civil society organizations, 3–4, 8, 10–11
Clarksdale, Mississippi, 123–129, 134–136
CNG. *See* Croatian National Guard
Coahoma Citizens' Council, 127
Coahoma County School Board, 128
coercion, 18, 24–25, 264–265, 283
COFO. *See* Council of Federated Organizations
Cold War, 10–11, 140–141
Cole, L. E., 121
Colectivos, 224, 232–236
collective action, 2, 7–8, 297–298
collective actors, 26, 102
Colombia, 218–219
color revolutions, 172–173, 179–180, 197, 231
Column Five, 62–63
Comités de Tierra Urbana (CTU), 225–226
Commission on Community Volunteers of the China Association of Social Work, 329
Communal Councils (CCs), 221, 222–223, 224, 230–231, 232–233
communism, 8, 10, 25–26, 27, 52
  anti-, 41
  influence of, 93
  mass organizations and, 25
  mobilization of concentrated social forces and, 13
  mobilization strategies and, 12, 15, 26
  party elites, 45–48
  proletariat and, 82

communism (cont.)
  student protests and, 80–81
  sympathizers with, 87
  vanguard revolutionary class and, 57
Communist Party Committee, 62–63
Communist Party Youth League, 70, 314, 315–316, 320, 331–332, 333, 336
community development, 96, 97, 98–99
Community Development Campaign, 86–87, 93, 96
  foundation for, 94
  impact of, 99–101
  results of, 101
  rural conditions and, 101–102
community development councils, 98, 99, 101–102
Community Development Eight-Year-Plan, 94, 96–97
Community Development Ten-Year-Plan, 94, 96–97
compulsory labor, 93–94, 98, 101–102
CONAVI. See El Consejo Nacional de la Vivienda
configuring enforcement, 134–136
Confucian idea of Mandate of Heaven, 11–12
Confucius Institute (CI), 331
El Consejo Nacional de la Vivienda (CONAVI), 225–226
contention, 194–197, 277–278
Council of Federated Organizations (COFO), 128–129
counterinsurgency subjectivity, 180
countermobilization, 8–9, 48, 54, 134, 222, 227
  anti-OCM and, 295–296, 298
  proletariat, 58, 59, 81
  standard forms of, 233–234
  tactics, 284–285
  vigilantist, 131
counterprotest, 31, 70–71, 72, 74, 231
counterrevolutionary mobilization, 141, 161–162, 264–265
  demographic features of, 154, 155
  effective, 141–142
  factors associated with participation in, 156, 157
  KIIS sample of, 158
  lifestyles of, 156–157
  Morsi and, 268–269
  Orange Revolution, failure of, 160
  Orange Revolution, survey data and, 149–154
  origins and purposes of, 142–149

  role in revolutionary processes, 142
  "thuggish" supporters of, 156–157
  Ukraine, composite character of, 158–160
  Ukraine, social sources of, 154–158
Crimea, 13, 193, 199, 200–201, 203–204, 213
Croatia, 239, 240, 241–242, 250–251, 254
  independence, 240–241, 242–243
  Knin, 256
  political dynamics in, 257–258
  Referendum Act, 251
  Sinj, 254
  Split, 254
  Zagreb, 254–255, 256
Croatian Armed Forces, 245
Croatian Government, 243–244
Croatian National Guard (CNG), 241–242
Croatian Policy Agendas Project, 244
Croatian Territorial Defence, 241–242
Croatian veterans' organizations, 9–10
Crouch, David, 140
CTU. See Comités de Tierra Urbana
Čular, Goran, 242–243, 249–250
Cultural Revolution, 8–9, 17, 73, 74, 317–318, 324, 334
  charismatic mobilization and, 81–82
  decades following, 314
  experimentation during, 69
  Marxism and, 65
  propaganda and, 59–63, 74
  Wang Hongwen and, 73, 80
  workers' patrols and, 74
cyber-attacks, 302, 309
Czechoslovakia, 29

Dahlmann, Hans-Christin, 46
Daily News (newspaper), 132
Day of Rage, 266–267
Declaration on Veterans in the Homeland War, 246
defensive mobilization, 8–9, 19–20, 28–29, 35, 212, 271–272
demobilization, 15, 26, 27, 291–292, 304–307, 310
democratic governance, 135–136, 286
democratic regimes, 6, 8, 11, 111–115, 135
Democratic Unity Roundtable (MUD), 229
democratization, 10, 241, 242–243, 291–292, 293, 295, 307
Deng Xiaoping, 69, 77–78, 82, 317–318
depoliticizing mobilization, 317, 338
desegregation mandates, 134–135

Index

development, 90, 98, 101, 105. *See also* community development
   agricultural, 90–91
   ARDP, 92
   infrastructural, 9
   legitimation and, 96
   promotion of, 102
   rural, 88, 95
   of Taiwan, 86
diagnostic framing, 299
Dick, W. Arsene, 119–120
Dickson, Bruce, 95–96
disability pensions, 243–244
Donbas, 201, 203–204, 213
   full-scale warfare in, 205
   network activity, 204
   Russian volunteers serving in, 202
   Ukraine and, 207
Donetsk People's Republic, 156, 201, 205–207, 209–210
Du Ping, 323
Dugin, Aleksandr, 175
Dziady (Mickiewicz), 24

Eastland, James O., 118–119
education revolution, 68–69, 70
Egypt, 8–9, 261–263, 276
   Arab Spring and, 284–285
   Cairo, 267–268
   Islamism and, 269
   police and, 264
   political landscape, 277
   pre-uprising politics in, 265–266
   protests during uprisings in, 266–267
   SCAF and, 279
   SMMs in, 265
   state agents and, 263–264
Eisler, J., 45, 50
electoral arena, 229–236
electoral technologies, 180
Eliasoph, Nina, 316
Emmerich, Oliver, 131, 133
emotion work, 183
empowerment, 97–98, 186–187
Eurasian Union of Youth, 172
Eurasianism, 198–199
Euromaidan Revolution, 160, 199–200, 203–204, 205
   criticism of, 205
   leaders of, 201
   period prior to, 205
European integration, 250–251

Factory Saemaul, 103–104
farmers' associations, 99, 101–102
fascism, 8, 34, 87–88, 93, 205–207
Federal Bureau of Investigation (FBI), 113, 127
Federal Youth Affairs Agency (*Rosmolodezh*), 171–172, 185, 186
Federation of Students, 301, 303
Fifth Republic (MVR), 220, 221–222
   dismantlement of, 229–230
   phases of, 222–223, 224
   skeptics of, 228
   social organization and, 227
First Party Secretary in Warsaw (KW PZPR), 44
Fishman, Robert, 114
Flying Tigers, 75
foreign policy, 196, 199
Francisco, Ronaldo, 280
Freedom Summer campaign, 1964, 118, 128–129, 130–131
Freedom Vote campaign, 128–129
French Revolution, 144–145
Friday of Departure, 277
Fundacomunal, 230

Gamson, William A., 279, 282
Gandhi, Mahatma, 299
Gang of Four, 324
GAR. *See* Grand Army of the Republic
Gartner, Scott Sigmund, 279
Gdansk Voivodeship Party Committee, 29–31
general strike, 226, 227–228
Georgia, 197
Gierasimow, Walerij, 5
Gierek, Edward, 33, 42
Girkin, Igor, 202
Glasnost, 202–203
Glaurdić, Josip, 249
Glorious Revolution of, 1688, 143–144
"Go West Plan" (*xibu jihua*), 333–336
"Goddess of Democracy" (statue), 78
Gold, Thomas, 92
Goldstone, Jack, 6–7
Gomułka, Władysław, 29, 34, 45, 53
   anti-Zionism and, 47–48
   letters of support sent to, 39
   nationalism and, 40
   Six Day War and, 40
GONGOs. *See* government-organized nongovernmental organizations
gongren jiuchadui. *See* workers' patrols
Goode, J. P., 202–203
Goodwin, Jeff, 143

Gotovina, Ante, 251
Gould, Roger V., 145–146
government-organized nongovernmental organizations (GONGOs), 4–5, 13–14, 197
Grand Army of the Republic (GAR), 247
grassroots organizations, 5, 12–13, 89, 223, 230
Great Depression, 102–103
Great Leap Forward, 90
Great Patriotic War, 177
Great Proletarian Cultural Revolution, 66
Griffin, Larry J., 278–279
Gross, Jan, 17–18
Guangdong Peoples' Congress, 332
Guangzhou People's Trolley Bus Company, 325–326
Guy, George, 110, 131, 132–133

Hague Tribunal, 250–253, 257–258
Hangzhou University, 68–69
Hankiss, Elmer, 15, 26, 338
HDZ. *See* Hrvatska Demokratska Zajednica
Help, Inc., 131–132
Hemment, Julie, 196–197
Henderson, Errol, 279
Henry, Aaron, 125–126, 127, 128
Henry, Noelle, 128
hierarchical mobilization networks, 37
high-risk mobilization, 213
Hillebrandt, Bogdan, 36–37
Hinton, William, 59, 63
HKSAR. *See* Hong Kong Special Administrative Region
Hobsbawm, Eric, 6
Hoffman, Nicholas Van, 132
"A Holiday Returned," 166, 179, 180
Holmes, Douglas, 182
Homeland War, 239, 240–241, 243–244, 246, 252, 253–254
Hong Kong, 8–9, 12–13, 291–292, 295, 327–328
  autonomy of, 302
  CCP and, 294
  civil society in, 292–293
  government of, 304
  party-state indirect rule over, 308–309
  political cleavage in, 19–20
  political control over, 309–310
  pro-democracy forces in, 295–296
  pro-democracy movement in, 292–294
  Silent Majority of Hong Kong, 298
  volunteerism and, 314
Hong Kong Economic Journal (newspaper), 296
Hong Kong Special Administrative Region (HKSAR), 295, 302, 307
Hoover, J. Edgar, 113
horizontal accountability, 219–222
horizontal diffusion, 26–27
Horn, Nancy, 274–275
Horvath, Robert, 173
household incomes, 71
Howard, Philip N., 195
Hrvatska Demokratska Zajednica (HDZ), 13, 239, 240–241, 244
  party leadership, 246
  party membership of, 242–243, 257
  protest arena and, 252–257
  veteran organizations and, 244, 246, 248–257
  welfare programmes from, 245
Hu Jintao, 104–105
human capital, 52
Human Development Index, 293–294
Human Rights Watch, 234
Hundred Flowers Campaign, 82
Hungary, 11, 26, 338
Hurley, Ruby, 125–126
Hurst, E. H., 130
HVIDR-a. *See* Association of Disabled Veterans of the Homeland War
hybrid regimes, 168–169, 263, 273–274, 286
hyperinflation, 232
hyper-mobilization, 301–302

"I Learn from Lei Feng, I volunteer" (*Xue Lei Feng, wo zhiyuan*), 321
identity formation, 16
Idushchie Vmeste (Moving Together), 169–170
Illinois Central railroad, 129
Impartiality (Tagarrod), 269–270
imperialism, 27–28, 40
incumbent regimes, 6–7, 161, 162
Indian tribes, 143–144
inducements, 18
industrial workers, 58, 72
industrialization, 91–92, 96
informal institutions, 89
informational management, 186
infrapolitics, 5
infrastructural development, 9, 220–221

Index

infrastructural mobilization, 87, 90, 101, 217–218
  local governance and, 225
  party-state and, 315
  use of, 236
  water provision and, 225
Institute of Sociology of the Ukrainian Academy of Sciences, 151
institutional change, 80–81, 115
insurrectionary plots, 144
interest groups, 89
international democracy, 168, 169
interracial cohabitation, 132–133
interstate conflict, 264
intra-elite conflicts, 33–34
intra-state conflict, 7–8, 113, 270–271
Iraq, 266
Irish Catholics, 143–144
irrigation associations, 99
Islamism, 269
Israel, 36, 40
Istúriz, Aristóbulo, 234

Jackson, Mississippi, 113, 118, 129
James V (King), 143–144
Japan, 86–87, 90–91, 94, 102–103
Al-Jazeera, 147
Jędrychowski, Stefan, 46–47
Jim Crow, 12–13, 20, 111, 114–115, 126
  banning of, 134–135
  breaches of, 117
  challenges to, 114, 118, 125, 134
  dissolution of, 111–112
  emergence of, 115
  enforcement of, 117, 125, 129–130
  logic of, 116–117
  maintenance of, 114
  preservation of, 118, 124
  state and civil pillars of, 115–124
  threats to, 122
  uncodified "rules" associated with, 115–116
Jiménez, Marcos Pérez, 218–219
Johnson, Paul, 122–123
Johnson, Paul B., 110–111, 113
Joint Commission on Rural Reconstruction, 93
Joint Declaration of Workers and Students in the Capital Region, 75–76
Jordan, 261
Josipović, Ivo, 255–256
Jowitt, Kenneth, 95–96
June Fourth crackdown, 74
June Uprising, 145

Kadyrov, Ramzan, 203
Kardov, Kruno, 249–250
Kennedy, Robert, 113
Kępa, Józef, 44
Kifaya pro-democracy movement, 266
KIIS. See Kyiv International Institute of Sociology
King, Martin Luther, Jr., 130–131, 299
Kitarović, Kolinda Grabar, 255–256
KKK. See Ku Klux Klan
KMT. See Kuomintang regime (Chinese Nationalist Party)
Knin, Croatia, 256
Kommersant (newspaper), 182
Korea, 95, 103–104, 105
Korean War, 317–318
Kremlin, 169–171, 188–189, 199, 203, 212–213
  Anti-Maidan drive and, 203
  civil society and, 198
  Color Revolutions and, 231
  managerial weapons of, 197–198
  Nashi and, 176–177
  objectives of, 213
  state television, 200
  Ukraine and, 193, 210, 273
Kristallnacht, 3–4, 20–21
Ku Klux Klan (KKK), 110–111, 113, 119–120, 127, 131
  bombing trial of, 133
  intra-KKK competition, 121
  law and order, flouting of, 122–123
  in Mississippi, 120
  organized vigilantism from, 134
  police and, 121, 132–133
  rise of, 132
  support for, 134
Kuchma, Leonid, 140–141
Kunming World Horticulture Exhibition, 330
Kuomintang regime (Chinese Nationalist Party) (KMT), 86–88, 95
  agricultural development and, 90–91
  founder of, 93
  political development of, 95–96
  political elite of, 92
KW PZPR. See First Party Secretary in Warsaw
Kyiv International Institute of Sociology (KIIS), 149–150, 151, 154, 158–159
Kyrgyzstan, 197

Labor Day, 34
labor protest, 196

labor reform, 69
labor unions, 12, 294
labour by obligation (*Yiwu laodong*), 326–327, 337
lad's logic, 182
Lake Seliger, 170, 178–179, 185, 186–187
Lam, Carrie, 304
land reform, 86, 91
landless peasants, 58
landlords, 117, 143–144
landowning employers, 116–117
Langer, Jacob, 146
laobaixing (ordinary people), 78
Latvia, 148
law 122 (Russia), 173, 174
Law and Justice party (PiS), 1, 239–240, 256–257
League of Equality (*Liga Spravedlivosti*), 181
"Learning from Lei Feng" (LLF), 324, 327, 339
  renewal of, 337
  slogans and activities, 321–324
  volunteerism and, 338
Lee Teng-hui, 86, 102
Leese, Daniel, 65
legitimation, 96
Lei Feng, 314, 320–321, 337, 339. *See also* "Learning from Lei Feng"
  depoliticizing, 324–326
  iconic image of, 321
  image and discourse of, 336
  shifting representations of, 315
Lei Feng Memorial Day, 323, 325, 328, 332
Lei Zhengxing. *See* Lei Feng
Leung, C. Y., 304
Ley de Consejos Comunales, 230
Li Peng, 74, 75
Liaison Office, 295, 297, 298
Liang Shuming, 93
Liberal Democratic Party of Russia, 172, 199
liberalization, 71, 92
Liberation Daily (newspaper), 74, 76, 79
Liga Spravedlivosti (League of Equality), 181
Limonov, Eduard, 174–175, 199–200
Linz, Juan, 88–89, 194, 195–196
Lithuania, 148
Little Red Book (Mao), 334
LLF. *See* "Learning from Lei Feng"
local governance, 223–224, 225, 227, 230
Local Improvement Movement, 102–103
Loga-Sowiński, Ignacy, 47
Łoś, Kazimierz, 42
Louisiana, 110, 129

Loyalists, 143–144
Lugansk, 205–207
lumpenproletariat, 145–146
Luo Ruiqing, 323
Luzhkov, Yury, 199
lynchings, 116–117

Maduro, Nicolás, 231, 232, 233–235
Magaloni, Beatriz, 196
Mahalla labor protests, 266
mainland China, 86
Malaysian airliner, flight MH-, 17, 203–204
Mallet, Victor, 310–311
managed campaigns, 336–338
Mandate of Heaven, 11–12
Mango Cult, 63–66
manufactured ambiguity, 13, 25–26, 48–51, 52–53, 60, 308–309
Mao Zedong, 59, 66, 79, 317, 323, 334
  blessing of, 62, 66–67
  campaigns under, 89
  Hundred Flowers Campaign, 82
  instructions of, 62–63
  loyalty to, 81
  market reforms post-, 71, 78
  National Day Parade and, 65
  organizational forms from era of, 314
  Tsinghua University and, 63
  veneration of, 65
Maoism, 104
March of Millions, 266–267, 277
market reforms, 15–16, 71, 78
market strategies, 13–14
martial law, 70–71, 75–76
Marx, Karl, 145–146
Marxism, 39–40, 65
Marxism-Leninism, 57
mass associations, 12–13
mass campaigns, 179, 315, 336
Mass Education and Rural Reconstruction Movements, 93
mass enthusiasm, 20
mass mobilization, 8, 95, 247, 253–254, 325
  capacity for, 241
  revolutionary, 10, 145, 316–317
  during World War II, 242
mass organizations, 25, 26–27, 35–37
Mass Task Force to Maintain Order in the Capital, 70–71
material incentives, 71
May Fourth Movement, 19
Mayer, Arno, 144–145

Index

MBR-, 200, 219
McAdam, Doug, 273
McComb, Mississippi, 110, 114, 123–124, 129–136
McDaniel, E. L., 120–122
Medvedev, Dmitry, 169, 171, 178, 185, 197–198
Mesas Técnicas de Agua (MTA), 225–226
Meyer, David S., 273, 274
Michnik, Adam, 24
Mickiewicz, Adam, 24
Middle East, 14, 261
Migdal, Joel S., 11
Mihalec, Ivica, 245
Milicja Obywatelska (People's Militia) (MO), 24, 45, 49–50
military crackdown, 70, 82
military suppression, 73, 82, 146–147
million-man march, 268
Mills, Erline, 126
Ministry for Croatian Veterans of the Homeland War, 246
Ministry of Civil Affairs, 314, 315–316, 330
Ministry of Interior (MSW), 36, 37–38, 45, 46, 48, 50–51
Ministry of Veterans, 255–256
Minsk Agreements, 207
Minsk Protocol, 210–211
Miraflores Palace, 226, 227–228
Mironov, Sergei, 174
mirror-image design, 217–218
Mississippi, 17, 110–111
  Clarksdale, 123–129, 134–136
  Jackson, 113, 118, 129
  KKK in, 120
  McComb, 110, 114, 123–124, 129–136
  officials governing, 112–113
  racist practices in, 114–116
  segregationist associations in, 122
Mississippi Highway Patrol, 121
Mississippi Movement, 129–130
Mississippi Progressive Voters League (MPVL), 125–126, 128
Mississippi State Sovereignty Commission (MSSC), 114, 118, 119, 127, 134–135
MO. See Milicja Obywatelska (People's Militia); People's Militia (Milicja Obywatelska)
Mobile Guard, 145–146
mobilization capacity, 26, 28–29, 247
mobilization challenges, 176–177
mobilization strategies, 176–177, 223
mobilization technologies, 12–14
mobilizational politics, 88
mobilization-social movement spectrum, 5–6
mobilizing affect, 183–184
mobilizing networks, 35–37
Moczar, Mieczysław, 29, 45, 46, 47
modernization, 101, 105, 185
Monitoring survey, 151, 152, 153, 154, 158–159
Morsi, Mohammed, 265, 268–270, 279, 283
Moses, Bob, 122, 129–130
motivational framing, 299
movement regimes, 88–89
Moving Together (*Idushchie Vmeste*), 169–170
MPVL. See Mississippi Progressive Voters League
MSSC. See Mississippi State Sovereignty Commission
MSW. See Ministry of Interior
MTA. See Mesas Técnicas de Agua
Mubarak, Hosni, 149, 261, 263, 267, 277, 283
  political hegemony of, 266
  resignation of, 266–267
  rule of, 265–266
MUD. See Democratic Unity Roundtable
Muslim Brotherhood, 266, 269–270
MVR. See Fifth Republic

NAACP. See National Association for the Advancement of Colored People
El Nacional (newspaper), 227
Nanjing Teachers' College, 69
Narodno-Oslobodilački Pokret (People's Liberation Movement) (NOP), 242
Nashi, 9–10, 20, 112, 166, 174, 212
  astroturfing and, 167–168, 178–179
  challenges to, 176–177
  contextualizing, 172–176
  founding of, 169–170, 273
  geopolitical context of, 189
  hybrid regimes and, 168–169
  inaugural rally, 170
  Kremlin and, 176–177
  offshoot projects of, 171–172
  Orange Revolution and, 172–173
  precursor to, 170
  Putin and, 171, 176–177
  SMMs and, 168, 188
  socially oriented work of, 183
  spoiler mobilization and, 175–176
  street technologies and, 178–179
  student protest and, 231

Nashi (cont.)
　summer educational camps, 170
　technologies of, 177–178
　trajectory of, 169, 188–189
National Association for the Advancement of Colored People (NAACP), 118, 125–126, 127, 128, 134
National Bolshevik Party (NBP), 172, 174, 178
　counterculture and, 174
　demographics of, 175
　founder of, 174
　potential recruits of, 175–176
　tactics of, 182
National Day, 65, 303
National Democratic Party (NDP), 265–266
National People's Congress, 291–292
National Police Day, 266–267
National Salvation Committees, 148
nationalism, 19, 27–28, 41–42, 51, 52, 257
　anti-Semitism and, 41–42
　civil society and, 199
　ethno-, 19, 52
　Gomułka and, 40
　Hindu, 8
　Slavic, 204
　xenophobic, 39–40
nationalist revolutionary movements, 88–89
nation-building, 202–203, 314–315, 336
natural resources, 197–198
Navalny, Alexei, 182–183
Nazi Germany, 20–21, 42
NBP. *See* National Bolshevik Party
NDP. *See* National Democratic Party
neighborhood governance, 102
neoliberalism, 189–190, 197, 316–317
New Community Movement, 103
New Life Campaign, 94, 102–103
New Life Movement, 93
New Orleans, Louisiana, 110, 129
New Strategic Map, 229–230
New Village Campaign, 102–103
New Village Movement, 103
NGOs. *See* nongovernmental organizations
Niedziałkowski, Jerzy, 36
Nikić Čakar, Dario, 242–243, 249–250
Nominating Committee, 299
nondemocratic regimes, 52, 54, 195, 263
nongovernmental organizations (NGOs), 3–4, 185, 250, 320
non-state collective actors, 7–8, 265
NOP. *See* People's Liberation Movement (*Narodno-Oslobodilački Pokret*)

Norac, Mirko, 251, 253–254
Novorossiya, 9–10, 20, 193, 203–211, 212–213
　constituencies making up, 213
　core community of, 204
　leaders of, 202
NPCSC. *See* Standing Committee of the National People's Congress
Number One Machine Tool Plant, 65

Occupy Central Movement (OCM), 8–9, 19–20, 291–292, 306, 308
　anti-OCM and, 295–296
　Beijing and, 297
　consequence of, 300
　failing to attract public support, 301, 306, 309
　nonviolent resistance and, 299
　prodemocracy movement and, 299
　weakness of, 298, 309
Occupy Central with Love and Peace (OCLP), 296, 297–298, 301, 302, 303, 304
Occupy Movement, 189
OCLP. *See* Occupy Central with Love and Peace
OCM. *See* Occupy Central Movement
Oddziałowe Organizacje Partyjne (OOP), 35
Office of Spiritual Civilization, 314, 315–316
oil industry, 226
oil prices, 197, 232
Olzak, Susan, 278
One Country, Two Systems White Paper, 302, 309–310
online communities of protest, 173
OOP. *See* Oddziałowe Organizacje Partyjne
Opening-up policy, 324
oppositional media sources, 210
Orange Revolution, 9–10, 140–141, 142, 162, 273
　aftermath of, 169–170
　counterrevolutionary mobilization, attitudinal profile for, 161
　counterrevolutionary mobilization, survey data and, 149–154
　demographic features of, 154
　failure of counterrevolution during, 160
　Nashi and, 172–173
　outcome of, 141
　political groupings in, 152
　success of, 162
　supporters of, 157–158
ordinary people (*laobaixing*), 78
organizational infrastructure, 12–13

Index

organizational weapons, 12–14
organized vigilantism, 129
ORMO. *See* Voluntary Reserves of People's Militia
Orthodox Christianity, 200–201
Osęka, Piotr, 37–38, 46
Other Russia, 199–200

Pakistan, 63
Palestine, 40
paramilitaries, 145
Park Chung-hee, 103
parliamentary arena, 248–252
parliamentary politics, 5
Partnership for Peace, 252–253
party-state, 304, 307, 308, 311
   agents, 15
   anti-OCM and, 298
   challenging, 292
   indirect rule by, 308–309
   influence, 294
   infrastructural mobilization and, 315
   Liaison Office and, 298
   mobilization, 26–27, 35
   proletariat and, 80–81
   rule of, 316–317
   Shanghai and, 73
   volunteerism and, 314
paternalistic culture, 124–125
Patriotic Education project, 177, 186
patronage networks, 17
Patterson, Joe T., 122–123
Patterson, Robert, 118
Patterson, Tut, 127, 128
Pavlin, Pamela, 245
Payne, Charles, 116–117
peaceful marches, 5–6
Pearl Revolution, 147–148, 149
peasantry, 89, 95
peer groups, 17
Peking University, 59–60
Peoples' Daily (newspaper), 323, 325–326, 327, 337
People's Liberation Army (PLA), 70, 72–73, 75–76, 81, 301–302, 304, 322, 325–326
People's Liberation Movement (*Narodno-Oslobodilački Pokret*) (NOP), 242
People's Livelihood Construction Campaign, 93
People's Livelihood Social Policy, 94
People's Militia (Milicja Obywatelska) (MO), 24, 45, 49–50

People's Republic of China (PRC), 58, 82
Perestroika, 202–203
Perry, Elizabeth, 183, 330, 336
Phillippe, Louis, 145
Pigee, Vera, 128
PiS. *See* Law and Justice party
PLA. *See* People's Liberation Army
Plan Bolívar, 2000, 221
planned villages, 90
plantation system, 111–112
"Please Hear What the Peasants Have to Say" (*Beijing Daily*), 72
Podstawowa Organizacja Partyjna (POP), 29–31, 35, 36
pogroms, 147
Poland, 8–9, 11, 20, 26–27, 52. *See also* Warsaw, Poland
   crisis in, 25–26, 27–28
   defensive mobilization in, 28–29
   destruction of, 41–42
   diversionist actions in, 51
   March 1968 campaign, long-term consequences of, 51–52
   mass rally, Gdansk, 31
   party organizations in, 53–54
   pre–World War II experience, 39–40
   reaction to student protest in, 52
   SMMs in, 27, 28, 33
   Upper Silesia, 31–34
police, 118, 121, 132–133, 146–147, 264
policy-making, 195
Polish Catholic Church, 1
Polish People's Republic (PRL), 47
Polish United Workers' Party (PZPR), 29–33, 43–44, 53–54
Politburo's Leading Group on Spiritual Civilization Building, 314, 320–321
political correctness, 57, 80
political manipulation, 181
political technology, 180
Poor People's Campaign, 118–119
POP. *See* Podstawowa Organizacja Partyjna
popular protests, 2
popular uprising, 302–303
populism, 19, 25–26, 39–40, 182–183
postcolonial world, 88–89
postcommunist regimes, 8
postmodern dictatorship, 189
postsocialist context, 168, 176–177
poverty, 87, 92, 97
practical labor, 68–69
Prague Spring, 82

355

PRC. *See* People's Republic of China
Prilepin, Zakhar, 175
principle-agent problems, 221
private property rights, 86–87
privatization, 152–153, 156
PRL. *See* Polish People's Republic
proactive mobilization, 9–10, 212, 217–218, 220–221, 236
　in electoral arena, 223
　SMMs and, 272
prodemocracy movement, 292–294, 299, 307
prodemocracy political parties, 297–298
productive labor, 39–40, 44
proektnyi podkhod (project approach), 185–186
prognostic framing, 299
pro-government demonstrations, 261
El Programa de Habilitación Física de Barrios, 225–226
project approach (*proektnyi podkhod*), 185–186
project design technologies, 169, 185–189
project implementation, 99–101
proletarian patrols, 69–70
proletariat, 57, 70
　Beijing and, 67–68
　bottom-up proletarian upsurge, 60
　Chinese term for, 58
　communism and, 82
　countermobilization, 58, 59, 81
　counterprotest, 74
　lumpenproletariat, 145–146
　party-state and, 80–81
　SMM and, 69
propaganda, 34, 39–40, 46–47, 54. *See also* Workers' Propaganda Teams
　anti-student sentiment and, 38–39
　apparatus of, 35
　astroturfing and, 193
　as bottom-up proletarian upsurge, 60
　campaign, 37, 51, 70
　counterprotest and, 72
　Cultural Revolution and, 59–63, 74
　infrastructure, 314
　student protests and, 44–45
pro-state demonstrations, 263–264, 267, 268, 273
　authoritarian rule and, 272–273
　domestic audiences and, 271–272
　frequency of, 269
　rise in, 277
　threat of, 280

protagonistic democracy, 217, 219
protest, 11–12. *See also* counterprotest; student protests
　data on, 275
　deliberately expansive definition of, 274–275
　disregard of, 264–265
　duration of, 280–282
　genuine, 8–9
　intensity of, 277–278
　labor, 196
　online communities of, 173
　popular, 82
　against Putin, 198
　social, 82
　states and, 4
　temporally dependent nature of, 275
　theories of, 4
　timing of, 277
　during uprisings in Egypt, 266–267
protest arena, 226–228, 231–236, 252–257
Provisional Government, 145
PSUV. *See* United Socialist Party of Venezuela
Public Chambers, 198
public criticism sessions, 68–69
Public Monitoring Commissions, 196–197
Public Opinion Programme, 297–298, 301, 305–306
public transcript, 15, 26
punishment regime, 196
Punto Fijo democracy, 218–219
Pushilin, Denis, 202
Putin, Vladimir, 167–168, 204
　first two terms of, 197
　foreign policy of, 199
　legitimacy of, 174
　Nashi and, 171, 176–177
　political crisis for, 173, 174
　popularity ratings of, 200
　protest against, 198
　support for, 193
PZPR. *See* Polish United Workers' Party

quasi-mobilization, 15, 26, 338
Quotations from Chairman Mao, 67

Rabaa' al-Adawiyah Mosque, 270
racial equity programs, 134–135
racial norms, 129–130
racial segregation, 111–112, 114–115
racialized norms, 115–116
racist practices, 115–116
Radnitz, Scott, 6

Index

RCNL. *See* Regional Council of Negro Leadership
reactive mobilization, 8–9, 19–20, 35, 212, 217–218, 220–221, 236
   pro-state demonstrations and, 271–272
   in protest arena, 226
Read, Benjamin, 102
Rebellion (Tamarrod), 269, 270, 277, 282
Red aristocracy, 68
Red Guards, 17, 58, 62, 66, 82, 317–318, 324–325
   contentious, 68–69
   demobilizing, 58, 80–81
   height of, 82
   suppression of, 73
Referendum Act (Croatia), 251
Regan, Patrick M., 279
Regional Council of Negro Leadership (RCNL), 125–126, 128
Relja, Marin, 245
repression, 10–11, 24–25, 161, 219–222, 285
   of civil society, 18
   concessions and, 279
   high intensity, 311
   insufficient, 274
   popular uprising and, 302–303
Republic of Korea, 103–104
resentments, 52
Resolution on Rights of Croatian Veterans of the Homeland War, 246
"Restore the Dignified Look of Tiananmen Square as Soon as possible" (*Beijing Daily*), 78–79
Revolution of 1905, Russia, 146
revolutionary challenges, 146–147
Revolutionary Committee, 66–67
revolutionary era, 314, 321–324, 339
Revolutions of, 1848, 144–145
Roach, E. L., 126
Robertson, Graeme, 147–148
Rodina, 199
Roman Catholic Episcopate, 27–28
Romanian revolution, 19
Rosmolodezh (Federal Youth Affairs Agency), 171–172, 185, 186
rural
   conditions, 101–102
   culture, 94, 95–96
   development, 88, 95
   incomes, 92
   infrastructure, 103–104
   living conditions, 91–92
   modernization campaigns, 88–90
   organizations, 105
   policy, 91, 95
   poverty, 87, 92
   resource extraction, 105
   society, 90
   transformation, 101
Rural Revitalization Campaign, 102–103
Russia, 5, 11, 157–158, 160, 189–190, 234–235, 261, 273
   apoliticism and, 176–177
   blogging factories from, 14
   contextualizing, 172–176
   Donbas, Russian volunteers serving in, 202
   foreign policy of, 199
   informational management by state, 186
   law, 122, 174
   Orange revolution and, 9–10
   Revolution of, 1905, 146
   Russo-Ukrainian crisis, 199–203
   SMMs and, 196–199
   social problems in, 187
   southern, 199–200
   state goals, 194
   Syria and, 213
   Tver', 166–169, 172, 180
   Ukraine and, 9–10, 193, 194, 200
Russian Federation, 169–170, 173, 198, 200–201
Russian Spring, 193, 203, 212–213
   constituencies making up, 213
   core community of, 204
   leaders of, 202
   media on, 211
   network activity, 204
Rwandan Genocide, 3–4, 20–21

Sadat, Anwar, 264
Saemaul councils, 104
Saemaul Undong, 103
Sanader, Ivo, 251, 254
Sanecki, Edward, 39
Sankya (Prilepin), 175
Saudi Arabia, 261
SB. *See* Security Service
SCAF. *See* Supreme Council of the Armed Forces
Scarbrough, Tom, 127
Schedler, Andreas, 10–11
schistosomiasis, 69
Scott, James C., 15, 26, 256–257
Scottish Highlander clans, 143–144

SDP. *See* Social Democratic Party
Security Service (SB), 38
self-determination, 310–311
self-improvement, 186
selfless sacrifice, 339
self-mobilization, 15, 26
separatism, 205, 207, 310–311
Serbia, 196, 197, 255
Serra, Robert, 235
SFRY. *See* Socialist Federal Republic of Yugoslavia
Shanghai, 58–59, 66–68, 73–74, 326
  Beijing and, 74–77
  industrial hub of, 72–73
  party-state and, 73
  workers' patrols and, 81
  Workers' Propaganda Teams in, 81
"Shanghai Must Not Become Anarchic; What Should We Do?" (*Liberation Daily*), 79
Shanghai's Workers' General Headquarters, 66–67
Shelton, Robert, 132
Shenzhen Civil Affairs Bureau, 327–328
Shenzhen Volunteer Social Service Federation, 327–328
Sichuan Earthquake, 314, 318, 329–330, 337
Silent Majority of Hong Kong, 298, 300
Silesian Polytechnic Institute, 44–45
Silicon Valley, 185
Sinj, Croatia, 254
Al-Sisi, Abdel Fattah, 270
Six Day War, 38, 40
Slater, Dan, 142–143
slavery, 124–125
Slavic people, 198, 204, 208
Slovenia, 251
Słowo Powszechne (newspaper), 46
Smerić, Tomislav, 242
Smith, Jackie, 6–7
Smith, Kerry, 102–103
Smith, Nicholas Rush, 142–143
SMMs. *See* state-mobilized movements
Smolensk plane crash, 239–240
SNCC. *See* Student Nonviolent Coordinating Committee
Snow, David A., 299
Sochi Olympics, 200–201
social control, 262, 263–265, 272, 286
Social Democratic Party (SDP), 242–243, 244, 248–249, 251, 252–253
social division, 306–307, 309
social media, 14, 297–298

social mobilization, 7–8, 87–88, 286
social movements, 2, 3–4, 7, 20–21, 142
  classic theories of, 2–3, 18
  formally organized, 278–279
  literature on, 6
  mobilization of, 7, 14
  students of, 194–195
social order, 11, 79–80
social organization, 225, 227
social protest, 82, 295
social services, 9–10, 52, 314
socialism, 26, 42, 50–51, 156, 176–177
Socialist Federal Republic of Yugoslavia (SFRY), 241–242
Socialist Patrols, 232–233
Sokolov, Evgenii, 185–186
solidarity, 1, 82, 183, 318–319
Song Renqiong, 323
Soule, Sarah, 278–279
South Korea, 86–87, 103
Southern Christian Leadership Conference, 118–119
Soviet Union (USSR), 1–2, 82, 167–168, 175–176, 199, 203
  collapse of, 149, 193
  color revolutions and, 172–173
  movement regimes and, 88–89
  nostalgia for, 204
  Palestine, support of, 40
  revisionism in, 59
  wartime songs, 167
  youth organizations in, 178
Špegelj, Martin, 245
spoiler mobilization, 9–10, 87, 175–176, 212, 272
Staggenborg, Suzanne, 273, 274
Standing Committee of the National People's Congress (NPCSC), 302–303, 304, 307
Starewicz, Artur, 46–47
state agents, 13, 263–264
State Highway Patrol, 118
state-building, 10, 241
state-insured pensions, 243–244
state-mobilized movements (SMMs), 2, 5–7, 8–9, 29–34, 261, 262–263
  in authoritarian contexts, 11, 284–285
  authoritarian regimes and, 15
  backbone of, 77
  broad contours of, 10
  broad terms of, 117
  China and, 18, 20
  civil society and, 294–295

Index

in comparative relief, 134–136
consequences of, 19–21
considerations associated with, 112
Cox proportional hazards models for, 281
definitional criteria for, 276
democratic regimes and, 111–115, 135
dynamics of, 272–274
in Egypt, 265
expectations of, 184
features of, 276
fluidity in, 58–59
framing, 39–40
full range of, 7
goals of, 285
improvised, 18
incentives for, 46
incidence of, 280–282
institutional change and, 80–81
intensity of, 277–278
intra-elite conflict and, 33–34
Kaplan-Meier survival estimates for, 283
limits of, 309
logic of, 218, 236–237
military suppression, 82
Morsi and, 269–270
motivations of, 270–272
Nashi and, 168, 188
nationwide, 66
new questions about, 285–286
onset of, 280
participation in, 16, 184
in Poland, 27, 28, 33
political geography of, 17
possibility of, 285
proactive mobilization and, 272
processes inherent in, 15
proletarian, 57
proletariat and, 69
purposes of, 142–143
by repertoire, 32
risk of, 282
Russia and, 196–199
Russo-Ukrainian crisis and, 199–203
under SCAF, 267–269
social control and, 262, 263–265
spoiler mobilization and, 272
spontaneity of, 62
strategic dilemmas of, 26–27
strategies, 13
student protests and, 25
symbolic framing of, 15–16
technologies of, 35, 58
timing of, 277
transformative policies and, 88
transnational, 5
variation over time in, 222–224
varieties of, 286
in Venezuela, 218, 220–221
states
civil society organizations and, 4, 11
complexity of modern, 18
components of, 264
conceptualization of, 6–7
effectiveness of, 10
interests of, 7–8
one-party, 27
protest and, 4
working class collaboration with, 57–58
state–society
concerns, 20–21
confrontation, 304
cooperation, 7
dynamics, 297, 311
equation, 4
interaction, 16, 20–21
interconnections, 6–7
relationship, 5–6, 18
state-sponsored organizations, 13
Stephenson, Svetlana, 182
Stola, Dariusz, 38, 47
Strauss, Julia, 95–96
street technologies, 169, 178–179
Strelkov, I., 202
Student Nonviolent Coordinating Committee (SNCC), 128–131
student protests, 24, 33–34, 43–44, 48–49, 51, 54, 77, 81, 229
Beijing and, 70
communism and, 80–81
main forms of countermobilization to, 31
Nashi and, 231
organizers of, 37
Poland, reaction to, 52
proletarian SMMs and, 57
propaganda and, 44–45
SMMs and, 25
working class and, 48, 49–50
subnational diversity, 58–59
subsidized publics, 12–14, 195
suburban rallies, 72
Sun Yat-sen, 93
Supreme Council of the Armed Forces (SCAF), 262, 267–269, 279

Surkov, Vladislav, 167–168, 172
surveillance, 10–12, 221
Sutherland, Donald M. G., 144
Świat (newspaper), 38
Syria, 213, 272
Szlajfer, Henryk, 24

Tagarrod (Impartiality), 269–270
Tahrir Square, 147, 261, 266–268
Tai, Benny, 296, 308
Taiwan, 9–10, 86–88, 90–102, 105
  community development policies in, 96
  development of, 86
  Korea and, 104
Tamarrod (Rebellion), 269, 270, 277, 282
Tan Jianguang, 320, 333, 339
Tantawi, Hussein, 267–268
Tanzania, 90
Tates, Leola, 126
technocratic rule, 87–88
tenancy rates, 91
tenant farmers, 124
terrorism, 14
Thompson, Allen, 118
Thornhill, J. E., 132
Tiananmen Democracy Movement, 58, 69, 76
Tiananmen Square, 70, 81
Tiananmen Square Management Office, 78–79
Tiananmen Uprising, 15–16, 17, 58, 81–82, 317–318
Tianjin, 328–329
Tilly, Charles, 4, 144, 274–275
Tito, Josip Broz, 242
Tocqueville, Alexis de, 111–112
Tong'il production, 103–104
Torres, Miguel Rodríguez, 235
totalitarianism, 15, 26, 195–196, 286
township coordination committee, 98
trade unions, 26, 35–37, 82
transformative policies, 88
transnational activism, 5
Traugott, Mark, 145–146
tribalism, 14
Triple Rustication, 334
Trump, Donald, 13–14
Trybuna Ludu (newspaper), 29, 34, 38, 43, 53–54
  anti-student sentiment and, 38–39
  names of protest organizers published in, 46
Tsarist authority, 146
Tsinghua University, 59–60, 62
  experimental farm and, 69
  Mao and, 63
  occupation of, 63, 68
Tsoi, Tony, 302
Tucker, Robert, 88–89
Tuđman, Franjo, 242–243, 245, 246
Turner, Denzill, 126
Tver', Russia, 166–169, 172, 180
Tyson, Tim, 116

UBCh. *See* Battle Units Hugo Chávez
UDVDR. *See* Veterans of the Republic of Croatia
UKA. *See* United Klans of America
Ukraine, 4–5, 41, 153–154, 197, 212
  counterrevolutionary mobilization, composite character of, 158–160
  counterrevolutionary mobilization, social sources of, 154–158
  Donbas and, 207
  Donetsk province, 156
  Euromaidan Revolution in, 160, 199–200
  geopolitical orientation of, 152–153
  Kremlin and, 193, 210, 273
  Orange Revolution and, 9–10
  political context in, 211
  political landscape of, 205
  Russia and, 9–10, 193, 194, 200
  Russo-Ukrainian crisis, 199–203
  trends within Ukrainian society, 151
  Yanukovych fleeing, 201
Ukrainian Supreme Court, 140–141
Umbrella Movement, 291–292, 303, 304, 308
  demobilization of, 304–307
  NPCSC, 309
UN *See* United Nations
Union of Communist Youth, 172
Union of Russian People (URP), 146
united front organizations, 298, 306, 307
United Klans of America (UKA), 120–121, 131–132
United Nations (UN), 94, 293–294
United Socialist Party of Venezuela (PSUV), 229–230, 234
United States South, 111–112, 115–124
unproductive labor, 44
"Upholding Social Stability is the Most Urgent Task, Critical to the Overall Situation" (*Beijing Daily*), 76
Urban Land Committees, 225–226
URP. *See* Union of Russian People
Useem, Bert, 274, 278–279
USSR. *See* Soviet Union

Index

Vanguard of Red Youth, 172
velvet revolutions, 172–173
Venezuela, 217, 228, 234–235, 261. *See also* Bolivarian Venezuela
  competitive nature of, 236
  local governance and, 223–224
  recall referendum in, 229
  in recession, 232
  SMMs in, 218, 220–221
  state crisis in, 221–222, 236
Venezuela, Indestructible Heart Campaign, 233–234
Venezuelan exceptionalism, 218–219
veteran organizations, 245–248
  HDZ and, 244, 246, 248–257
  NGOs, 250
  protest arena and, 252–257
veteran population, 241, 249
  Homeland War and, 243–244
  interests of, 248
veteran protests, 253
Veterans of the Republic of Croatia (UDVDR), 245, 246
VI Congress of Trade Unions, 40
Victory Day, 252, 256–257
vigilante violence, 127, 131, 133, 135, 147
village improvement projects, 93–94, 104
VKontakte, 202, 203–211, 212–213
Voivodeship Committees, 31–33, 36–37, 46
Voluntary Reserves of People's Militia (ORMO), 24, 48–49
volunteerism, 9–10, 314, 322, 336
  China and, 315–316
  emergence of category of "volunteer," 327–329
  institutionalising, 329–333
  LLF and, 338
  official discourses on, 318–320
  youth volunteer work, 332
Volunteers in Action, 318
Vukovar Remembrance Day, 239, 240, 252, 255, 256, 257
Vuković, Vuk, 249

Wade, Robert, 86–87
Wafd Party, 266
Wałęsa, Lech, 36, 37
Wang Hongwen, 66–67, 73, 80
Wang Xiaoping, 65
warfare, 5–6
Warren, R. R., 131, 132–133
Warren, R. W., 110

Warsaw, Poland, 1–2, 3, 31, 42, 239–240
Warsaw Committee, 37, 39
Warsaw National Theater, 24
Water Tables, 225–226
Watkins, W. H., Jr., 133
Wedeen, Lisa, 272
Weiss, Chen, 196
welfare programmes, 245, 247
Wen Wei Po (newspaper), 308
Western media, 78
Weyland, Kurt, 144–145
White, Tyrene, 89
white elites, 125
White Knights, 120–121
"whites-only" restaurants, 115
Williams, John Bell, 119
Worker-Peasant-Soldier Trainees, 68–69
Workers' General Headquarters, 73
Workers' Mao Zedong Thought Propaganda Teams, 59
workers' patrols, 69, 70, 81
  Cultural Revolution and, 74
  dispatch of, 79–80
  historical significance of, 77
Workers' Propaganda Teams, 62–63, 67, 68–69, 81
working class, 42, 43, 48, 49–50, 57–58, 63, 76–77
"The Working Class is the Primary Force in Upholding Social Stability" (*Liberation Daily*), 76
"The Working Class Must Lead in Everything" (Yao), 66
World Bank, 293–294
World Trade Organization (WTO), 252–253
World War II, 39–40, 86, 102–103, 170, 204, 242
WTO. *See* World Trade Organization
wuchan jieji. *See* proletariat

Xi Jinping, 68, 104–105, 296–297
xibu jihua ("Go West Plan"), 333–336
Xinhua News Agency, 75, 76
Xinhua Printing Plant, 62
Xue Lei Feng, wo zhiyuan ("I Learn from Lei Feng, I volunteer"), 321

Yakemenko, Vasily, 169–170, 171–172, 179
Yan'an period, 317–318

Yang, M. C., 91–92
Yanukovych, Viktor, 140–141, 150–151
  campaign of, 141
  commitment to, 154–156
  demonstration for, 151
  fleeing Ukraine, 201
  home base of, 156, 162
  rule of, 205
  support of, 153–154, 156
  "thuggish" supporters of, 156–157
Yao Wenyuan, 66–67
Yashin, Ilya, 182
Yeltsin, Boris, 180, 199, 202–203
Yen, Y. C. James, 93
Yiwu laodong (labour by obligation), 326–327, 337
youth organizations, 26
Youth Service Corps (YSC), 325–326
youth volunteer work, 332
YSC. *See* Youth Service Corps

Yugoslav war legacy, 243–244
Yugoslavia, 199
Yung Chow, 298
Yushchenko, Viktor, 140–141, 150–151
  demonstration for, 151, 154–156
  lifestyle of supporters of, 156–157
  support of, 153–154, 156, 159

Zagreb, Croatia, 254–255, 256
Zakharchenko, Aleksandr, 202, 207
Zald, Mayer N., 274, 278–279
Zhang Chunxia, 319–320
Zhirinovsky, Vladimir, 199
zhiyuan, 328–329
Zhou Enlai, 323
Zhu Rongji, 73–74, 76–77
Zieleniewski, Marek, 36
Zionism, 34, 40–41, 44, 45, 48. *See also* anti-Zionism
Znak, 34

Books in the Series (continued from p.ii)

Lars-Erik Cederman, Kristian Skrede Gleditsch, and Halvard Buhaug, *Inequality, Grievances, and Civil War*
Christian Davenport, *How Social Movements Die: Repression and Demobilization of the Republic of New Africa*
Christian Davenport, *Media Bias, Perspective, and State Repression*
Gerald F. Davis, Doug McAdam, W. Richard Scott, and Mayer N. Zald, *Social Movements and Organization Theory*
Donatella della Porta, *Clandestine Political Violence*
Donatella della Porta, *Where Did the Revolution Go? Contentious Politics and the Quality of Democracy*
Mario Diani, *The Cement of Civil Society: Studying Networks in Localities*
Nicole Doerr, *Political Translation: How Social Movement Democracies Survive*
Barry Eidlin, *Labor and the Class Idea in the United States in Canada*
Todd A. Eisenstadt, *Politics, Identity, and Mexico's Indigenous Rights Movements*
Olivier Fillieule and Erik Neveu, editors, *Activists Forever? Long-Term Impacts of Political Activism*
Diana Fu, *Mobilizing Without the Masses: Control and Contention in China*
Daniel Q. Gillion, *The Political Power of Protest: Minority Activism and Shifts in Public Policy*
Marco Giugni and Maria Grasso, *Street Citizens: Protest Politics and Social Movement Activism in the Age of Globalization*
Jack A. Goldstone, editor, *States, Parties, and Social Movements*
Jennifer Hadden, *Networks in Contention: The Divisive Politics of Climate Change*
Michael T. Heaney and Fabio Rojas, *Party in the Street: The Antiwar Movement and the Democratic Party after 9/11*
Tamara Kay, *NAFTA and the Politics of Labor Transnationalism*
Neil Ketchley, *Egypt in a Time of Revolution: Contentious Politics and the Arab Spring*
Joseph Luders, *The Civil Rights Movement and the Logic of Social Change*
Doug McAdam and Hilary Boudet, *Putting Social Movements in Their Place: Explaining Opposition to Energy Projects in the United States, 2000–2005*
Doug McAdam, Sidney Tarrow, and Charles Tilly, *Dynamics of Contention*
Holly J. McCammon, *The U.S. Women's Jury Movements and Strategic Adaptation: A More Just Verdict*
Sharon Nepstad, *Religion and War Resistance and the Plowshares Movement*
Olena Nikolayenko, *Youth Movements and Elections in Eastern Europe*
Kevin J. O'Brien and Lianjiang Li, *Rightful Resistance in Rural China*
Silvia Pedraza, *Political Disaffection in Cuba's Revolution and Exodus*
Héctor Perla Jr., *Sandinista Nicaragua's Resistance to US Coercion*
Federico M. Rossi, *The Poor's Struggle for Political Incorporation: The Piquetero Movement in Argentina*
Chandra Russo, *Solidarity in Practice: Moral Protest and the US Security State*
Eduardo Silva, *Challenging Neoliberalism in Latin America*
Erica S. Simmons, *Meaningful Resistance: Market Reforms and the Roots of Social Protest in Latin America*
Sarah Soule, *Contention and Corporate Social Responsibility*

Sherrill Stroschein, *Ethnic Struggle, Coexistence, and Democratization in Eastern Europe*
Yang Su, *Collective Killings in Rural China during the Cultural Revolution*
Sidney Tarrow, *The Language of Contention: Revolutions in Words, 1688–2012*
Sidney Tarrow, *The New Transnational Activism*
Wayne P. Te Brake, *Religious War and Religious Peace in Early Modern Europe*
Ralph A. Thaxton Jr., *Catastrophe and Contention in Rural China: Mao's Great Leap Forward Famine and the Origins of Righteous Resistance in Da Fo Village*
Ralph A. Thaxton Jr., *Force and Contention in Contemporary China: Memory and Resistance in the Long Shadow of the Catastrophic Past*
Charles Tilly, *Contention and Democracy in Europe, 1650–2000*
Charles Tilly, *Contentious Performances*
Charles Tilly, *The Politics of Collective Violence*
Marisa von Bülow, *Building Transnational Networks: Civil Society and the Politics of Trade in the Americas*
Lesley J. Wood, *Direct Action, Deliberation, and Diffusion: Collective Action after the WTO Protests in Seattle*
Stuart A. Wright, *Patriots, Politics, and the Oklahoma City Bombing*
Deborah Yashar, *Contesting Citizenship in Latin America: The Rise of Indigenous Movements and the Postliberal Challenge*
Andrew Yeo, *Activists, Alliances, and Anti-U.S. Base Protests*

CPSIA information can be obtained
at www.ICGtesting.com
Printed in the USA
LVHW020441280721
693844LV00010B/1355